D1061911

"An international excursion into the byways of the military mind . . . [with] special significance as one of the few books to seek to set, let alone succeed in setting, the Latin American military in a broader international perspective. . . . It will become standard fare for students of Latin America, [and] of military affairs worldwide." —Frank D. McCann, author of *The Brazilian-American Alliance, 1937–1945*. "One of the most important works ever written on the subject. . . . It will be the standard against which all future studies will be measured and will become required reading for everyone even marginally concerned with the military in society." —Thomas M. Davies, Jr., Director, Center for Latin American Studies, San Diego State University.

The quarter century from 1964 to 1989 was the "time of the generals," the most clearly defined era of military rule and influence in the history of Latin America. The effects of this rule were most evident in Argentina, Brazil, Peru, and Chile, where French- and German-style military professionalism developed into professional militarism. Frederick M. Nunn shows that the mentality of Latin American generals is typical of a worldwide military ethos but that its application is unique in the context of individual countries. In detailing the pervasiveness of this ethos worldwide, Nunn enables a better understanding of the willingness of Latin American military leaders to intervene in government, and of their activities once in power.

Frederick M. Nunn is a professor of history and international studies and associate dean of the College of Liberal Arts and Sciences at Portland State University. His books include the award-winning *Yesterday's Soldiers: European Military Professionalism in South America, 1890–1940* (1983), also published by the University of Nebraska Press.

THE TIME OF THE GENERALS

Latin American Professional Militarism in World Perspective

Frederick M. Nunn

University of Nebraska Press *Lincoln & London*

Manufactured in the United States of America
The paper in this book meets the minimum requirements of American National Standard for Information Sciences—Permanence of Paper for Printed Library Materials, ANSI Z39.48–1984.

Library of Congress Cataloging-in-Publication Data
Nunn, Frederick M., 1937–
The time of the generals : Latin American professional militarism in world perspective / Frederick M. Nunn.
p. cm.
Includes bibliographical references and index.
ISBN 0-8032-3334-5 (cl : alk. paper)
1. Latin America—Politics and government—1948– 2. Latin America—Armed Forces—Officers—Attitudes. 3. Civil-military relations—Latin America—History—20th century. 4. Latin America—Military policy. I. Title. II. Title: Latin American professional militarism.
F1414.2.N83 1992
322'.5'098—dc20 91-39896
CIP

To the memory of Edwin Lieuwen
and to Gonzalo Mendoza Aylwin

CONTENTS

PREFACE

In the later years of the twentieth century generals presided over a majority of Latin Americans. Some generals achieved such power that they left marks on their countries that may never fade.

On March 31, 1964, the armed forces of Brazil seized power from populist President João Goulart, who assumed the presidency in 1961 under most controversial circumstances. Two and a quarter years later, the Argentine armed forces overthrew the government of the Radical Party's Arturo Illia. Although they relinquished power to a civilian administration ultimately led by General (ret.) Juan Perón in March 1973, they forced his successor and third wife, Isabel, from the Casa Rosada three years later, in March 1976.

In October 1968 a *golpe de estado* in Peru had resulted in the fall of another populist, President Fernando Belaúnde Terry, and the proclamation of the "Revolutionary Government of the Armed Forces," and there ensued a twelve-year experiment in what was initially termed "military socialism." Five years after the Peruvian *golpe,* on 11 September 1973, the Chilean army, navy, air force, and *carabineros* violently destroyed the government of Marxist Salvador Allende Gossens. The leaders of these military movements did not topple civilian governments because they wanted to reconstitute them; they took control of national affairs with the idea of governing for years.

By the end of 1989 all four countries were either once again under civilian leadership or shakily on their way to being so. In Bolivia and Uruguay similar military-civilian clashes had occurred during the same period, that is, from 1964 to 1989. In the meantime Nicaraguans had put an end to the Somoza dynasty and entered into a state of military-civilian relations similar to that of Cuba in the early stages of the Castro revolution; Paraguayans had freed themselves from the grip of Alfredo Stroessner; and Guatemalans, Salvadorans, Hondurans, Panamanians, and Ecuadorans continued to experience military-civilian strife in various forms, in some cases with serious international complications, and at levels never before achieved. In Mexico, Costa Rica, Santo Domingo, Colombia, and Venezuela civilian government plodded on amidst unsolved problems.

The 1964–1989 quarter century constitutes what we might call the "time of the generals," the most clearly defined era of military rule and influence in the history of Latin America. Obviously the same kind of military-civilian relations did not obtain everywhere. Not all Latin American countries shared the kind of special conditions in which the military profession could exert its influence over the rest of society as pervasively as it attempted to do in Argentina, Brazil, Chile, and Peru. Nor had all shared in the kind of past in which the military profession could develop to the point where long-term military rule could be contemplated, much less realized. In *Yesterday's Soldiers: European Military Professionalism in South America, 1890–1940,* I revealed the long history of professional development prior to World War II. French- and German-style military professionalism had prevailed in Argentina, Brazil, Chile, and Peru since the late nineteenth century. In these countries professionalism became the state or condition in which corporate self-interest, specialized expertise, and a sense of mission (not to mention the concept of *career*), came to influence the armed forces' thought, self-perception, and political actions. In other parts of Latin America professionalism either prevailed to a lesser degree or was overshadowed by domestic conditions that precluded or redefined it.

This book shows that, despite differences in professional development, army officer corps thought and self-perception throughout Latin America were more comparable than not following World War II, especially during the 1964–1989 quarter century. It explains how the ideas and attitudes of "yesterday's soldiers" still prevailed decades after their passage into the pages of institutional and, sometimes, political history. The primary explanations for such comparability and perdurability are really quite simple. Military professionalism at all levels is characterized by adherence to traditional values and time-tested, familiar, simple explanations. There is, in fact, such a thing as a military mentality, or its equivalent, military spirit. "Military spirit," said Chile's most sagacious officer-author, in an interview about the imminent publication of one of his books (*Hoy,* May 9–15, 1988), "is in the final analysis the *oriflamme* that distinguishes and, in a special manner enisles the armed forces from the rest of society." Don Tobías Barros Ortiz, a retired colonel, knew better than most just what made up this "spirit." A distinct spirit, or mentality, often dating from the early years of the twentieth century, pervades the profession and its literature, especially that portion of it produced for internal consumption.

Adherence to traditional ideals and values and the essentially conservative nature of military organizations lend to official military literature a quality of timelessness. Officers are allowed to base their arguments on the accepted wisdom of militarylore, meaning that there is a good measure of continuity and commonality in officer corps thought and self-perception. This also means that officers are able to perpetuate, by transmitting to their subordinates and their men, their own educational and career experiences. This has been historically the case throughout the region, not just for those countries where professional militarism was so starkly evident between 1964 and 1989.

The thought and self-perception of "yesterday's soldiers," men steeped in the late nineteenth-century European military tradition, were transmitted from one generation to the next so that they still obtained, in large part, during Latin America's time of the generals. The process of transmittal was not orderly but did abet the metamorphosis of professionalism into militarism there. This is important historically, for it indicates that while a firm base of military professionalism is necessary for professional militarism to exist in other than latent form, there is no established pattern for the development of its intellectual or ideological core.

Professional militarism is the willingness and propensity to provide solutions for national (and sometimes international) problems based on a military ethos, what Barros Ortiz called "military spirit" and what I think of as "mentality." The professional militarist is guided by his profession's ethos—or spirit, or mentality—when he seizes power, or when he condones its being seized, for the purpose of applying his expertise and fulfilling his sense of mission for the greater good of his fellow citizens. That practice has often fallen far short of theory goes without saying; that not all officers are comfortable with either is plain to see.

In Latin American countries where professionalism was not yet a reality following World War II, or where it existed but was tightly bound to historico-political tradition, there were no institutional *golpes de estado,* no attempts to apply a professional ethos to national problems. In such countries a continuation of military-backed personalism or an often intricate balance of civilian and military interests precluded metamorphosis of professionalism into militarism.

This book demonstrates that comparability of military thought and self-perception does not necessarily lead to similar political behavior.

Professional militarism emerges as a contextual phenomenon, both manifest and latent in the entire region—and beyond it as well, owing to wide differences in the state of the profession and in the strength of civilian institutions.

Professionalism, clearly, can be a shared experience; so can militarism. Recent Latin American history attests to this. If this is the case in Latin America, goes the question begged, might it not also be in other parts of the world? How do Latin American military-civilian relations in general compare and contrast with military-civilian relations elsewhere? Why are there differences within a given region? Are differences and similarities merely variations on some great theme? Are some countries of Latin America more comparable with non–Latin American countries in terms of their military-civilian relations than with other countries in Latin America? And where there is professionalism, does militarism lurk beneath the surface, retarded by other than military influences?

Adequate study of professional militarism in Latin America requires answers to such questions. In order to provide intellectually satisfactory answers I decided to study Latin American professional militarism in world perspective by comparing and contrasting officer corps thought and self-perception. To do this is to challenge Latin America as a structural framework for both intellectual exercise and comparative institutional history, and doing this makes the recent role of the military profession there both more understandable as unique and more recognizable as typical. Typicality and uniqueness are by no means mutually exclusive, these chapters show.

Studying Latin American professional militarism in world perspective is in a way a natural result of my having examined European military professionalism in a South American context. It is similarly a logical end to earlier studies of military-civilian relations in Chile. But mere extension of frameworks utilized in previous efforts could not expose professional militarism, manifest and latent, to be both unique to parts of Latin America and typical of much of the world. I do not believe the metamorphosis of professionalism into militarism can be convincingly discussed without comparing and contrasting officer corps thought and self-perception both within and without Latin America.

The countries selected for study here are noted in the Introduction. The classical time of the generals was unique to the four South American countries whose armies had retained a continental European professional heritage—Argentina, Brazil, Chile, and Peru. But the quarter century in which it took place was a time in which other Latin American officers, as well as North Americans, Europeans, Asians, and Africans, evinced many of the same ideals and values that generated professional militarism in these four countries. Officers everywhere recurrently expressed the same thought and self-perception in their professional publications well before and during the time of the generals in Latin America. In these publications lies the definition of Latin American professional militarism in world perspective. This book, then, is about what army officers thought and how they perceived themselves in Latin America and elsewhere, not what they actually did or failed to do. It is as much about their literature as it is about them. All translations from this literature, unless otherwise indicated, are mine.

I could not possibly acknowledge by name all those who helped me during the elaboration of this book, but some names must appear. Those who do not see their names below will understand; they know who they are and that I will never forget them. My wife and esteemed colleague Susan Karant-Nunn inspired, listened, commented, and understood. My daughters Jessica and Marianna endured a lot of my wondering out loud. My parents and in-laws did the same. My entire family was of great support and comfort during the years of research and writing.

These efforts would have been most difficult without another kind of support, a timely fellowship awarded by the John Simon Guggenheim Memorial Foundation. A twelve-month sabbatical leave granted by Portland State University in 1985–1986 was thus all the more enriching, for I was able to devote myself exclusively to research in Washington, D.C., Santiago de Chile, and London. Words cannot express my gratitude to the Foundation and to those who supported my application for a fellowship.

Portland State University has provided assistance, usually for research trips of varying lengths to South America, where I began to assemble some materials on the post–World War II era, even while concentrating on earlier times. The fruits of those labors form much of the background for this book; therefore I also think it fitting to thank again the American Philosophical Society and the Joint Committee on Latin American Studies of the American Council of Learned Societies and the Social Science Research Council for their important past support. Assistance from the Portland State University Research and Publications Committee, and a Travel to Collections Grant from the National Endowment for the Humanities made possible a final bibliographical search in the summer of 1991.

No one who spends much time in Latin American archives and libraries can overestimate the value of those in charge of repositories there. To those who over the decades have helped me in Argentina, Brazil, Colombia, Mexico, and Peru, I owe a great debt. The individual who more than any other, for over a quarter century, has made Chile a home from home is named on the dedication page. He has enabled me to make the Biblioteca Central del Ejército de Chile in Santiago my principal research center in Latin America. *Te agradezco mil veces y más,* Gonzalo.

On the same page there appears another name, that of the person responsible for my setting out, over thirty years ago, in search of the time of generals. The "tie that binds" cannot be weakened, neither by passage of time nor by death. For his counsel, friendship, and support, I will be ever grateful to Ed.

And then there are the scholars and colleagues, in this country and abroad, with whom I have exchanged ideas on my work. Principal among these are Thomas M. Davies, Jr., Robert A. Hayes, Brian Loveman, and Michael C. Meyer; the late Harold Blakemore and Fredrick B. Pike; Gustavo Cuevos Farren, Tomás P. MacHale, and Augusto Varas; and David A. Johnson and Craig E. Wollner. Thanks to these valued friends. This book is better for their ideas and advice, and for the comments and suggestions of hundreds of army officers with whom I have exchanged views over the years.

I want William W. Paudler, Dean of the College of Liberal Arts and Sciences at Portland State University, to know how much I value his patience in allowing an associate dean the time to write this book. Several members of our College office staff helped make this effort a pleasurable one. Jennifer L. Hulse, my former administrative assistant, factotum, and conscience, was a real help all along the way. Donna R. Kiykioglu, the dean's own administrative assistant, Gwendolyn J. Hodges, and Kirsten Seeborg made the final stages of word-processing much more tolerable than they might have been. Debra Z. Gahlhoff provided invaluable assistance during the final editing stages.

Joni Marie U. Johnson processed (again) one of my manuscripts through several drafts. Her wisdom and skill are inestimable, her patience amazing, her advice sage, her scholar's sense invaluable, her indexing meticulous.

Duran Dodson's copyediting improved the final version markedly. My profound thanks to her. All those at the Press who worked on the production of this book, and the anonymous experts who commented on it, also deserve my gratitude.

In addition to research in Santiago, a great amount of work was done at the Hispanic Division, Library of Congress, Washington; the British Library; the library of the Ministry of Defence; the Royal United Services Institute for Defence Studies; and the International Institute for Strategic Studies, London. I extend heartfelt thanks to directors, bibliographers, and other personnel of these places. What follows could not be without their assistance.

INTRODUCTION

It is easy to imagine an enthusiastic affection existing among soldiers for the colonel. Not so easy to imagine an enthusiastic affection among cotton-spinners for the proprietor of the mill.—John Ruskin, "The Roots of Honour" (1862)

The general asked what time it was and an aide-de-camp quickly ran to his side and mumbled: "Any time you wish, Mr. President."—G. Cabrera Infante, *Vista del amanecer en el trópico* (1974)

The presence of the military as a politically deliberative force is a major theme in modern Latin American history.[1] During the 1964–1989 quarter century professional militarism appeared in South America as the culmination of increased military interest in providing solutions outside normal political procedure for serious economic and social problems the armed forces saw as the result of changes wrought in the postwar years. The officers who masterminded the movements of this time openly sought to impose their ideals and values on the rest of society. They were professionals. They were also militarists.

The eight chapters that make up the main body of this book deal with the principal ingredients of professional militarism and how they evolved during 1964–1989 in Argentina, Brazil, Chile, and Peru. By interpreting and comparing the military profession's own literature, I demonstrate that professional militarism can exist in a latent as well as a manifest state almost anywhere.

This literature comes in various forms. I have purposely chosen that form which most actively and consistently transmits the thought and self-perception of officer corps from instructors to pupils, superiors to subordinates, generation to generation, branch to branch. Official military journals do not speak for all officers, for there are no monolithic officer corps—ever, anywhere. No *golpe de estado* ever has unanimous support, either, especially one designed to really change things. But in critical times as well as under routine circumstances officers are able to fall back on what they have learned, read, committed to rote memory, and discussed: words that have influenced them and their superiors. There are a select few published memoirs and political chronicles that do this. The number and quality varies from country to country and from context to context. But all officers have their own professional journals. These periodical publications are better than any other type of military literature for providing evidence of long-term, widespread consistency in traditional, mandated approaches to life. Across continents, across generations—across space and time, that is to say—military journals portray military ways that mark off the profession from the rest of society. If the distance between theory and reality that emerges from the pages of this literature seems great—at times amusingly, at others frighteningly so—it is all the more representative of the profession.

Articles and essays in military journals have endowed officers with a corpus of "militarylore." Individually they serve as "guides," in ways comparable to those written by Machiavelli and Castiglione, in fact. Collectively they influence the "proper officer" to think about the world and perceive himself and his fellows as parts of a historical process.

It would be unwise to think that things unspoken or unwritten are never thought about. Some things often have to be left unsaid or unwritten, but this does not mean officers are ignorant of them. Studying professional literature thematically over time enables one to see more clearly things that, although unspecified, did find their way into argumentation. Often this may occur through allegory or analogy; sometimes it may be just a matter of timely allusion or reference.

Repetition over time leads to an accumulation of lore that strengthens the conviction that an officer is *a part of*, yet *apart from*, the rest of society. This conviction can be seen blending with other themes; thus sometimes it reinforces beliefs in military superiority. Latin American references to the "gift" of leadership or command exemplify this. However much they may be convinced that the world around them changes, most officers have some idea of a tradition. Historians know that paradigm changes are few and can be far between, that pressures of the present color interpretations of the past. They know, if only in retrospect, that historical change often comes in the form of blendings and blurrings that do not affect all those conscious of change in the same way. *The Prince* and *The Book of the Courtier* can be construed as both medieval and Renaissance works, yet they are timeless in their usage. Much of the content of military journals, and certainly the material dealing with characteristics and roles of officers and armies, is equally timeless. Often tedious, simplistic, fatuous, and repetitive to the outsider, it is conveniently like scripture to the insider, hortatory, comforting, and justificatory.

Conveyed in the pages that follow is the clear impression that officers of the second half of the twentieth century, regardless of their continent or country of origin, thought and wrote about many of the same things. They did this throughout the forty years between the end of World War II and the mid 1980s (at which point both documentation and perspective end), just as they had for decades prior to the war. What was good for military professionals of the past, that is, would be good for the professional militarists who revered them.

The reader will also have the equally distinct impression that there are essential differences in thematic and topical emphasis in this literature, that typicality and uniqueness are not incompatible, and that thought and self-perception do not lead simply to the same results in different national contexts. Some things, in short, can transcend space and time, and some cannot.

During the twentieth century two preeminent exogenous influences were brought to bear on Latin American military organizations: Western European and North American. Having striven to shed as much of their Iberian heritage as possible, Spanish South American and Brazilian elites looked for inspiration to France and Germany late in the nineteenth century, and in the middle of this century the four South American "powers" still had European-style armies. While civilian sectors of their countries (and other regions of the continent) fell increasingly under the influence of the United States, not all professional officers would gladly acknowledge the United States' hegemony from the 1940s forward.

The difference between Argentine, Brazilian, Chilean, and Peruvian professional military development and that of, say, Colombia, El Salvador, and Ecuador, or of Venezuela, Bolivia, and Uruguay, is qualitative.[2] For the latter, French and German influence was diluted, secondhand, or downright negligible. The difference between areas subjected to European influences, whatever their intensity, and those that were not is also qualitative. In most of the Caribbean–Central American region professional development came as a result of the United States' influence in the early twentieth century, precisely when Europe was influencing South America under contrasting military-civilian conditions. Professional development in Mexico would be a unique case. Not all Latin Americans would live through the 1964–1989 period in the same way, therefore, but the glaring weaknesses of the Latin American structural framework do not preclude an impressive, substantive comparability of officer corps thought and self-perception on a number of themes and topics.

Most *uniformados*, or men in uniform, of the late twentieth century were not men of letters, but they did try to be; although their ability to express themselves was routinely limited, this did not dissuade them from making the attempt. Often their professional reach exceeded their intellectual grasp of the nonmilitary subjects they essayed. A few were both learned and literate, and their efforts show it. A few approached their subjects in Montaigne's way, as a response to intellectual challenge, as a test of memory, and as a means of exercising skills of argumentation and reasoning. Over time, their writings would add to the lore of the profession, and when the time came for political involvement on an institutional scale, militarylore served both as stimulus and ex post facto justification of actions carried out. Where political action did not occur, militarylore was nevertheless extant.

The period from 1964 to 1989 cannot be defined by simply extending the study of the continental military heritage in Latin America. An international and comparative approach based on other means suggests itself. Despite the results of World War II, French and West German officers would find it necessary to continue grappling with most of the same problems that had bedeviled their predecessors. They were, then, in a situation similar in some respects to that of Latin Americans. Spaniards, Italians, and Portuguese had to deal with the difficulties of "modernization," and British officers concerned themselves with some of the same issues that their continental and transatlantic colleagues did. Australians were forced to contemplate new geopolitical roles similar to those being considered by Latin Americans. Soviet officers showed no less interest in their role as molders of youth than Latin Americans always had. United States officers would be forced to keep pace with changing times from V-J Day through the Korean and Vietnamese debacles, into the "post-NATO, post–Warsaw Pact" era and the Panama and Andean drug wars controversies. Africans and South Asians would deal with some of the same issues that had characterized early twentieth-century Latin American military literature. Everywhere officers would strive to hold on to the past, confront the present, and prepare for the future.[3] The ways in which they did this and the reasons why they thought they had to do it shape the world perspective from which Latin American professional militarism is examined here.

The first two chapters deal with officers' perspectives on the past and present from their vantage point of a disconcerting "new world paradigm," the postwar era. The post-1945 world was one in which two great wartime allies became peacetime ideological antagonists and wartime foes became ideological bedfellows: a most egregious paradox to many Latin American officers.

Chapters 1 and 2 show how professional officers portrayed idealized pasts for their readers, how they confronted their present, and how they often found the two as irreconcilable as their predecessors had. Hitherto concerned chiefly with traditional defense (but always desirous of an internal role), some armies would now become more enmeshed in frustrating endeavors for which they were ill-suited professionally. Those used to internal constabulary activities hardened their traditional stance. The perdurability of traditional attitudes is treated in these and later chapters. Just as in the pre–World War II era, there would be consistency and continuity in post–World War II military literature. Changing times merely increased the attraction of the past, its examples, its disasters. Change of the "wrong sort" would continue to trouble men in uniform everywhere. Insufficient progress, development, or modernization also alarmed them. In most cases later twentieth-century Latin Americans differed little from either their contemporaries or their predecessors. Cold war politics and diplomacy reinforced traditional geopolitical thinking of Latin American military professionals, allowing and even encouraging officers to proffer solutions to national and international problems of all kinds. One wonders how future generals will differ from them? One wonders, too, just what past it was that military writers yearned for. Sometimes a specific time is mentioned, most times not, but always it is an idealized one.

John Ruskin's words at the beginning of the book speak of a time when social and economic institutions in industrial nations were reflecting a shift from an (idealized) communal, paternalistic social context to a materialistic, individualistic one in which just as many great decisions would be made in market places as on the field of battle or in the corridors of state power. It is not hard to understand why officers one hundred years later longingly wrote about an "enthusiastic affection" existing between their men and them and still perceived the rest of society as divided against itself by politics, class conflict, and economic struggle. No such rifts existed in armies, where generals could order up any time they wished (especially if they held civil power), as does Cabrera Infante's fictive chief of state.

In *The Crisis of Civilization* Hilaire Belloc lamented the effects of the Protestant Reformation ("a rising of the rich against the poor") on western society and culture. He viewed the sixteenth century's great upheaval as ending an age of spiritual and temporal unity, albeit one with its own problems, and giving rise to an era of exaggerated materialism, individualism, capitalism, and ultimately communism. Belloc would be cited more than once by officers from Latin America who shared his idealization of the pre-modern era, and Ruskin's idealization of intra-service relations would be shared by men in uniform who would never read him.[4] "Any time you wish, Mr. President" was what many officers yearned to hear. Epigraphs such as these from Ruskin and Cabrera Infante provide "texts" indicative both of the intensity of Latin American feeling and of the universality of themes discussed and compared here.

Chapters 3 and 4 address the perceived and practiced roles of officers and armies and show how officer-authors struggled to adapt old ways to new situations. Armies had once been "nations in arms," a symbol of national greatness. Officers everywhere had seen themselves as role models, paragons of virtue, inspirers, knights, teachers, confreres. They portrayed their life as a servitude of grandeur, a gilded poverty, claiming to serve state, nation, and society, God and man, in all possible ways. Through obligatory service, Latin Americans had long ago convinced themselves, they had inculcated in peasants, workers, Indians, and the wayward youth of the bourgeoisie morals and ethics befitting responsible, disciplined citizens of modern countries. Now some found themselves performing "community service," devising public relations campaigns, scrambling for recruits, catering to individualistic, disrespectful youth. Few officers anywhere had ever thought of themselves as "managers," faceless bureaucrats in olive drab or field gray. Many, therefore, wanted to maintain as much of the past they idealized as possible, clinging to old ways.

Chapters 5 and 6 deal with officer-corps thought on politics, ideology, religious faith, wisdom, and nationalism, subjects that permeate all other themes as well. By discussing the arguments used by officers to get their readers to react to the world around them, these chapters show how a blending of thought and self-perception can lead to professional militarism, both manifest and latent. They also help us to understand the gap between present and past by revealing the mutual influence of traditional self-perception and thought on current events in Latin America and elsewhere.

Few officers are polymaths. Their profession demands clear thinking, but few are called to become true theorists and ideologues. Some of those who do, of course, are responsible for the literature discussed in this book. Their writings contain varying definitions of "democracy," defenses of religion, opinions on Marxism and nationalism, observations on education and the proper use of wisdom, each and all in relation to traditional military values. In revolutionary situations—in Mexico and Bolivia, say—ideological expedience might overwhelm professionalism. The same could be said of the USSR, at least until events of the late 1980s made the future of Marxism-Leninism and the Warsaw Pact subject to professional questioning. Professional commitment to "democracy" influenced what Colombian, Venezuelan, British, North American, Australian, and Indian officers would be permitted to say. Strong doubts about both "revolution" and "democracy" were already evident before those who would express them took power in Argentina, Brazil, Chile, and Peru. Adulation and personality cults dominated writing in Paraguay, Nicaragua, Santo Domingo, Cuba, and the Philippines. Spaniards, Portuguese, and Italians did their best with the hurly-burly world of parliamentary politics after decades of authoritarianism. So did Germans, now locked into a new kind of military-civilian relationship. French officers would grope their way toward *entente* with new leaders. Pakistanis would strive to reconcile Islam with the creation of a modern nation-state and the technological age. By the end of chapter 6 all the essential ingredients of professional militarism—from both the past and present—will have been introduced and analyzed.

Chapter 7 focuses more intensely on what those who held power in Argentina, Brazil, Chile, and Peru between 1964 and 1989 would identify as national priorities of a cultural, economic, political, and social nature. Here, resort to retranslations from the Spanish and Portuguese confirms that officer-authors would lose perspective the nearer they got to actually applying their ideas (and ideals) to extra-professional situations. They lost the ability to express themselves clearly because much of what they now tried to express was only partially thought out. By the end of this study it ought to be clear that consistency of professional thought and self-perception could not lead to comparable militaristic results in other parts of the region, much less in other parts of the world. Traditional Latin American military attitudes and those expressed contemporaneously elsewhere notwithstanding, the professional militarism of the 1964–1989 "classical period" was indeed a contextual phenomenon. In this chapter uniqueness finally overcomes typicality, making the time of the generals truly Latin American.

The final chapter includes a discussion of professional militarism's place in the unfolding of recent history and elaborates further on why it was manifest in some countries and only remained latent in others. It speculates on newer themes and significant alterations of traditional ones. Its orientation is present-future in contrast to that of the first seven chapters. It speaks to "times of change," as opposed to "changing times," and to recent events that might presage another "new world paradigm" for men in uniform.

In the greater scheme of things, if there be such, professional militarism may prove to be a negligible set of coincidences, an aberration, an eddy in the flow of history, a period piece. It was at the very least evidence of an inchoate assertion by Latin Americans of increasing cultural independence. Demographic explosions, populism and polarization, economic instability, "redemocratization"—these all present Latin Americans with domestic problems of major proportions. The functional (if not structural) weaknesses of the Inter-American system—now evidenced by heightened hostility toward the U.S. following the Falklands/Malvinas conflict, inconsistent U.S.–Central American policies, invasions of Grenada and Panama, and the sending of military personnel to Andean countries to help rid the region of drug traffickers—may lead some Latin Americans to wonder just against whom and what they should be defending their countries.

At times we must resort to describing officer-corps thought and self-perception in terms of a timeless stream of consciousness. The final chapter suggests that it may not be coincidental that the "new novel" and professional militarism appeared together in "Invertebrate America," a term derivative of Ortega y Gasset's classic study of Spain and descriptive of Latin America. Militarism manifests itself politically, not in cycles, attractive as that analogy may seem, but rather more like chapters in a long story. Linear time, diachronic development, evolution—these appear to be interrupted over and again in the recent history of Latin America. Time's passage there, and in some other places as well, has not been orderly, nor has the military profession's experience in it.

Both foreign and Latin American savants have noted Latin America's unique blending of cultures, eras, and styles—the area's capacity for adaptation. Others have emphasized the region's inability to resist cultural, technological, and ideological penetration. The latter assessment may mistake short-term vulnerability for long-term flexibility. It will need to be examined in light of both the quincentennial of Latin America's existence in history and its time of the generals.

ONE

Changing Times: Confronting a New World Paradigm

Don Alfonso was excited and warm; he stuttered and fanned himself with his bowler. The purpose of his visit, he said, was to give the General a warning. He knew someone, he said, who had the confidence of Gamelin. He advised the General's immediate departure.—Ludwig Bemelmans, *Now I Lay Me Down to Sleep* (1942)

The phrase "the good old days" does not mean that bad things happened less frequently in the past, only—fortunately—that people simply forgot they happened.—Ernesto Sábato, *El túnel* (1950)

When Ludwig Bemelmans' fictional General Leonidas Erosa left his Biarritz villa for his home in South America, a new era began. The real General Maurice Gamelin's French Army shortly thereafter suffered its most humiliating defeat ever: the disaster of 1940 at the hands of Hitler's army. The idealized and the real "good old days" of European–South American military relations came to an end, and all over Latin America army officers confronted past, present, and future at once. They were not entirely alone, for officers everywhere soon realized they were living in a new world paradigm.

The Second World War changed many things, and Latin American military leaders were as acutely aware of this fact as civilians, perhaps more. The lessons of protracted intercontinental conflict convinced most officers that now, more than ever, there was a need for close military-civilian cooperation. This would threaten civilian control of the military in countries where politicians previously had eschewed close cooperation with the military and where officers had long espoused an internal role of sorts. In Latin America the concept of military-civilian cooperation would, with the exception of Mexico, be realized with detailed proposals for economic development, civic action, and internal reforms based on military-civilian efforts.

European officers likewise believed that they had a critical role to play internally, but, owing to the lessons of war as well as to the renewed strength of civilian institutions, civilians had little reason to fear military political action. Officers everywhere soon became aware of the logical extension of the 1939–1945 conflict: the Cold War. Confrontation with the internal enemy, usually leftist groups, soon became linked to classic geopolitics based on Cold War rivalries. In much of Latin America geopolitics also became inward-oriented owing to interest in military-civilian cooperation in internal development and national security policies. This, in turn, would promote figurative "declarations of independence" whenever national priorities were not seen as harmonious with those of the bastion of Western democracy and values, the United States of America.

This chapter concerns itself with what army officers thought about the changing times of the post–World War II era and how they perceived themselves as part of the new world paradigm. In their grudging acknowledgement of change as a permanent phenomenon, most Latin American officers betrayed themselves as fearful of its rapidity and of the disorderly passage of time. In attempts to cope with change and time and to confront perceived newness, they fell back on ideas and values from the past, their "good old days," and on traditional doctrines they could adapt to their own situations. If ideals and values could not be adapted, then they were not worthy of becoming part of professional militarylore; if the times could not be shaped by tradition alone, then they had to be confronted with some kind of direct action. To confront the early stages of the Cold War and champion the cause of closer military-civilian coordination of national activities, many officers used geopolitical theories originally devised in Europe for other purposes that nonetheless had become very popular in Latin American circles. In doing this they routinely evinced concerns about the United States' concentration on European affairs by expressing doubts about U.S. capability to strengthen democracy in Latin America.

In the material discussed here there is evidence of a growing Latin American military distrust of the United States as well as a hatred of communism and anything that resembled it. Both distrust and hatred emerge as responses to things considered alien, non–Latin American. The relatively rapid rise of the U.S. as a hemispheric and then a world power did little to improve relations within the hemisphere, even less among members of the military profession. From the outset of the postwar era Latin American officers were aware, to varying degrees, of the multiple dangers of a North American hemispheric hegemony. They would not be amicable military partners with their U.S. counterparts. What made this situation conducive to the metamorphosis of military professionalism into professional militarism is the fact that Latin Americans were aware that the reconstruction of Europe (a process they might have termed "development") was based on armed might, economic aid, and the consequent fusion of military and civilian priorities with regard to communist expansionism. They saw it as something less than the maintenance of democracy and more like what they were advocating for their own countries.

Their own protestations of support for democracy become all the more suspect when juxtaposed with European military literature dealing with the new order of things. Latin American or otherwise, military writing on changing times indicates discomfort with current trends, be they of the 1950s or 1980s; fear of an uncertain future; and nostalgia for an often idealized past. This is exaggerated in the military literature of countries where professionalism was an essential part of the historical past. But in some places the present actually provided a more comfortable "time" with which to identify. And in yet others only the recent past provided the gestation for professionalism and for idealized military-civilian relations. The influence of idealized and selective pasts on the present is everywhere evident in this literature, as is the influence of perceived presents on the past; but in all cases military literature is rife with suggestions for how armies, in close coordination with civilian authorities, can control change and thus shape time's unavoidable passage.

The degree to which all this is successfully presented in military publications of course varies, and to show this variation, I will compare and contrast Latin American sources with sources from other regions. Principal themes emphasized here are the lure of the past, change itself, military-civilian coordination to confront change (in the form of the internal enemy of tradition and stability, the heightened need for national security policy, the tenuous position of the United States as democracy's champion and communism's foe, and the reawakening of geopolitical theories), and a framework for the role of an army in the new paradigm.

The Argentine general Joaquín Aguilar opened the 1966 academic year of the *Escuela Superior de Guerra* by summarizing his version of the new paradigm. Whereas traditional political confrontations had been between democracy and dictatorship of the right, especially during the 1930s and until 1945, there was now a conflict between Western, Christian democracy and international communism. One of the principal reasons for this, he wrote, was decolonization and the spread of communism in non-Christian countries.[1] This set the stage for generals to champion the cause of the West and Christianity versus the East and atheistic socialism. But before generals could do this they had to be satisfied that their own brand of military-civilian unity was unsuitable to politicians. The literature indicates that they did convince themselves of this prior to rising up in the 1960s.

Even during World War II, Brazilian officers had become aware of the need for close military-civilian coordination. General José Pessoa informed his readers that there was now a necessity for integrated "psychological mobilization of the domestic front and public opinion" against Brazil's enemies. Civilian institutions were not doing the job, he insisted, and the stakes were higher than ever before.[2] Colonel João de Segadas Vianna concurred.[3] The very fact that the *Força Expedicionária Brasileira* (FEB) was participating in the European theater, they convinced themselves, justified what they wrote and made it imperative for them to propagate their ideas.

Shortly after the war the Argentine General Jorge Giovanelli urged the creation of a single defense ministry to coordinate defense "under one roof." The war had proven the value of unified command, and, furthermore, Argentina's neighbors, Brazil, Uruguay, and Chile, all had centralized defense planning. The inference was clear, even if the logic was poor.[4] A Bolivian colonel, Humberto Torres Ortiz, used such logic in his essays on the coordination of military education.[5] So did Peruvian Colonel Luis Bustos G., who wrote that "in order to be able to count on a capable army, it is necessary above all to properly educate and prepare the mass of the population," for total war demanded total mobilization against ideological enemies. "Pacifism," he went on, "undermines in the form of systematic propaganda . . . the patriotic will of the people [and constitutes] a grave danger to the future of the fatherland."[6] An editorial in *Armas,* the Mexican "Revista Continental" of hemispheric solidarity, maintained that only an "unbreakable alliance between the armed forces, the people who serve in it, and the government that represents us all" could preserve sovereignty, maintain order, and continue the "transformational action of the Mexican Revolution."[7] Mexico's military-civilian fusion would never be the type preferred by South American officers, but it did nontheless indicate a certain degree of postwar consensus.

In the 1950s other Latin Americans would evince concern for unity—of a sort. Colonel Santiago Baigorria and Lieutenant Colonel Julio César Salvadores implored their Argentine colleagues to insist on governmental assurance that the military have all it needed to defend the nation against external and internal enemies.[8] A Peruvian, Colonel César Pando, reminded his readers of the "real reasons" for the fall of France: lack of military preparedness, military-civilian consensus, and home-front preparation.[9] General Giovanelli of Argentina continued his propaganda efforts by stressing the internal military-civilian cohesion of all participants in World War II (omitting reference to the Soviets, of course), and Argentina's need for such cohesion, albeit in a different context.[10]

By the 1960s Latin Americans were discussing many things in terms of "national security," defined by some as the only guarantee of the survival of human beings.[11] The Peruvian major Romualdo Sarango Zapata exhorted his colleagues to devote themselves to the development of Peru and thus assure its security.[12] During the next decade, now in the time of the generals proper, the theme of military-civilian cohesion took on more sophisticated dimensions. In the pages of Argentina's *Estrategia,* edited by the influential, outspoken retired general Juan Enrique Guglialmelli, military intellectuals from various countries would render opinions on internal unity, development, and security—most of them framed in geopolitical terms.

In the September–October 1973 issue, for example, Peru's General Edgardo Mercado Jarrín, one of Latin America's foremost military minds, wrote that the armed forces "constituted for the state the guarantee of its sovereignty and its independence. Historical circumstances have changed," he continued, "but the *razón de ser* of our armed forces is still the same."[13] Could there be any doubt that changing times bore the influence of the past?

Certainly not in the mind of Brazil's General Breno Borges Fortes. The army, he stated in an address to the Tenth Conference of American Armies, had to engage in the battle for the minds of the people, to combat the indiscriminate use of electronic media by their enemies; the evil influence of pornography, eroticism, and violence; and the decline of the traditional family. In the schools, he wrote, "there is even serious discussion of sex education in lustful and irresponsible ways."[14] In his own address Argentina's Lieutenant Colonel Jorge Raúl Carcagno was less concerned with that than he was with the need for "a harmonic equilibrium between the improved general welfare of our fellow citizens and their spiritual well being."[15] Brazilian Lieutenant Colonel João de Araújo Ribeiro Dantas saw the world becoming an *aldeia global* (global village) owing to rising anti-nationalism, the spread of communism, and the reluctance of the United States to defend against these evils, owing to its own lack of internal cohesion.[16] The world was not growing together but rather was coming apart at the seams.

There were also those who saw the need for military-civilian cohesion in the stricter sense of economic diversification and development. Early on in World War II, as a matter of fact, a Brazilian major had told his readers that despite progress achieved at the Volta Redonda steel plant, Brazil would need to go further to fulfill her future needs; true independence would come only through coordinated industrialization, greater availability of transportation facilities, importation of technology and capital, and close cooperation between government, citizenry, and the military.[17] Close to the end of the war a Peruvian major would say much the same about his country,[18] and in 1946 Captain Nelson Werneck Sodré, a prolific Brazilian military writer, looking back on the 1930–1945 Vargas-era industrialization, called on his fellows to take advantage of the war's lessons and make use of its scientific and technological advances for further development of the national economy.[19] Brazil, he asserted, must not be left behind the rest of the world for lack of military-civilian cohesion. As an Argentine captain put it in 1946, "The armed forces win or lose battles or campaigns; they can fall without the fatherland being defeated . . . but the opposite, when it occurs, is beyond remedy; the fatherland can fall even though the armed forces are on the march."[20] The message to civilians was pretty clear.

Less than a decade later, professional militarism could be seen already in the making. A Peruvian essay, "El departamento de movilización integral de la nación: Elemento básico del ministerio de la defensa nacional," describes, in terms dripping with innuendo, national coordination of total defense under the aegis of a unified defense ministry. Defense was a permanent problem, economic, industrial, financial, and sociopolitical, as well as military in nature, this essay claimed. Peru had faced both internal (leftist) as well as external (Cold War) threats to stability earlier than other South American countries, but "our country," the writer concluded, "has lost the opportunity for leadership owing to lack of political vision and administrative incapacity." He also decried Peru's inherent handicaps: her regionalism, climatic variations, topography, demography, lack of transportation and communications infrastructures, all evidence of a lack of "organic cohesion."[21] Typical of Peruvian military literature, this essay offered a challenge to civilians by pointing out what they were ignoring in the new post–World War II paradigm: close military-civilian cooperation was important for a multitude of reasons.

Were Latin Americans alone in their recognition of change, in their advocacy of close military-civilian ties? Are the points discussed above merely early evidence of meddlesome militarism? Of course not. In one context they are evidence of mainstream thinking; in another, of merely a continuation of professional thought and self-perception brought to bear on changing times. The fact that officers from other parts of the world were also concerned with the new paradigm corroborates such assertions.

Even before the end of the war the British were being made aware of changing times. A 1944 essay, "The Training of the Young Officer," discussed government preparation for a postwar world that was yet to be.

"In fact," the author said, "we appear to have learnt our lesson from the 'hugger-mugger' period which followed the last war, when no apparent plan existed, and when the country drifted into one crisis after another."[22] Great Britain was not Peru, to be sure, but its military leaders were just as cognizant of the impact of changing times. So were Indians, for that matter. In that part of the waning British empire, "demobbed" officers had problems at war's end returning to civilian life. An editorial in the *Journal of the United Service Institution of India* advised those with reentry problems to learn how to write a good business letter, to improve their grammar, to avoid using too many acronyms, and above all to write clearly. Thomas Babington Macaulay's *Indian Penal Code* was put forth as a good guide to writing, for "it is a model of clarity."[23] Potential civilian employers, it was hoped, would respond favorably to evidence of such writing skills, and an officer's passage to Indian civilian status, however unpleasant to him, would be facilitated.

French officers were soon told that France's "general impoverishment no longer permits giving the army all that which it needs," and that "results" will dictate the army's fate and sacrifice will create a better image in peacetime."[24] Canadians were informed that maximum preparedness for the 1950s and beyond would depend on an integrated industrial effort and military readiness. Canadians could not expect to maintain their freedom if they were caught unprepared as in 1914 and 1939.[25] Ex post facto mobilization, even of volunteers, would not suffice.

Beginning in the 1950s leaders of the German Federal Republic's reconstituted defense force, the *Bundeswehr,* would begin to grapple with their own new paradigm. An oft-translated and republished piece by retired General Erich Dethleffsen argued that Germans must "build not *again,* but *anew.* An army is not democratic by virtue of a democratic organization, but only when . . . its officer corps stands firmly on a democratic foundation, and is ready to fight for it . . . [when] human virtues—freedom and dignity of the individual soldier—are protected . . . [and] the armed forces are not suspended in a vacuum, but draw their strength and morale from the fact that they consider themselves that part of the nation which is serving with arms."[26] Germans would emphasize these points numerous times and for various purposes in years to come. They would also decry the loss of prestige and glamour of the military career, because of its lack of appeal to Germany's youth. The remilitarization of Germany would soon become a major factor in the creation of a new paradigm for all of Europe.

"Tomorrow's war begins today," wrote General André Zeller at the end of the 1950s. Zeller discounted the *grandeurs* of the past and called upon Frenchmen to understand that military service promoted a necessary beneficial "fusion and camaraderie of citizens from all walks of life."[27] France's army, like most in Latin America, would face political crises steadfast in its self-perception as the nation's unifier and defender.

By the 1960s officers in those countries involved directly in World War II again faced anti-militarism head on, and nowhere more than in the United States. "We laud the American scholar, the American businessman, the American scientist, the Yankee Trader—but it rarely occurs to us to boast of the American soldier. Why?" So queried General Maxwell Taylor. Taylor's eloquent "The American Soldier" bluntly presented the case of the misunderstood, mistreated man in uniform. "We still have trouble," he wrote, "distinguishing between what is military and what is militaristic, between what is peaceful and what is pacifistic."[28] Latin Americans were saying things like that too. Peacetime brought its own peculiar changes.

Germans had problems similar to those of their new allies. "The gulf and the contrast between the frock coat of the politicians and the brass hat, between civilian and military thinking, is in the nature of things,"[29] wrote General Leo Freiherr von Geyer, who blamed the United States for breaking up the remnants of the *Wehrmacht,* thus making the defense of the West a more difficult task. Politics, he insisted, was to blame—during Weimar times, under the Third Reich, and then again under the *Bundesrepublik*—for destroying morale.[30] The Germans had lost their tradition principally because the army had obeyed civilians too much.

Generational change and new civilian attitudes toward the military profession, it would be alleged, complicated things and alienated civilians and the military on many levels. In the United States no historical tradition of military-civilian unity of purpose had ever been established comparable to that which the French and Germans still imagined their tradition to have been. As Defense Secretary Clark Clifford would write of the United States in 1968: "This nation has never had much time for the past and is forever impatient with the present. From the very beginning our chosen time-frame was the future."[31] Civilian Kurt Hesse's counter to Geyer's traditional militaristic argument above confirmed all the more that things were not well with men in uniform. A different political system, a different society, generational change in the form of a *skeptische Generation,* the transnationalism of NATO, and absolute control by the German parliament, he insisted, meant that "the spirit of the soldier is now the same as that of the people."[32] That is to say, professional officers and their men were different only because of the uniform they wore—when they wore it. Ironically, unity of purpose of the military and society, lacking in the land of the victors, could be viewed as detrimental in the land of the losers.

By the end of the 1960s Germans would be overwhelmed by their new unity of purpose. *Innere Führung*, inner leadership by strictly defined democratic principles, became the *Bundeswehr*'s ideology, its *Geist*, its *Weltanschauung*. The *Bundeswehr*, wrote military affairs commentator Wilfred von Bredow, became officially "an army of democracy and an army for democracy." *Innere Führung* had no historical foundation, according to von Bredow, but it now belonged to German history.[33] Military officers and writers, it seemed, had set out to create instant tradition, and thereby instant unity.

As Germans struggled to establish new traditions while rearming, their former foes just to the west were also agonizing. Malaise gripped the French army in the 1960s in the wake of disasters in Asia and Africa.[34] Americans now faced their own Asian debacle, too. General William Westmoreland told readers that integrity and competence were necessary to bind the military to the rest of society and reestablish a shaken unity.[35] French officers were told much the same, and their army, they were given to understand, was no longer the principal expression of national power and influence.[36] For Americans the plight of the 1970s did not constitute a great fall, but for the French it was worse than that of 1940. Only in Germany could one still get away with calling military service "the price of freedom" and expect an immediate response. There, argued Colonel Adolf Reinicke, there simply could be no "cleft between an industrialized society and a modern army if both were to survive."[37] Neither the United States nor France, however shattering the experiences of Vietnam, had to share a frontier with a hostile armed camp in the postwar years.

Far away from the Atlantic world, from Western Europe and Latin America, armies confronted the new paradigm, with mixed results. Indonesians achieved a sort of cohesion through dictatorship,[38] Russians maintained their unity of purpose through ideology,[39] Australians strove for it through exhortations to consensus and common values.[40] Elsewhere beyond Europe military–lower class linkages could be stressed.[41] But in Europe certain arguments for unity used in the developing world would also prevail. Italians were told that their reconstituted army was "the safeguard of free institutions and the intervening agent of the people in the event of emergency."[42] The Italian army also served as the ideal place for what one writer called structural *confronto* of the old and the young, past, present, and future.

By the end of the 1970s, changing times saw American officers and civilians emphasizing unity in more prosaic, historic terms.[43] Officers in Europe and the Western Hemisphere were (officially, in some cases) now reconciled to democracy and aware of the dangers of militarism, especially with the availability of *Atomwaffen* (atomic weaponry).[44] They were both conscious of the need for internal order and concerned for the future of the United States as democracy's champion and arsenal in the age of the Cold War. Of course this had repercussions throughout the world, especially in Latin America.

This concern reinforced South American worries about the internal enemy. South Americans were sensitive to subversion and ideological warfare before the war in ways now historically comparable to Cold War convictions that led directly to the time of the generals. In a 1952 essay an Argentine lieutenant colonel acknowledged the importance of an "internal front,"[45] and shortly thereafter Peru's General Felipe de la Barra revived the old axiom *si vis pacem para bellum*. Barra emphasized the need for preparation of the civilian population for psychological warfare and propaganda attacks by Peru's enemies.[46] These cold warriors were linking military-civilian unity to the internal enemy issue; they were also building a case for the threat of sustained outside interference in national affairs. This would soon come to mean any kind of outside interference, not just that of the left, and it would provoke significant responses cloaked in the guise of professional militarism.

Colonel Víctor Odicio T., a Peruvian, continued this line in a 1957 essay. The fall of France, World War II, and the Cold War, he believed, made it imperative for Peru to adopt a combined defense ministry. National defense, military tradition, coordination, and the internal threat to security all justified an enhanced role for Peru's emerging professional militarists. A 1958 article in the Peruvian *Revista de la Escuela Superior de Guerra* hardened this line and indicated a reliance on the past in lieu of a more suitable, present-day model.[47] The more intensely Peruvians concentrated their attention on the present, the more they relied on historical examples to assure their country a future of their liking. And the present suffered for it.

Marxism was of course the primary concern of most Latin Americans. The Argentine colonels Arturo Pasqualis Politi and Osiris Guillermo Villegas were typical in attacking its subversion of traditional values and structures and its destructive impact on the family and social discipline. They branded the USSR as the source of encroaching evil, and they were more than skeptical about the ability of the United States to defend the

West.[48] The well-published Peruvian officer-author, Víctor Sánchez Marín, had earlier analyzed what he considered the new paradigm's major menace to mankind. Atomic war, he noted, merely made use of the disintegrative force of the atom; revolutionary war, on the other hand, relied on the disintegration of society and soul.[49] Sánchez Marín's concern for the subversion of social harmony by the revolutionary left was shared by the vast majority of his colleagues in the Peruvian military in the 1960s—a time when Peru was beset by guerrilla warfare in the Andes. It posed a far greater threat to Latin America than atomic weaponry could ever pose.

In the early years of the new paradigm, most officers outside the River Plate and Andean regions were wary of making too many direct comments of a political nature. Military-civilian unity, "internal security," the fragility of democracy—these were their emphases. Italians, interestingly, did get right to the point by the early sixties. General Giorgio Liuzzi told his readers in the pages of the *Rivista Militare d'Italia* that war per se was now "localized, limited, subversive, civil."[50] His examples ranged the world: Greece, Cuba, Indo-China, Korea, Algeria, the Congo, and the Suez. Nonatomic armies still had an important role to play, and their identity and legitimacy would often depend on that role.

The internal enemy issue cropped up, of course, in numerous essays dealing with other subjects, in most places linked with the perceived reluctance of the United States to confront the Soviet Union in the manner Latin Americans and others thought it should. Thus the new world paradigm entailed sporadic "declarations of independence" from the hegemony of the United States. Often taking the form of routine expressions of nationalist fervor, the perception of U.S. decline reached a zenith with the institutional *golpes* of the 1960s and 1970s. Professional militarism, thus, follows closely upon the brief rise of the United States' influence as an epoch in Latin American history.

Even when the U.S. was still held in esteem generally, and before Latin Americans began to the feel the internal pressures of both the Marxist left and economic change, between 1935 and 1945, say, criticism of the United States was routine fare. The *Revista Militar Brasileira* editorialized before Pearl Harbor that although the British were holding their own, the United States was as yet an untested power. For Germany not to succeed in Europe, the editor continued, "we must be strong to be respected,"—with or without the United States, readers might have inferred.[51] An unsigned Bolivian essay of 1948 fairly sermonized on the plight of an America dominated by *any* alien forces. "America is—after Jerusalem—

lost to a mankind that never learned how to deserve it—the only promised land [it remains] unworthy as long as it knows not how to free itself from its own sins."[52] This cumbersome and melodramatic description indicated a growing sense of despair in prerevolutionary Bolivia, an awareness of the role of North Americans in Latin America's "fall from grace."

Still favorable to the United States was one of the founders of Peru's *Centro de Altos Estudios Militares* (CAEM), General José del Carmen Marín. He praised the U.S. military mission in Peru for inculcating a sense of unity and coordination so desired by his confreres, but he did not yet see the vast differences in internal roles. He did observe that "Russia . . . would not vacillate in encouraging a Third World conflagration if it were not for the spiritual and material power of the United States."[53] By the late 1950s the internal enemy and concern for the future stature of the U.S. were both prominent in essays focusing on the now plainly visible East-West conflict.

The prolific general-author Jorge Giovanelli described the *Guerra Fría* as an essentially psychological one,[54] the logical result of World War II. Giovanelli did not think the U.S. capable of winning this kind of war. In 1958 Lieutenant Colonel Mercado Jarrín stated unequivocally that despite the good intentions of the United States, Peru could not benefit all that much by following the U.S. model of organization and doctrine. Peru, he thought, ought to look inward and consider doctrinal content before concerning itself much with organizational form.[55] This piece of Mercado Jarrin's probably signals the beginning of a marked decline of the United States' influence over the Peruvian army. It coincides with a decline of U.S. influence elsewhere.

Colonel Tomás Sánchez Bustamante, an outspoken Argentine, thought he understood the East-West conflict fully in 1962. "Intrinsically perverse" communism had been behind every bit of trouble since the war, from the Greek civil war to the *Bogotazo* (the violent popular upheaval that rocked Colombia's capital in 1948 and degenerated into nearly a decade of constant civil war), to the war in Indo-China.[56] His list of world trouble spots was a long one, and he found Soviet influence at the root of all evil, large or small. Most interesting of all, perhaps, is that he made no comment on the United States, a conspicuous omission. But Lieutenant Colonel Carlos Bobbio Centurión, one of Peru's military firebrands, did the following year by rejecting the U.S. as military role model. In "¿Qué ejército necesita El Perú?" he echoed Mercado Jarrín's line: "What we need is an army like none other in the world."[57] Peru's army should fight in the East-West conflict by defeating *all* the internal enemies, including underdevelopment, poverty, illiteracy, and regionalism. The list of enemies, both internal and external ones, was getting longer, but the South American emphasis was on the internal, not external.

Maintaining something of a regional dialogue, General Giovanelli continued to take a "global community" approach in a 1963 essay in which he discussed the diminution of distance by technology and communications and the transmittal of ideas. Ideas had changed Turkey and Japan a half century before, he wrote, and they were changing the entire world now.[58] The West was at risk, owing to the speed of propaganda and psychological war. One reason for this, according to Giovanelli's dialogist Mercado Jarrín, was the break-up of the West, and especially the Western Hemisphere, owing to what he called "military nationalism." Because armies were the most important shapers of "national personalities" the Inter-American system was breaking up.[59] Latin Americans would have to go it alone.

This meant the Inter-American system required swift mobilization to attack communism, opined Argentina's commander-in-chief, General Alejandro Lanusse—in the very same year that Mercado Jarrín was seeing that system as an affront to sovereignty. Lanusse saw armies as leadership groups, and if communism was to be defeated, if the Church were to be saved from atheism's "coopting . . . the faithful and the clergy who believe in its social mission," there had to be an Inter-American commitment not only to develop economies but to smash all internal enemies.

In "Gran América" Lanusse told an audience that the military was "the vanguard of the union of nations, the cohesive representative of our historic past."[60] He saw no loss of sovereignty in a U.S. role in the Inter-American effort against Marxism. Colonel Abraham Granillo Fernández was less circumspect, more representative of traditional Argentine aloofness toward the United States and the Organization of American States. The Soviets were on the make, he believed. They had intervened in Czechoslovakia in 1968, then stayed on. The United States had intervened three years earlier in Santo Domingo, then had left. The Soviets were resolute, the U.S. was ambivalent. "Two examples, one conclusion," he observed.[61]

By the mid 1970s disappointment and indignation at what appeared to be a wavering United States position in the Cold War had given way to the heaping of blame on the U.S. for failures to curb subversion throughout the hemisphere. Diplomacy and détente were unsuited to Latin American reality. "There is no such thing as a Latin American power, owing to the fact that Latin America cannot function as a bloc; interaction in Latin America is uncoordinated and unharmonious."[62] Here, Mercado Jarrín was again affirming his position as Peru's ideologue and as a spokesman for the nonaligned nations. An as yet undefined "Invertebrate America" was slowly emerging from the shadow of the northern colossus, and the United States was to blame for the region's ills.

The United States was also charged with making the transition to developed status virtually impossible. Bipolarity, insisted Brazil's General João Baptista Peixoto, had created the Cold War, and the transitional stage in which third world countries, as well as Argentina, Brazil, and Mexico, found themselves made further development extremely difficult.[63] Peixoto's intent was plain: the East-West conflict was impeding a natural flow of history. It was an aberration. Latin America, certainly Brazil, was being victimized by both the United States and the Soviets. His colleague, General Alzir Benjamin Chaloub, concurred. Both he and Peixoto were writing during the high point of Brazil's time of the generals, so they were less influenced by a need to restrain their arguments. Theirs was the distillation of Brazilian thought on the new paradigm, and they were by no means lonely voices.

Chaloub saw the military as the last hope in the war between Marxism and democracy. That was the reason, he believed, that the *golpe* of 1964 had occurred. Marxism, perverted by Lenin and Stalin, had become the "mental poison of the twentieth century," and the *abertura* carried out under Generals Ernesto Geisel and João Baptista Figueiredo in the late 1970s and early 1980s recognized this fact. The military would tolerate no soft line toward communism, come devolution, but would continue to cooperate with the civilian sector in all ways possible in order to assure the protection of democracy.[64] This made things pretty understandable to military readers: they would play a political role regardless of who held power.

The East-West conflict fueled ambivalent attitudes toward the United States, obviously, during the time of the generals, but not just in those countries where professional militarism flourished earliest. Argentine, Brazilian, and Peruvian officers could be expected to evince such ambivalence, but others did too, each stressing his own country's singular strategic importance.

One Chilean officer minced no words in defending the 1973 military coup that overthrew Allende. Chile, he wrote, was a geopolítical cornerstone in an inevitable East-West struggle for control of the South

Pacific and of Antarctica's resources. To date, he averred, the United States response was inadequate.[65] To Chileans the nature of the struggle was critical, not nebulous.

Likewise, in Colombia, Lieutenant Colonel Alfonso Plazas Vega saw the Soviets as near-victorious in the Cold War (despite the impasse in Afghanistan) in a 1984 contribution to the *Revista de las Fuerzas Armadas de Colombia*. All over the world, in Africa, Asia, and Europe, events since 1945 had resulted in communist victories through *guerrilla,* subversion, and terrorism, through psychological manipulation and exploitation of democracy's inherent weaknesses. "The United States must fully grasp the totality of this war," he asserted, "for the technological advances in armaments will not be of much benefit."[66] The arms race did nothing to win over the minds and hearts of peoples of developing countries, and this was what would count in the long term. The validity of Plazas' argument remained to be seen, but it was one that had been made for years, and not just by Latin Americans.

Less than a decade after VE Day Europeans began to comment on this aspect of the new paradigm, especially on Germany's place in the new order. "It is an obligation of all German soldiers," wrote Maxime Mourin in the *Revue Militaire d'Information,* "to establish clearly, honestly, objectively for themselves and their Western allies, a basis upon which a new *Soldatentum* (soldierhood) can be established." To be a successful contributor to the defense of the West, the new German army, could not again become *un état dans l'état,* as it once had been.[67] The French (and others) were not yet reconciled to NATO's and the United States' encouragement of, and acquiescence to, German rearmament. *Innere Führung*'s substance was not yet seen as a dynamic in the confrontation between democracy and marxism.

Across the Atlantic, Americans in uniform also were thinking seriously about the impact of the recent war on their profession. John W. Masland and Lawrence Redway acknowledged in 1957 that the training of army officers prepared them to assume "command and staff responsibilities of units much larger than could be assembled in peacetime," and argued that the "American experience in the second war . . . made a heavy impact on professional military education. Officers . . . found that the management of fighting forces on a global scale was an even more complex undertaking than they had anticipated. . . ."[68] But one might ask, while Latin Americans began to see both the limited and broader ramifications of the Cold War, and Europeans began to grapple anew with ideological-military issues, were North Americans simply counting divisions and guns and ignoring the human factor? Had they lost sight themselves of their new responsibilities?

Some British officers thought this was the case—giving them further cause to suspect the Johnny-come-lately North Americans might not be welcome abroad, both figuratively and literally. Brigadier C. N. Barclay (CBE, DSO) hinted at this in a 1963 essay on Cuba in *The Army Quarterly and Defence Journal,* claiming that "to a conventional [North] American or Western European, it is inconceivable that a man of Castro's background, negligible political and administrative experience . . . could be a popular figure. . . . This has led us to misjudge him." "The United States," he added, "was fortunate to have escaped unscathed from the 1962 missile crisis."[69] Beyond Castro's singularity, North Americans and Europeans certainly faced many other new and unfamiliar choices. Reginald Hargreaves, writing in the same journal a few years later, would chide both the United States and Great Britain for being so anxious to "demob" following World War II. In both countries "do-gooders, political panderers, and uplifters" had forgotten that "it is futile to yap, yap, yap about *social* security until you have first made sure of *national* security."[70] Hargreaves' argument sounded very much like that of Latin Americans, who at this point physically confronted Castro's emulators, and like that of the Europeans, who could actually see the Iron Curtain.

Germany's General Geyer would put it succinctly in 1970: "No one looking back on the last decade would describe the policies of the USA as being politically successful. A historical appraisal of Soviet policies would, however, be quite different."[71] To this old German—and, as noted above, to a number of young and old Latin Americans—the East-West struggle was indeed being lost, and the United States was the chief culprit in this dismal state of affairs.

There was also a question of the power of ideas, thought the historically minded Colonel Arturo Baldini. The "political-ideological action of the East" and Soviet expansionism had combined to accelerate a Spenglerian decline of the West. Communist ideas amounted to an offensive that could not be stopped, certainly not by a West that had "spiritually and intellectually lost its way." The situation demanded "reinvigoration of [the West's] moral forces."[72] A review of European and Latin American military sources shows the emerging belief that the United States was either doing too much and doing it wrong, or not doing enough, and that poorly. The results, for Latin American officers, were perceived to be ominous indeed for the future of the military profession and civilian institutions.

Meanwhile, "declarations of independence" continued to be issued, sometimes from the most unexpected places. In 1970 Corelli Barnett wrote, "Since 1945, American strategic fashions have exercised on Whitehall and Downing Street the same powerful but belated influence that Paris clothes exercise on the women of Manchester."[73] His turn of phrase could hardly have been more appropriate, for it addressed a temperate zone culture lag reminiscent of the true gap between Europe and Latin America. And it serves still as a reminder of just how limited support for the United States' military influence can be. Several years later, Jean Larteguy would berate the United States for failing to come to France's aid at Dien Bien Phu.[74] And if former allies could show such disgruntlement, why should not hemispheric clients who had never really felt comfortable with their mentor, who had resisted its imposition in the midst of World War II? European critics might complain that the United States could have done so much more, but by the early 1970s the attitude of many Latin Americans was that it should now do more nearer its own shores.

Critics were not all one-sided, of course. Corelli Barnett did not fail to criticize his own countrymen, and Larteguy's lamenting of French shortcomings is, as it were, history. The European powers were not immune from criticism themselves, and their critics made their own "declarations of independence." One well-known African nationalist and Occident-baiter went so far as to claim that military professionalism in Uganda, of all places, owed little to foreign influence (one wonders whether similar assertions could be taken seriously if made on behalf of an analogous Latin American country). The English language, Ali Mazrui claims, was less suited to military bearing, less representative of manliness than Swahili. The "commanding heights of the military profession, unlike any other major profession in Uganda," he writes, "did not require any special fluency in the English language. . . ."[75] This makes about as much sense as do Latin American arguments that military traditions evolve from Aztec, Inca, or Mapuche times; from conquest, occupation, and exploitation at the hands of sixteenth-century Spaniards and Portuguese. The idealized past and selective memory were often brought to bear on the present in unfortunate ways, as a review of military literature demonstrates over and again in dramatic fashion.

The perceived decline of the United States, the East-West conflict, military-civilian unity—all aspects of the new paradigm—were seen as responsible for the creation of a Latin American phenomenon, a new independence.[76] This phenomenon, not surprisingly, would be most prominent in South America, where a historical tradition of international conflict had enriched the military profession's development. Professional militarism, while a contextual phenomenon and a form of cultural independence, could be a latent as well as a manifest force, influential in different ways beyond hemispheric shores. A good way to demonstrate this is by comparative examination of the literature on geopolitics per se, wherein themes already discussed figure ever more significantly in the metamorphosis of professionalism into militarism.

One of the Third Reich's most prominent champions of *Geopolitik*, General Karl Haushofer, was to geography and politics what Richard Wagner was to music and mythology. Each transformed ingredients into wholes somehow greater than the sum of their parts. Geopolitics in Latin America, and South America especially, became to military men of the twentieth century what positivism was to reformers and modernizers of the nineteenth: an explanation of, and justification for, almost all they had ever wanted to do for their country. When linked to security doctrine and development schemes, geopolitics would become a potent part of professional militarism, and thus an explanation, justification, and rubric for much of what the South American military would attempt to do.

In postwar Latin America, geopolitics came to have internal as well as external applications. Military-civilian cooperation, unity, the internal enemy, the East-West confrontation, and the perceived decline of the United States each had geopolitical ramifications. So did development programs and security doctrines. Geopolitics was not at all new to army officers of the second half of the twentieth century, for they were well aware of the theories of Rudolf Kjellen, Halford Mackinder, Karl Haushofer, and others. Their diplomatic and military histories were replete with geopolitical implications, so influenced were they by European diplomatic and military tradition. They read the literature of their profession, in short.

Connections between the external applications and internal implications of geopolitics were evident early on. Already in 1942, Brazilians understood the connection between control of their coastal sea lanes (or lack thereof) and the alternative of interior lines of communications (or lack thereof). Chileans and Peruvians were reading up on the subject, and Argentines had begun in the early 1950s to appraise their position as a maritime power strategically located astride the route from the Atlantic to the Pacific,[77] something of which Chileans were also more than a little aware.

In the interior, Bolivians were told that their land's very existence was *una experiencia geopolítica*—by an Argentine, no less. Bolivia, wrote Alfredo A. Kolliker, was the "Tibet of America," a country astride a continent and bordering on all the major powers; and any Argentine route to the Pacific, by sea or through Bolivia, would be a "breach in the Chilean-Brazilian wall."[78] Argentines were encouraged to intensify their contacts with pivotal Bolivia for purposes of internal development and external security. The fact that Bolivia now had no coastline only encouraged Sr. Kolliker to see that country as a strategic counterpoise to Brazil and Chile. It certainly did not dissuade Bolivians from wanting to regain the one they had lost in 1879. Lieutenant Carlos Eugenio de Moori-Koenig discussed the application of *la concepción haushoferiana de la geopolítica* (i.e., *Lebensraum,* expansion) to Bolivia's case in a 1951 essay.[79] One of the most important themes of Bolivian history and historiography could thus be recast in terms of power politics, twentieth-century style.

By the mid 1950s, geopolitical theories were also used to recast Inter-American affairs. Peru's Colonel César A. Pando Egusquiza paid only lip service to Pan-Americanism in 1956 studies of the Inter-American Defense Board and continental defense.[80] Colonel Enrique Rottjer of Argentina contributed sections of several *Revista Militar* issues devoted to "Oriente y Occidente," in 1956 and 1957, and the Peruvian major W. Contreras A. published essays in 1959 and 1960 dealing with geopolitical lessons of the recent global war.[81] And in 1960 a Brazilian major would reveal a new conception of Haushofer's doctrines and associate it with criticism of the U.S.

In "América del Sud: Salvaguardia de los EE. UU. de Norte América,"[82] Brazil's Major Octávio Tosta tied geopolitics to the East-West conflict and the role of the United States on the defense of the free world. South America, he wrote, was now the United States' "heartland," but the North Americans were still more concerned with European reconstruction than with their own neighbors. South America, especially, was being ignored, and the consequences could be dire ones for all.

Tosta's argument was original only in his heavy use of the "heartland" theme. Nearly a decade earlier, Tosta's Argentine colleague, Captain Agustín P. De Elía, had written that world domination by the USSR and communism could only be prevented by concentrated U.S. attention to the problems of underdeveloped countries. South America, he had argued, should now begin preparations for World War III. Another Argentine, Colonel Jorge Atencio, assailed the teaching of geography in his country's schools as being dominated by a "simplistic, ponderous, and descriptive atavism." Geography had to mean something, serve some purpose. The Southern Cone concept should guide all aspects of Argentina's foreign policy, he argued. Determinism and fatalism, on the one hand, antideterminism and skepticism on the other, should give way to practicality and pragmatism in the application of geopolitics. In another 1950 essay, Lieutenant Emilio Radamés Isola linked internal and external applications of geopolitics in his essay, "Las influencias geopolíticas en la formación de nuestro estado." Isola wrote that Patagonia still was not Argentine enough. Too many "immigrants" still lived there, and Buenos Aires needed to be more closely tied to the far south. The Magellanic sea link between the oceans needed greater protection. Argentina's Antarctic claims had to be assured. "Applied" geopolitics was leading South Americans toward a new conception of their continent. The Southern Cone was, as it were, taking shape.[83]

So was a South Atlantic policy for Brazil. Professor Américo Matheus Florentino pointed to Brazil's economic potential in a 1966 essay,[84] and by the early seventies geopolitics was an essential theme of military literature. Lieutenant Nelson Freire Lavenere-Wanderley's "Hemisfério Sul" of 1972 is a good example. In it he traced Brazil's historic ties with Europe and her traditionally peaceful relations with neighboring countries. Brazil was, he claimed, at once a hemispheric, South American, South Atlantic power, as well as a bastion for the defense of western civilization and culture. To boot, Brazil was a Southern Hemispheric nation, in fact the largest of the countries of the meridional world. Owing to this status, Brazil should be the leader of the Southern Hemisphere. Second in population, first in area, second in gross national product, Brazil was—dynamic.[85] Major Agneldo Del Nero Augusto's "A Política Militar Francesa" cast an educated military eye on francophone Africa, where Brazil now had diplomatic ambitions. General Carlos de Meira Mattos' "A Evolução do Conceito do Poder e Sua Avaliação," assesses Ray S. Cline's intelligence- and policy-oriented study of world power.[86]

Brazil's ambitions were somewhat more grandiose than Argentina's with respect to expanding her influence in South America and in the South Atlantic. Generals like Carlos de Meira Mattos and Golbery do Couto e Silva would wax eloquent on Brazil's imagined potential as a leader of a South Atlantic Treaty Organization that would include Argentina, Uruguay, Chile, the United States, and the Union of South Africa, a coalition for the protection of the West from Marxist encroachments in Africa—and elsewhere.[87] Navy Captain Luiz Sanctos Döring focused on Angola in a 1978 essay. The West must be protected from "Black Marxism" in Angola and possibly South Africa, he argued, yet the West (i.e., the United States) remained ineffective there.[88] Brazil, therefore, should take up the challenge. In "Quo Vadis Africa" the civilian geopolitician Therezinha de Castro urged her countrymen on to action in Africa, an underpopulated, vulnerable, backward, poorly governed, and politically immature continent led by "pseudo-leaders, Marxists who spoke in the name of nations formed of non-nations."[89] If Brazil did not act, the South Atlantic would be lost. Castro and others wrote prolifically on Brazil's self-styled expanding sphere of would-be influence, far more frequently than they wrote on the specifics of their own country's internal problems.

Over on the western slopes of the Andes, Chileans also saw geopolitics as both explanation and justification for the simultaneous application of internal and external imperatives. Like Argentines and Brazilians, they applied it to defense and security in an increasingly widening range. Colonel Gerardo Cortés Rencoret's 1977 "Control de armamentos en Latinoamerica" dealt with geopolitics from the standpoint of the arms race and potential for renewal of the nineteenth-century Bolivia-Peru-Chile territorial conflict. "It is an undeniable fact," he said, "that inter-American relations must be based on a strict compliance with existing legality. To stir people up . . . to reoccupy territory belonging to another country by virtue of a treaty is the same as an attack." *Uti possidetis,* say, of 1800, was an unrealistic doctrine for Latin America, he insisted.[90] Cortés spoke bluntly to Chile's border conflicts with Mediterranean Bolivia and Atlantic Argentina, but couched his words in terms that would appeal to the pacific, if not Pacific, interests of all. His confrere, Colonel Florencio Zambrano, expanded Chilean thinking on geopolitics in the very same journal. He echoed the arguments of Argentines and Brazilians on the dangers of Marxism's encroachments on the West and tied post-1973 Chile ever closer to the East-West rivalry as justification for reliance on geopolitical thinking in both domestic and foreign policy. Owing to the United States' defeat in Vietnam, he believed, North Americans no longer wanted to lead the West. Her power had diminished to a point where the U.S. actually carried on amicable relations with most of the Marxist world, he complained.[91] Other Chileans would concur with this complaint, especially navy Captain Luis Bravo, who wrote in 1979 that "in reality the United States has beaten a retreat since World War II; she has no vocation for leadership. . . . and lacks both a philosophy of power and the internal cohesion to create one."[92] Chileans used geopolitics, then, to justify their own "defense of the West," to the point of turning it inward so as to focus on *internal* security as General Julio Canessa Robert blatantly did in his 1983 "Visión geopolítica de la legislación."[93] Here he used geopolitical rationalizations for the administrative reorganization of Chile under the leadership of geopolitician General Augusto Pinochet Ugarte. Geopolitics had come a long way.

But Chileans were by no means the first to apply geopolitics directly to all internal affairs. Argentines, for example, will never forget their claim to Las Malvinas. Early in the postwar era the Argentine *Revista de Informaciones* published a lengthy summary of the Anglo-Argentine struggle over the South Atlantic archipelago.[94] Colonel Julio Sanguinetti then revived a prewar emphasis on industrialization and overall economic development in a 1949 essay, "La producción de materias primas esenciales en la hipótesis de un nuevo conflicto mundial."[95] Sanguinetti discussed this familiar issue in terms of Argentina's potential in a global conflict, not a South American one.

Up north in the Andes and over on the Pacific, geopolitics also became a catch-all for most thought on internal development. General Felipe Viscarra opined that Bolivia's cold, dry *altiplano* ought to contribute to its growth as a center of developmental activity. If Northern Europe, especially Scandinavia and England, could become economically developed and socially progressive, if Siberia's wealth could be tapped, why not Bolivia's? Bolivia's landlocked status and the extremes of altitude should be seen as a challenge, not as a curse, though he added that the devolution of "at least a strip giving access to the Pacific would be helpful."[96] Despite offering no sophisticated discussion of the effects of altitude, soil types, and the like, Viscarra pressed on in his challenge to Bolivians. Extending his climatic determinism to the *yungas* (valleys descending from the Andes toward the interior) and the *oriente,* he claimed that with respect to sexual mores, the heat there "provokes irritability, making men and women very sensual. Man's will is weakened, his intelligence is limited." The ways of the *altiplano* should be extended to the plains, rivers should be dredged and cleaned for transportation and communication purposes. The Indians and *cholos* (here meaning *mestizos*) had to be integrated into the mainstream, for these proletarian classes, totaling eighty-five percent of Bolivia's population, were ripe for communism. Bolivia's Indians had great potential but were also easy prey, especially for Protestant sects like the Seventh Day Adventists, who, after all, had done much to regenerate them. Shades of positivism and *indigenismo,* both couched in terms of geopolitics, testify to the durability of ideas.

Peruvians had also begun early on to apply geopolitics internally. Three essays published in 1955—in the early days of the Centro de Altos Estudios Militares (CAEM), and the final year of the dictatorship of General Manuel A. Odría—discussed Peruvian nationalism in terms of penetration of the interior, industrialization, and creation of a "national mentality" among the lower classes in the provinces.[97] The next year Major Augusto Cáceres Echeandía used geopolitics to link national defense with internal development. In "¿Se justifican los gastos para la defensa?" he argued that Peru's were soft frontiers. Brazil's *marcha al oeste* menaced Peruvian security, for the eastern giant coveted the raw materials and petroleum of Peru's *montaña* and *selva*. Ecuadorans still smarted from the loss of some of that valuable terrain in the 1941–1942 war with Peru, and Bolivians kept muttering about *acceso al Pacífico* and *fajas* of land necessary to regain their national dignity. Chile, ever the jealous expansionist race, would do anything to hinder Peru's growth as a copper-producing country.[98] Such writing is indicative of paranoia, perhaps, and of geopolitical determinism, assuredly, but Peruvians under the influence of CAEM mentality would use inverted Haushoferiana at any turn in their attempts to remake Peru, both in theory and in practice between 1968 and 1975.

Major Edmundo Rey Riveros seized upon the organization of a national census to ascertain just how many inhabitants Peru's *selva* did have.[99] He estimated there were a half million Amazonians who needed to be turned into Peruvians for the same essential reasons Argentines wanted to "nationalize" Patagonians. His prolific colleague, César Pando Egusquiza, extended Peru's frontiers out to sea, thereby expanding geopolitics–turned inward by two hundred miles, in order to establish a defensible frontier: inversion of inversion to take into account expanded definitions of national security. In "La declaración de las 200 millas de mar territorial frente a la defensa nacional y al derecho," he described for his readers the potential wealth from subsoil and sea life on the continental shelf and below it. During World War II there had been a 300-mile defense zone, after all, and in 1952 Chile, Peru, and Ecuador had all claimed 200-mile sea frontiers.[100] Peruvian national security demanded geopolitical input, even from Brazilians, if the *patria* were to hold off so many hostile neighbors.

Bolivians, the least militarily potent of Peru's potentially hostile neighbors, continued to apply geopolitics to internal development and link it to maritime access during the heyday of the *Movimiento Nacionalista Revolucionario* (MNR), 1952–1964. Early in the 1960s an entire issue of the Bolivian *Revista Militar* was devoted to the army's labors in opening up the country's remote interior for *La Revolución*. Now couched in geopolitical terms, the argument had been raised over a half-century before. Bolivia's frontiers were not controlled by the central government, and communications and transportation there were inadequate. In terms echoing those of his Peruvian counterparts, one author enviously noted the great potential of the Beni, Mamoré, and Madre de Dios rivers as transportation and communications routes—all of which were used by Peruvians and Brazilians more than the highlands-huddling Bolivians. Bolivia's revolutionary agrarian reform legislation of 1953 had already served the interests of more foreigners than Bolivians in those valleys, he claimed, owing to the low number of nationals living there. He argued that a "fluvial army" to complement Bolivia's riverine flotilla would protect the fatherland from the incursions of undesirable foreign elements.[101]

Colonel Humberto Costas Escobar claimed that Bolivia ought to take advantage of riparian access to the Atlantic: "God grant that given the reality of the situation, our present and future leaders, and the armed forces as well, tutelary institution of the fatherland, will know [how] to fulfill this unavoidable civic duty, for the welfare of our dismembered but immortal Bolivia."[102] Another officer also saw Bolivia's need to dominate the vast fluvial northwest as far more important than any outlet to the Pacific. Not only would skeptics and counterrevolutionaries see the benefits of such activity as positive evidence of the 1952 revolution's commitment, but control of the Beni, Mamoré, Madre de Dios, and Madeira rivers was a "theme of more importance than acquisition of Arica, even more so if those rivers open Bolivia's ports to foreign trade via the Atlantic."[103] Bolivians thought big, as big as any other officer corps on the continent ever would.

In 1965, the articulate, well-published General Juan Enrique Guglialmelli opened the session of Argentina's *Centro de Altos Estudios* at the *Escuela Superior de Guerra* by putting the Southern Cone in a (then) new, if transitory, perspective. "Confrontation is a thing of the past. The Southern Cone, with a commonality of policy, is not only from the military standpoint a living perfection of a system of security, but a counterpoise to that great power of the north, [aligned] with it, nevertheless, in the quest for a world of peace, progress, and liberty."[104] Guglialmelli stressed the shrinking of the world owing to science, technology, communications, transportation, and economic interdependence, as characteristic of the nuclear age, exploration of space, and the end of colonialism. Much of what he said about the Cone would remain wishful thinking, like most geopolitical theories, but it bespoke an already widening scope of geopolitical thinking in the new world paradigm.

So too with General Edgardo Mercado Jarrín's 1972 "El tercer mundo." Published at the zenith of Peru's championship of nonaligned nations, this essay pointed out the difference between political and economic sovereignty. The former, Mercado Jarrín claimed, was nonexistent without the latter. Third World countries had to strike an independent course in their internal development in order to avoid being dominated by either communism or capitalism.[105] Concomitantly, Bolivian officers read that the government of General Hugo Banzer was Bolivia's salvation. An editorial in the *Revista Militar* stated the new government's case: "The privileged situation occupied by Bolivia in the heart of the continent, which makes it a factor of continental equilibrium, even more her mediterranean condition, combined with her vast potential wealth, demands the maintenance of an efficient and capable army, ready to defend the territorial patrimony of our republic against foreign ambitions or interventions."[106] Overall underdevelopment, strategic location, expanded and extended frontiers, landlocked status: all these factors begged a geopolitical interpretation and military-political action.

By the time generals actively brought thought and self-perception to bear on their countries' politics, inward-directed geopolitics had fused with an essentially European military ethos. This is best seen in the works of the South Americans Juan Enrique Guglialmelli, Claudio López Silva, Carlos de Meira Mattos, Golbery do Couto e Silva, and Mercado Jarrín. Perhaps the Peruvian summed it up best in 1973, bringing into his argument other issues already discussed in this chapter. By the time he wrote "Reflexiones sobre la seguridad y el desarrollo en América Latina," Mercado Jarrín believed the world to be truly a multipolar one. The East-West conflict had been overshadowed by the rise of China and Japan as world powers and by the combined economic strength of Western Europe. Mutual defense of the Western Hemisphere was a dated concept, dated by the nuclear age and the accompanying balance of terror. All Third World countries needed to work together to confront the industrial powers—not fight among themselves. The United States, he believed, was now incapable of defending Latin America against Marxism. North Americans had other commitments, and it was up to Latin Americans to look out for themselves. Peru, specifically, should look west, to the Pacific, "that basin toward which world powers are shifting their interest."[107] In all of this, naturally, Mercado Jarrín saw a key role for the army. So would officers from other Latin American countries.

And so, of course, did others beyond Latin America. Changing times and their attendant subthemes would conspire to maintain the credibility of geopolitical explanations and justifications for European officers who really should have known better. At least their references to Haushofer and his *Zeitschrift für Geopolitik* were not as frequent and blatant as those of Latin Americans.

Europeans turned inward quickly following the war. They did not apply geopolitics to their domestic situation but rather used it to explain the withering of colonial empires. While Latin Americans would proceed, in the name of national security, to "invert the inversion" of geopolitics and begin to focus on the 200-mile maritime frontier, Antarctica, the Pacific Basin, and the South Atlantic, Europeans had to avoid direct applications of tainted doctrines. Their thinking along geopolitical lines did, though, indicate general confluence of thought and self-perception. This is best shown by the tone of the writing on non-European areas—Asia, the Indian Ocean, and Africa—by Europeans and their former colonial pupils. Such geopolitical attention often took the form of "the essay of responsibility," a frequently used military prose form outlining a problem, providing a challenge or a warning, then proffering a military solution. Much of this "responsibility" has been historically self-conceived—both in Latin America and elsewhere. It has the potential to encourage the already mentioned metamorphosis of professionalism into militarism. It is a form of noblesse oblige, a remnant of the past that has not worn away, not in Latin America, at least.

France's withdrawal from Asia and Africa—Algeria most dramatically—was already in the works by the time General de la Tour published "La progression de la sécurité sur les routes du Sud Viet Nam" in 1950. He and most of his colleagues still had high hopes they would defeat Ho Chi Minh's insurgents. "If we apply ourselves with vigor we will be able to present the government of His Majesty Bao Dai a pacified Cochin-China and reestablish peace and happiness in the bosom of his fatherland and in the French Union."[108] Four years later the French were licking their wounds, and dreams of the French Union's Asian component were no more. France's next backward military step would be in Algeria.

Asia, despite all, remained a focal point of interest after World War II—every bit as much as Peruvians and Chileans hoped the Pacific Basin *would become,* and as much as Argentines and Brazilians saw the South Atlantic *becoming.* S. P. Sharma, writing in the *Australian Defence Journal* in 1951, described the Indian Ocean as a "landlocked" body of water. He noted that access and egress were controlled: Suez–Red Sea–Bab al Mandeb, the straits of Hormuz, Singapore, and Malacca, and the Cape of Good Hope. India, his homeland, had the best land access to the Indian Ocean; and India, as many of his readers no doubt remembered, had long been coveted by Russians. He depicted the Soviet Union as hovering behind the mountains of Central Asia, waiting to pounce on heedless new states of South Asia.[109] The quest for subcontinental warm water ports and the "Great Game" went on, but not so blatantly as to attract domestic attention.

Africa, too, came to the attention of Europeans and ex–colonial powers. René Grandchamp, one of the more frequent contributors to French military literature, showed that Gallic optimism for former possessions had not faded, at least not by 1952. His "L'Eurafrique doit constituer l'un des plus solides bastions de la paix"[110] extolled the virtues of the French Union in Africa. In terms that sharply contrast with those of soon-to-be fearful Brazilians, he wrote that "French Africa's" population was increasing, and longevity was greater owing to France's contributions in the fields of medicine and hygiene. European immigration was still changing the face of Africa. Africa was becoming a "New Europe," and her resources and location made the "New Europe" strategically important. Grandchamp saw great things in Africa's future: agriculture replacing herding as the chief economic activity, European-inspired stability conquering Arab-inspired anarchy; centralized bureaucratic government erasing millennia of tribal dominance. From the Arab north through *Afrique Noire* to the Union of South Africa, French, Belgian, Portuguese, and British colonialism had left a legacy of civilization and culture: "New Europe." Grandchamp's wishful thinking might be contrasted with Latin American insistence on geopolitical solutions and explanations for most security and strategic questions. The difference between his wishful thinking and their assertions of "independence" was great, but each was based more on fancy than fact.

His 1953 observations on Latin America itself were rather more astute.[111] The United States, he now asserted, was taking Latin America for granted—a hint of ideas soon to come from Latin Americans themselves—by concentrating so much on the communist threat. The major threat, he believed, was really from neofascism—just what was General Juan Perón doing on his recent state visit with General Carlos Ibáñez de Campo? What did the Argentine and Chilean presidents have in mind? Specifically, not much, as time would show; but in general the visit was symptomatic of anti–U.S. feelings.

The United States became a prime geopolitical concern of Europeans at about the time South Americans began to question North America's commitments to their problems. A 1953 *Wehrwissenschaftliche Rundschau* piece made it evident that defense of the West would be impossible without careful international coordination of matériel production. The United States would of necessity play a major role to keep Marxism and Soviet imperialism at bay.[112] *Bundesrepublik* defense minister Kai-Uwe von Hassel put it as boldly in a *Wehrkunde* article of the early 1960s. Geopolitics ("geography" and "politics," he wrote), placed the BRD under an increased pressure from the USSR; the defense of the Atlantic world depended on permanent resistance to that pressure through a strong Germany.[113] Geopolitics in the classic European form still reigned.

By the early 1960s the *Volksarmee* of the *Deutsche Demokratische Republik* was also the subject of Western interest. Essays in the *Revue Militaire d'Information, Soldat und Technik,* and *Wehrkunde,* reprinted for U.S. readers in the *Military Review,* all stressed the buildup of the German armies as both a potential threat to peace and an unfortunate necessity. Charges of Soviet imperialist manipulations were countered by the likes of DDR defense minister Otto Grotewohl, who called the *Bundeswehr*'s existence evidence of Western "revanchism."[114]

Of course, to those in the West, NATO and the *Bundeswehr* were seen as wholly legitimate. General Beaufré put it succinctly: "The fundamental purpose of the alliance is the safeguarding of the liberty, the common heritage, the civilization of the peoples of the NATO countries."[115] Geopolitics had become an actual as well as a historical phenomenon, made more important because of the East-West conflict, national unity and international coalition were necessary. Pierre Maillard's "La défense nationale de nos jours," published in 1966 in the *Revue de Défense Nationale* extended Beaufré's (and others') arguments, discussing national defense in terms of military-civilian cooperation, and political, diplomatic, economic, and psychological preparedness: total readiness for total war.[116] Only the terminology was new; territorial integrity and sovereignty demanded defense against all forms of aggression, internal as well as external. France and her allies had to come to grips with the "internal enemy." But some French readers would always wonder if they should not be wary of the trans-Atlantic ally, for American-German cooperation would approach new heights by the late 1960s,[117] and France's role as defender of the West could change if Germans were allowed to rearm. Familiar geopolitical arguments still appeared in mid 1970s supplements to *The Army Quarterly and Defence Journal,*[118] but "geostrategy" had become the euphemism in vogue.

Meanwhile, back out on the extended frontiers of the "old Europe," some former colonials were confronting the new world paradigm geopolitically. In 1962 an Australian staff sergeant discussed his country's new place in the world in these terms: "Gone are the days when Australia was a piece of Europe in exile or isolation. Australia is a part of Asia. . . ."[119] He saw a great need for "Asian Studies" in military and civilian curricula so that "White European" Australians could learn to deal with Asia and communism there. Such reasoning is not altogether unlike that characteristic of Latin American independence statements.

A decade and a half later, in 1978, a Thai general would see Southeast Asia as divided against itself, torn by factionalism, preyed upon by Soviets and Chinese—not altogether unlike the way some Latin Americans now saw their own region.[120] Geostrategic concerns, pointed out one Australian essay of 1978, nevertheless made Australia more an Indian than a Pacific Ocean country, but defense policy makers still failed to take this into account. After all, Australia had the longest coastline of any Indian Ocean country.[121] Chileans and Peruvians, Argentines and Brazilians would all have understood such a frame of reference.

Zara Dian, an *Asian Defence Journal* correspondent, pointed out that the West, by retreating from Southeast Asia, had left the door open for the division of the area into communist and noncommunist blocs, a kind of East-West confrontation, Asian-style, consisting of Vietnam, Laos, and Cambodia versus Thailand, Malaysia, Singapore, Indonesia, and the Philippines—but not Australia.[122] Another zone of confrontation existed in South Asia proper. General Mohammed Zia-Ul-Haq called for Indian-Pakistani cooperation, for a "rational partnership in the geostrategic sense. . . . Culture, heritage, history, geography, language, and values, like the seas and the oceans, can unite or divide, depending on your capacities and intentions in regard to their use."[123] These two historic antagonists should act together to confront the common foe, he argued, in a vein that South Americans again could have understood. Far to the west and well into the new world paradigm, an Israeli general voiced his concerns based on basic Middle Eastern geopolitics: "The revenues available to our smallest competitors, the Fatah . . . , are far greater than those we possess."[124] Beset on all sides, and not blessed, like Australians, with a briny frontier, Israelis also faced geopolitical uncertainties of historic dimensions. At about the same time we can find an essay by the Italian social scientist Franco A. Casadio ("La conflittualità mondiale nel periodo 1954–63") ascribing all intra- and international conflict in Latin America, the Middle East, South and Southeast Asia to geopolitical factors of similar significance.[125] Military political involvement in these regions, he wrote, distinguishing them thus from the West proper, was prima facie evidence of serious internal problems. Geopolitics was just another part of shared professionalism that became a weapon for professional militarists to wield in their arguments. Beyond Europe geopolitics would become more than any European had ever foreseen.

As they confronted a new world paradigm, military men the world over would continue to write on the same themes even though the particular events they had in mind differed from one another. Change continued to threaten them all. Power realignments menaced their status quo, however uncomfortable they might have previously found that status to be. Their attraction to geopolitics—not unreasonable, given its flexibility, illusory utility, and superficial simplicity—often led them to fall back on it as a panacea. Its apparent applications to national security and developmental programs encouraged Latin Americans (and others) to believe they could blend theory and practice and thus solve the dilemma of social and cultural change and their unsettling effects on their countries. This dilemma is the subject of the next chapter. There the process of metamorphosis will be examined for what it must be regarded historically, one of accumulation and continued self-enrichment. Change in whatever form became a challenge and a threat to the officer, the army, the nation. The distinction between challenge and threat often marks the distance between professionalism and militarism. All change could be, and often was, reflected in the society and culture of which the officer considered himself *a part,* but from which he would also come to see himself *apart.*

TWO

Sociocultural Change: Reconciling Tradition, New Ideas, and the Generation Gap

Rauffenstein: "I was a fighting man and, now, I am a bureaucrat, a policeman. It is the only way left for me to try and serve my country."

Boeldieu: "I am afraid we can do nothing to turn back the clock."—"La Grande Illusion" (1937)

If we'd only prevented them from learning all those wild dances a few years ago, they wouldn't act the way they do now, so totally crazy. . . . If only they couldn't publish all that stuff about sex, forbid them from undressing on the stage and in the films and on the beaches, those disgusting hippies smoking their marijuana and flaunting their filth in front of all the news cameras—they shouldn't be allowed to show things like that.—Ivan Ângelo, *A Festa* (1976)

Probably the most sharply focused and forcefully argued literature dealing with changing times covers the sociocultural shifts given impetus by World War II and its aftermath. Naturally, associated social and cultural change became the major internal foci of military writers. Such change, after all, could affect the very souls of officers and men.

This chapter shows how attention directed toward social and cultural change influenced both the metamorphosis of professionalism into militarism and the very elaboration of professionalism itself. When military writers chose to deal with social and cultural changes, they could not avoid discussing traditions and the impact of new ideas on them. When viewed in the context of the themes treated in the previous chapter, sociocultural change became, in the minds of officers, associated with instability. Officers typically continued to champion stability, associating it in many cases with tradition. Professional militarism, tradition, stability, and aversion to sociocultural innovations would prove inseparable.

This chapter also leads toward the conclusion that military literature of a nontechnical nature limits itself in breadth and depth. A perpetual self-enrichment of militarylore lends both timeless and boundless qualities to the officer's lament—and to the justifications of his actions.

Self-enrichment through persistent repetition across time and around the world made the post–World War II mix of officer corps thought and self-perception a more complex and volatile one than that which characterized the prewar era, both in Latin America and elsewhere. The importance and legitimacy of the past and tradition proved at times difficult to maintain. Certain topics would be omitted from the literature of the profession. Yet though they were off limits, they were not forgotten. Variations in past experience and traditions, continent and country, made for variations in present reality, real and perceived. Professionalism varied, of course, and militarism could be latent as well as manifest. Nowhere is this clearer than in works dealing with sociocultural change. At times this literature seems to constitute an intercontinental dialogue on like themes which are nevertheless germane to different times and places.

Some South American professional military men could legitimately hearken to echoes of an idealized Europeanized past. Despite all, there were still some good old days for Argentines, Brazilians, Chileans, and Peruvians to remember. Their writings, juxtaposed with examples from beyond Latin America, show comparable concerns for the decline of the social position of officers and for a perceived lack of civilian respect for tradition, ceremony, and hierarchy. Social and cultural change was destroying them and their fatherlands. Throughout Latin America, as well as elsewhere in the world, social patterns, cultural mores, rampant individualism, excessive militarism, and Marxist propaganda virtually took on a life of their own, so prominent were they in military literature. Yet there were important differences, despite broad consensus. In Europe and North America, for example, tradition could not be propped up on a crumbling pedestal any more, as an idol to be revered for the sake of reverence. Beyond Latin America, in fact, there existed a more firmly stated (if not genuine) acceptance of change per se as at best beneficial, at worst tolerable. This recognition of the inevitability of change would be reflected in essays that discussed in calmer terms the changing relationships between the classes, between officers and men (and women), generational differences, race relations, and the altered roles played by family, school, and church. Latin Americans were not as charitable when and if they dealt with such specific aspects of sociocultural evolution.

In fine, sociocultural change meant quite different things in different parts of the world and not too surprisingly was appraised and dealt with in varying manners by military writers. Whether change was real or perceived often did not matter. Where professional militarism became manifest, officers convinced themselves that the social and cultural content of the new paradigm was destroying the good old days. Even where militarism was merely latent officers would often write about all that was new as destabilizing, encouraged from the wrong quarters, and indicative of civilian failings. Societies and cultures in transition attracted more than passing attention from military writers everywhere.

Before most Latin Americans could even begin to idealize the good old days, South Americans were already looking back to *prusianización* and *afrancesismo,* to the glories of the *Força Expedicionária Brasileira* (FEB), to the establishment of schools and academies, to the founding fathers of their profession, national and foreign, and to errors of the past. Mexicans began to look back to *La Revolución* as their foundation—certainly they could not go much further back than 1910.

Officers molded in the image of their predecessors saw their past as preparation for the role of stabilizers of national affairs. It became a standard, if simplistic, maxim that the army was a rational, organized institution. "Let us remember that the army is an oasis of comparative sanity. The world is going through turbulent times . . . to date, anyway, we have maintained a wonderful officer-soldier relationship . . . values . . . old fashioned virtues; we in the service are perhaps still unique in our standards within the nation and should still be able to [repeat] what we have done before."[1] No Latin American colleague could have said it better in 1975 than this British general.

Back when the war began, Latin Americans were already looking to their heritage. In 1939 the first issue of Brazil's *Nação Armada* extolled the late-nineteenth-century Goltzian concept of *Volk in Waffen,* the nation in arms, and used it as justification for military-civilian unity and preparedness.[2] The Chilean general Indalicio Téllez fondly recalled the birth of Chile's professional officer corps in a 1942 essay that urged postgraduate training for officers in order that they, as "professional public employees," be always able to defend their country.[3] That same year, Brazilians paid homage to one of their founding fathers, Marshal Hermes da Fonseca, and looked back with nostalgia to their French connections.[4] They also read the essay by then Captain Nelson Werneck Sodré urging them to rewrite Brazilian military history using their own standards.[5] Bolivia's Colonel Enrique Vidaurre told his readers that they should rectify some of their own past errors. However prosaic his keen interest in the right kind of uniforms for multiclimatic Bolivia may have appeared, his point was well taken. The army's consciousness of its Bolivianness made reordering of at least part of its past necessary. Bolivian uniforms, with their "bright colors and head plumage, made the troops visible and vulnerable."[6] The time for adoption had passed; the time for adaptation had arrived.

Even the Dominican Republic's finest officers recognized this. "The army is no longer a uniformed rabble characterized by cannon fodder, ready for sacrifice. Today to wear the uniform is an honor, and our boys from the best classes are enrolling in military schools with as much enthusiasm as they enroll in other schools." Military service had become, this writer claimed, "a religion of loyalty and honor."[7] "Passing along the

Haitian frontier," one foreign scholar would later observe, "one is struck by a number of crenelated observation points seemingly designed under the influence of the 1930s French Foreign Legion movies."[8] So much for change there. Bolivians and Dominicans might indeed have had reasons to recreate their pasts. In the Andean nation political meddling had damaged the army's prestige. In the Caribbean country, Trujillo's grip on the army had made it a good place to make a living, but not much more.

Peruvians, like their Brazilian neighbors, would often recall fondly the French missions. The *Revista Militar del Perú* edition of November 1946 was devoted to the Franco-Peruvian military experience.[9] A Brazilian colonel wrote a paean to France six years later in which he blamed French politicians, youth, and subversives for France's 1940 collapse, and in 1954 General Francisco de Paula Cidade recounted the history of the 1919 French mission.[10] Also during the 1950s, Colombians recalled their experience with Chilean second-generation Prussianization.[11] Peruvians would also read that since the days of Alfred de Vigny accelerated change in all sectors of society had destroyed far too much of the past. Industrialization, another South American opined, had destroyed the very best of the past: "What do industrialization and honor have in common?" he asked.[12] Brazilians were also treated to a revival of interest in Olavo Bilac, the nationalist poet who pled the case of the military so eloquently in the post–World War I decade. Bilac would be compared to Luiz de Camões and Gabrielle D'Annunzio, "soldier poets."[13]

Peruvians were reminded in 1960 that the CAEM was, after all, modeled after the *Centre des Hautes Études Militaires,* Marshal Ferdinand Foch's advanced-studies brainchild; and in 1961 Brazilians recalled the revolution of 1924 and read anew of the continuing need for a Brazilian version of military history.[14] In the very same decade Mexicans read (as if they did not already know by then), that the army was "the people," and had been ever since "the era of the pre-conquest civilizations,"[15] then again briefly in the days of *La Reforma,* only to be perverted by the dictator Díaz.

Somewhat less grandiose in historical sweep was the Colombian Gonzalo Canal Ramírez's assertion that the professionalization of his army had removed it forever from "those days in which the landowner made himself a brigadier general, made his majordomo and foremen into a staff, armed his peons with muskets, shot guns, or farm tools, and issued *pronounciamientos*."[16] The establishment of Colombia's military academy in 1907, he wrote, had ended the era of spontaneous martial improvisation that had contributed to Colombia's state of collapse in the past century. A Venezuelan colonel used Foch's model—which was not a U.S. example—as his justification of a military higher studies center for his own country as late as 1967,[17] and that same year Peruvians once again traced their military history from the days of the Incas through the disgraces of the nineteenth century to the days of French deliverance.[18]

In the 1960s Salvadorans, who, like Colombians, were the benefactors of Chilean Prussianization, looked back on their own history. So much political activity by the Salvadoran army demanded some kind of justification of institutional existence, and Chileans who served in El Salvador even after World War II came in for a heavy dose of praise. Salvadorans tended to compare themselves to Chileans at every turn in their speeches and essays.[19] Mexicans, by this time, were systematically elevating Lázaro Cárdenas (President, 1934–1940) to the lofty position occupied by the likes of Brazil's Hermes da Fonseca, the Argentine Pablo Riccheri, and French and German mission leaders in South America: that is, a founding father of the profession.[20] Mexicans also continued to remind themselves of their Colombialike nineteenth-century history and their own preconquest heritage.

Peruvians of the late 1960s had begun to view the founding of the CAEM and of military preparatory schools in the same terms they once used to recall their French origins. The Colegio Militar Leoncio Prado, the setting for the former cadet and author Mario Vargas Llosa's *La ciudad y los perros,* celebrated its silver anniversary in 1969. Military writers insisted (as Vargas Llosa's officer-characters had) that Leoncio Prado turned out "young men who disdained childish frivolity and ideas that smacked of decadence."[21] Lieutenant Colonel José Zárate Lescano added another dose of the pre-Colombian past to the wholly idealized mix: the army had its origins in the Chavin culture and was the "most autochthonous of Peruvian institutions."[22]

Venezuelans received steady doses of another kind: maxims by the score, published in the *Revista de las Fuerzas Armadas*. Xenophon, Puffendorf, Plutarch, Machiavelli, Comte, Corneille, and others found their way into the pages of the *Revista*.[23] Readers were also reminded of a (tenuous) Prusso-Chilean link dating from early in the century. Brazilians in the 1970s read still again of French influences on the FEB. By participating successfully in the struggle against the Axis (at the behest of an authoritarian regime), the FEB became the "manifestation of the national democratic consciousness solidified against the dictatorship that suffocated Brazil," and that created the conditions for the revolution of 1964.[24] The 1964 movement, the initial case of professional militarism in flower, thus became a product of the idealized past as much as a response to the troubles of the present. The author of that passage went so far as to remember that: "*Sob a metralha, dentro das trincheiras, em pleno 'blackout' eu ouví noites inteiras uma canção no ceu vibrar. Era o inimigo a recordar: 'A ti Lilí Marlene, A ti Lilí Marlene.'*" Ah, how good it must have sounded. Brazilian officers read still of their colonial military origins, too, which only encouraged them to think of themselves as part of a continuum that somehow included the army in every aspect of Brazillian history.[25]

By the 1970s Mexicans had jumped backward, beyond Lázaro Cárdenas to Aztec chieftains who had organized and sought the counsel of selected nobles in something like a general staff.[26] Chileans were, for obvious reasons, more realistic. They still traced their doctrine of national security back to the 1920s in order to show that what they had done in 1973 was merely the logical extension of a previously assigned and partially fulfilled mission.[27] Everyone had a right to a past, even if that past was an idealized one.

In his Fordham Lectures of 1937, Hilaire Belloc argued that Christian civilization had reached a crisis. One Argentine interpreted him as saying that the Reformation, "that cataclysmic rupture," had caused most of the social and moral evils that led to revolution, "that is to say that doctrine that pretends to structure society according to the will of man instead of the will of God, that doctrine that pretends to de-Christianize a world and a society that embraces Christianity."[28] Whatever the past may have been in reality, there was for everyone some *time before* when things had been better, if not ideal, a time before so much change had outpaced the army's ability to exist as an "oasis of sanity."

Officers from other regions likewise would look to the past with fondness and relief, but in some ways distinct from those of Latin Americans. Major General A. C. Duff (CB, OBE, MC) reminded his readers in 1949, for example, that whereas "the position of an officer used to have much in common with that of the governor of a prison . . . the present position of an officer, and of a junior officer in particular, has much in common with that of the captain of a team."[29] Duff thus began one of the long debates that mark military literature outside of Latin America for much of the post–World War II era: leadership versus management. An Australian officer raised the issue in a different way, juxtaposing mercenary and missionary ambitions. "Formal education," wrote Lieutenant Colonel A. Green, "is apparently not so essential as a high basic intelligence, which must be combined with drive and a love of the profession."[30] Simple team captains were not good enough for that sports-minded Aussie.

At about the same time, continental Europeans again were casting their eyes on the past. One German recalled uniforms of the past and lamented that the new *Bundeswehr* kit made Germany's soldiers look like lift boys, stewards at parties, and, for good measure, South Americans.[31] A French general warned his countrymen against trusting too much in treaties with former enemies and thinking too much about the past. Another would recall the bygone days in a more partisan way by writing of the contributions of Black Africans to victory in the Great War.[32] A German even advocated using Jean Jaurès' *L'armée nouvelle* as a starting point for rearmament, to commemorate the centennial of the Frenchman's birth.[33] As the 1950s drew to a close, one French general concluded that the days of *la grande muette* ("the great mute") had ended and officers were now regarded not as men of Vigny's *grandeurs* and *servitude,* but as mere technicians, affected by a *malaise de l'armée.*[34] *La muette malade,* as it were, had barely survived the crisis of Dien Bien Phu and was about to confront that of Algeria.

Africa, whence had come Mangin's *armée noire,* would serve also as a decidedly ungeopolitical source of nostalgia for the French and the Belgians. *Tropiques,* the journal of Francophone Africa, published paeans to both Lyautey and Joffre and their colonial exploits during the 1950s and 1960s.[35] The Belgian Congo's *Force Publique* was touted by one officer as the only institution capable of holding the Congo together as a nation at the time of independence.[36] Islamic and Sub-Saharan Africa—Grandchamp's "Eurafrique"—were already by this time beginning to experience the agonies of transition from colonial to neocolonial status, and this may have been more evident to Europeans than to Africans themselves.

Meanwhile, the East-West confrontation of the 1960s drew further attention to the pre–Berlin Wall continental European past. Now rearming, Germans still fretted about tradition as a basic component of all military organizations, a dangerous one to some. "Responsibility to comrades, company, regiment, division, army—and even *Volk und Vaterland,* this is the duty and the obligation of the soldier, be he grenadier or general." The spirit and morale of the troops "were traditional, yet timely to an army." Tradition "had nothing to do with militarism."[37] Germans sought to build on, not rebuild, the past. To do so, they began to remember selectively. One 1962 essay managed to ignore the entire Third Reich experience and yet recall the glories of the Napoleonic era quite clearly.[38] Obviously, selective memory of idealized pasts was by no means exclusive to Latin America.

Nor were admonitions to officers to hit the books and keep apace of change. One North American article reprinted for Australians reminded an open-minded reader of the Chilean Indalicio Téllez's comments on the need for advanced study. Since soldiers had usually not gotten the respect they deserved in peacetime, it was incumbent on them now, during the Cold War, to prove their worth all the more vigorously: "An officer who expects to make a significant contribution in his calling must continue to study throughout his career."[39] Professionalism meant proficiency; the peace of the Cold War demanded preparedness.

This was especially so on the European continent in the face of German rearmament. Writing for British readers, H. W. Koch stated that "the future of German democracy—in contrast to Weimar—will still depend upon its parliamentarians rather than its generals." But, he also reminded them, compared with the other NATO forces the West Germans looked like "underprivileged mercenaries," whereas the *Nationale Volksarmee,* "smartly goose-stepping in jackboots . . . dressed in what amounts to a replica of the old *Wehrmacht* uniform," was a force to contend with.[40] Germans would confront differing, often contradictory, visions of past and present across the Iron Curtain and the Berlin Wall far more often than would officers throughout Latin America. To officers from all backgrounds, appearances may be as important as tradition in enhancing self-perception.

Near the end of the decade that saw the Wall go up and the Vietnam debacle take its final form, a Canadian officer would write that "it must always be axiomatic that the military profession is the agent of national policy and not its manipulator. It exists solely to serve the interests of the state and not to determine what those interests should be."[41] The world balance of power had shifted from Pax Britannica to Pax Atomica, this man believed. China and the Third World now had to be reckoned with. Canada and other countries, like it or not, could not live in the past. He was not alone in his thinking. Europeans and Latin Americans, Asians and Africans knew it too. In the 1970s they would show this by refining earlier arguments.

Vice Admiral Fritz Ruge raised the question of *Tradition* when he worried that the "new tradition" of *Staatsbürger in Uniform*—not *Volk in Waffen,* mind us all—would not easily be established. Germans must emphatically deny any intent to recreate a *Wehrmacht* or *Reichswehr* mentality. The cultivation of tradition through symbols, displays, ceremonies, and veterans' organizations had been sanctioned, well and good. Defense Minister von Hassell had affirmed the importance of preserving tradition in 1965, including the use of traditional flag colors, marching (no goose-stepping as in the DDR, Soviet Union, and Latin America), and the erection of museums devoted to "past" glories. All this, after all, was history, and "man without history is easily manipulated, he is part of a shapeless mass."[42] But that mass must not be given its past forms. By 1970 the distant past had again become important; history needed greater emphasis in German schools in order that soldiers who "did not yet understand their place in society might understand it better." Ruge's essay summarized neatly the German dilemma. It confirmed the attraction of an idealized past, the importance of tradition and of appearances in the form of symbols and dress.

Far off in former imperial domains where the sun could now set, Indians struggled with their colonial tradition and their independent present in the 1970s. Major K. Brahma Singh told his readers that soldiers ought to maintain strict rules of appearance, for "the current hippy trend among the youth of the country is beginning to show itself in the armed forces. Girlish hair styles with locks of hair delicately positioned on the forehead, though only practiced by a small minority in the armed forces, are egregiously visible."[43] The British, he coldly maintained, would never have permitted such shenanigans; and if "the masses have certainly awakened to assert their rights and privileges . . . few understand their responsibilities." Permissiveness and ignorance, he warned, in tones comparable to those of Argentines and Brazilians, would ruin India. Britain's Major D. M. R. Esson insisted in the same vein, at about the same time, that "a commission is a form of property . . . of no financial value to the holder, . . . inalienable, and . . . akin to a dignity."[44] How times had changed. Or had they?

In the 1970s French officers would still reflect on Dien Bien Phu, Algeria, and now on the emergence of a French stand against U.S. influence in NATO. Too many French officers, claimed Pierre Demeron, still thought in Lyauteyesque terms, and used Father Charles de Foucauld and Marshal Lyautey of African imperial fame to justify behavior such as that of General Pierre Massu and the anti–de Gaulle *Algérie Française*. De Gaulle's own metropolitan and Free French past, though, would become rallying points for others who repudiated colonialism and much of the past associated with it. On the other hand, General Raoul Salan's *Fin d'un empire* blamed France's problems, all of them, on France's withdrawal from the exotic lands of the *Outre-mer*.[45] Others of the decade were less strident in their assessment of the impact of past on present and, by implication, of the present on the future. But most Frenchmen were aware of both, for France's was still an army divided, and her past was still divided too.

Britons dealt with analogous issues. Lieutenant Colonel J. F. Stone, writing in the *British Army Review,* recognized fully the limitations of past British military organization, recruitment policies, and institutional stratification. He observed that the British army had been an imperial, European force, not much of a domestic one.[46] Britain's new role on the continent and its new nonrole in the old outer British Empire strained her abilities and will to maintain traditional ways, just as it had strained France's. Stone's colleague, Major P. G. Frances, noted that the same problems affected military-civilian relations in the armies of emerging African states.[47] But Frances was as optimistic about Africa's Sandhurst- and St. Cyr-educated officers' ability to defend and administer as Stone was pessimistic about Britain's younger generations' ability to adequately serve the mother country and its army's ability to influence youth. Britain's was an army in search of a job description, her officers were in search of a past.

The past always gives way to the present, if not figuratively, then certainly literally. Military literature of the late 1970s indicates this poignantly, often reluctantly. In a Hegelian vein, Colonel Johannes Pfeifer attempted to show how leadership, *Führung,* was a constant; its essence did not change. That to which it was applied changed constantly, however, making it necessary for leadership to adapt itself to changing times.[48] Italy's General Andrea Viglione lamented the "progressive demolition of values of the past" in his beloved country, and urged the army to balance tradition with innovation in an attempt to maintain the past's best aspects.[49] A Pakistani lieutenant colonel, Qurban Ali Barlas, attacked the increasing bureaucratization of his beloved profession. Valor, character, and self-sacrifice, he wrote, had been replaced by management skills and opportunism.[50] In "Demain et hier," Colonel F. Menonville summed up the dilemma of his time rather well: "The coexistence of a need to be led and the capacity for leadership makes the obligation of the commander one that is of benefit to all."[51] The similarity of these arguments to those made in the half-century preceding the fall of France is startlingly close. Pasts gave way grudgingly, especially where traditions were worth retaining.

"Man cannot do without tradition," wrote *Bundestag* member Jurgen Molleman in 1978. Military service was to him an "obligation to fellow Germans to maintain their freedom." Fulfilling it would create new traditions to replace those no longer suitable to the new *Vaterland.*[52] Tradition was not just "history per se," asserted General Harald Wust, but something that withstood change and remained in the hearts and minds of men.

The content of tradition was constant, and military tradition was something Germans needed, given all the change now going on around them.[53] An Indian colonel, Y. A. Mande, wrote in 1979 that whereas a civilization might undergo profound change rapidly, cultures only changed slowly. "Look around," he warned, "all over the world the elite are busy in money making and sex. Philosophy knew it long before; man is addicted to women and property." Mande believed that it was up to an elite to save India from the catastrophe of contrast between the culture of the majority—the eighty percent that was still village-based—and that of the westernized minority.[54] His elite, of course, was a uniformed one, and its past was a noble one.

Across the frontier, in Pakistan, Lieutenant Colonel Muhammad Hafez's "Islamic Renaissance in Muslim World" drew sharp distinctions between his world and that of the West. Western "progress" had given Muslims an "inferiority complex," he claimed. In an argument akin to those in Edward Said's *Orientalism,* Hafez accused westerners and westernized Pakistanis of attempting to adapt a conceptual framework derived from the Protestant Reformation to the entire Islamic world. He linked Luther's "revolt" to the rise of the secular state, to the theory of evolution, to Positivism, to Utilitarianism, to dialectical materialism, to Marxism, to atheism, all in such a way as to make the West and its style of change anathema to all good Muslims.[55] His essay won first prize in a military writing contest and is not all that different from some Latin American military commentaries on religion as a constant cultural force in a world undergoing profound changes.

In the "satanic occident," Lieutenant Colonel Gustav Lünenborg strove to show, in somewhat dialectical terms, how it was youth that found itself a temporal synthesis of military and civilian society. Without youth (i.e., the present generation) the military could not flourish, the future could not come to be. "The spirit of the young generation is a reflection of the under-officer and officer corps."[56] *Innere Führung* (inner leadership), of course, guaranteed the soldier's (or youth's) rights; democracy was its civilian counterpart, or, by implication, should be. This sort of present-oriented argument would never gain currency among tradition-bound Latin Americans or ex-colonials in South Asia, for they simply could not accept sociocultural change.

In what is one of the most splendid examples of recent military literature, one that ranks with works of Mercado Jarrín, et al., the retired Pakistani General Shaukat Riza commented on change and its complexities at the beginning of the 1980s. He claimed that the measure of a nation's honor and the worth of its sovereignty was the soldier, a remark that stands as clear evidence of the perduration of Colmar Freiherr von der Goltz's ideas in a most decidedly non-Goltzian land. It is equally reminiscent of arguments made by Chile's grand old soldier, Tobías Barros Ortiz. The anguish in General Riza's pages epitomizes the dilemma of his generation of soldiers—yesterday's soldiers in every sense—who saw the old ways and the old world pass before their eyes and who were uncomfortable with the ways of the new.

"Forty years ago," Shaukat Riza said, "even a high-class entertainer could not dream of sitting at the same table with a military officer. Today a general officer cannot afford to enter restaurants crowded with low-class entertainers."[57] Workers now sniffed at what used to be high wages, and inflation had not protected the career soldier. The past was past, and the present was alien to this general.

The past and tradition still appealed to so many, and in so many ways. Well into the 1980s Germans clung to theirs. *Innere Führung* often led them back to Jaurès' 1910 study, *L'armée nouvelle* as the example par excellence of a citizen army—a "purest image" of a "nation in arms." If Germans needed examples, argued *Bundesrepublik* president Theodor Heuss in 1984, they should now look to the knightly martyrs of 1944, "the *Ritterlichkeit* (chivalry) that triumphed over defeat."[58] In short, he was suggesting that Germans might find a spark of tradition amongst the ashes of yet another idealized past.

Change in terms other than strictly geopolitical orientation even affected the antipodes. "New Zealand," opined one acerbic authority, "has exported frozen meat in peacetime and live meat in war."[59] Civil war against the Maoris and war abroad one year in every three had kept the country on war footing for most of its history, but were not New Zealanders, he asked, finally tired of having to prove themselves part of an empire that no longer existed? Were not officers everywhere troubled by time's passage and its sociocultural consequences? Could the past change because of thought or action in the present?

At this time answers to such questions are conjectural. South Americans were involved in redefining their various pasts. Where the military profession still kept its distance from political action, as in Colombia and Venezuela, or was entwined with personalism, as in Paraguay, the thought and self-perception of officers did slowly come to resemble that of Europeanized South America. The past, in a sense, recurred in the minds of some officer-authors, convoluting the kind of "tropical culture lag" once experienced by Claude Lévi-Strauss.[60] The professional militarism of Europeanized Latins might also be viewed in the way that Mexicans like Octavio Paz have viewed the Mexican Revolution: an attempt to revive the past.[61] Elsewhere, in Cuba, say, national traditions of any substance were lacking. There the army could "not claim ties with the *Ejército Libertador,*" and, "lacking historicity, grew increasingly estranged from national traditions."[62] The results, certainly comparable to those that characterize some of this century's other national military creations, do not merit elaboration here.[63] But they may someday, and in the interim they are disturbing, for they presage continued mental confusion of an idealized past and a troubling present.

"The price for living in a stimulating period," wrote the North American Lieutenant Colonel Anthony L. Wermuth, "is that a period of stimulation is also likely to be a period of transition, and transition is always partly painful. The clock cannot be turned back, nor can it be slowed down." "Mass man," he continued, with an understanding of Ortega y Gasset's use of the term, "has gained a long-fought-for, long-deserved economic and political equality, but has not yet achieved maturity in many fields in which his voice is thunderous."[64] Those Ortegan masses posed problems for Latin American military thinkers wherever painful transitions demanded resetting cultural and social chronometers. Perceived problems resultant from changing times dramatically influenced how officers and armies fulfilled roles and how they justified that role fulfillment. Wermuth could have been writing about armies in Latin America—or elsewhere.

There really did exist, for many officers, a spiritual malaise in the world around them. Romanticism, according to the Argentine Lieutenant Colonel Manuel A. Estol, had given way to crass materialism. "Now more than ever, there is a lack of Quixotes, and the Argentine officer should allow himself to be one. His activities might be less sensational, but they demand a good amount of will, spirituality, and austerity; acceptance of moral compensation in lieu of material; willingness to follow a routine that affirms over and over that military life is one of honor, austerity, and abnegation."[65] This was the stuff of Alfred de Vigny, of Hubert Lyautey and Charles de Gaulle. Its realization in the Argentina of Juan Perón was something else, of course.

The impact of GOU and Peronist-military thought on Argentina is important in tracing the impact of past on present, for Argentines had little more than an idealized military past with which to confront a present that was, to say the least, one of "painful transition." Chaplain Lieutenant

Colonel Roberto A. Wilkinson, the army's vicar general, saw the world of the 1950s as one of disorder, doubt, malaise, insecurity, and crises of faith. Social change had begun, he believed, having accepted Belloc's dicta, with the Reformation, until which point men had lived for the most part in peace. Had not even war always resulted in religious conversions, even for the likes of Attila? And had not Christianity embraced the entire western world?[66] But Protestantism, capitalism, and materialism had done their destructive work. A colleague of Wilkinson's boldly attacked the problems of social and cultural change by noting how the recent war had made necessary "a nation in arms" precisely at the moment that society was changing. Therefore, he concluded, the two phenomena must necessarily go hand in gauntlet.[67] During the rest of the 1950s Latin Americans would grapple with this perceived coincidence in terms both prosaic and dramatically obtuse.

Peru's Major Abel Carrera Naranjo thought that education methods should both keep pace with social change and maintain cultural continuity and patriotism. Too much of what soldiers and students learned in school bored them and did not help them to relate to authority and leadership. He specifically advocated text materials in the form of decalogues and the *Exercitia Spiritualia*—rote learning.[68] Students likewise worried Mexico's Lieutenant Colonel S. Rangel Medina. The increased reliance on technology required officers with skills better learned at universities, and this brought into the corps individuals who lacked a true military mentality. This situation is reminiscent of observations on social change and the attendant effects of increased bourgeois membership in French and German officer corps of the late nineteenth century. Pushing another oft-heard argument, Rangel wrote that "a Pemex [petroleum] worker can earn more than an army officer."[69] Social and economic change had placed a higher value on technology than valor, a tragedy for mankind, let alone defense, he averred.

In the past, officers often had likened their calling to a vocation. Their worries about social and cultural change would give them the opportunity to keep doing so, as Wilkinson and other chaplains testify. In a similar vein, an Argentine lieutenant wrote in a 1959 essay on education that officers needed to be educated now more than ever before, in order to become moral and spiritual leaders.[70] Social change had widened existing educational lacunae, making a longer stay in the ranks a good idea for the country's youth. The *sacerdocio castrense,* Wilkinson and other chaplains would argue, could show them how to better deal with the temptations of the modern world. This was another old argument, only the setting was different. Morality, materialism, temptation, and individualism all worried officers. Lieutenant Colonel Monsignor Ramón Lizardi of Venezuela was sure that love itself was no longer either profound or meaningful. It had been cheapened by movies, magazines, advertising, "and even television, poisoned by commercial interests."[71] Some technology was necessary to heighten defense capabilities; some was bad because it destroyed the old ways. Even love itself was the worse for "bad" technology's influence.

By the 1960s most sociocultural change was usually associated with Marxism, often confirming to officers the negative quality of change, per se. Communism threatened home, family, fatherland, church. It threatened to destroy Argentina, for example, to undermine her fragile industrial base (conceived in a disorganized neocolonial manner), to reinject into politics a "totalitarian tendency" akin to that of the recent past, according to one writer of the early 1960s, when "to our great disgrace there arose Perónism, with its demagogy, immorality, and incompetence, becoming a national calamity."[72] Thus the negative results of change could be ascribed to recent domestic as well as international influences, making the provision of remedial measures all the more conducive to the maintenance of a nationalist professional ethos: better education, planned development, cultural stability, faith, clean politics, national security, avoidance of materialism, better conditions for workers. Argentina had wasted too much time flirting with totalitarianism; her urbanized industrial society needed stability if the nation were to survive.[73] The army, thought most officers, should be a primarily stabilizing agent.

Such was the position of officers who justified the Brazilian *golpe* of 1964, the event which marks the beginning of this book's eponymous quarter century. President Emílio Garrastazú Médici himself opened the 1970 *Escola Superior de Guerra* session by excoriating pre-1964 leadership and faulting the economic boom of the 1950s for creating more problems than development and progress could resolve. "The decision of the majority of the Brazilian people to appeal to the armed forces opened a new era in our democratic revolution that, even though it still lacks perfect definition, has certainly laid to rest a political liberalism incompatible with brusque changes of socioeconomic structures."[74] Brazilians, like Argentines, could selectively associate the wrong kind of change with the (wrong kind of) recent past.

This became a norm as generals picked their time to assert professional military viewpoints in crisis situations. The evils of change multiplied and transmogrified in their minds. "The corruption of traditions, psychedelic drugs, dissolution of family ties, popularization of the 'hippy,' 'yippy,' and 'beatnik' movements should be observed carefully; measures should be adopted to preclude their corruption of the integrity of our national soul."[75] In the 1970s social and cultural changes were interpreted as threats to all good citizens.

"In this age of hedonism and uncontrollable sensuality; in an age in which obscenity and pornography assault with license our contemplation of God's creations and man's labors," wrote one Argentine, "cheating, lying, swindling, murder, torture, assassination, terrorism, materialism, individualism . . . are destroying society."[76] In this age of *guerra sucia,* one might have asked, how could an army officer have dared make such an assertion?

Not all officers, however, were so fanatically committed to stopping change and tying it to satanic forces. At Brazil's *Escola Superior de Guerra* officers were told early in 1972 that social stability simply depended on organization and the inspired use of it to carry out great projects. "Without inspiration a society will stagnate; it will lose its capacity to adapt itself to new circumstances or to generate new objectives."[77] Inspiration and organization, innovation and tradition needed to be in balance. But too much organization, they were also informed, led to bureaucratization; too much inspiration was destabilizing. The Brazilian compromise was to attempt control and management, sometimes a challenge to men who fancied themselves leaders first and foremost.

Brazilians would also be subjected to arguments as extreme as those that became routine in Argentina. A 1973 piece lashed out at family disintegration, decline of paternal authority, rapid urbanization, and disregard for human life. The latter fostered disrespect for virginity in all aspects, improper use of contraceptive devices and stimulants, individualism, materialism, and the cult of "*Os Hippies,*" all of which had brought Brazil to the brink of crisis in 1964.[78] Too much of this sort of thing had been allowed to continue out of control even after 1964.

A majority of Latin American officers of the 1970s probably would have agreed, to an extent, with Lieutenant Colonel Ernesto Repetto Peláez of Argentina, who wrote that all change was not bad; a positive change can come about "when the present is a reaffirmation of the tendencies of our historic past."[79] The most visible, palpable reaffirmation of the historic past was, needless to say, the army. Most idealized historical pasts by the 1970s were those in which communism, individualism, libertarianism, egalitarianism, lack of discipline, and disorder just did not figure.

For this reason student demonstrations, ideologically inspired violence, liberation theology, and crime were all antihistorical, illogical. The media, popular culture, and technology had been perverted by antinationalists. The evidence was clear to General Hélio Lemos, who wrote in the mid 1970s: "Communist penetration of popular music has come about through the introduction of alterations of the scale and new concepts of harmony and rhythm. Along this same line there is also the popularity of music based on exotic sounds produced by animals and natural phenomena."[80] There was, apparently, no limit to the corruptive influence of change, at least for the hardliners in Brazil and the Southern Cone. Since the end of the war, Argentina and Brazil had been the sites of the most vitriolic attacks on society's new profile. By the end of the 1970s demagogy and violence, poverty and exploitation, individual freedoms and foreign influences, movies and television, drugs and even the Church were all being blamed in one way or another for national problems.

Over on the Pacific shore, Chileans likewise saw sociocultural change as the root cause of the problems that led to the *golpe* of 11 September 1973. Colonel Carlos Castro Sauritain's 1976 essay, "Desarrollo social chileno," even portrayed some clergy and Catholic faithful as naively serving the interests of subversive organizations, "engaging in dialogue, thinking it possible to defang the tiger, forgetting that having tasted human blood the tiger only thirsts for more."[81] The military hoped to make 1973 Chile's last "year of the tiger." Two of Castro Sauritain's colleagues blamed drugs for most of Chile's post-1973 problems. The Allende administration, they alleged, had actually protected pushers and users, encouraged the trade and addiction, thus contributing to the destruction of Chile's human resources.[82] Chile's immediate past, not its historic one, now became justification for military political action. The idea of rapid change of any sort had become anathema in Chile and elsewhere throughout the region; the ability of technology to influence time's passage and perceptions of it was considered largely to blame.

"The cinema," explained Brazilian Major João Aveiro Carneiro, "brings to us directly a world of emotions, more easily than theater or literature; it places us instantaneously in contact with the distant past and future. From the psychological point of view it is a means of compensating for the limitations and frustrations of real life."[83] Too much television, he thought, kept people from work and creative activity, from reading and reflecting, and from sleep. The tube had became an opiate of the masses.

General Ramón Camps, who achieved notoriety during Argentina's *guerra sucia*, tried to draw the line between humanism—in the Renaissance sense—and individualism. In the name of humanism, he insisted, small groups of subversives were manipulating the people, "creating unduly raised consciousnesses, trying to destroy the traditional structure of society."[84] Camps would do his very best to prevent that.

Brazil's General Gustavo de Morães Rego Reis still saw things that way at the beginning of the 1980s. He believed that only through the action of elites could his country achieve a modern version of *ordem e progresso*. Individualism—manifest in terrorism, civil disobedience, subversion of public order, uncontrolled exploitation of national resources, and general poverty(!)—was ruinous to the country. Pollution, the disruptive effects (not causes) of rapid urbanization, violence, and crime made Brazil vulnerable to alien influences of the wrong sort. The elites he had in mind, of course, were the same as those alluded to by officers from other developing countries. Tying sociocultural change to geopolitics, he went on: "Brazil is not an island in this world. . . . On the contrary, Brazil has yet to define the character of her population and their potential in order to guarantee development and security." Brazilians needed to make "a pact with their future."[85] It was not yet too late, but time was awasting, for the struggle to survive alone made men easy prey for propaganda, and public opinion was now too easily shaped by insidious demagogues.[86] A Brazilian colleague writing that same year cited illiteracy, poor schooling (for those lucky enough to get any at all), scanty resources for vocational training, decline of religious convictions, dissolution of the family, political factionalism, pornography, television, cinema, and "the influence of exotic cultures" for Brazil's problems.[87] Causes and effects began to blur for the generals of this period, to the point where officers were unable to point to a single cause—ideological, technological, spiritual, or sociocultural—for any national problem. They would no longer agree on simple solutions to the effects of change in their countries. In the cases of Brazil and Argentina it is safe to say that a real identity crisis among the military had developed. Who had the right to determine just what was a national identity?

Certainly there was building, in differing degrees, a wariness of "exotic cultures." What had once seemed so necessary for progress or development or modernization (the terms varied), now seemed to menace a present that was out of control. Cultural imperialism and subversion transmitted via screens, airwaves, needles, "joints," propaganda, and violence were equally dangerous. "Modernization imposed from without," a Canadian political scientist could attest, "produced a crisis that demanded confrontation: the summons to revolution."[88] One Brazilian general of the 1980s insisted there was indeed a simple structural explanation. Developed countries, he argued, had established mechanisms, bureaus, and agencies, to assure proper use of, and access to the electronic media. Developing countries had not.[89] His call for regulatory agencies as a way of establishing state authority fell on deaf ears. His plea for educational programming as the proper method of utilizing television made no mention of ratings. His solution was too mild; it was too late for halfway measures.

It is apparent that in the latter part of the century in those countries where the profession had a long history, the army officer corps ceased to represent a specific sector of the population and became increasingly a sector in its own right.[90] Officers needed no ties (illusory always) with the aristocracy or linkages with the bourgeoisie (wishfully construed by Marxists and many social scientists) to spur them to action for the sake of saving society and culture from time's onslaught.

In countries where sociocultural change was not so profound, where the officer corps lacked a proper history, where professionalization was a post-1945 process, or where it was generated by a pre–World War II United States presence, ties to civilian sectors still heavily influenced military thought and behavior. Change was no less threatening but was perceived in less sophisticated terms. A decided lack of professional sophistication can be discerned in post-1973 Chile where a professional army with a rich past but little political experience initiated one of Latin America's most controversial authoritarian regimes. Results of a highly sophisticated blending of thought on social change with other issues and the subsuming of them all under professional militarism can be seen in the Peruvian experiment of 1968–1980, where another army with a long past absorbed civilian reformist programs and created Latin America's purest military regime in one of its most backward countries. Variations on the primacy of sociocultural change as a cause of military concern and political action are limitless, to the point where we should simply conclude that military organizations can always find a reason to oppose most kinds of change.

Examination of non–Latin American sources that deal specifically with perceptions of changing societies and generational differences leading to cultural conflict lends perspective to the opinions rendered on Latin America thus far. Some non–Latin American arguments can be seen as entirely consistent with those just discussed; others obviously cannot. Some arguments are anecdotal, some universal, but all are the products of deep concern, beginning to appear as soon as the war ended.

This was as true for Asian and Australian professionals as it was for

Europeans. "In the future we shall see mobs better organized than in the past," wrote an Indian editorialist in 1946. "A disturbing factor is the manner in which women have begun actively to participate in civil disturbances. The power of the press, with its leaning towards sensationalism, is also not a help to the army; and the weapon of propaganda has also made our task increasingly harder."[91]

Australian officers realized they could no longer lead if they remained as aloof from their charges as they had in the past.[92] They would have to learn to use psychology, for the social order had changed. Moreover, claimed one Aussie in 1949, "the [Australian] army should appeal for recruits on a higher, loftier plane in order to avoid getting men morally and intellectually incapable of fulfilling the tasks which will fall to them when the bottom drops out of the present uneasy peace."[93] Already in 1949 perceptions of change and its liabilities were being sharpened. Technological change, too, now forced armies to adjust to the present, to the rising status of scientists and engineers, and the declining status of fighting men.[94] These assertions from the mid 1950s would be refuted,[95] but the debate would continue as military men discussed the specifics of their army's roles.

The Cold War allowed Europeans to discuss at least social change in fairly blunt terms without being accused of meddling in civilian affairs. Civilians were free to do the same in the name of defense studies and national security. In the Europe of the 1950s lines were drawn sharply between East and West, less so between military and civilian, as long as social change remained the specific issue.

"The politically naive soldier is no more than a target who is unfit for warfare, given all its malicious psychological and militaristic dimensions,"[96] opined one German as his countrymen were embracing *Innere Führung*. Some officers felt that naiveté in one form or another marked the postwar generations of European youths that filled the ranks. Still others saw the major effect of change as one of the decline of an officer "class," a loss of prestige.[97] Merchants, technicians, managers, entertainers, and workers—these all had gained status at the expense of officers.

Major J. E. Colbeck wrote in 1958 that "a soldier's sense of his own status and that of the army is keenly affected by his impression of the importance of his officers."[98] Managers and bureaucrats were not leaders; today's youth would not follow them. This was what had led to the British army's recent recruiting difficulties. In the same decade, a German civilian traced the sad plight of contemporary armies to antimilitarism and pacifism, psychological warfare, and an exaggerated sense of individualism and egalitarianism. The state had a right, a duty, to exact military service if freedom, law, and values were to be upheld.[99] This appealing argument was not unlike those soon to be made throughout Latin America.

Throughout Europe there was a perceived shortage of officer material during the first quarter century following World War II. Lieutenant Colonel Lunt believed that the military was no longer attracting enough scions of "old army families." If indeed there were fewer "Colonel Blimps" around now, it was even more difficult for dedicated career officers to maintain a decent living standard on army pay. Recruits were staying away in droves. Britain's welfare state made it unnecessary for youths to seek socioeconomic refuge in the service. There was no more "adventure" to it. Two world wars had changed the composition of the officer corps so that now, with greater opportunity in civilian life, less prestige in uniform, and more exposure of military shortcomings by the press, neither the corps nor the ranks were attracting the right sort.[100] "Dash it all!" one can imagine old-guard officers muttering.

An American lieutenant colonel, John E. Lane, was somewhat more optimistic than his European colleagues. In a 1960 essay he called America's young men "a veritable gold mine of potential."[101] If conscription or enlistment was just a step toward vocational training for those who donned the uniform, so much the better. They were better men, better educated, more worldly, more physically fit, more religiously inclined. One wonders just what was the sample group on which he based his findings?

More and more, in the 1960s, non–Latin Americans were turning to psychology, to human factors, in order to explain and then prescribe for the ills of change. An anonymous Italian believed that attitudinal and motivational research—modern versions of *Lebensphilosophie*—would allow men to serve according to their capacity.[102] New European values and transnational culture had changed man, wrote another Italian, and armies had to take this into account.[103] Societal change was, in the opinion of one Frenchman, *une mutation extraordinaire*.[104] Armies were becoming scientific and technological. Like society, they too were changing. The past was becoming simply a collection of selected memories, a concept which threatened some traditionalists.

"In the twentieth century," wrote one British die-hard traditionalist, "there are very few men who do not shave once—or wash twice—a day, or have a bath at least once a week. To them the hardship of the dirt is in great contrast to the lives from which they have come, and it causes considerable discomfort and lowered morale."[105] Men were becoming softer and softer, it would seem, by paying attention to personal hygiene. Some traditions were probably worth discarding.

Men were also becoming hardened all right—hardened against military service. Social change, according to India's Major K. S. Kapur, led to questioning of authority. Job opportunities in the cities ("lost village life" being a familiar theme of officers from the Indian subcontinent) and the expansion of the civil service had convinced Indian youth that the military was a second or third choice. "The rapid growth of industries has resulted in a general migration of the population to the cities," he wrote. "This, coupled with more amenities and a better standard of living, has tended to reduce the natural hardihood of the soldier, who previously was a son of the soil."[106] Reduced hardihood turned men against the military; social change made them into poor material. Better educated, politically aware men who had drifted from their faith, were not very good soldiers, especially if pitted against a disciplined, ideological, propagandized, atheistic foe. Soft Indians, in other words, were no match for Chinese hordes. Nor were soft west Germans a match for toughened Warsaw Pact troops.

Major K. H. Lorenz even saw new marriage customs as signs of sociocultural change in Germany. Time was, he wrote in 1967, when officers asked permission of their superiors if they wanted to marry. No longer, though, and officers did not take into account that military life changed dramatically when they took a wife without permission.[107] Young officers, wrote a German lieutenant in 1967, now had vastly different social views and values from their superiors.[108] They were of another generation, and the gap between theirs and that of their superior officers appeared to be widening in the BRD.

"Modern soldiers, especially in advanced countries, are not illiterate hordes, but intelligent and educated men with strong convictions and mature ideas,"[109] stated an Indian officer in yet another broaching of a new reconciliation of sociocultural change with established tradition. An Irish cadet put it rather neatly from the standpoint of a more advanced country: "The raw material of future armies," he said, "is hostile to authority, has access to information, is individualistic." Universal free education was now within reach of all; soldiers were now educated men, just like their officers. "The student-soldier of the future will not lightly subject himself to superiors who are no longer his superiors in education."[110] More opportunities for education in civilian life in general meant less interest in a military career or voluntary service, and this was a universal attitude, limited neither by region nor loss of culture.

"The younger generation," as Captain Herbert Keller called it in 1969, showed more "interest in prestige gained from success than from honor gained from wearing the uniform."[111] Keller's view of sociocultural change was not unlike that expressed by Captain Jesús Baeza López. Writing for fellow Spaniards, he lamented that his country's consumer society was not a good breeding ground for "vocations that demand attitudes of obedience and abnegation."[112] Spanish society, he thought, was changing for the worse. So was French society, for that matter, according to a sympathetic civilian author who wrote that changing times had brought about too much questioning of authority and polarized military and civilian sectors.[113] The fact that French officers had been writing such stuff for at least ninety years did not deter him from dwelling on the immediate past quarter-century. In 1970 in Australia Captain J. B. Dishworth could say that an "affluent society has tended to soften us, and we see a marked contrast between war and peace."[114] General Hans Speidel, one of *Innere Führung*'s principal advocates, saw social and technological change as both threat and challenge. "The commander of the present and future must be able to lead a modern technological army," but he also had to have charisma, foresight, and personality.[115] Barely a quarter century after the war's end officers outside Latin America were showing as much interest in their future as they were in their past.

Concern for the wearing away of even the idealized past and the implications of this process for the future continued to appear in military journals well after it had been seemingly covered. Lieutenant Colonel C. L. Proudfoot's "The Indian Soldier: Cornerstone of Democracy," published in 1970, kept the flame flickering nicely in India. "The observer on the sidelines, watching the decline of fundamental values and the erosion of discipline in high places, is genuinely perturbed. For whilst discipline thrives on example and imitation, indiscipline is a dread disease that spreads quickly downwards and outwards."[116] Metaphorical mixing aside, Proudfoot lamented the spread of indiscipline and politics in the service. "Hallowed traditions" were under pressure; professionalism and democracy were therefore both endangered.

"Man is a social creature," concluded Lieutenant Harald Schlieder in 1971,[117] and the army provided a good atmosphere for the tempering of exaggerated individualism and restrictive collectivism, sinister results of social change. Leadership, *Kameradschaft*, and esprit de corps were healthy, restorative phenomena. The army was still "the only tangible expression of national power," claimed French psychologist Jean Paul Moreigne.[118] But social change, economic growth, and pluralism were threatening the equation, for industrial output and intellectual activity were also "expressions of power." Echoing Goltz, Moreigne tied national defense capabilities to social health through the structures and organizational schemes of each. The vocation of career, lamentably, might be a thing of the past, and what counted in the 1970s was "contractual relationship." This was all right as long as defense could be assured. The question was, could it?

Could it, indeed, wondered Lieutenant Colonel Ijaz Ahmad of Pakistan. Individualism, materialism, laziness, resistance to authority and routine, diminishing allegiance to religion and country, increasing psychological and emotional pressures, addiction to drugs and other such vices, urbanization, progressive attitudes, varying ideological and political affiliations, pacifism, and antimilitarism were all the results of cultural and social modernization.[119] And they were evil. They also made the assurance of defense virtually impossible. Pakistanis and Indians, not surprisingly, responded to the challenge in ways slightly more comparable to Latin Americans than to Europeans: European-based tradition influenced by a non-European environment.

"Techno-societies" was the term used by Colonel J. O. Langtry of Australia to describe what had happened in Europe and Japan. Most of these were "white" countries, whereas most of the developing and underdeveloped world was "colored," he informed his readers. Urbanization, increased use of energy sources, the explosion of information science, affluence, and overall ease of life were signs of bad times, not good ones.[120] In a "techno-society" technology dominated culture, and because it did, there was a rise in both social consciousness and disillusionment with the status quo. Developing countries would face this soon, he thought, but they would lack the resources of developed ones. "Whatever policies may be adopted, the application of modern science and technology to developing nations can cause only limited beneficial effects, which will do little to close the gap between them and those nations now entering the techno-society or superindustrial stage." Argentines and Brazilians were already confirming this in their literature dealing with sociocultural change.

At least one "techno-society" faced unique problems in the early 1970s. Captain Julius T. Crouch's "The Black Soldier in Today's Army" provocatively raised the question of U.S. Black consciousness in the pages of the *Military Review*. Crouch pulled no punches. "Uncle Toms" and "Oreos" were fair game for activists; officerhood was difficult to attain, let alone enjoy, for Blacks. Whites too often bent over backward to patronize those whose qualifications were marginal. Above all, identity was critical. "The Afro hair cut, the black power salute, and the 'dap' are all things which relate to . . . blackness, and they have no effect whatsoever on being a good officer." "Black," not "negro" or "colored"—the equivalents of "boy," "son," and "nigger"—was to be used. Life was difficult for Black officers in all ways, and artificial differences were often seized on by whites to keep them from mixing. "The primary difference between whites and Blacks is that the latter will usually barbecue pork ribs, whereas most whites will barbecue steaks or other types of beef," he noted sarcastically.[121] Dietary preferences aside, there were no legitimate reasons, Crouch believed, for whites and Blacks to "serve separately."

By the 1970s permissiveness, lifestyle, and individualism were also established issues outside Latin America. "Old ideas on homosexuality, capital punishment, abortion, free love . . . have ceased to have social sanction. Authority in all [sic] is the first target and is constantly challenged. In educational institutions persuasion has replaced . . . authority," wrote one Indian officer.[122] Permissiveness and individualism had also contributed to a "loss of hardihood," to effeteness and "flabbiness." Peace bought by treaty or money fostered *pacifism,* not *peace,* he added.

The recognition of such problems by governments was often as bad as the problems themselves. Lieutenant Colonel William Hauser's *Parameters* article, "The Impact of Social Change on the U.S. Army," published in 1972, listed five major problems of his army: The Vietnam debacle; domestic problems (such as race relations, urbanization, environmental protection, education, transportation, and the handicapped and disadvantaged); the Cold War stalemate; challenges to authority in all spheres; and a negative attitude toward volunteer service.[123] America's increasingly liberal, permissive society was producing a new kind of youth, and the well-educated ones were not showing up in uniform. Those who did enlist needed improved living conditions, remedial education, and vocational training—benefits, in short—to keep them from visiting "honky-tonks" and "crash pads."

Some officers wrote as if overwhelmed by change. "The officer of today [1973] cannot remain the aloof martinet of yesteryear, and men are no longer content to hear and obey,"[124] one Canadian offered. "There is no getting away from the truth that the army tends to hold on to old values, even after the expiring of their influences,"[125] an Indian figuratively replied. Unlike the United States, he hoped, India would not rush headlong into "a rabid craze for change," but would retain an affection for the humanities, lasting peace, and internal development, all for the sake of national defense. One Italian argued that individualism, pacifism, and materialism must be strictly channeled if Italians were to defend themselves, but he did not say how it could be done.[126] A Pakistani, Brigadier Mohammad Sardar Hussain, called for attention to "motivation" as a way of overcoming negativism in the younger generation. Human factors, job content and context, and career planning all had a place in the modern military milieu he envisioned.[127] He saw no "technological threat" to Islam. It was the sine qua non of national power. Perhaps foreshadowing Pakistan's nuclear program development, Hussain's work also plumped for research and development, education, and modernization of his country. Fundamentalists obviously would have trouble with his views, thus creating a dynamic tension more akin to the struggle between tradition and change in some Latin American countries than to that characteristic of "techno-societies."

In the final analysis, it all came down to the accommodation of traditional ways to present-day situations and contemplated futures, and naturally there was a good deal of variation in the specific accommodations proposed. Germans and Frenchmen, Pakistanis and Indians, Australians and British, Brazilians and Argentines, Chileans and Peruvians, Americans and Canadians could agree with that. "Discipline based on unquestioning obedience is totally at variance with the ideals and practices of a free democratic state." A soldier's lot is, "by conditioning and upbringing, to reason why," wrote one Englishman.[128] Thinking soldiers, ones who understood the proper meaning of discipline by motivation, were indispensable. They were better soldiers, were they not? By virtue of their continental European orienatation and their love of tradition, most Latin Americans were intellectually and emotionally incapable of considering such a thought.

A few other European officers might have disagreed. In "An Officer and a Gentleman,"[129] one retired British brigadier lamented that in the 1970s "codes of honor" no longer held. Modern officers cut corners and played by their own rules. Permissiveness led to tolerance of abuses and lowering of standards. In "Behind the Times,"[130] another retired brigadier blamed parents, schools, and churches for failing to inculcate discipline in youth. The specter of unionization haunted this writer, for he could see no good coming of a mooted soldiers' union; it was unnecessary and undesirable in a real army, he asserted. One Spanish officer charged unbridled capitalism with the destruction of the younger generation:

"The current opposition to the army is fundamentally an ideological conflict and one of generations, a product of the consumer society."[131] This author saw all Europe in turmoil, not just his beloved Spain.

By the early 1980s the arguments had firmed up even more. Beyond Latin America it was now evident to all but the toughest diehards that "the leader must earn a heavier percentage of the necessary respect than his predecessors of twenty years ago."[132] Things really had changed in the short span of a third of a century. A survey of military literature shows that sociocultural change, perceived or real, had altered significantly the face of an army. A German civilian would write, "it is certain that the social profile of the *Bundeswehr* officer corps between 1955 and 1962 already differed from that of the past."[133] A Spanish general would observe that "the armed forces, conservative in principle, but progressive with regard to material advances, not only have incorporated technology from the civilian sector, but often are the first to apply technology to useful progress."[134] The Spanish general lamented the decline of traditional military values, but he did see the army as still capable of mitigating the disruptive aspects of change by being technologically advanced. Any army could become more socialized in more than one way, could it not?

No, countered an Indian participant in the ongoing dialogue that same year. His ideal army was by nature an authoritarian institution set into a democratic, pluralistic matrix—civilian society. During peacetime, he thought, this created a "dissensus" between civil and military authority. In civilian society money had assumed a godlike power, and corruption was widespread in the civil service. Soldiers got no respect during peacetime; civilians considered them just an expensive burden. But in the army traditional values and honesty prevailed. Peacetime—what most citizens of any country would hope for as a norm, after all—was not conducive to what this officer saw as an absolutely necessary close relationship between officers and gentlemen, soldiers and citizens. This closeness—what most military men everywhere had always hoped for—was necessary for an army to be effective.[135] One inference we might draw from the argument only summarized here is that the only conditions under which an army could now exist as it had in the (idealized) past were those of conflict.

The fact that other arguments, *lapsus logicae* notwithstanding, often came close to this one in intensity, indicated that peace, democracy, pluralism, libertarianism, egalitarianism—things men in uniform supposedly fought and died for between 1939 and 1945—might be viewed as less than conducive to the proper care and maintenance of a real army. This begs the question: Just what was a real army, anyway? Sociocultural change in its various manifestations makes this question of necessity multipartite. And it raises still other questions frequently asked in Latin America. Might not the old ways be restored, despite the onset of the new world paradigm? If so, what would the military's role be in that restoration?

"In the Hispanic tradition the military sees itself as the guardian of the morals of the government and hence feels obligated to assume political power when political ineptitude and corruption become excessive," wrote retired Admiral Henry Eccles in 1979. Was the assumption of political power, often in the midst of internal conflict, a proper military role? "The [North] American tradition," Eccles countered, "is quite different; the military has sworn to defend the constitution, not the morals of the state. It can, however, set an example of competence, dedication, and integrity. Furthermore, the military can even be the core of an overall system of national service that can provide a sense of social responsibility." Admiral Eccles went on to remark on the decline of authority in government and education and in the family and the churches. He saw clearly that violent crime and the lack of "moral and community responsibility" pervaded a society motivated by wealth and material gains, "libertarian youth culture . . . evident in dress, hairstyle, music, theater, moral values . . . the new musical style of loud rhythmic, overtly sexual, partly political rock music," excessive salaries paid the musicians who created it, and leftist politics—all scourges of modern society.[136] But however starkly comparable such a statement might be to utterances of Brazilians, say, or Pakistanis or recalcitrant Britons, Eccles and the vast majority of his other non–Latin American colleagues would never experience a time of the generals like that which already obtained in South America. Reasons for this will become apparent in chapters to come.

In some ways Latin Americans did perceive both the new world paradigm and sociocultural change like non–Latin Americans did, but their mindset was obviously as distinctive as it was comparable. Latin America was Iberian before it was "Europeanized"; the United States' influence never penetrated the entire region. Latin America is part of the Third World, but only one part of it, a unique region in so many ways. Hence comparability of thought and self-perception—a major feature of these chapters—need never be taken to mean inevitable comparability of action.

At the end of World War II, when the cultural influence of the United States appeared to increase in Latin America, there had already developed reactions to it, reactions already termed "declarations of independence." The Mexican Revolution had become institutionalized. Bolivia's revolution came and went. Cuba headed down the revolutionary road, as did Nicaragua later. Elsewhere, democracy and capitalism, as imported items, proved expensive to maintain in working order and were not particularly effective means of providing a better way of life or allaying discontent. Nationalist populism fared no better. The literary movement known as "El Boom" began. Then the Brazilian institutional *golpe* of 1964 gave light to that most formidable form of reaction: professional militarism.

Although the uniqueness that led to professional militarism could be noticed from mid-century forward, it would be decades before comparability within the region or with other parts of the Third World would be so clear, before both comparability and contrast with United States', European, and Asian military thought and self-perception could be properly defined. Professional militarism studied in world perspective is but one way to solidify Latin America as a structural framework and to give substance to cultural differences that matter to scholar and nonscholar alike.

Christopher Isherwood, of all people, portrayed the Anglo-Saxon–Latin American culture clash in 1949.[137] Remarks made by this neophyte in things Latin American on his encounters with North American businessmen, on the British as teachers, and especially on South Americans as wary of all but French interests in their affairs, are timeless. André Maurois, writing at about the same time, lamented both the passing of France's cultural hegemony, because of the break in continuity after 1939, and the now seeming omnipotence of the United States.[138] But *lo europeo* did live on, just as did vestiges of the Iberian past. The forms of tradition engendered by non-Iberian Europeans helped enrich the comparability/contradistinction mix that is so important in modern-day Latin America. (As naive as Isherwood's "travel-diary" shows him to have been about Latin America and its culture, his observations vividly portray countries in the throes of the new world paradigm. Maurois' more learned reflections shed light on the beginnings of uncomfortable Western Hemispheric relationships.) "Why do things European survive better in Latin America than North America?" asked Count Keyserling in 1932. *The reason is that the Spaniards as opposed to the Anglo-Saxons surrendered to the new soil.*[139] Spaniards and Portuguese, he implied, had no choice. Their cultural descendants still had few options, for they were by then products of environment as well as inheritance. This makes them both comparable and distinct in myriad ways, some unfamiliar to non–Latin Americans.

In 1964, Colonel Mercado Jarrín published the seminal "El ejército de hoy y su proyección en nuestra sociedad en período de transición." In it he touched on all the themes dealt with in this book. He championed the army as the only institution qualified to run his country, to modernize it, to educate it, to introduce technology to it, to develop its economy, to maintain law and order. The army was way ahead of the state and free enterprise in all these spheres, he claimed. The phenomena of change had "permitted the formation of a nucleus of officers with modern attitudes, new techniques, renovating spirit, social consciousness, and inclined to maintain law and order."[140] And change it was that generated the revolutionary program and *golpe* of 1968 in Peru.

Six years later a Chilean major, soon to play a more significant role, published "Las fuerzas armadas en el tercer mundo." Claudio López Silva bluntly stated that in the developing world the army, perforce, as it were, played an internal development role of considerable magnitude. This role was not the cause of political action, but political action became a responsibility by default; it was an effect, not a cause. It was a natural phenomenon, for the army's external role was, for the time being, less important.[141] Here, peacetime offered the military opportunity, not stagnation, and a month after this essay was published Chilean officers seized their opportunity.

In the same year that Peru's Mercado Jarrín became a military ideologue par excellence, Argentina's General Jorge A. Giovanelli and Colonel Tomás A. Sánchez Bustamante would put a finer point to their own army's new role.[142] Writing on national security and national defense in "modern times," they both saw defense as a necessary peacetime burden. The general welfare of the population was to security what development was to defense. Unity, tradition, liberty, modernization were now all parts of the equation. Without unified action—and Sánchez, like other impressionable Argentines, drew his convictions on this from Belloc's *The Crisis of Civilization*—foreign interests and ideas would destroy his country. Two years later Argentines would begin the long, hard experience of military political action that ended only with both internal and external war.

In 1975, a good decade after Brazilians had begun to apply military solutions to their country's problems, General Adolpho João de Paula Couto, summarized what he thought it all meant for the nation. In "A Guerra Política"[143] he explained how communism—through subversion, infiltration, corruption, manipulation of the press, perversion of the definition of democracy, demoralization of society, and the sham of détente—sought to destroy the culture and civilization of the entire West. Brazilian officers were simply not going to let that happen.

Each of these essays published between 1964 and 1975 indicates a concentration, a crystallization of thought on numerous issues. Each points to the arrival at a stage where professional militarism eclipsed military professionalism, where metamorphosis ended. Elsewhere in the developing regions of the world, Africans had just begun to face the dilemmas dealt with in these initial chapters. Civilian corruption justified military intervention, but this only served to exacerbate regional and tribal rivalries, and one form of authoritarianism begat another.[144] By the 1980s an African could ponder as justifiably as any Latin American that "in talking about coups, must one not make a qualitative distinction between 'progressive' coups and the 'reactionary' ones . . . ?"[145] The military in most of Africa had probably become a sector, representative, in a sense, of one scholar's assertion that "'left/right,' 'progressive/reactionary,' 'reformist/conservative': these are all loaded terms."[146] Even South Africans, whose strategic position was now of great concern to Brazilians and Argentines, were well aware of *apartheid*'s explosive qualities. Their defense policy changed accordingly, bringing the military much further into public life than ever before in that country's history.[147] The South African military was on its way to becoming more than just an adjunct of the government; it was becoming more comparable to a Central American security establishment. Asian and Middle Eastern armies were asserting themselves politically in ways roughly comparable to those of Latin Americans. "If one sees the situation as being calm and steady, it is [because we are] like a duck in a pond moving on its course with its head and body serene and still. But underwater its two legs paddle furiously unseen. That is how we work," stated Tan Sri Ghazali Shafie, Malaysia's Home Affairs Minister, in an address of 1981.[148] The entire Third World was "paddling furiously," not just Latin America.

Stillness and serenity prevailed in Europe and North America, albeit sometimes at considerable expense. Not all Frenchmen—civilians or officers—were at ease with de Gaulle's anti-NATO heritage, the loss of empire, the *force de frappe*.[149] Soon Spaniards would have to awaken from nearly forty years of a civil war mentality and make dramatic adjustments to life without *El Caudillo*.[150] Germans would learn that *Innere Führung* made it only slightly easier to "reconcile the new army with the new Germany."[151] The *Bundeswehr* was by no means an institutional sector yet. Both British and U.S. officers would serve their countries beset by professional quandaries. But in none of these places was there anything like the time of the generals, all the changes notwithstanding.

Everywhere a comparable military ethos, the raw material of professional militarism, could be discerned. In those countries of Latin America where the military profession had a formal tradition, the time of the generals would come to pass. Elsewhere in the region attempts to reconcile change with tradition were still expressed in more elemental ways, often only in discussions of the roles of the officer and the army. It is now time to turn to specific and comparative discussions of the role of army officers in a changing world.

THREE

Steadfast Officers: Maintaining Basic Attributes, Vocation, the Social Role, and the "Gift"

The red and gold on his cap and the ribbons on his breast marked him off as one far different from themselves . . . a general was an object of interest, about whom they felt curiosity but little else.

—C. S. Forester, *The General* (1936)

To Gustavo Morante, the Army was an absorbing vocation. He had chosen it as a career because he was fascinated by the rigorousness of the life and the security of a stable future, and because he had a taste for command as well as a family tradition.

—Isabel Allende, *De amor y de sombra* (1984)

Keyserling wrote that soldiers are "the most secure of humans."[1] By this he meant that their values and ideals were so steeped in tradition that choices were simpler, decisions easier, solutions less complicated. He also thought that the soldier, less conscious of fear (or of the consequences of his actions), should be expected to display more courage (i.e., act more decisively), than civilians. In Latin America army officers have been less conscious of the consequences of their actions and have acted decisively (rashly, some would say) out of conviction that theirs is the right way to address national problems.

However much the world was changing under the malevolent influence of the new paradigm, some things would always remind military leaders of their place in the grand scheme. The post–World War II literature of the military profession makes it clear that officers believed they and their armies would always have important roles to play worldwide. Throughout the postwar decades professional officers would stress their importance to the well-being of the state, nation, and society in essays specifically devoted to their work and its unique qualities.

In this chapter army officers speak of specific ways in which they could be a stabilizing force in a destabilizing world. They speak of continuity in the face of many different kinds of change, for the times, they convinced themselves, should not be allowed to dilute the essence of an army officer's role. They repeatedly stress the need to maintain their role in all its established forms. This chapter provides some of the best examples of both the self-enriching and -perpetuating qualities of militarylore, the profession's accumulated wisdom and its transgenerational currency. At all times before and during the time of the generals, then, officers maintained that the essence of their particular way of life and the responsibilities it entailed were resistant to change and to time's passage.

Officers did this by clinging steadfastly to the ways of their own predecessors and their role models (regardless, at times, of national origin), and by portraying themselves as more necessary to the national well-being than ever before. Everywhere officers touted a set of common ideas about their role and common convictions about the rectitude of their stand on matters of moment. The degree to which their convictions of rectitude overshadowed their acceptance of civilian supremacy often differentiates the professionals from the militarists.

In order to demonstrate this there follows a comparison and contrast of the attributes officers believe they need in order to succeed in their profession. Throughout Latin America the basic attributes of all officers are the same, regardless of the level of professional development. In the rest of the world officers claim the same attributes, well and good, but their measure and blend varies more. Three specific examples of basic attributes are discussed to illustrate the telling divergence between Latin Americans and others. Divergences adumbrated in the first two chapters become even more discernible in this chapter.

All officers believe they are (or should be) paragons in terms of leadership and discipline, and their definitions of these qualities are quite provoking. Latin Americans place far more emphasis on the military man's ability and obligation to lead civilians as well as soldiers. Beyond Latin America the officer's roles vis-à-vis the rest of society are debated, but, with few exceptions, in terms far less intense and provocative. Everywhere the idea of vocation, in the sense of commitment, emerges as a basic attribute of a true officer. Yet only in a few places outside Latin America does a military writer ever portray a military vocation as a spiritual one. Most officers see themselves as managers of sorts, but in Latin America the term rarely appeared in print. Leadership and management would never be synonymous with professional militarists there. Both in Latin America and elsewhere the social role of the officer, perhaps the most all-encompassing role of the man in uniform since the late nineteenth century, continued to absorb writers and, one presumes, readers. Differences in intensity within Latin America and between Latin America and other parts of the world mark off the region, and help us chart the metamorphic process of professionalism into militarism.

Nowhere beyond Latin America is there anything as pronounced as the devotion to the "gift" of command and leadership, *don* (or *dom*) *de mando*. This peculiar, almost mystical concept, defined in André Maurois' 1925 work *Captains and Kings*, bound together in a unique way leadership and discipline, vocation, the social role, tradition, and aversion to change.

Themes discussed in the first two chapters, in fact, lend themselves to the rise of professional militarism chiefly through belief in the "gift." This peculiar endowment distinctly separates Latin Americans, especially the South American militarists, from colleagues elsewhere whose literary efforts evinced more of a desire to simply be current in new techniques of leadership (i.e., "man-management") that appeared more in line with changing times and all that ensued. Most non–Latin Americans wrote in practical terms about human relations, about exercising a role much like that of social workers in contrast to the almost sacerdotal role affected in Latin America. Through the "gift," the uniqueness and typicality of officer corps thought and self-perception arise as characteristics of both professionalism and militarism.

All Latin American officers perceive themselves, in various combinations and proportions, as possessed of self-discipline, initiative, tact, professional knowledge, courage, patience, personal appearance, a sense of justice, enthusiasm, ethics, industriousness, demonstrable ability, energy, and good will.[2] They think they must be educators, leaders, and organizers.[3] They must practice abnegation, be honorable, spirited, and physically fit. They have to be morally pure and intellectually motivated. They must be reflective and show initiative.[4] They must demonstrate self-control.[5] They must be gentlemen.[6] They must be efficient, and they must know their men. They must be many things—to many different kinds of people. "Youth instinctively looks to its elders and leaders either for models of good behavior or in order to justify its own immaturity and bad behavior," wrote Colombia's Lieutenant Colonel Alfonso Novoa in 1956.[7] Officers thus had a transcendent responsibility. Novoa's activist confrère, Brigadier General Alberto Ruiz Novoa, opined that "the officer must be a man of strict morality, and his efforts must serve as examples for the rest of the citizenry, which in Colombia and all countries should be far more demanding than those of his compatriots in the public employ."[8] Officers, in short, were expected to stand above it all, to be superior in all things.

Officers were to be teachers and leaders because total national defense demanded more than simple field command abilities.[9] They were to "fear being afraid"; their valor, discipline, esprit de corps, their tradition, all made them role models, wrote Osiris Villegas in 1959. If he had not read Keyserling, he surely wrote as if he had. Officers, added Nicaraguan Colonel Carlos Prera in 1961, should ever maintain "the tradition of conquering any and all temptations and impulses to commit acts that their conscience tells them are wrong."[10] This member of Somoza's praetorian guard cited Napoleon, Bolívar, San Martín, and José Moscardó as examples of officers who had conquered temptation and had always respected both the law and the rights of others. Oddly, he did not include a single Somoza in his parade of paragons.

A Colombian major, Mario Ortiz Ayala, thought the basic attributes of any good staff officer were innate, like "inspiration in a poet, like the precious gem hidden in the heart of a large stone."[11] An officer first had to be inspired, then shaped by other officers; this meant, without having to say it, that an officer had to have a true vocation.

In the first quarter century following the war Latin Americans would continually emphasize intellectual capacity, physical fitness, moral superiority, patriotism, religious conviction, valor, self-discipline, initiative, obedience, and leadership ability.[12] On occasion, they blended geopolitics, national development, and the like with basic attributes of all good officers. The Guatemalan lieutenant colonel, Lotario Nuila, argued in 1967 that in order to be a true leader the officer must know his own country's geography, population characteristics, natural resources, and industrial capacity. Military technology, he wrote, was a perpetual cause of historical change, and knowledge of one's own fatherland was indispensable to the assessment of its technological capabilities.[13] The long-standing interest of South Americans in the relationship between security and development was, by this point, spreading throughout the region, beginning to pervade the thought and self-perception of all officers. Owing to this, South American influence on the region's military thought and self-perception probably outweighs North American technological influence in the long run.

Officers fulfilling an educational social role were expected to have the same attributes as any other officer. Peru's Major Víctor Santander Salas, writing at the end of the 1960s, in a country where knowledge of the fatherland had become a justification for Latin America's most significant exercise in professional militarism, made his own list of the good officer's basic attributes. He thought officers should be demanding but reasonable, severe but fair, in dealing with their charges. They should be fully cognizant of their men's personal problems and concerned for their welfare. They should always behave correctly, be self-sacrificing, bold, valiant, tireless, communicative, modest in deportment. They should seek to instill patriotism, discipline, camaraderie, and fitness in their men.[14] Taken figuratively, and in some instances literally, these constitute an institutional apologia for the 1968 institutional *golpe de estado*.

Sincerity, equanimity, loyalty, conviviality, willingness to sacrifice, strength of will, confidence, vocation—these were all essential ingredients of true officer material, wrote the Salvadoran colonel, Julio Campos Sepúlveda in 1969.[15] Campos believed as well that while many wanted to lead, only a few were able to do so. Those who possessed the abilities to lead, should; those who did not should not. Officers, by definition, did; civilians, by exclusion, did not. A colleague, Lieutenant Colonel Carlos Flores Benítez, asked fellow officers if they kept up to date with technological changes, if they read frequently, if they ensured that all equipment in their charge was up to date and well maintained, if they, themselves, maintained close relations with civilians in their area of responsibility, if they got along with their fellows while on duty. "Do you lead by example or by fear?" he queried.[16] As if in reply to his question, a colleague cited Panama's Omar Torrijos: "Soldiers are the reflection of the man who leads them."[17] By implication, if they were not, the officer was at fault—unless, of course, the followers were civilians. Self-serving statements such as these on the officer's role would permeate the literature during the 1960s and 1970s, becoming part of the professional lore. So being, they were winked at as much as observed.[18] By the end of the decade recognition of more mundane attributes was beginning to appear in Latin American's military literature.

For example, Brigadier General Athos Cézar Baptista Teixeira's 1979 "Chefia e Liderança" stressed administrative capacity, organizational skills, planning ability, coordination, and analytical capacity as complementary (not supplementary) to moral character, basic professional expertise, intelligence, good health, patriotism, et cetera.[19] By the time South American professional militarism manifested itself, capacity for management of professional and national affairs had become as essential to the Latin American officer as his more traditional attributes, but he would never admit it as candidly as others did.

Latin Americans certainly were not alone in maintaining certain basic attributes of those men who led and managed their land forces in the new paradigm, organized and supervised obligatory military service in times of accelerated social change, and stood ever-ready to play some peacetime role. Attributes discussed above were consistently lauded in Europe and elsewhere from the 1950s forward in much the same type of essay. An army officer continued to be an army officer.

Sometimes concurrence appeared in essays designed as mini-manuals of conduct, such as Spanish Captain Bernardo Perdomo y Granela's "Virtudes militares."[20] It found its way into other manuals emphasizing a specific attribute, like Portuguese Captain Virgílio Vicente de Mattos' "Pela disciplina," or French Colonel Suire's "Peur et courage."[21] These all date from the 1950s and 1960s. Out in the further reaches of European influence some officers demanded even more of their fellows. Lieutenant Colonel Ihsan ul Haq's "System of Recruitment and Initial Training of Officers," a *Pakistan Army Journal* essay of 1964, decried the recruitment of officers from British-style prep schools and cadet colleges, for it resulted in "soft, smooth, and comfort-loving" officers.[22] He wanted "rough and tough" leaders of men who understood better the rigors of life and who could relate more closely to their men. There were, of course, Europeans who agreed wholly.

There would always be those who believed there was still a place for intangibles like "style" and "character." The "officer class," no longer found its civilian counterpart in the nobility, but rather in the "citizenry, from which came also sub-officers and men."[23] "Style" and "character" would never completely be relegated to the past. Spaniards would still look for spiritual qualities as well as the more telluric ones, especially while *El Caudillo* still represented both to them. Don Quixote regularly figured as a combination of a Spanish officer's attributes.[24] Sancho Panza did not. Spaniards were not the only ones who looked for intangibles. The French had Lyautey. Battalion Chief E. Walter, in a *Revue de Défense Nationale* article of 1970, advised his readers to model themselves after Marshal Lyautey, for whom service was a "joy" and, as he claimed Emerson would still put it, *accrocher son char a une étoile*.[25] Emerson may not have had the French army in mind when he wrote such words, but then Cervantes never envisioned Francisco Franco either.

Contrapuntally, Red Army officers of the postwar years were still expected to love their profession, be morally pure, honest, disciplined, good family men, efficient, restrained, proficient, good teachers, daring, confident—and modest, to boot. "Authority," in the official Soviet view, was "a consequence of the objective relations existing in the collective and personal qualities of the people. Officers are the embodiment of unprecedented military traditions and enormous combat experience."[26] Taken at face value these 1970s' sentiments do not seem any more high flown than those appearing in noncommunist military sources. They certainly do not contrast all that vividly with those expressed by Spanish officers. General Mateo Prada Canillas offered a too-familiar litany in his "Permanente vigencia de los principios morales," published in *Ejército*. Commander Luis Arturo Pamplona echoed him in his own *Ejército* piece, "El capitán hoy (y siempre)."[27] Nor did Soviet sentiments differ significantly from those of French officers,[28] Germans,[29] or Italians.[30] On the continent the basic attributes of the postwar army officer were as unsurprisingly comparable in the present as they had been in the past.

Of the British and Commonwealth armies the same can be stated. As early as 1944, Major J. D. Lunt of the Indian Army was arguing that officers of the future would have to be adaptable, eager to lead, and both physically and mentally tough. They would have to possess a sense of duty, be disciplined, loyal, proud, and possessed of "smartness in turn-out and bearing."[31] Appearances would always count for something, despite technological, social, and political change.

So would character, one of de Gaulle's favorite qualities. Early in the 1950s General Sir Harold E. Franklyn (KCB, DCO, MC) wrote that "the qualities needed by a supreme commander are more those of character than of the highest military skill." Franklyn saw personality, tact, firmness, thinking and planning skills, coolness, good judgement, ability to listen to the advice of others and discuss it, adaptability, freedom from jealousy, and controlled ambition as the most important attributes of a leader. "It is above all necessary that he should possess the type of leadership which brings forth willing cooperation from subordinates."[32] These British of the early postwar years were not yet managers.

In less-tradition-bound Canada, human relations as an aspect of leadership was gaining currency. Lieutenant Colonel F. E. Anderson, writing in the *Canadian Army Journal*, contrasted the successful officer with the successful business executive. The latter had to understand his subordinates, and it was sometimes hard for officers to do this.[33] It was felicitous that this was not yet a major problem for Canadians, nor did it ever appear to be. Lieutenant Colonel W. A. B. Anderson, writing years later in *Canadian Forces Sentinel*, would stress these same essential qualities but warn that the encapsulated nature of the profession might produce "that most horrible of all phenomena, 'the military mind.'"[34] Such an argument, by sharp contrast, would never be made in Latin America, and rarely elsewhere either.

Back in the 1950s, Englishmen like Field Marshal Sir William Slim were stressing as much as any others those traditional basic attributes common to all officers.[35] But by the 1960s human factors, psychology, and sociological approaches found their way into more discussions of "the good officer" and his leadership.[36] Human factors, particularly the recognition that changing times were dictating the adoption of new techniques, would become a significant topic in most parts of the world in the 1970s, but not in Latin America.

All the while officers would maintain their claims to social and educational roles they had striven to fulfill for decades. Thus, while allowing for human factors and acceding (openly or silently) to a management capacity, most officers both continued and increased their advocacy for roles first assigned them in the past century. Traditional qualities of the officer, therefore, would still be brought to bear on the rest of society through the leader's influence on his men—under the right conditions. One Indian officer, as early as the 1950s, saw this as a very good thing. Lieutenant Colonel B. L. Raina, in "Leadership," ticked off the usual prerequisites, then averred near the close of his essay that "officers and men . . . should be brought up to have one political faith—loyalty to the government, and one fanaticism . . . the country and the armed forces."[37] This was latent professional militarism.

Officers of the postwar Australian and United States armies differed little from their contemporaries (Latin Americans or no) when it came to those things they believed an officer should be, have, and do. Aggressiveness, confidence, preparedness, responsibility, honesty, moral and physical courage, understanding of men, and professional expertise were the attributes emphasized by retired Lieutenant General Samuel T. Williams in a 1961 *Military Review* essay.[38] Seventeen years later, though, Captain Donald R. Turkelson, a chaplain, saw the officer as more than just a leader of men. The American officer must be, he thought, "a model of ethical conduct."[39] "Whether he wants to be or not," Turkelson cautioned, "the officer is looked up to, and because of that he must show concern for his men, maintain their morale by allowing them to express opinions, be a person of unquestioned integrity in order to inspire a sense of loyalty and discipline among them, and at all times be credible as a leader." These basic attributes all served more than simply a military function; they responded to modern times by taking into account human factors. They asserted a social, educational role—within a strictly defined military-civilian relationship.

Traditional, widely shared attributes of the officer prevailed in North American literature well into the 1980s. So did the social and educational role, strictly defined. General E. C. Meyer would argue that officers "should think of themselves as a combination of leader and teacher, not one of leader and director." They should avoid "bureaucratic leadership."[40] The attributes were in essence the same; their application and their importance relative to each other adjusted to time and place.

There was, therefore, an unmistakable, timeless, and boundless consensus of thought and self-perception about the essential qualities of all army officers. The meanest army could claim through its official sources to have (or need) officers with the same attributes as those of a superpower. Leaders were leaders. Discipline was discipline. Or were there distinctions, innate ones, owing to specific, inherited military traditions? Were there, perhaps, ad hoc ones, imposed by individual, environmental conditions? Were those who led and inculcated discipline as distinct in some ways as those who were led and disciplined? The notions "leadership" and "discipline" could bear scrutiny if we attempt to respond to these questions and place Latin America and its individual countries in world perspective.

From the very onset of the postwar era, Latin American officers wrote forcefully about leadership and discipline as inseparable, as aspects of military life that might bear application to the nation as a whole. That constructive leadership and discipline of a sociopolitical nature were lacking in most of Latin America might not be questioned; but that an army should be the source of national leadership and inculcate its style of discipline certainly must be. This never dissuaded Latin American officers from seizing opportunities to prescribe for their troubled countries in ways others would not dare essay. They did this throughout the postwar era.

"Discipline is the soul of the people and the army," wrote Bolivia's Lieutenant Colonel Sinforiano Bilbao in 1947,[41] and Bolivia needed both, he was convinced, if she were ever to regain her lost access to the sea. The Mexican, Eduardo Sáenz, also a lieutenant colonel, stressed the benefits to all citizens of leadership and discipline in a 1948–1949 series.[42] In 1949 Peru's Colonel Ricardo Pérez Godoy charged his fellows with the establishment of discipline based on mutual acceptance of hierarchy and subordination. Pérez Godoy wrote that a "sense of collective duty will be nothing more than a latent force, thereby ineffective, if it is not controlled by [a hierarchical, structured] organization."[43] The leader of Peru's 1962 *golpe de estado* was already representing the aspirations of Peruvian military nation-builders.

Other examples of early postwar writing on the national applications of military-style leadership and discipline include those of Dominican General Antonio Leyba Pou and Venezuelan Major Martín García Villasmil. García called psychology the *bagaje imprescindible* (indispensable equipment) of leadership and urged his readers to study human behavior in order that they might know their subordinates' reactions to leadership.[44] French and Germans, of course, and other Latin Americans too, had long acknowledged the importance of psychology. Guatemalan lieutenant colonels like Jorge Hernández and L. Felipe Baldezón Valle also linked "productive discipline" to proper leadership—however unspecifically.[45] Still others of Trujillo's proud fighting force linked the two. One, Lieutenant Colonel Viterbo Peña Medina, saw discipline as a generator of patriotism and loyalty, which made men become "as one with the fatherland." Like others of his service, he saw General Rafael Leonidas Trujillo Molina as an ideal role model.[46] Needless to say, such adulation stood one in good stead, even in such a "highly professionalized" army as Trujillo's.

In a series of essays appearing in 1955, Mexico's Captain Mario Murillo Morales would join the growing number of Latin Americans arguing that inculcation of military-style discipline through effective leadership was good for the entire nation. Relying on Numa Denis Fustel de Coulanges' *La cité antique* for corroboration, he wrote on one occasion that "the army is the nation as a whole disposed to defend its independence, secure its territory, preclude any transgression of its legality, and, in fine, maintain secure and happy the beloved fatherland."[47] Murillo's argument was echoed by a retired Venezuelan colonel, Pedro García Gil, in 1956 and 1957. To García, the army was a national reservoir of patriotism, a morally superior force owing, principally, to discipline.[48] In Latin America, it is obvious, military leadership and discipline were seen early on in the postwar era as prime political and civic qualities as well.

To Argentina's Lieutenant Colonel Osvaldo Ameiva Saravia, discipline was necessary to hold not just the nation but civilization itself together. "Folklore," he argued, proved that discipline really meant tradition and culture; it was, of course, the "oral transmittal of knowledge, of man's thoughts, acts, and experiences."[49] There could be no lore if man did not have the discipline to transmit his wisdom, heritage, and experience. The army had its own lore, of course; moreover this was "part of the 'id' of the nation," "guarantor of its existence." Militarylore was becoming perforce an integral part of national collective memory, in Argentina and elsewhere.

Dealing as they had to with a perpetual revolutionary experience, Mexicans strove to depict their army as one of many collectivities or sectors, as a way of encouraging acceptance of leadership and discipline as "revolutionary" by those in mufti. Mexicans assured readers that a unit came before its commander and that intense preparation was necessary for leadership to result in the right kind of discipline.[50] Mexican military authors discussed many of the same themes found in the rest of Latin American literature, but in muted tones, in an avowedly "revolutionary" context. This served the needs of preserving a national collective memory founded on military-civilian union.

General Alfonso Corona del Rosal, for example, cautioned his readers in a 1960 essay that valor—bravery—conquered fear, but it served colleagues, subordinates, and others as an example of good behavior only if it was to the benefit of the collectivity. Heroics—individual actions—meant nothing if they did not serve the needs of the whole.[51] Soldiers, in other words, were merely a part of the collectivity. The same distinguished Mexican, whose ill-advised actions exacerbated the unfortunate popular movement of 1968—thus probably doing a disservice to the collectivity—had already made a case for discipline in an earlier essay. Writing on discipline back in 1960, he stressed its value as the binding agent of any society or state. Lack of discipline destroyed societies, disrupted or destroyed governments. To the army, discipline was everything. To a government, state, and society, all products of *La Revolución,* the breakdown of discipline (like the popular one that occurred in 1968) was intolerable. A Mexican thus faced, along with his own professional *compadres,* what Argentines, Brazilians, Chileans, and Peruvians (and Bolivians and Uruguayans) faced in the 1964–1973 epoch: the breakdown of much of what they held sacred.

Leadership and discipline of an army, of a collectivity, were based on hierarchy and subordination, on obedience. These in turn were predicated on willingness to submit. Without esteem and admiration for the leader, discipline might become a matter of fear and intimidation. And these had been disdained in print regularly since the early years of the century. In Mexico, just as in other countries, men "were not automatons, but men subject to emotions, feelings, complexes, and passions."[52] That the collectivity was an agglomeration of individuals affected dramatically by changing times and subjected to many pressures was something officers everywhere were finding out all too often.

Eighteen years before the Somoza dynasty crumbled, a *Guardia Nacional* article on leadership urged Nicaragua's finest to know their men, to seek out talent as Joseph Simon Gallieni did when he met the young Lyautey upon his arrival in Indo-China.[53] Somozan Nicaragua was a far cry from late-nineteenth-century Annam and Tonkin, but military men all over Latin America have been told about the unique blending of leadership and discipline of those French officers who were enjoined by Bugeaud, Gallieni, Lyautey, and their disciples to "know their men," the terrain, the citizenry, the total dimensions of both friend and foe.

The true leader, believed Peru's Colonel Gastón Ibáñez O'Brien, in his

1966 "Reflexiones sobre comando y estado mayor," uses psychology and initiative in leading and planning. Initiative—with no reference here to its effects on the well-being of the collectivity, but rather evocative of the same examples held up to Nicaragua's crack fighting legions—was the sine qua non of a good commander.[54] Nation-building in the here and now demanded discipline as much as empire-building had in the there and then.

Nation-building, wherever it went on, was supposed to result in a disciplined society or collectivity. "Discipline is the base upon which rests the success of any organization, whatever its nature . . . it is the sum of the individualities that compose it," wrote a Venezuelan in 1969. "Therefore, it is necessary that we begin by disciplining ourselves."[55] Without a disciplined army there could be no disciplined society; without discipline the collectivity could not realize its potential. The connection could be understood by any right-thinking officer.

By the 1970s most of the cogent (and vapid) arguments had been made, most of the perceived effects of sociocultural change on discipline experienced. Refined Latin American arguments now found their way into other, broader discussions. The pieces published during the 1970s iterated and reiterated these arguments on discipline, but in new contexts. Dominicans ceased to use the deceased Trujillo as their model of discipline and leadership.[56] Venezuelans came no nearer to indicting the lack of civilian discipline than they ever had,[57] and neither did Guatemalans[58] nor Mexicans,[59] even after the violence of 1968.

Early in the 1980s a Chilean would argue that however much times had changed society and culture, charisma would always be vital to leadership and discipline.[60] Late in the century Latin Americans were still reciting lists of basic attributes of all successful officers, still striving to maintain traditional essentials of leadership and discipline. Without them no officer could fulfill his obligations, play his role. As that role became more extraprofessional, or was defined more broadly, his attributes and essentials would of necessity be brought to bear on civilians. And leadership and discipline were precisely what many officers thought civilians needed most. The 1964–1989 quarter century gave generals both the opportunity and the time to provide it.

In most of the world such an opportunity would never present itself, although around the globe officers steadfastly held with certain convictions about leadership, discipline, and authority with regard to the civilian sector. "Study them," advised Australia's pseudonymous "Soldier," when he described how officers could mold men into a "good unit."[61] Take human factors into account, urged French writers.[62] Apply psychology, a Spanish army psychologist recommended.[63] "Be exacting," offered Colonel S. Titov of the Red Army, in a 1970 essay.[64] According to Lenin, Titov hastened to inform his readers, discipline was "based not on fear of punishment but on high political motives." Leadership reflected the same inspiration and was based on classless relationships between leaders and led: contrasting means, comparable ends.

By the 1970s, European military men, unlike their Latin American counterparts, were promoting the importance of psychology, human factors, and management techniques. Colonel Günter Ohme even used the latter term in his 1970 *Wehrkunde* essay "Führung, Verwaltung—Management."[65] Compliance with discipline (obedience) came through example, not force; both were critical to social harmony (peace and order). Without good leaders there could be none of this, wrote Lieutenant Colonel Vincenzo Morelli in 1971.[66] Two countrymen agreed with him in essays of the next year. Psychology, example-setting, and propriety were noted as essentials.[67] With this combination, the old and the new might become compatible—or so at least they thought.

Lieutenant Colonel D. Chavanat, writing in 1973 on the topic "Pour réhabiliter la discipline," described two types of discipline. The discipline of action, tactics, and strategy was characterized by efficiency, initiative, cooperation, and effectiveness. Harmony, equilibrium, good will, and love for one's fellow man all characterized a "discipline of life" applicable to civilian affairs.[68] Chavanat implied that the two disciplines were compatible, or at least they ought to be.

"Is leadership learnable?" queried Major Sigurd Boysen, in a *Truppenpraxis* essay of 1974. Sometimes, he reluctantly concluded, but leadership defied the ability of many teachers and practitioners. Leaders were "born and not molded."[69] Lieutenant Colonel Pietro Regni agreed. "The superior," he wrote, must be "superior, first in all things, in courage and virtue." *Nobilità* was the word Regni employed to indicate the intangible quality of leadership necessary for the successful use of psychology (and everything else, for that matter), on subordinates and troops.[70] De Gaulle, as noted, had used "charisma" and "character" to denote essentially the same thing. Colonel Serge Douceret echoed both him and Boysen and Regni four years later.[71] The old and the new complemented each other in this special way, as military writers believed that they ought to.

"In a certain way the individual in our society considers it almost his right to be asked to serve, and the quality of his response at a given time depends on his desire to be needed,"[72] wrote General Paul Arnaud de Foiard early in the 1980s. He believed that military and civil discipline and leadership were now gravely threatened by rampant individualism and consumerism and that while modern ways might be considered useful, they should by no means replace traditional standards of leadership and accomplishments of discipline. There was still time for old ways.

But leaders had to be responsible for their actions. Discipline should be constructive, as anyone should know.[73] As if anyone doubted it, one Russian would observe in the mid 1980s that "years of practice show that the best organized and orderly [units] are those in which the commandos themselves strictly and exemplarily fulfill their service duties. The servicemen consider it an honor to serve under an industrious, just, and exacting officer."[74] Over time East and West could agree on many basic attributes. As Field Marshal the Viscount Montgomery of Alamein had once written, "An army," after all, was but "a fighting weapon molded by discipline and controlled by leaders; the essence of the army is discipline. Good morale is impossible without good leaders; both are impossible without good discipline."[75]

Montgomery's transcendent conclusions of 1948 held fairly firm in the British Isles and the old empire. The Irish, in their journal *An Cosantoir,* would never disagree with Monty,[76] and nor would the Canadians. Some years later Captain N. A. Petty would affirm Montgomery's conclusions and see fit to advise his own fellow officers that they should "not rate popularity too highly. It is an ever changing trend, like the tide at sea; it may surge with power, but it soon changes direction."[77] Distance from one's men was still a good thing. *Mol an oige agus tiocfaidh si:* "Praise the young and they will improve," reminded Lieutenant P. T. P. Ua Caoindealbhain, in his Lyauteyesque essay of 1966, "'The Old Man' and the Young Officer." "Set an example, inspire, know your subordinates."[78] The argument was old, the logic familiar. Men were always the "key element," and human "details" counted heavily in dealing with men, as one Australian asserted.[79] "If you want to be a leader," an Englishman later offered, "and you hate your job, there is only one remedy; you must change it."[80] Leadership was full time and demanded total immersion; anything less was insufficient. Officers were, regardless of their nationality, officers.

Thought and self-perception from the Indian subcontinent support this assertion. Leaders needed, according to one Indian, "an elastic and adaptable mind if they are not to crack under the stress of battle."[81] Rigorous preparation could preclude such infelicity by preparing leaders, but only experience could make an officer a finished leader; and only total removal from politics would keep him one. Pakistan's Captain Sondha Khan Malik concurred with this 1946 argument but averred that only a devout Moslem with "character" could be a proper leader.[82] Major Amir Zafar Ali Khan both reinforced Khan Malik's argument and agreed with officers worldwide that a leader had to know his men. "Any attempt to understand men," of course, involved "acceptance of the people as they are." Frailties, inconsistencies, and the like did not mean that understanding of men conflicted "with the established military order and discipline."[83] Among the true believers, too, the old and the new could be complementary—in the army.

"God in the heaven promises great rewards to those who die in His name," Khan Malik wrote in 1963. "The Holy Quran tells us that those who die in the name of Allah never die."[84] Leaders, then, might rely on faith to render their men fit for discipline. Leadership based on faith and understanding of one's men actually made a commander's job easier, for commands need not be subjected to discussion or debate. "Zero added a hundred times equals zero. The collected wisdom of a hundred donkeys similarly equals that of one. That it is less than one man conclusively proves the futility of conferences and the value of orders."[85] So much for the "understanding" of one's fellow *citizens*. Leadership and discipline were ordained—in civilian affairs as well as military, some Pakistanis—and many Latin Americans—maintained.

But of course they were not alone. India's Major K. Brahma Singh singled out officers and their leadership as vital to the nation's discipline. It was the officer who had to civilize, motivate, and, in effect, "nationalize" Indians.[86] Relying on the inspiration of John Ruskin, Gandhi, and Nehru, Lieutenant Colonel Y. A. Mande urged his readers to fulfill a social and educational role through leadership and application of discipline.[87] Indians and Pakistanis plainly were not alone in the Third World. A. F. J. Viesse de Marmont of the Congo's *Force Publique* had told his readers back in 1954 many of the same things officers from the subcontinent were now saying—minus the theological suggestions, of course.[88] Army minister Sadou Daoudou of Cameroon did the same nearly twenty years after,[89] and Major General Muhammad Gamel El-Din Mahtouz recapitulated his Pakistani countrymen's arguments in a brief 1982 contribution to *Islamic Defence Review*.[90]

With but minor emendations to allow for culture and new-nation status and with the major qualification occasioned by the spread of Islamic fundamentalism, leadership and discipline meant essentially the same to army officers from Europe and its former colonies as they did to Latin Americans. Tradition still tempered innovation. Intangibles were still important. Civilians still "cried out" for leadership and discipline. We might ask, did this hold for the United States, a place where innovation tempers tradition historically?

"An officer must never think as a white officer, a Catholic officer, a West Point officer, a Negro officer, a Reserve Officer Training Corps officer, or an Officer Candidate School officer. An officer must think only as an Army officer,"[91] wrote Major De Reef A. Greene in 1965. In the midst of one of the United States' most turbulent eras of domestic division and foreign involvement, traditions were exposed as vulnerable. U.S. officers knew they had to respond to change and find ways to lead men where they did not want to go, and they learned what it meant to fail in many painful ways.

Yet, even at this time, leaders like retired generals Omar Bradley and Matthew Ridgway could still discuss leadership in ways quite comparable to their foreign counterparts. All the basic attributes and essential qualities still counted for these two Americans.[92] In 1970, Lieutenant Colonel (ret.) Fielding L. Greaves, could still find inspiration in Machiavelli.[93] That same year, Lieutenant Colonel Thomas A. Rehm noted the complexities of, and constraints on, leadership and professional commitments in his discussion of "Ethics and the Military Establishment."[94] To General Maxwell D. Taylor the ideal officer was he who carried out all assignments and missions while getting "the most from his available resources with minimum loss and waste."[95] Taylor ticked off most of the attributes and qualities and deviated little from the definitions of leadership discussed herein, but he allowed that the good leader need not be perfect. "He may be loyal to his superiors and his profession but disloyal to his wife," he concluded. Better to let down one's bride, one surmises, than let down one's side.

By the 1980s other works reiterated the mainline arguments on attributes and essentials of officers and leaders, still emphasizing the personal nature of leadership, the impersonal nature of management, and the difficulties of professional life in an era of rampant careerism, and consumerism.[96] "Leadership, like pornography," wrote Colonel Thomas B. Vaughan in 1984, "is relatively easy to recognize but relatively hard to define."[97] This spoke far more to the situation of the United States than it did to that of Europe or the old Commonwealth countries or Latin

America. If this were so, how could North American concepts of leadership have ever been much of an inspiration to Latin Americans clearly convinced of their own ability to define a leadership role so precisely?

"The military career is not, should not be, simply a way of living, but an elegant form of service," stated one Colombian editorialist. "The military is not some trade of drudges for whom it means nothing more than the expenditure of energy, for in the career of arms much thought is necessary in order to act."[98] Officers needed vocation. On numerous occasions over the years, Latin Americans have written of this vocation and its significance to the military man, often in essays dealing with the basic attributes of all officers or those emphasizing leadership and discipline. Vocation provides the strongest link between attributes and qualities, leadership and discipline, and the officer's educative and social roles. It is that special aspect, as officers see it, that distinguishes their profession from most others. Even if it does not, it lends dignity to their chosen path, and it places them on a level with the clergy as representatives of a higher calling.

Nothing that does not derive from *la vocación profesional* should influence the behavior of officers, stressed one Argentine back in 1948.[99] General José del Carmen Marín, lauded for his efforts to launch Peru's CAEM (and often associated with pro-APRA factions in the army), and his confrere, Lieutenant Colonel Pando Egusquiza, confirmed the importance of calling and vocation in articles of the mid 1950s.[100] The Guatemalan, Colonel Manuel Antonio Aguilar Letona, writing slightly later, lamented the lack of calling, or *Beruf,* among his fellows. "The military career," he said, "along with those of the physician and the pastor, are those that most demand a vocation, and therefore in the career of arms that natural inclination we call vocation defines the military spirit of the professional, from whose moral and intellectual formation arises the officer."[101] Aguilar based most of his remarks on ideas gleaned from Alfred de Vigny's *Servitude et grandeurs militaires,* always a favorite source of inspiration for Latin Americans.

"Without that special vocation," wrote a Venezuelan colonel, "there can be no officer; one cannot pursue the profession of arms as a way of getting by, nor carry out its educative function in a languid and nonchalant way; this is a profession of abnegation and self-denial."[102] He would also make it clear that because the army was the nation (in arms), it naturally had a vocation relevant to all citizens. His fellow countryman, Lieutenant Colonel (monsignor) Ramón Lizardi, concurred: "The officer . . . knows how to blend the virtues of knight, gentleman, and soldier, as well as those of the Christian and the humble citizen."[103] In a 1960 essay resembling ever so much the classic *Vigilia de armas,* Colonel Aníbal Suárez Girado advised young Argentine officers that only a true vocation would allow other attributes and qualities to flower fully.[104] His evocation of the venerable Barros Ortiz's 1920 treatise on the military spirit was but one more example of heavy professional reliance on the past and precedent in dealing with the present and preparing for the future.

Venezuelans, striving to shed the onus and erase the stigma of the Pérez Jiménez years, would endlessly compliment themselves on their hard-won (or new-found) vocation. In an exchange of 1967 their commander-in-chief and defense minister asserted that the military vocation had enabled Venezuelans to buttress democracy and defeat insurgents.[105] Vocation in Venezuela now signified belief in a military-civilian partnership of mutual benefit not unlike that of Mexico's.

As the decade of the 1970s dawned, an obscure Guatemalan colonel, José Efraín Ríos Montt, speaking on the occasion of the ninety-seventh anniversary of President Justino Rufino Barrios's founding of the *Escuela Politécnica,* exhorted his listeners to genuinely evince the basic attributes of an officer through a true calling, "for if the cadet-gentleman feels an uncontainable and authentic vocation, he will make of his profession a veritable priesthood at the beck and call of the fatherland."[106] A Protestant-fundamentalist military professional like Ríos Montt could easily be as vocation-oriented as his Catholic *compadres.*

Cadets hear a "call to duty," a call "to serve to the death," wrote Lieutenant Roger Vergara Campos, a Chilean. This calling enabled them to devote themselves to their studies and drill and to develop all the necessary qualities and attributes of an officer. It enabled them to serve their God, their country, and their family in all the proper ways. "The life of an officer cannot be separated from the life of a citizen, for he is the citizen par excellence."[107] Vergara also allowed that the officer ought to be willing to serve in the government if needs be—a timely vocational suggestion for a Chilean of the late 1970s.

Mexicans of these same years were warned editorially that "the military career in Mexico more than any other country, is not attractive to the ambitious, the egoist, to he who pursues his own agenda. As with teaching, it is a career marked by constant dedication, by sacrifice, by devotion, by constant efforts toward improvement. It is an exhausting career that demands the total surrender of one's self, without denying one's self as a man and as a Mexican."[108] Revolutionary commitment was every bit as intense as Catholic, Protestant, or nationalist vocations.

Like Mexicans, Venezuelans now knew the liabilities of a past marked by military and authoritarian abuses, a past without a significant residue of professional militarylore to patch over the errors or justify (however weakly) the excesses of the past. President Luis Herrera Campíns continued the tradition-building process begun in the 1960s by praising the military in a 1982 speech: "In a pyramidic and hierarchic organization like the military, the importance of examples established at the highest echelons . . . is inexpressible."[109] Such examples included a virtuous personal life, self-discipline, moderation in speech, discretion in actions, fond respect for the profession, and "respect for the democratic system that has enabled the country to live in liberty and dignity." Vocation in Venezuela could now be defined by civilians. But did it really mean the same to civilians as it did to officers? This question still goes unanswered.

Nearly twenty years after the Brazilian *golpe* of 1964, and just prior to the return of civilians to political power, General Octávio Pereira da Costa urged a comparable democratic vocation on Brazilian officers. "You must develop a solid democratic conviction, one which repudiates and combats forms of totalitarian thought, especially that of a Marxist-Leninist type, our most tangible menace."[110] Despite his claims that the democratic vocation should be manifest in all ways, his argument was clearly one that limited the concept of democratic vocation to the struggle against communism. Civilians, especially politicians, did not exert the same influence in Brazil that they did in Venezuela. Different pasts had led to different presents.

Overall, then, one's vocation had to be something of an inspiration, something innate, perhaps of divine origin. Certainly one had to have a "feel" for the military life, a commitment to endure a life less soft than that of one's civilian coevals. An officer might look forward to certain institutionalized benefits, a structured career, and a decent standard of living. He might do less well for himself than others, yet be better off than the vast majority. The vocation had to be channeled—not stunted or smothered—and refined. Military schools were where channeling and refining processes began. Vocation depended on schooling for its application.

Officers had to be cultured in order that they could raise the cultural level of others.[111] Officers ought to think of themselves as "Knights of the Round Table," ready and willing to "do justice, punish the guilty, feed the hungry, give strength to the weak, and never abandon a damsel in distress."[112] This early postwar Bolivian creed, somewhat reminiscent of the Boy Scouts' motto, allegedly came from oaths sworn by Arthur's own men.

Guatemalans, too, were told that moral and spiritual education were as important as technical military training they received in school.[113] Argentines of the mid 1950s were reminded that changes affecting the military profession demanded constant changes in course content, that their efficiency as leaders of men still depended on their overall intellectual and moral standing.[114] They would also read that they should constantly seek to expand their cultural horizons, to learn more about the world around them, especially in their professionally formative years.[115] "El oficial completo," as a *Guardia Nacional* reprint of 1961 put it, "read[s] regularly." He read three newspapers daily, regularly read a half-dozen nonprofessional magazines, three to six professional journals, a book every three weeks, and several technical journals.[116] Vocation, over the years, had become complex and demanding; it was now associated with intellectual activity.

But only a handful of officers ever pressed the case for ranging too far afield in the world of letters. Argentina's Lieutenant Colonel Venancio Carullo's 1966 essay on culture and technology dealt with *ciencias humanísticas* as a vital ingredient of all *ciencia militar* courses.[117] Thus equipped, the successful officer, owing to a true vocation, might know his men. Colombian Colonel Jaime Barberis Romero also urged his comrades to read, to read the Bible, the Koran, the *Communist Manifesto*. Books were the best way to learn about life.[118] Argentine Colonel Homar Segrista saw reading as cultural and intellectual renewal,[119] and constant renewal as evidence of vocation. In Latin America it was constant training and formal coursework that turned vocation into application, not familiarity with belles-lettres.

In 1974 Major Richard P. Diehl's "El profesionalismo militar en el cuerpo de oficiales del ejército de Estados Unidos," stressed to Peruvians the importance of broad-based education in the postwar period as a way of dealing with the Nuclear Age and the Cold War.[120] Of course this merely confirmed what Peruvians and other South Americans had accepted for years. "The military man," wrote General Alzir Benjamin Chaloub, some years after Diehl's article appeared, "must be formed, specialized, perfected, and developed, all of which constitute the essence of military education, whose basic parameters are man, the future, and war."[121] Vocation, well and good; but without the necessary training and proper grooming, vocation was insufficient to assure a conflict-free future for mankind. The extraprofessional implications of this line of thought are obvious. The potential for alienation of military and civilian sectors from each other owing to assumption of leadership roles and presumption of political obligations by officers was enough to deter many professionals from becoming militarists.

Nevertheless, vocation and lifelong learning per se counted for a lot beyond Latin America—where political action would never take place. "In the service the officer is on duty and must seek and accept responsibility every hour of the twenty-four, day in and day out for a lifetime," Canada's Colonel A. G. Chubb had noted back in 1951. His essay, yet another reminiscent of *Vigilia de armas,* went on to discuss the tendency of Canadians to think of themselves as military-minded and nationalistic.[122] It showed that Canadian officers also believed a vocation made the basic attributes of an officer stand out. Just after the war ended, Major J. D. Lunt advocated some service in the ranks as proof of vocation. He thought it would encourage the soldier to look upon his leader as a "capable edition" of himself.[123] Brigadier B. S. Gill continued this argument for Indians in 1950. Commitment to the highest standards "assured a good officer corps." Viewed in this light, he claimed, "the average officer becomes not just a measure of the vast majority of his fellows, but a superior being on a higher level that does not now exist but must soon be made to exist."[124] Levels of training and performance, he thought, must be continually raised, thus pushing the officer on to greater things, a kind of "dialectical militarism." "As the level of quality achieved rises, the level of the ideal must be lifted higher and higher, and the real desire to follow close behind it."

Lieutenant Colonel H. C. B. Cash believed that the best leaders came from the National Service, not from Sandhurst, where, he complained, the "rather academic education" produced good staff, but not good field commanders.[125] Cash and other British and Commonwealth officers confronted a peacetime fraught with controversy over the best way to assure preparedness: the merits of conscription versus those of a standing force. This controversy affected their thinking on maintaining high standards of leadership and discipline. Officers with a vocation might be found among those who initially entered the military as a ranker or through candidates' courses, might they not? Should the officer of the new world paradigm be a respected professional or something less? Such a question would not be asked by Latin Americans.

"In a highly competitive and materialistic society he stands barely on a par with the efficient artisan and below the successful small businessman," wrote Lieutenant Colonel A. Green, an Australian, in 1954.[126] Only a few officers, thought Green, could stand with the learned professions economically and socially. Medicine had come a long way since the time of the "barber-surgeon," he thought; the military, alas, had not. But in Australia, rebutted Major General S. F. Legge, social elitism had never really flourished, and therefore the officer had not really lost much in prestige over the years.[127] At Green's urging of more scientific training and orientation—"an officer and a scientist," was the desired result—Legge replied that the military did indeed serve now to make gentlemen of officers, whereas in days gone by it had made gentlemen into officers. Legge thought that this meant the profession was acquiring prestige, not losing something it had never had. The Green-Legge debate (so typical of the *Australian Army Journal*) was evidence of antipodal uncertainties comparable to those now manifest in most parts of the "European" world. It also kept alive the debate over leadership and vocation versus management and career, so common beyond Latin America.

A French general, L. Loizeau argued in 1956 that an officer needed to read constantly in the field of international affairs: "He does not have any right to confine himself to the area of his specialization."[128] The officer-reader, he believed, committed himself to a constant educative process and led through the expertise he gained from it. That same year A. Green continued to advocate his own "Green revolution." His scientifically trained officer had to be blessed with innate intelligence and true vocation. "The modern officer," he insisted, "has an opportunity to become a great force for social good in his role of trainer of youth under National Service. This is nation-building work, by the inculcation of manly ideals of service and of high standards of conduct, hygiene, and social cooperation, and, in particular in present-day Australia, in helping in the assimilation of young trainees into the body politic."[129] The social role he had in mind—reminiscent, as are so many noted herein, of Lyautey's—was not for just any officer-to-be. Those attracted to a commission by pay were "little better than the old Asiatic, starveling 'monkey nut recruit.'" Officerhood was for the select, the few good men; no monkey nut recruits need apply. Still in the 1950s, Lieutenant Colonel J. D. Lunt commented that vocation was all the more a necessity now, for peacetime soldiering was, frankly, dull. Lunt's army was still deeply traditional, even during peacetime, and men often retired as majors or captains owing to slow promotion. At the age of 45–47 the retired officer had a modest pension, only effective at age 60, and not all that many second career choices as a middle-aged retiree.[130] It took a true vocation to face these possibilities.

"A free man is not judged by his life style, but by his value as a human being," wrote France's Lieutenant Colonel Etienne in 1960. His discussion of military life as one of "grandeur through servitude," and often unpleasant, was still another modeled on Vigny's classic.[131] The paraphrasing of Vigny and Lyautey, Clausewitz and Goltz, de Gaulle and Seeckt, and the Barrosian qualities of many works on the profession ought not surprise the reader. Lectures, readings, mind set, and the essential comparability of so many aspects of military life make charges of plagiarism plausible yet fatuous. It is as if officers unconsciously spoke to and answered each other from afar.

In 1961 the Pakistani lieutenant colonel, Shaukat Riza, urged young officers to demonstrate their professional zeal by working to improve themselves through constant study. "What we omit from a single hour is lost to all eternity," he wrote.[132] Further, "unless the young officer is an irredeemable moron, reading must provoke him to articulation. He will begin to express his opinions on subjects other than mess food without fear of ridicule." Riza insisted that officers think, show initiative, and dare to be original. Only in this way would the army in which "routine is fatal" become a progressive institution and attract the right sort of officer candidate.

A 1965 reprint from the *Military Review* appearing in the *Australian Army Journal* urged Australians to still more self-improvement. Real professionals still read and studied. "An officer who expects to make a significant contribution to his calling must continue to study throughout his career," for the age of technology still had not rendered broad-based knowledge useless.[133] Australians, Pakistanis, Frenchmen, and others read frequently in their professional journals of the importance of further study, beyond staff and specialty school assignments. Even so, four years after Riza's article appeared, his colleague, Colonel S. A. Maqsood, wrote that "the military career has an unmistakable overtone of a 'calling' with a sense of mission, which implies a deliberate rejection of the limited horizons of the business world."[134] Maqsood's argument was standard professional opinion. It displayed in yet another context the clash of a mystical calling with ties to tradition and the past and the careerism of a crass world where struggles took place in bloc, boardroom, and *bourse* and involved the likes of politicians, merchants, bankers, and brokers. Numerous references to the consumerism and materialism perceived as rampant in civilian society in changing times appear throughout these studies. That true believers in vocation should also reject certain aspects of the socioeconomic matrix is significant. Calling was not careerism. It never had been—and never should be, they thought.

As they moved from the 1960s to the 1970s Italians would read of the differences between calling and career and of the importance of vocation as opposed to opportunism.[135] Pakistanis read of the advisability of having officers serve time in the ranks.[136] Frenchmen still read that a military career was the "highest expression of the constant desire to serve the fatherland" (from, of course, a confessed disciple of Lyautey) and that the military was the extension of a vocational devotion to France.[137] Australians were told repeatedly by one of Lunt's disciples that a military career was now quite risky.[138] Americans would read Diehl's claim that "as long as conceptualization is encouraged and rewarded, the vocation will maintain its professional status."[139] Is it any wonder that Diehl's work (and not some of the others just noted) was translated and published in Latin America? Once true vocation had been enough, but no longer, for in the world of the 1970s expertise, knowledge, and the ability to apply them technologically were absolutely necessary. In Latin America devotion to study was an effect of true vocation; elsewhere it might be a cause.

Soviets would read that their officers, "because they embody the most noble qualities of the Soviet man, high ideological conviction, exactingness, principledness [sic], irreproachable honesty . . . and a number of other qualities, are held in high respect."[140] Vocation, allowed Captain (1st Rank) V. Drozdov, indicated a "calling," but meant as well being a true Marxist-Leninist: ideology before vocation. Spaniards read that vocation resulted from a dislike of social disorder, a love of security, family tradition, and the appeal of all aspects of military life: tradition before vocation.[141] Britons read that "perhaps only the Church appears to ask so much of the individual."[142] The most secular of armies could relate to traditional vocations.

Still and all, the 1970s ended with some officers still torn between maintaining true vocation and reconciling it with the changes around them. In 1979 Pakistanis were still reading excerpts from Seeckt's venerable *Gedanken eines Soldaten* on both calling and vocation;[143] but they also had to deal with Shaukat Riza's poignant lament that whereas civilians had in the past dressed to imitate officers, "today most of our officers try to imitate some low-class entertainers, in their hair style, in their plunging necklines, carefully turned sleeves, and in their exhibitionist tights."[144] Had the military profession come to a crossroad? With so much change, individualism, materialism, opportunism, technology, careerism, loss of prestige, was vocation anything more than just chimerical?

Ever since the publication of Lyautey's "Du rôle social de l'officier," vocation's most widely acknowledged praxes have been through the social, educative role of the officer. The attributes and qualities that army men claim as theirs, the calling that propels them into lives of (relative) abnegation, of servitude and (relative) grandeur, that which makes of them a nation in arms—all these link their past to their present, and can bind them to each other, regardless of nationality. Fulfillment of the social role not only allows officers to maintain tradition, it encourages them to do so.

In most of South America the social role was a significant result of the inculcation of European military professionalism. Its application came about in two ways. It was a peacetime function of military service in countries where the development of society and the uniformity of culture were retarded, and it would come to serve as a pretext for certain actions before and during the time of the generals, when men in uniform made the rules for the rest of society. Consequently, throughout Latin America the social role of the officer has always found its way into printed sources dealing with many other themes. *El rol social* in the late twentieth century was no longer a role that had to be pointed out so boldly; most essays devoted specifically to it differ only slightly from those of the prewar years. Ideas on the subject change minimally between, say, 1910 and 1980; World War II did not change them at all. This is still another way in which officers, to varying degrees, could confront, the new world paradigm, reconcile the old and the new, and maintain their status vis-à-vis society.

Peruvians would thus continue to read about the integration of the Indian into the mainstream of society, an idea first brought to their attention in the first decade of the century and discussed in myriad contexts since. "Besides his purely military preparation, the officer has an unavoidable obligation to assist in the integration of the Indian." To do so the officer had to know about Peru's indigenous population. Indians (most of whom were illiterate) gained much from their service in uniform, this source insisted, and Peruvians were thus more unified.[145] Argentines were convinced that the military was a social sector that had a positive impact on the rest of society because of the constant mix of recruits and conscripts who returned to civilian society the better for having worn the uniform.[146] They were also advised that their mission was a synthesis of the "most worthy ideals and aspirations," and of "the most authentic vocation."[147] Soldiers were role models for all Argentines.

Bolivians would know that "to be an officer is not only to practice some profession; it is to discharge a ministry."[148] This assertion, appearing in a French article of 1943, was buttressed by citations from Maurice Gamelin, Lyautey, Weygand, Ernest Psichari, Pétain, and other devotees of *le rôle social.* On the eve of the uprising of 1952, an editorial would inform Bolivian officers that the army officer "is an educator and teacher of national youth." Military life had a civilizing effect on the "huge indigenous majority, which once sent home from the barracks possesses new knowledge and better habits, all acquired from the service."[149] The Bolivian military, like that of Peru and Argentina, was striving to convince itself that it was of the people. Venezuelans and Colombians also convinced themselves that theirs was a profound social role.[150] Wishful thinking could triumph over substance in many ways.

In the 1960s Paraguayans were also told that they were "of the nation," and that General Alfredo Stroessner was the example they should follow in their quest for "total consecration to the higher interests of the nation" and to national social and economic development.[151] Only Somoza and Trujillo would ever receive commensurate treatment. Hondurans read Captain Jorge Alberto Arguello Moncada's charge that "an army officer is a citizen who must set a dignified example and know perfectly his duties and rights. . . . The professional officer is obligated to teach his subordinates the fulfillment of their civic, and the basis of all their military, duties."[152] The professionalism of most Bolivians, Hondurans, Nicaraguans, Dominicans, and Paraguayans was apery and nothing more, however. Their political actions since World War II had little of the theoretical base characterizing those of Argentines, Brazilians, Chileans, and Peruvians.

Discussion of the military's traditional social role after World War II was widely treated in a self-congratulatory way, in essays directed at self-reinforcement. The fact that it remained an issue to be treated separately from civic action and obligatory military service—modern vehicles for the social, educational role—indicates that tradition still counted for a lot when it came to putting ideas into practice in South America where professional militarism became manifest. How much did it count elsewhere?

"Too often we soldiers live in the past with the resultant loss of enthusiasm and desire, both of which . . . are necessary to respond to the needs of the future." Lieutenant Colonel I. B. Ferguson (DSO, MC) wrote these Lyauteyesque lines in 1955 in an exhortation to officers to be mother/father, sister/brother, military genius, tyrant, and inspiration to the soldier.[153] This Australian's view of the traditional social role would be shared by colleagues worldwide.

The French, of course, had never forgotten that exhortation. Squadron Chief Chaudessais advised his readers in 1950 to remember the three essentials of an officer-educator: self-knowledge, spirit of inquiry, and the practice of meditation.[154] An officer should be all things to his men. Captain Boyer reminded fellow officers in 1957 that they were like priests, that they earned their "grandeur" through "servitude."[155] The profession's mystical qualities were vital to social progress. Still in the 1950s a French lieutenant colonel told his readers that real men "were developed through suffering, not through that which they enjoyed."[156] The officer was responsible for making military life rigorous for his men. François Kuntz evoked Vigny, Lyautey, Gallieni, and Psichari in his "L'officier dans la nation" of 1960. Officers were "at one and the same time knights, technicians, and exemplary educators."[157] And so we see there were still some Frenchmen who thought like Latin Americans; many, after all, were attempting to preserve as much of their European heritage as possible.

Innere Führung certainly obliged Germans to be educators, but youth had to be dealt with gingerly, given Germany's controversial military legacy.[158] German officers were above all teachers and trainers now, wrote Lieutenant Colonel Joachim Feist in the early 1960s.[159] Writing the next year, Colonel Friedrich Schmidt allowed that the army was the *Schule der Nation,* for a military-service-bolstered democracy.[160] "Captain as confessor, father, and social worker," was the way Wido Mosen would describe an officer's role in the barracks, the home from home, in a 1970 book.[161] Germans, like Frenchmen, saw the officer as educator, who should fulfill an important, traditional, albeit limited, social role.

Red Army officers were "educators and friends to their men, too."[162] They were, after all, from the same class and different only owing to their respective responsibilities. Officers were the "sons of the working people." They showed "paternal concern" for their men as proof that men from the same levels of society could both educate and lead, as opposed to "imperialist countries . . . where the monopoly over military education and leadership of the army is firmly in the hands of the ruling elite, of the most faithful servants of big capital."[163] Moreover, "the Soviet officer corps is a friendly family composed of sons of the peoples from all the national republics," asserted Captain A. Skrylnik in his 1972 essay, "Our Strength Is in Friendship of the Peoples."[164] For all his concern for "the Peoples" of his far-flung motherland, Skrylnik mentioned no Asiatic figures in his discussion of heroes of the Great Patriotic War, belying his assertion of "friendly family" conditions. Other essays from the *Soviet Military Review* would focus on the educative role, stressing ideological purity as necessary to its fulfillment.[165] Red Army officers, therefore, fulfilled a social and educative role prescribed strictly by ideology rather than one emanating from military tradition.

In Asia and Africa the social role was discussed in terms resembling those of both Western Europe and Latin America, terms comparable even to those used by Red Army officers, without the ideological rigor of Marxism. Filipinos repeatedly professed commitment to a social role. Lieutenant Eduardo T. Guingona, for example, discussed it in terms of civic action in a 1956 essay appearing in the *Philippine Armed Forces Journal.* Captain Fidel Ramos, who later achieved political stature with the fall of Ferdinand Marcos and the rise of Corazón Aquino, discussed the social role in the same terms. Lieutenant colonels Reynaldo Mendoza and Lucano Gunabe, in their 1956 "Leadership is Preventive Maintenance," saw the social role in practical terms as well. Officers needed to be involved with, and learn from, civilians. An officer did not have to be the best "cha-cha dancer," Mendoza and Gunabe argued seriously, but he should be a part of the garrison-town social scene.[166] "A company commander is partly a chaplain, a doctor, a lawyer, a psychologist, a psychiatrist, a financial expert, an educator, a moralist, a father, a special counsellor, a magician . . . depending on the situation and circumstances in which his organization finds itself." He should even read a lot, added Brigadier General Mateo Capinpin in 1956,[167] in one of those generic essays on responsibility, which could have been written almost anywhere by anyone.

Commandant T. Counet and Major Marliere advised *Force Publique* officers in the Congo to learn all about their men, their language, their villages, their religion, and their families in terms similar to those once used by Frenchmen and now used by Latin Americans.[168] In the Philippines and the Congo westernized minorities and their professional sectors confronted indigenous majorities, and their cultures clashed. As in such situations in Latin America—Peru and Bolivia, say—army officers would see themselves as nation-building go-betweens. In Europe officers still saw themselves as representatives of the state, of democracy, as providers of civic education through their social and educative role, with or without ideology and tradition behind them.

In 1974 Lyautey's "Du rôle social de l'officier" appeared in a *Military Review* translation. Its impact was modest, its meaning blurred by time's passage and the quaintness of its origins. Other essays appearing in the same journal dealt with the same subject in less controversial (or quaint) terms.[169] Only in Latin America and the least developed countries of Africa and Asia was a full-fledged tradition-based social role still either contemplated or pursued to its fullest extent.

In André Maurois' 1925 *Captains and Kings,* a lieutenant tells his friend, a philosopher, that "A Lyautey, a Gallieni, a Pétain are not obeyed out of fear." Later he avers: "When I stand at attention before my colonel (and I do it with a keen pleasure, I assure you) it is not to a man that I click my heels. It is to a principle of authority which I regard as salutary and worthy of respect, and without which human society, the guardian of our precious liberty, would never have existed at all."[170]

All the Latin American officer's attributes and qualities, his vocation, his social and educative role, seem as nothing without that other intangible, almost mystical "gift" (or "knack") of command and leadership. Latin American essays dealing specifically with the gift of command border on treatments of political activity, for they deal with authority and its exercise in such a way as to convince the officer that leadership is more than an obligation, more than a result of training, more than a strictly professional function. It emerges as a divinely inspired mandate to enlighten, deliver, and improve. In Latin America officers always have been made to think of themselves as natural leaders in a natural order, different from, and superior to, civilians. The "gift" would lead some generals to believe the time had come to testify to their vocation by leading entire countries.

Early on in the postwar period the "gift" had become a favorite theme in its own right, often set apart from discussions of vocation or leadership. In Cuba, Mexico, Bolivia, and Argentina, he who did not know how to follow was unworthy of leading.[171] Essays of the 1950s consistently pointed out that almost anyone, given the proper education and training, could be a leader, but that only leaders with the necessary attributes and vocation could truly possess the "gift."

By the 1960s military-style leadership was being tied to politics and government. Politicians, argued one Guatemalan lieutenant, were goading the military into politics owing to their own desire to maintain their positions while doing nothing for either civilians or the (gifted) military.[172] Major Augusto Baldoceda, a Peruvian, discussed the "gift" in a 1961 essay in which he stressed every attribute and quality of vocation mentioned in this chapter.[173] Major Trevor Swett, Jr., of the United States' military mission to El Salvador, portrayed it as a worthy goal of divisional commanders.[174] *Don de mando* would appear as both a critical ingredient of, and a public service to, Venezuelan political life in 1964. Democratic Venezuela needed its military leaders in order to protect its wealth and sovereignty.[175] Paraguayans would perceive it as both aspect and guarantee of loyalty and patriotism.[176] The Mexican *Revista del Ejército* put officers on notice in 1968 that they should not permit their family or the family of a subordinate to participate in official military matters or to render advice on such matters, "for as well intended as they may be, they are ignorant of military affairs." Leadership was for gifted officers only.[177] Officers were in charge of men, and those who truly had the "gift" took care that their men were always well cared for, advised Lieutenant Colonel Julio González Palomo, a Salvadoran.[178] Writing in the Argentine *Revista de la Escuela Superior de Guerra* at the end of the decade, General Hans Speidel, one of the *Bundeswehr*'s spokesmen for *Innere Führung,* stated his case for true leadership as the successful inculcation of democratic ideals.[179] In Latin America the political implications—links between professionalism and militarism, between theory and practice—would become even clearer during the 1970s, when tradition and heritage became so important to generals who thought their time had come.

The Argentine Luis Gozzoli's *Reflexiones sobre el mando,* a two-volume work derived from Captain André Gavet's *L'art de commander* (Paris: 1899), stressed charisma as the essential ingredient of the "gift." Charisma made the leader "an attractive individual to the subaltern, thus creating in the latter a sense of emotional equilibrium and stability propitious to unconditional obedience." "Virtuous leadership ennobles obedience," he continued, "while defective leadership debases it, for it leads inevitably toward acts of indiscipline."[180] Gozzoli (whose work contains one of the most outrageous discourses on the natural inferiority of women) will stand for a long time as an example of Argentine military intractability, a quality responsible for the tragic military-civilian confrontations of recent times.

"He who believes that military leaders spring forth like mushrooms is sadly mistaken," wrote a Venezuelan in 1971.[181] Leaders must demand much and give much in the way of role model. "We need to see in him who gives us an order not just a leader, but also just a little of our own father. The officer must not allow himself to be used for purposes that are not 'national' or constructive, not based on progress or welfare of all, but are for the benefit of a few, a small circle," he insisted. Lieutenant Colonel Carlos Bobbio Centurión's "El ejército, el oficial, y la política," of 1970 bluntly defended the military profession against all civilians and their political machinations.[182] *Don de mando* was a monopoly, a military monopoly. Bobbio, like so many others, was directing his arguments toward all politicians, not just those of the left or right.

Criticism of political leaders was at the core of Brazilian statements on *dom de mando,* as well.[183] And even Mexicans, faced with troubling times in the 1970s, were led to believe that, owing to the "gift," military leadership was now superior to that of politicians (certain ones, anyway).

To Major Víctor Raúl González Rodríguez, it might be acquired by almost anyone, even civilians, through the right kind of education and training.[184] If civilians could not acquire the ability and the will to lead in a democratic ambience such as Mexico's, something must be wrong, was the unstated conclusion. Essays of the late 1970s from Bolivia and El Salvador dealt with *don de mando* in a more traditional way.[185] Cumulative conviction after decades of discussion and definition was to link military leadership to national leadership in Latin America through the gift.

"I do not exercise the highest responsibility of any citizen because of some simple personal wish. I have always had in mind that 'one swallow does not make a summer.' I mean by this that I govern with the people because the people have decided I should. And I would not hold on to power for a minute if I lacked that popular support for my work for the good of Paraguay."[186] Thus spoke Alfredo Stroessner, self-styled posessor of the "gift," in 1982. At about this same time, General Paul Arnaud de Foiard's frequently reprinted article, "Lo específico del mando militar,"[187] tersely lumped civic action, geopolitics, close relations with civilian society, attributes, qualities, and vocation together, indicating that military leadership by any name or definition might now mean far more than just command of troops. Military leadership meant just about anything officers wanted it to mean. The "gift" made it that in Latin America.

Outside Latin America, or wherever the peculiar blend of Iberian and other European influences did not give rise to the concept of *don (dom) de mando,* there is no representative body of literature dealing with the "gift." The ability to command or lead simply did not encourage political action. For example, Germans were encouraged to stay abreast of national and international affairs, well and good, but, as Walter Rehm wrote in 1956, "the officer must be a willingly apolitical being."[188] An officer's leadership ability was no *Gabe* setting him apart from others. Frenchmen consistently advised each other in similar fashion, even while they were keeping up on extramilitary affairs and recalling their idealized past.[189]

Spaniards, allowed a lieutenant colonel of the *Guardia Civil,* Juan Antonio Núñez, and an army commander, Martínez Tenreiro, should make sure political and national leaders were well informed of all the military's needs.[190] Commander José Frías O'Valle [sic] even claimed the military had a permanent duty and right to intervene in civil affairs "when permanence is threatened."[191] Frías' essays on the military and politics and leadership appeared in 1975, the year the Spanish army's consummate leader went on to his final reward. Another Spanish commentator was just as bold: "The military spirit demands surrender and service, altruism and sacrifice, while the characteristics of bourgeois life reflect naturally egocentric and egoistic inclinations."[192] However removed from Spanish politics and government the army might have been by 1979, some of its officers still believed they enjoyed a special status and possessed special qualities: the "gift."

Red Army officers, of course, saw "politics" as a fitting and proper activity, but to them politics meant participation in Marxist-Leninist unity of officers and men—something impossible in capitalist countries.[193] At least for men such as Colonel-General Ivan Mikhailovich Chistakov, a veteren of fifty-years' service, it was as simple as saying, "for a military man it is indeed good fortune to serve the interests of the people and to defend the lofty ideals of peace, freedom, independence, and socialism."[194] But such interest in "politics" had nothing to do with the "gift."

In fact, singular as their attributes and qualities, vocation, or specific roles might be, officers from Europe only rarely evinced attachment to the "gift" as something applicable to national leadership. The same is true for most of the old Commonwealth lands and the United States. Circumstances—not the least of which were the primacy of civilian political and governmental leadership and the selective success of postwar political and economic systems—made it unseemly as well as unnecessary for officers in most of the world to forge their professionalism into a theoretical justification of seizure and exercise of power. There is some evidence, nevertheless, that non–Latin Americans envisioned for themselves a kind of extraprofessional role. Missionary roles, not unlike those assumed by South Americans prior to World War II, would appeal to some Europeans and North Americans. Officers everywhere were aware of independence and nationalist movements in the colonial reaches and of challenges from the left in new states, particularly the African ones. Officers in developing countries beyond Latin America would begin to play a role—often termed developmental or modernizing—that some in both the Third World and the developed world saw as necessary to the advancement of what they considered to be retrograde societies and neocolonial economies.

French officers—and it should be remembered that the influence of French military thought on Latin Americans was a profound one throughout the century—were greatly concerned, for example, with all things African in the postwar era. Publications like *Tropiques* and *Frères d'Armes* were devoted to Franco-African relations. A special issue of the *Revue Militaire d'Information* in 1956 dealt with the Algerian question in depth,[195] and in it the Indigenous Affairs Service, descended from the old *Bureau Arabe*, was portrayed as a place where the officer could be all things to all men. The story was an old one; French colonial officers had written about it often over the years, and the Algerian crisis brought it to the fore once again. A sense of *mission civilisatrice* was still in their thoughts, and they bear most of the responsibility for its appeal in both Latin America and Africa.

British officers would concern themselves with what had once been theirs in Africa and India and with threats to neocolonial stability posed by Marxism and nationalism. African shortcomings, primarily the results of training limited to elite, westernized bureaucracies and officer corps, were most glaring when these elites ran into trouble dealing with premodern societies and cultures. "The colonial power taught well in local training depots the elementary principles of armed forces' work," wrote Major P. G. Francis in 1969, "but they rarely built locally higher technical training schools or an officers' training college, much less a staff college. Instead they sent the few African officers who were commissioned to study at Sandhurst, St. Cyr . . . or at a staff college in Europe."[196] African officers, for that reason, might no longer be considered representative of their societies or cultures, but Latin Americans, who had studied both abroad and at home, would convince themselves that they were and always would be.

Latin American military professionals, in fine, saw themselves much as did officers from Europe, the Commonwealth countries, and the United States. They all had certain basic attributes and essential qualities. They viewed leadership in many of the same ways. They all had a calling, a vocation. They fulfilled social and educative roles. Only in Latin America did all this fuse uniquely through *don (dom) de mando*. The distillation of military heritages and the intellectual and emotional influence of European military figures and authors made Latin America distinct from any other part of the Europeanized (or North Americanized) world. Uniqueness and typicality both marked the literature of the profession devoted to basic attributes and the true vocation of all officers. Only in Latin America was the "gift" so mightily stressed. And nowhere in the region would there emerge a body of literature lauding North American contributions to professional advances like the plethora of materials alluding to French and German inspiration for basic attributes and vocation. Nowhere would officers seek to lead North American style.

The "gift" could not figure prominently in the metamorphosis of professionalism into militarism everywhere, for the circumstances in which officers became professional militarists would not obtain throughout Latin America. Perhaps they never will. But that is not certain, for time passes and change occurs at different rates of speed there. Because this is so, it is now fitting to examine the armies themselves. For without armies, where would officers be? Where, indeed, would men become citizens, and how would countries stay free and sovereign? What was it about armies that linked them to past, present, and future, that made them institutions of social and political action?

FOUR

Steadfast Soldiers: Adapting Purest Images and Nations in Arms to Harsh Reality

For by arms states are defended, kingdoms preserved, cities protected, roads made safe, seas cleared of pirates; and, in short if it were not for them, states, kingdoms, monarchies, cities, ways by sea and land would be exposed to the violence and confusion which war brings with it.—Miguel de Cervantes Saavedra, *Don Quixote de La Mancha,* I (1605)

A nation without heroes is a house without doors.
—Gabriel García Márquez, *El otoño del patriarca* (1975)

No steadfast officer would be able to confront, reconcile, and maintain without an army. All armies are the products of historical processes, influenced to varying degrees by the political circumstances under which professionalism comes to be. In Latin American countries, where institutional history could withstand the influence of partisan politics, military traditions became firmly entrenched. Where personalism or partisan politics unduly contributed to institutional history, military traditions would have to be created in an ad hoc fashion. In the former, professional militarism became manifest; in the latter, it would be latent at best.

This chapter examines the images created by officers for the institutions they led: the symbols, the metaphors, and similes of military literature. Throughout Latin America and elsewhere, armies were portrayed by their leaders as fulfilling civilizing, educating, and synthesizing roles. Regardless of the level of institutional development, all Latin American armies would be seen in nearly identical terms. Beyond the region, the emphasis was on armies as military-civilian catalysts, as teaching institutions where, in theory, men (and later women) of all stations lived, served, and learned together as a group, for the betterment of all, not just the individual. One of the chief reasons for the difference between Latin America and other parts of the world was the pervasive influence of the "gift," for nowhere else did officers presume so much—about their privileged position, the responsibilities it entailed, and those they led. Only in a few places would officers see themselves and their armies as so ubiquitously important to the peacetime well-being of the whole of society.

Always in theory (if rarely in practice) officers would see obligatory military service as the prime agent of education and synthesis of the citizenry. Obligatory service would be viewed by officers as the arena in which leadership and discipline were professionally blended to produce citizens better able to both preserve tradition and withstand the temptations of the new world paradigm. Real citizens (only later did this include women) had their education topped off while in uniform, and purely military capabilities often figured less prominently than did the sociocultural benefits allegedly derived from their happy times in barracks. On occasion the soldiers of these times would be depicted as having become superior to the mass of the society whence they came. In most discussions symbols, metaphor and simile, and references to sacrosanct tradition outweighed the substance, practice, and objective reality of either lifetime or short-term military service. Arms were still important in peacetime. So were heroes.

Because officers had maintained so much of their own past, so would the armies they led into the new world paradigm. There was not always consensus on what of the past should be held on to and what should be discarded. There was not even agreement on where to begin or end the past. There was agreement, though, that if it were not for the army, there would be no fatherland; if not for heroes, no hope.

Military writers would use various metaphors and similes to describe their armies. In Latin America "school of democracy," "purest image of the state," and "nation in arms" have been favorites since the initiation of obligatory service schemes late in the last century and early in this century. In the school of democracy conscripts received directly the benefits of the social role of the officer and took part in the civilizing mission. They would one day become party to civic action, internal security, and development. Stripped of their descriptive terminology and technical jargon, these activities would be but historical extensions of the social role and civilizing mission discussed throughout *Yesterday's Soldiers*. These *modernized* the role(s) of armies, but they did not introduce all that much that was *new*. Symbolically, the roles of armies were essentially the same at century's end as they were when Europeans began to professionalize South Americans a century ago. Times had changed, but had armies had not.

Professionalism has various base points and beginnings in Latin America. In Mexico the 1910 revolt is the base point—for Mexican authors. Central American and Caribbean professionalism, if it ever existed, was a post–World War II phenomenon. In Venezuela and Colombia it accompanied the rise of political systems established or revived in the late 1950s. In Bolivia, pre- and post-1952 professionalism, such as they were, would clash. Professionalism had emerged far earlier, of course, in Argentina, Brazil, Chile, and Peru.

This chapter provides a comparative study of how leaders of Latin American armies depict themselves, followed by a comparison and contrast of the ways in which the roles of armies in the United States, the USSR, Latin Europe, France, Germany, and the former British imperial domains have been depicted. Following this, thought on the institution of obligatory service will be traced, beginning with Europe and ending with some ideas on its relationship to a nation-building role back in Latin America. The study then turns to official views on security, peacetime defense, and integrative action. Country studies in an order directly contrasting to that just noted will draw a clearer picture of functions perceived and realized, of ways in which symbols and substance were blended, by evoking tradition, to justify political action. From the writings described in this study there emerges a military dilemma. Was the army, in order to do its job, *a part of* or *apart from* the rest of society? Here symbols and substance begin to blur, and the answer becomes "perhaps both."

"Young men," wrote Émile Auguste Chartier (Alain), "are separated from their families, they are made captive and exiled. They are suddenly thrown into a community which is the most brazen, the most cynical, and also the most corrupt in humanity."[1] Such was a French intellectual's view of barracks life in the first third of this century. Alain's is a timeless comment. To hear most officers tell and retell it, the military experience is something altogether different, no matter the time and place. In the barracks, on the drill ground, on maneuvers the conscript and recruit learn how to live with their fellows. They learn the meaning of cooperation, sacrifice, and discipline. They become men (and, more recently, women) of valor and character.

Socialization, cooperation, sacrifice, and discipline are important attributes for all citizens. The way in which they are inculcated dictates the way in which they are understood and defines how they are turned into practice. To leaders of armies, cooperation, sacrifice, and discipline and the purposes of socialization mean things they do not mean to politicians. They mean the perpetuation of the fatherland, the nation in the strictest of terms. They mean the perpetuation of tradition.

The relationship between army and nation does not always make clear which is most important. Without discipline and hierarchy there is no army, all officers agree. Without the army there is neither authority, order, nor fatherland, a Spanish colonel would note in 1978.[2] His construct was by no means a new one, for the same argument had prevailed before

World War II. It serves to indicate that the idea of the military's preeminence is neither uniquely Latin American nor confined to an era.

Soldiers led by officers make armies all they can be. Without the latter the former are nothing. Hence, one should expect to learn that good soldiers also make good citizens if, after all, the army is a truly representative one. This, too, has been a fundamental tenet of both professionalism and militarism. The army allows a citizen to "be all that one can be." The relationship between a good army and an advanced country, then, has been a constant, certainly from the times of Goltz forward.

By the 1960s all Latin American sources subscribed to the concept of the army as democracy's school, the state's image, the people's civilizer, and national developer; the soldier, likewise, was seen as both a fundamental component of the esteemed institution and the perfection of citizenry. There is a stricter concurrence on these points throughout Latin America than on any others dealt with in this book. "The soldier's abnegation is a cross heavier than that of the martyr; let us carry it with resignation, for only the greatest of men earn both cross and Calvary."[3] This is how an Ecuadoran lieutenant extolled the virtues of his country's heroes of the 1941–1942 conflict with Peru.

Alain, the Spanish colonel, and the Ecuadoran lieutenant used symbols, metaphors, and similes typical of those offered by the foes and advocates of armies and military service. Few officers have ever agreed with Alain; if they have, it has been for political purposes; most have written as forcefully, some as floridly as others already cited. In blending their army, its soldiers, and *La Revolución,* Mexicans have done as much or more with symbol, metaphor, and simile as other Latin Americans.

Mexican officers would tie the army to the people early on in a revolutionary-institutional sense. The army was made up of soldiers, one general claimed, who "not only are symbolic of abnegation and patriotism, but are at the same time the most solid links [in the chain of] national unity." Moreover, "a people that entrusts its future to the loyalty of its army has a definitive guarantee of its independence and of the consolidation of the desiderata that serve as the basis for all authentic democracies."[4] The army of Mexico, according to a captain writing in 1965, was "mute and blind"; it sought only to serve the people of which it was composed.[5] The *grande muette* ("great mute") metaphor was, of course, a favorite of many prewar South Americans who borrowed it from nineteenth-century French authors.

Even in the 1960s, General Abel Orozco linked the Mexican army and other services to *La Revolución,* the living revolution. "The armed forces," he wrote, "not only participate in this civic crusade because of their historic legacy, which is profoundly revolutionary, [but] from our very roots we are an institution born of the people, formed by it, and with which we form a brotherly bond of solidarity, sharing its aspirations."[6] In short, the army was the purest image of society. Colonel Bruno Galindo would reinforce and amplify this in a 1970 essay by asserting that the army was the guardian of sovereignty, exponent of civic education, the symbol of Mexican nationality, and the servant of the civilian population. From its inception (19 February 1913) the army of *La Revolución* had been an integrative force, "a great family in which we Mexicans should be united as brothers."[7] Force, power, and achievement of Mexico's goals were the results of military-civil union.

Nothing legitimate should ever be allowed to drive a wedge between the army and the people: "The armed forces of our country contribute in an exemplary way to the strengthening of national unity, in which is based the happiness of Mexican families and their hopes for the future."[8] No one could deny legitimately a military-revolutionary-nationalistic mix that could make all Mexicans happy, could they? Soldiers, after all, were "dynamic organs of the people and the state, to which [the army] owes its existence, and for whose protection it became necessary."[9] As the people go, so goes the army, was the essence of this 1976 opinion. By the end of the 1970s such was the essence of Mexican military literature treating the army and society. The soldier was symbolic, as was the entire army, of all Mexico; but he was not just an "armed citizen." He was no "partisan" of any particular faction. He was "the people itself . . . a select citizen who dedicates himself to the service of Mexico and the Mexican people under norms of discipline and devotion. . . . He is purely and simply the product of a social concept . . . the Mexican Revolution."[10] Mexico's soldiers were more than just human beings.

And so were soldiers of those Central American military powers, those whose histories boasted no revolutions comparable to Mexico's, but where soldiers and armies would nevertheless be portrayed as the very same kind of symbols of more recent political and social movements. History was a relative thing. Time in Latin America is relative. Just after the successful movement against Jorge Ubico, Colonel Carlos Castillo Armas, yet to rise to his country's highest post, would write that "the Guatemalan army, fully comprehending and feeling the anguish suffered by the people, threw itself into the fray, fully convinced and disposed to carry out a vindicating *revolution,* not simply an ambitious barracks revolt."[11] The fate of Guatemala's "revolution" would indicate that Castillo Armas' words were hardly ones of substance, but this did not dissuade his colleagues from pleading their case in terms similar to Mexicans and other Latin Americans. Colonel Bonifacio Ixcaragua believed that the soldier had a *dual,* not *divided,* personality. He was a citizen-soldier: "People and army form a marvelous conjunction."[12] All great nations and cultures, from ancient Greece to the present, had been blessed with military strength, he reasoned. This is a standard cause and effect relationship employed in modern military literature.

Years after their own claim to revolutionary status had failed to prove true, Guatemalans still referred to it, justifying all possible military-political stances. "It is obvious," stated an editorial of 1967, "that in the struggle of 1944, just as in our independence movement, military action had the unanimous support of the people, without political factionalism, as one single goal of liberty, justice, and law."[13] The next year, Guatemala's (still) fledgling professional army was being referred to as the "coordinating force of equilibrium and stability."[14] Its *golpista* behavior notwithstanding, this army and its men were being made out to be as patriotic and historically legitimate as any other group. "To be a soldier is, after all is said and done, to belong to an institution that is, with regard to politics, something akin to religious orders as they relate to that which is spiritual."[15] Soldiers and their officers, just like monks and their abbots, cumbersomely concluded Major Mamerto Marroquín, obeyed rules, wore uniforms, and were beyond reproach—all the while purporting to be a popular, nationalizing, integrating force.

In adjoining El Salvador the army would also seek to justify its existence as an extension of the society surrounding it. Following the 1948 "revolution" there, the army was to be restored to, and maintained in a condition of, apolitical behavior as guardian of liberty and sovereignty of the republic, as both defender and observer of the law.[16] Most of the metaphors applied to other Latin American armies found their way into the early issues of the new bimonthly *Boletín del Ejército*. And Nicaraguans had their own base point: the rise to power of Anastasio Somoza García in 1934. This did not dissuade the Nicaraguan military, however, from claiming a state of professional grace for the National Guard, that combination of constabulary and private band bequeathed to Nicaragua by the United States. "An army without discipline will always be defeated by a disciplined one equally armed, even unequally armed," wrote one patriot.

Such truisms were not limited to Nicaraguan military literature, but they are ever so much more fatuous when they appear there, just a few pages prior to such statements as: "Despotism is always detestable, and this is the reason he who truly knows how to lead and deal with his men is always obeyed with greater consistency."[17] The piece from which that citation is taken also made the case for great nations having great armies: Greece, Rome, France, the United States, Nicaragua. Nicaraguans were also treated to the Mexican Alfonso Corona del Rosal's words on military-civilian relations in 1960,[18] indicating that *Guardia Nacional* readers at least had something with which to compare their country's fighting force. Only a traitor could claim that a soldier could be anything but a sacrificing patriotic servant of the freedom-blessed Nicaraguan people. "The enemies of the people, anarchistic demagogues, those with ambitions of leadership, the eternally frustrated by politics, the resentful," these were the ones who spoke out against the army and the fatherland.[19] Even Hondurans would be given doses of the essential, vital relationship between a healthy, sane, thriving society and fatherland, and a strong army.[20] Isthmian armies and constabularies thus tried to propagate the idea that they really were equal to other armies.

Over in the island nations as well, officers propounded views of military-civilian fusion, the soldier-citizen, and the military as the people in uniform, but also as something even more special. A Cuban essay of 1952, a paean to Fulgencio Batista Zaldívar, nearly as absurd as anything written about Stroessner, Trujillo, or the Somozas, referred to the army as "the most worthy symbol of our civility," to soldiers as "the vital fluid of this renovative movement" and as "the last redoubt of morality and discipline."[21] Cubans by this time were used to referring to their army and its soldiers in terms of high praise: "school of patriotism and dignity"; "university of character, will, and discipline"; "incarnation of the people"; "spoiled child of all nations, of all vigorous countries."[22] "It is the soldier," the same author wrote, "who has the best concept of the fatherland; he who proudly wears the uniform is the priest of that religion called patriotism, pure religion, unique and true."[23] Such stuff was appearing in countries where military professionalism was little more than an afterthought in the second half of the century.

To Dominicans, the army would be portrayed as "a light come down from Sinai." A thing of rare beauty was the "citizen in uniform," for he served the entire nation. The army, through its soldiers, was the "armed right arm of the state," the "incarnation of the people" and, not surprisingly, "should be treated as a spoiled child."[24] These stand out as glaring, but by no means the only, examples of professional plagiarism, so clearly derived were they from J. F. Alcorta's 1952 essay just cited. The Dominican army was, moreover, the "moral representative of the people," the appropriate institution to lead citizens out of the "shadow of the past" into the "light of the future." It was a "superhuman force of justice and national integration."[25] The army was the "noble expression of democratic culture,"[26] the "white corpuscles of the nation."[27] All this (and more) was the army of General Rafael Leonidas Trujillo Molina, who along with Fulgencio Batista Zaldívar and the Somozas made a mockery of military professionalism.

In the wake of Venezuela's brief postwar experiment with democratic reform her officers had been told that their movement of 1948, the one that resulted in the rise of Marcos Pérez Jiménez, was "in accord with the [army's] legal faculties to seize power for the purpose of reestablishing internal order."[28] The Venezuelan army, Lieutenant Rafael Angarita claimed, had never involved itself in politics, and, to a degree, this was true, for Venezuela's long history of *caudillismo* left little room for the development of military professionalism. Owing to this, Venezuelans would start fresh, and they did, once under Pérez Jiménez, by justifying their seizure of power as noted above; then again after his fall, in an attempt to break completely with the past, they would create traditions ad hoc and accommodate themselves to democratic ways. In both situtations Venezuelans would be portraying their institution very much as Mexicans, Central Americans, and Caribbeans were doing. The army, according to one major writing in 1953, was the "reservoir and guardian of national traditions." The armed forces were the "people who can"; the army was the symbol of nationalism.[29] Pérez Jiménez himself would say that national greatness always depended primarily on military strength,[30] placing himself in the mainstream with those who linked a country's greatness to the strength of its fighting forces.

"Today the army continues its glorious role of vanguard of national security. Ours is a prudent army that adapts to modern realities. Ours is the custodian of a tradition of courage, competence, sacrifice, and total devotion to the nation,"[31] agreed a Paraguayan lieutenant colonel just three years later. Soldiers, the human figures making up the vanguard of national security, were indispensable heroes: "Men without arms in modern warfare are without doubt somewhat powerless, but arms without men to use them are useless," continued this Paraguayan, in terms quite comparable to those employed in Central America and the Caribbean.

Ten years after the fall of Pérez Jiménez, Venezuelans had to return directly to the same theme. The concept of *nación en armas—Volk in Waffen* being by any other name this and much more in Spanish America—was still valid, insisted Colonel Hernán Delgado. "Our sons," he averred "must learn the moral values that prevail in our world; we must awaken in them the faith in democratic principles, but simultaneously prepare them to defend such values and principles when the moment comes; let us remember that the most practical way of preserving peace is to be ready for war." *Si vis pacem para bellum* (one form) was still a popular slogan in Latin America. Soldiers and the people whence they came must realize, claimed Delgado, that "when a people shows a civilized abhorrence of war, it quickly receives a punishment for its failing: God changes its sex, denies it its virility, transforms it into a *pueblo-mujer*, then sends conquerors in order that its honor be stolen."[32] To be against the army was to be traitorous, atheistic, effeminate, and otherwise repugnant to real men.

In the 1970s other metaphors would prove more popular in Venezuela, but the point was still quite the same. "The armed forces is a thermometer indicative of the power of the nation, and it is just that they be prepared for the purpose of being an indisputable guarantee of the sociocultural and economic patrimony of a democratic Venezuela."[33] Democracy thus still owed its existence to military strength, and this relationship pervades the literature of the 1970s, for by this time Venezuela's political system had evolved to a state where consensus dictated a sharing and alternation of power among the two major civilian parties, *Acción Democrática* and the Christian Democratic *Comité de Organización Política Electoral Independiente* (COPEI). Like Mexico and like Colombia after 1957, Venezuela was fortunate, with regard to its new post-caudillo, military-civil relationship, in having a consensus among civilian leaders that precluded and, indeed, obviated the necessity for resort to military assistance for the purpose of achieving political ends. "The practice of the profession," said General Gustavo Carnevali Rangel, "also implies a responsibility and stewardship."[34] Venezuela's soldiers were now expected to keep their country what it had become.

A quarter century after Venezuelans began the reconstruction of civilian consensus, army officers could look backward with a measure of pride, encouraged by civilian leaders like Senator Pedro Pablo Aguilar. In words reminiscent of those uttered by Mexicans, Central Americans, Bolivians and Caribbeans about their "revolutionary" and "democratic" achievements, he told officers that the military movement of 1958 had been dominated by democratic values. It was the genesis of democracy and military professionalism; it had replaced dictatorship with genuine national unity.[35] Pérez Jiménez merited no mention by name, but there was explicit criticism of his regime for having soiled the army's reputation.

By the 1980s military professionalism in Venezuela, therefore, was tightly bound to a relatively new civilian political system. In 1982, President Luis Herrera Campíns could tell graduates of armed forces academies that "the military career is a hard, severe, difficult one. It requires temperance, character, courage, decisiveness. It is no place for cowardly actions or faint-heartedness, but for strong will, intelligence, and men of vocation."[36] These were values that military men all believed in, but the question arose, could they continue to believe in a troubled political system when it fell on hard times?

To the west, Colombians were being told much the same as Venezuelans. In 1959 they were exhorted to bind their military service to the cause of preserving democracy and to the inculcation of democratic principles among those who temporarily wore the uniform. "To be a member of the armed forces is today probably the greatest personal responsibility that can devolve upon a Colombian," wrote one editorialist.[37] Abnegation, vocation, and sacrifice were as necessary to civilian democracy as they were to a military career, closed President Alberto Lleras Camargo, in an address of 1959.[38] Like armies of other countries, Colombia's, indeed the armed forces in toto, were "by nature the armed arm of the people, the community, society, the nation, and the state, the guarantee of external sovereignty and internal security,"[39] wrote one lieutenant colonel. Colombia's Liberal-Conservative accord and anarchic rural and provincial situation made the maintenance of the army a sine qua non of any civilian endeavor to bring order to the country in the aftermath of the Rojas Pinilla dictatorship and the years of *La Violencia.*

Colombia's army would "physically represent the sovereign power of the people, the guarantee of fulfillment of its desires and aspirations, those that can be no other than national welfare, buttressed by the two pillars of security and development."[40] These 1981 opinions of a Honduran serving in Colombia represented what by then had become the principal role of the army there: maintenance of sovereignty through internal security and development—civic action. Colombians had rapidly entered the age of national security and civic action, key ingredients of professional militaristic thought and self-perception. The "good sons of the fatherland,"[41] having rid the land of dictators now had to keep it safe for democrats. That democrats themselves would not do much to keep it safe for citizens in the long run needs no elaboration. Fledgling democracies and ad hoc or restored professionalism would make for a delicate balance in northern South America.

Like Venezuelans and Colombians, who dated their professionalism from recent postdictatorship revolutionary experiences, and Mexicans, who bound themselves to an earlier postdictatorship experience, Bolivians also would use a revolutionary heritage as base point for role definition. No matter that the Bolivian movement of 1952 (like the Mexican Revolution) was moderate almost from inception. Never mind that it became a mockery before the 1960s were history. It was a beginning. Long before 1952 officers had assigned the army a role comparable to that of most other armies discussed herein.

In 1948, a decade following the dramatic "revolutionary" military actions of the 1936–1939 epoch, and only two years after the 1943–1946 "revolutionary" epoch, and just four years before the ultimate rise of the MNR, Captain Guillermo García would call Bolivia's rag-tag army the "spinal column of the nation." "In Bolivia, our fatherland, we must have in our army more brains than brawn, wills more than willingness, heads more than arms," he wrote.[42] "Unity means power," exhorted Lieutenant Colonel Sinforiano Bilbao Rioja that same year. Only with a strong army could Bolivia ever be more than the "mutilated fatherland" it was. Echoing Tupac Amaru II, leader of the eighteenth-century Inca revolt against Spanish rule, and early-twentieth-century Peruvian officers, and antedating Juan Velasco Alvarado and his Incaphiles, Bilbao also told his readers to teach their men: *ama sua* (do not steal), *ama llulla* (do not lie), *ama kkhela* (do not loaf), and urged that Bolivia's Quechua-speaking conscripts carry these teachings with them "when they returned to civilian life."[43] He did not, of course, urge them to think much about changing their miserable lot in that life.

Nor did Captain Guillermo Zuña in 1950. Like Bilbao, he encouraged his readers to teach their men discipline.[44] It made for a good army and, certainly in 1950, it made for an orderly society. Well into the *Sexenio* (1946–1952), Bolivia's army showed its essential conservatism; writers, nevertheless, were assigning it a role not altogether unlike that of other countries in the throes of "revolutionary" circumstances. In 1952 an editorial again referred to the Bolivian army as the "spinal column of the nation"—poignant in an invertebrate land such as Bolivia, a land so internally divided culturally, ethnically, geographically, and socially—and as the "heart of the nationality." Anatomical and physiological metaphors were by now quite common in Latin America. The people, moreover, had been "consubstantiated with its army"—(not to be confused with *transubstantiated*)—thus becoming "the synthesis of the people in arms." "The army is to the nation what the father is to the home, the teacher to the school, in fine what the priest is to the temple."[45] Such heady stuff may have appealed to some officers, but it is doubtful that it sounded very convincing to those unfortunate enough to serve obligatorily, consubstantiated, as it were, by spending time in barracks.

The year 1952 would bring changes for them all. Just after the overthrow of the government, Colonel Francisco Barrero reminded his readers that the army was "still the soul of the nation, symbol of the fatherland," Bolivia's "oldest formal institution of order." He warned them that unscrupulous politicians were trying to subvert discipline. It was the politicians, he continued, who had pushed the country into the disastrous Chaco conflict, "the ruling class," who wanted to "step boldly in the Chaco." That war had molded Bolivians into a nation.[46] The army, destroyed by the 1952 uprising, was now born again, free from the nefarious influence of the old ruling class. Army officers could always find a way to maintain tradition and justify existence of the institution through selective memory of idealized pasts.

Colonel Clemente Inofuentes' "Necesitamos un ejército que sea síntesis del anhelo popular," of 1953, anticipated the arguments of Peru's CAEM products.[47] The Bolivian upheaval of 1952 would be seen much as Mexicans saw their own of 1910—as a political catalyst for the development of professionalism where an institutional genesis was lacking. Though subsequent events would both tarnish Bolivian professionalism and make professional militarism politically farcical there, a distinct military mentality would manifest itself, similar in essence to that of other countries with regard to cultural, economic, and social underdevelopment.

Inofuentes pulled no punches. He expressed outrage at "the brutal inhuman attitude of the privileged ones [the tin barons Hochschild, Patiño, and Aramayo] and the *camarilla* at their service [i.e., politicians and bureaucrats], which, with the power of a savage beast, stood on the neck of its victim, the Bolivian people." No civilian would ever define *La Rosca* so well (literally meaning "yoke" or "yoke pad," a term applied to the tin barons, *hacendados,* and their allies, who constituted a burden on the backs of the people). International capitalists, traitors, rightists, sensationalists, all still conspired against the army. Sophists had merely mouthed slogans before 1952 to keep the army docile and servile, Inofuentes claimed. But things had changed. Bolivian officers now meant what they said. The army was determined, one young officer claimed, to become "the pedestal on which rests the monument of nationalism."[48] It now marched side by side with all the other revolutionaries (as if a pedestal could become pedestrian). Colonel Inofuentes repeated his 1953 excoriation of the tin barons in 1955. They had used the army for their own evil purposes and had prohibited the establishment of a truly nationalistic military doctrine in order to maintain the army as their own police force.[49] But now the army was truly Bolivian—and revolutionary to boot.

Further south, in Paraguay, the army would continue claiming to be just as authentic a representation of national aspirations, but there in a decidedly nonrevolutionary ambience. "No one ignores the fact that the Paraguayan soldier has been the forger and sustainer of our fatherland in difficult and anguish-filled times, and for that reason we must never fail to do everything to assure the felicity of its destiny," asserted one citizen in 1959.[50]

No matter the circumstances, armies from Mexico to La Plata were of the people, historical institutions, sometimes guarantors of social progress, ever responsive to civilian needs, ever symbolic of national greatness. In revolutionary Mexico and Bolivia, newly democratic Venezuela and Colombia, or under the likes of Somoza, Batista, Trujillo, and Stroessner, armies were described first and foremost as faithful servants of the people.

In Argentina, Brazil, Chile, and Peru, men in uniform had quite different base points from which to mark their professional status and national profile. Their associations with civilians and their symbolizations of fatherlands had longer histories and had begun long before the upheavals of the twentieth century—or so they claimed.

"Whereas political organizations may well see the military as 'afunctional' and the nation may view officers as simply 'professionals,' the fatherland looks upon the army as its sons, in whom it has placed its honor, its integrity, and its life," wrote Major Venancio Carullo of Argentina in the mid 1960s.[51] He distinguished between political groups and the nation as a whole, as true manifestations of *argentinidad*. The true Argentine would see things from the point of view of the nation, the fatherland. "The armed forces," he quoted Perón as saying, "are the synthesis of the people. They do not belong to any party or sector, nor can they serve as the instrument of anyone's ambition. They belong to the fatherland, which is our common home, and to it they owe their all." Certainly the army had not served Perón's own personal ambitions, had it? Officers and soldiers had been told in the *Decálogo* of 1954 that they were the "synthesis of the people," and had been instructed to remember that Perón ("the conductor of New Argentina") steadfastly affirmed this.[52] The "conductor" also reminded them that they were the heirs of San Martín. He mentioned no intervening heroes by name but did make some invidious comparisons.

Nothing much would change following the "conductor's" flight from

Buenos Aires in 1955. In an article published in 1957, Lieutenant Colonel Matías Laborda Ibarra told his readers that the armed forces were "the nation in arms." This was so, however, only if they were united and could count on total support from the civilian sector.[53] If they could not stand together with civilians, Argentina would never be a great nation. History had proved this, according to another source. The Argentine army had liberated Chile, conquered the Argentine southland, contributed much to economic development and technological advance, all the while performing many other services to the civilian population.[54] Argentines owed a lot to their men in uniform. Lack of gratitude constituted treasonable behavior.

The army was a "priesthood of armed men," and soldiers and their officers were spiritually representative of the fatherland.[55] The army "reflected the civilization and culture that makes it up," and the soldier was a veritable *homo duplex,* "for underneath all the glitter, ribbons, medals, and braid was hidden great sensitivity, tenderness, affability, and aesthetic feeling." The army was nothing less than a "religion of armed men."[56] If the metaphors began to sound familiar to uniformed readers, this was the purpose of propaganda in a milieu where repetition and rote led to acceptance. Officers wanted their subordinates to feel different from, yet be accepted by, civilians.

Selective publication of foreigners' views that coincided with theirs served to solidify Argentine self-perceptions. The army was a school, too, "a school of citizenship and an energetic guardian of the security and integrity" of the fatherland.[57] The armed forces, all of them, were *of* the fatherland because of the ingress and egress of male citizens, these all being part of a "global society . . . responsible for an incessant osmotic process."[58] It was as if wearing the uniform lifted men above being merely Argentines, made them superior, and encouraged others to emulate them. By the 1970s military and civilian sectors were, officers hoped, inseparable. The well-published Juan Enrique Guglialmelli even resorted to hackneyed metaphoric cant in 1980 by referring to the need for "communal vertebration" and the army's critical role in it.[59] What he meant was the army's role in establishing and maintaining internal security and fomenting economic development.

Across the estuary, Uruguayans, though not prolific on the subject, would argue similarly from World War II forward.[60] Across the Andes Chileans would do no different. "Soldiers are the genuine representation of the people in arms. They are the people itself, recognizing no distinction of social class," claimed Major Gustavo Díaz back in 1948.[61] With few exceptions, postwar Chileans eschewed blunt and inflammatory comments on the army's potential internal roles, but they rendered opinions nevertheless. Political realities and the strength of the civilian system militated against candor—and bombast. No revolutionary movement would demand justification of the army's nation-saving role, no dictator would require ego massage, not until the 1970s at least. Certainly the past had not been unkind to the profession. Tradition was still on its side.

"In peacetime there is no part of our national life that does not bear the obvious stamp of [the army's] presence, forged in the will of the fatherland."[62] So stated President Salvador Allende Gossens in his Armed Forces Day address of 19 September 1971. As uniformed Chileans still mourned the assassinated army commander, René Schneider, and began to worry about Allende's own plans for their institutional future, they would also think more seriously about their role. Lack of its definition in other than the strictest of terms, and the lack of ad nauseam repetition of metaphoric exaggeration would not militate against their decision to rise up in 1973. Allende's own words could have been used to justify what they thought they were doing.

Brazilians were no more original in their self-perception than were their continental neighbors. "The cross and the sword will ever dominate our origins and our destiny," grandiloquently asserted General Heryaldo Silveira de Vasconcellos in 1970.[63] Soldiers were, after all, "the legitimate representatives of the Brazilian people." Owing to the presence of all races, colors, and classes, the army was authentically, indisputably Brazilian. Moreover, the barrack was "the legitimate symbol of our national territory. . . . It is impossible to consider the barrack as simply a center for military instruction." In the barrack young men were made literate, learned trades and civics, were acculturated to democracy, became moral, gained confidence. Barrack life "brought youths rich and poor; white, mulatto, and black; worker and student together in the same atmosphere of work and discipline."[64] The army reflected the true soul of the nation, the most authentic aspirations of each generation, a leap to the future without risk to the present and without negation of tradition.[65] The army blended Brazilians and banished class conflict from the national vocabulary.

Like Chileans, Brazilians had written comparatively less, in terms of quantity, than Argentines prior to the seizure of power; and, like Chileans, they would make up for it afterward. Even while their generals ruled, Brazilians still saw a need to justify institutional existence. In 1984, on the verge of leaving things to civilians once again, Brazilians were still writing about the army as the country's main instrument of education and culture for the citizenry. Public education was so inferior that the barrack still had to fulfill the social and educative mission of the schoolroom. The army's political involvement had been an unfortunate experience, opined one writer, but an inevitable one owing to both the manifest incompetence of civilians and the professional qualifications of officers.[66] If the army had been able to deliver on promises, this argument might have had some substance. Their shortcomings did not dissuade Brazilian officers from continuing to champion themselves, however. What better place to learn about life but in barracks? Where better to prove one's worth but in the army? "The soldier as symbol! The soldier eternal! The soldier of yesterday, today, and forever! The soldier of land, air, and sea! The man in uniform! The soldier-citizen!"[67] Where would Brazil have been without her soldiers?

Although Peruvians had long, and very specifically, advocated an army role in social and economic development projects (i.e., civic action) they never forgot its overall educative and civilizing role, its identity as symbol of the nation. The old ways did not slip the minds of the CAEM's graduates. Quite to the contrary, causes championed by officers of the pre–World War II years ended up as adjuncts of programs administered in the 1960s and 1970s.

"From its origins [the army] was an expression of *peruanidad*, of national reality, of rebellion against the injustices of the past, of integrity and virility in its efforts and sacrifices to serve, and of faith and optimism in the destiny of the fatherland." The army's work was depicted as the "synthesis of the country's will, a synthesis of healthy manhood, formed in the school of *loyalty* and *duty*."[68] "The army is the great school of the nation, foundation of the social edifice, solid guarantee of the people. Within it vibrate the purest sentiments of love for the fatherland and the most exalted civic virtues. Its high and noble mission assures national sovereignty."[69] Captain Erasmo Herrera was as unrestrained as the Brazilian expert on "the soldier!" cited just above. The army was a "granite column sustaining the people, the dike against all excess, the cornerstone of national progress, the lighthouse that guides all defenders of that nation, the national pride." Only in its ranks could a citizen truly achieve, understand, and practice citizenship.

All other symbols, metaphors, and similes aside, perhaps Peru's Colonel Carlos Bobbio Centurión would overstate it best: "The army is to the state, in a sense, as the rifle is to the marksman, with the difference that if the latter aims poorly the bullet does not hit the mark; whereas the army, because it is composed of intelligent individuals, can arrive at its objective even if it has been poorly armed."[70] Bobbio first published those words in 1962; by 1972, when they were reprinted, his colleagues more than metaphorically hit the mark, for they were attempting to *re*make their country according to professional priorities.

Many of these same images, however "barrack-worn" they may seem, would characterize military writing beyond Latin America. This reconfirms the consistency, both intercultural and intercontinental, of recent professional thought and self-perception. It may also substantiate the assertion that latent professional militarism can exist in areas where the very idea has been considered ridiculous. Once again the comparison and contrast of Latin American thought and self-perception with that of other regions serves to demonstrate the existence of both mainstream military mentality and its idiosyncratic features.

Soviet military thought for example, is both like and unlike that of non-Marxist countries. Russian officer-authors insisted that capitalist, imperialist, bourgeois armies are incapable of representing either the nation or the people. They are *apart from* the people. Only the Red Army and its Warsaw pact equivalents, or armies of other socialist countries, were viewed, during the Cold War, as *a part of* the people. S. Titov would put this succinctly in 1968, insisting that "imperialist armies are composed and maintained at the expense of the popular masses. An increasing majority of their personnel is composed of workers and peasants. At the same time these armies are used against the working class. This is the essential contradiction inherent in the army of every imperialist state and shows the antipopular character of their politics."[71] K. Moskalenko would agree in 1969.[72] General Semion P. Ivanov put things in terms more compatible with those of Latin Americans in a 1975 essay published in *Estrategia*. "The armed forces of the Soviet Union," he proclaimed, "are an inseparable part of the state. They are called upon to support the pacific work of Soviet citizens, assure the liberty and independence of our fatherland, defend the great cause of Communism."[73] Ivanov went on to discuss the army's labors on behalf of the people in all cultural, social, and economic endeavors in which good citizens engaged.

The Red Army, according to a 1972 study, was the "flesh and blood of its people," "totally united by common fundamental interests of workers, peasants, and intelligentsia of our nation, materially and spiritually a part of Soviet society."[74] According to General V. Novikov, the armed forces were "of the whole people"; and in V. Borsov's opinion they were "an embodiment of the Soviet people's staunchness and heroism."[75] What Soviets wrote about the Red Army and the entire armed establishment of the Soviet Union was (at one time) at least as plausible as what Latin Americans said, certainly if ideological intensity and orthodoxy are taken into account.

North American opinions were necessarily muted. Lieutenant Colonel Paul B. Parham could write in 1974 that citizen-soldiers performed many services for the rest of society and always had. The army's apolitical existence, he believed, was a prerequisite for the continuation of the American way of life: "The role of the military professional in our society is to ensure that heritage is never lost."[76] On both sides of the century's great ideological divide armies symbolically assured fulfillment of heritages, revolutionary or postrevolutionary, at least according to officers and ideologues.

Obviously this was the case for those in between, in Latin Europe, say. Early on in the postwar era a Portuguese major revived the classical allusions to the *nação armada*.[77] In his view the Portuguese army was inseparable from the society of which it was composed. Mediterranean views would be much the same. "The armed forces in a democratic country are the immediate and genuine expression of the nation . . . the first and the largest *scuola della nazione*."[78] And another Portugese would write in 1968 that without an army there could be no sovereignty, without sovereignty, there could be no law, without law no authority, and without authority no state.[79] Across the border in Spain thought on the role of the army was evolving in much the same way. "Today, the symbiosis of army and society cannot be just theoretical, but forcefully the safeguard of principles that vitally affect the state," wrote one Spaniard in 1968. Another believed the army had dual roles, one strictly of national defense, the other a spiritual one. "This double mission inherited from, and mandated by, the Spanish people . . . has ever obliged [the army] in its various avatars to labor with a spiritual guidance that gives form and substance to its actions."[80] The Spanish army's role was spiritual, educative, and always had been.

And why not? As Generalissimo Francisco Franco y Bahamonde himself stated in his last New Year's address: "In a world traveling down the road to anarchy, violence, and licentiousness those traditions that faithfully conserve spiritual values are so much more necessary, for only discipline and unity can stand against them. Because of this my feeling of satisfaction today is great, for I can feel that intermingling of the armed forces, the fatherland's greatest safeguard."[81] Franco was not alone in

Latin Europe, for by this time Italians, under decidedly different political conditions, were writing in a surprisingly similar way. The Italian army was perceived as part of Italy's social structure as well as a fighting force: "In a nation like ours, in general, in all modern democratic countries, the strategic picture has changed the concepts of consensus and legitimacy of the military institution."[82] In Italy, too, then, the army was portrayed as a source of stability, of tradition, of sensibility. Despite political constraints or those necessary for the maintenance of continental credibility, Latin Europeans saw themselves playing roles awfully similar to those of their American cousins.

The French (Latin Europeans to a degree, after all) were both outspoken and subtle in making their case. In 1959 Captain Usureau tied the army to the nation in a way true to tradition: "Army-nation! The association of these two words today is more an appeal than what it once was."[83] Usureau believed that democratization of the army, for which there was clamor everywhere following the war, could only succeed if there were a concomitant militarization of society. He meant that a workable obligatory military service system must be maintained if democracy were to flourish and France remain strong. Captain Yves Hervouet would boldly assert an overt political role for the army just the next year. This political role was one in which the army would be "at the disposal of the government."[84] Hervouet was arguing that the government, as legitimate representative of the state, must be able to avail itself of defense against all types of warfare, including ideological.

Politics and politicians had always been worrisome to French officers, and little would change after the demise of the politically intense Third Republic. The troubled times of the Fourth Republic merely represented a continuation of military-civilian tensions of the late nineteenth and early twentieth centuries, leading one general to warn against too much political activity. In a 1954 essay significantly entitled *Du rôle idéologique de l'armée,*" he asserted that the barrack was not a forum, as some would now have it be, but must remain a *lycée* wherein the social role could be fulfilled. With history and philosophy as men's guides, and electoral programs and partisan politics banned, barracks would be perfect schools. He allowed as how men now came to barracks far more politically oriented than in the past, but insisted that this constituted no excuse for the institution to ever return to the time of Dreyfus or to that of the controversies raging for years after. The army was better off not being mute and ever-neutral, for in that condition it had been unwittingly dragged into political battles: "It is time that the army ceases to be *la grande muette*." Through their service in the ranks Frenchmen would now be indoctrinated in the ideology of democracy—an *Innere Führung* argument in France—in order that they be prepared for a possible struggle to come with Marxism.[85] Lyautey's *rôle social* writ large was now being incorporated into Cold War *mentalité*.

Her army would save France, one writer insisted, because "the army is the emanation of the nation." In a time when France was experiencing a "grave absence of good citizenship and ideals and a tendency toward materialistic neutralism," it was up to France's uniformed citizens to provide the example of patriotism to civilians. Soldiers were rightfully critical of civilians because of the lack of ideals and courage shown by them, and for their failure to provide the means necessary to fulfill the military imperative. In turn, civilians now scorned the military, owing to the apparent mediocrity of the service—which, in turn, was the result of civilians' lack of attention.[86] Civilian hostility, then, was still both cause and effect of the army's plight, an argument used often by Latin Americans.

France's armed forces, argued another writer (a civilian), had to be insulated from party politics—what Latin Americans would call *politiquería*—yet be very much a part of the high-level deliberation of national and foreign policy—*grande politique*.[87] Nationally and regionally the army was very much a part of France's future, technologically, commercially, socially, culturally, and for defense purposes, of course. "An army," Claude Delmas would write, "is nothing less than the expression of the nation, and history provides no examples of a country triumphant over all, that has no organic accord between civilian and military."[88] Given France's problems of the late 1950s and early 1960s, these were not unexpected sentiments, however they may strike the reader. They were eminently comparable with Latin American arguments. Involvement in Asia and Africa, the collapse of the Fourth Republic, the Cold War, European defense commitments—all these kept French military leaders believing that the army had a definite internal peacetime role.

Most civilians took issue with these sentiments. From the French left, predictably, came the opinion that "the army preserves a privileged place, against wind and tide, protected against all criticism by an arsenal of [bourgeois] laws and decrees, by its own code of justice."[89] A version of what Spanish Americans had once known as the *fuero militar* appeared alive and functional in France, if one subscribed to such views. "But the army," claimed one loyal defender, "existed before us and will exist long after, in new ways adapting to the times."[90] To civilian and uniformed advocates, France's "timeless army" would always represent past, present, and future. Individuals, factions, political regimes could make no such claim to timelessness.

Bürger in Uniform and *Integrationenmodel* were typical terms employed by Germans to discuss the new military-civilian relationship. Pluralism in politics and integration of the new army into the whole of society in *Partnerschaft* were the orders of the time. However, "a 'democratic' army is in and of itself nonsensical," argued one German. "Only in a democratic state can such a thing exist."[91] Only in such a state could anything remotely resembling "civilization" of the military be accomplished, and then only to a certain degree. Germany's new way, *Innere Führung,* continued to be the subject of constant interest. It would even interest North American observers watching closely the rearmament of their erstwhile foe.[92] From villains to heroes was no easy march, but "*Bürger und Soldaten,* insisted one German politician, "was no contradiction."[93] Soldiers were, after all, citizens first, and all citizens had a responsibility to defend the *Vaterland,* surely not as part of a *Staat im Staate,* as one Red Army officer warned,[94] but rather as patriots and members of a free society.

Away from the continent, officers echoed the words of the Europeans and Latin Americans. Some meant what they said; some probably did not. "There is often no dividing line between civilian and military interests," President Ferdinand Marcos of the Philippines would write in 1973, "for civilian authority orders the military, and the military may often perform civilian functions."[95] There was not much doubt, years later, as to what Sr. Marcos really meant. But for the time he sounded like proarmy authors everywhere. And everywhere soldiers and civilians were indeed moving closer together, at least that is what military writers and promilitary civilians wanted their readers to believe. India's Singh, in his memorable essay, "The Wind of Change,"[96] noted that "the present-day soldier has become soft like his civilian counterpart, who is leading a more comfortable life." Thus soldier-citizens were not altogether a happy prospect. In Pakistan, as already noted, Sardar Hussain had written that "the armed forces mirror national capabilities in every field of endeavor. Personnel are a cross-section of the people and display in ample measure their strengths and weaknesses."[97] General Shaukat Riza, author of "The Pride and the Privilege," agreed, and in unabashed Goltzian terms linked the quality of the army with the "character of society."[98] Things of the same sort were being said about Indonesia's armed forces: "Since it played a major part in the achievement of independence, it believed it had the right to a similar part in the political course of the new state."[99] The armies of Latin America, of course, assured themselves they had the same right. Less outré in terms of symbols, metaphor, and simile, non–Latin Americans nevertheless depicted their armies in comparable, if at times idiosyncratic, terms.

One major "part" in the political course of all states was obligatory military service, that program in which officers theoretically carried out their social and educative roles with the soldiers who help make the army into the servant of the state, nation, and society. The raw material of this process of institutional self-perpetuation has always been, needless to say, youth.

In France, where the social role was first defined, the ideas of Lyautey long outlived him—as they have his early disciples in Latin America. Post–World War II French officers, as already noted, were still invoking his name or his teachings in justifying the army's various roles.[100] To some, obligatory service superseded all other allegiances, even conscientious objection. It would still be seen as providing young men with their initial contact with the mechanisms of the state. It benefited the entire nation, for it prepared men for a more productive civilian life. It was still the way in which French youth could repay a debt to their country, a debt incurred simply by being fortunate enough to be born French. It was "psychological rearmament," a process in which men learned what it was they were to defend as well as how to defend it: western culture, democracy, European common interests, freedom. It still created an esprit de corps that carried over into civilian life and permitted young men to "find themselves" and help unify all citizens. It was a constant assurance of defense, hence of peace. It was ever necessary to provide youth with a "civic sense." It had become the army's *rôle sociologique*.[101] By any name it was much the same. By all names it was more in theory than in practice.

Across the Channel, where most officers had eschewed lofty (and silly) metaphoric role definitions assiduously, concern endured over obligatory service from the onset of the postwar era. National service, prior to its elimination in the late 1950s, was usually thought of as unquestionably necessary to national defense. A few years later it would become more a benefit to young men not yet "contaminated by the domesticating influences of an affluent society, in which marriage and 'settling down' take place around the age of twenty: "The wives and fiancees of these young men rarely look upon joining the army as conducive to settling down, the problems of the young married soldiers are painfully evident."[102] "It is noteworthy," Corelli Barnett would write later, "that the upsurge of student discontent in this country can be roughly dated from the ending of national service."[103] Though the cause and effect relationship should be questioned, reactions of the military "lobby" to youth movements of the later years of the century were quite understandable. Uniquely British though they might have looked, set in a world perspective they were as typical as not.

Back on the continent, *Bundeswehr* officers and their own civilian defenders would argue the same case, with less emphasis on history, of course, and in less Blimpish terms as well. Some thought *Allgemeine Wehrpflicht* was unnecessary in a technological age. Others now saw it as essential to the survival of German democracy; as a barrier against military fanaticism; as unifier of home, society, and fatherland; as service to God; as blender of all social classes; and as confirmation of all the benefits accruing to the *Staatsbürger in Uniform.*[104] As one historian put it, it assured that there would never again be a danger of "a lot of square-brushing zombies" being called upon to defend Germany's new democratic order.[105] Obligatory service in Germany had become democracy in action. This just had to be.

This held true in the Soviet Union as well, for it provided young citizens there with "the honorable right to defend the revolution with arms in hand." Had it not done so ever since imperialist powers had unsuccessfully intervened in the attempt to overturn Lenin's new government? Obligatory service would be cited as mass evidence that the "enjoyment of basic rights and duties by servicemen and all other Soviet citizens is proof of the truly democratic character of the socialist system."[106] "Democracy" was even part of the military way (and vice versa) in socialist states. This also just had to be.

Democracy was alive and well in the countries of the old Commonwealth—if one believed military writers—owing chiefly to the vigilance of armies stocked with troops provided by obligatory service systems. Australians would grapple with military service much as did the British, while they watched their regional, intercontinental defense roles expand in the 1960s. So would Canadians and Irishmen.[107] In fact most "ex-colonials" would link service in uniform to citizenship. They were doing so in the Philippines, where Captain Fidel Ramos advocated reforms in the 1950s; in India, where "national integration" would become a by-product of preparedness; in Pakistan, where it was seen as a way to make ready for partisan warfare in the likely event of an invasion (by India), and where it created "national spirit" and better focused the efforts of all citizens, "now struggling after the oasis of wealth . . . in the desert of immoralities."[108] Obligatory military service was nationalism in action where democracy was a secondary or as yet unattained feature of politics and government. And this, too, had to be.

Of course where democracy was as new as it really was in Germany, or where it was an idiosyncratically defined ideal, as in Latin Europe, military service was seen most clearly by officers as the duty of all men to serve the nation, an integrating agent, a way to learn a skill or trade, a means of inculcating values, the mission through which citizens could fully realize their obligations and privileges to the fatherland, and learn the true meaning of "democracy."[109] Almost everywhere beyond Latin America, then, citizenship and defense, whatever the local specifics, still required some kind of national commitment by all citizens.

From the beginning of the century, as is well documented, military service had been extremely important to Latin Americans. French and German arguments and models already prevailed before World War II. In the second half of the century Latin American champions of obligatory service compared more in their arguments with those who saw it as a form of nation-building, a civilizing, integrating process. In other words, they remained within a worldwide mainstream, but now recognized more fully the internal dimensions of the total army experience.

"Military education is the topping off of the educational process begun by parents and teachers, and, because of this, the virtues demanded by the military are lofty ones acquired only by men [both] virile and pure of heart."[110] Major Alejandro Medina, who wrote these lines back in 1946, in effect set a tone for Latin American treatments of military service—and he was only discussing "premilitary" training in public and private schools.

Obligatory service per se would be viewed in ways that, by this point, must be obvious: by Peruvians as vocational training, inculcation of patriotism, civic action, and elementary education; by Argentines as an obligation to one's countrymen; by Venezuelans as a force for national integration; by Mexicans as an honor to the individual and the fatherland: emulation of the *Niños Héroes* of the war with the United States.[111]

It would be described by Colombians as a natural way in which youth could look with pride to elders for guidance and advice; by Brazilians as an indicator of national strength.[112] It would be discussed in Goltzian and Lyauteyesque terms by Argentines as a prerequisite for Argentina's social, moral, and economic stability;[113] by Guatemalans as evidence of social equality, and Salvadorans as adjunct to internal security.[114] It would be portrayed as insurance against the disastrous results of an army made up of "senseless, agitated inebriates, who end up being struck down by the first shots fired";[115] and linked to entire national histories.[116] To think of any other way of providing for national defense, wrote one Brazilian colonel in 1944, would be "equivalent to altering the national mentality, and to thrusting it into the future without an understanding of the past."[117] Military service was, above all, another of the many time-defying links between the early twentieth century, the days of yesterday's soldiers, and the time of the generals, 1964–1989. There was no original argument or theory presented in its favor in the second half of the century. For this reason further discussion is unwarranted.

All armies, thus, have been portrayed as many things. Symbolically they have been made out to represent schools, homes, machines, temples, melting pots, equalizers, integrators, evidence of strength and virility, guardians of all that is good against the forces of evil, and as sundry parts of the human body. In practical terms armies have been discussed in a more detailed, less lofty manner as defense organizations, as developmental tools, as agents of national security and integrative elements in societies badly in need of organization and development. Often symbols and traditions would blur with substance and actions, and theory and practice became confused in the metaphoric process.

Twelve years into the post-Allende regime in Chile, three Venezuelan colonels published a book that gained wide circulation among Chilean officers. With regard to national security, they wrote that "the armed forces are not an end in themselves, but a means destined to contribute, along with the rest of society, to the confrontation of all that menaces security."[118] Nearly forty years before, in 1947, at a time when Chileans were confronting an unruly Marxist left (and preparing to outlaw the Communist Party), a Chilean major had advocated an obligatory national labor system. His idea, a sketchy version of prewar German *Arbeitsdienstpflicht,* did go into effect in 1953 but never amounted to much. It would be seen much as premilitary education schemes were, as a way that an army, summarily excluded from political participation, could somehow legitimize its existence as a national force: a "spiritual communion" of citizens.[119] Public works and other mundane activities, emphasized since the 1920s and given new emphasis after 1938, would benefit all Chileans, if supervised by the army, enthused the major.

In 1958 another Chilean major would write that "the people themselves" ought to play a greater role in internal development. "Chile is what her armed forces are," opined a colleague, but, he countered, a national labor scheme ought not detract from the warrior spirit of Chileans and the necessity to have an army ready for defense against foreigners.[120]

Chilean officers were struggling with role definition in very basic terms at this point.

Then, twelve years later, in an article published shortly before the election of Salvador Allende Gossens, still another major boldly asserted that "the armed forces of the state" had both manifest roles—including those of defense, education, civic action, national catastrophe activities—and a latent one—that of saving the country from extremism through a *golpe de estado*. "In such cases," he wrote, "the behavior of the armed forces is legitimate, the result of subjective evaluation of the situation; whether this corresponded to the reality of the situation is another thing."[121] Citing liberally from sources on military involvement in the politics of the developing world, and relying heavily on Edwin Lieuwen's incisive *Arms and Politics in Latin America*,[122] Chilean Claudio López Silva argued persuasively, as events would later confirm, for a significant participatory role in all aspects of Chilean life. His application of "manifest" and "latent," though not in accordance with the usage in these chapters, is nevertheless highly indicative of cautiously applied emphasis by a military writer who was aware of his service's delicate situation. Just two years later, another Chilean would state that "wherever and in whatever way a modern state projects itself, it will need armed forces capable of supporting its decisions; owing to this irreversible premise it cannot have misunderstandings with the military and avoid failure."[123] Like López Silva, this individual spoke in broad terms, avoiding specific prescriptions for military-civilian relations in his own benighted land. Soon Chileans would be sounding like their colleagues in other countries, for the Chilean army was soon to become, in one officer's words, "the spinal column of the fatherland." It had overcome all "misunderstandings" and assumed its "latent role."[124] Chile was now in the grip of professional militarists.

From the Caribbean to the Southern Cone there was general consensus that, whatever its symbolic and traditional roles, an army had to be a bulwark against ideological aggression. Defense meant exactly that to Venezuela's Monsignor José María Pibernat.[125] To a compatriot, the army could not win total victory with arms alone; victory over all Venezuela's enemies was achievable only through total civil-military cooperation in civic action projects. "The concept of the 'nation in arms,' which clearly von der Goltz bequeathed us, is still valid, having widened its theater of action to include the moral and spiritual mobilization of materialism."[126] All Venezuelans would benefit from military service, wrote General Martín García Villasmil, for it was the way to foment national progress through civic action and internal security.[127] Venezuela's counterinsurgency campaigns of the post-Castro decade both justified the army's multiple roles and obviated the necessity to assume the "latent" one alluded to by the Chilean López Silva.

Much of Venezuela's national territory was either still marginally occupied or untapped. Insurgency festered in remote, undeveloped parts of the country. The army ought to be in the vanguard of postpacification development programs, wherein a "consciousness of citizenship" would replace lack of national identity and patriotism, wrote a colonel in 1967.[128] Out there in the mountains and forests, "officers and soldiers die so that Venezuela will not fall into the hands of foreign powers," wrote a chaplain major the next year.[129] "Far from being a danger, the military is a powerful guarantee of the fatherland's liberty," a confrere would add a decade later.[130] Defense Minister General Tomás Abreu Rescaniera could say with pride in 1980 that the armed forces were now entirely conscious of national realities, tied to no interest group or party, and had defended Venezuela well against insurgency.[131] Between the fall of Pérez Jiménez and the 1980s, symbolism had achieved a certain substance in Venezuela. But how long could the mix endure?

Far to the south, Argentines, on their own march toward the flourishing of professional militarism, also consistently merged symbolism with substance, relying on World War II as a base point. There would be no counterinsurgency campaign there to weld citizens to their defenders. The war against totalitarianism, according to the writings of General Jorge Giovanelli, had been won because the allies made good use of military-civilian unity.[132] This concept would prevail in military literature, regardless of specific theme, throughout the postwar decades, but it would never reflect Argentine sociopolitical reality.

The army, its general staff would claim in 1964, was the prime mover of national material, spiritual, and cultural progress. Far from being a parasite and a consumer of wealth, the army actually produced wealth. Engineering projects, scientific research, manufacturing, exploration, technical training—all these activities proved beyond doubt that Argentines owed much to their armed forces. The military, after all, had been involved in economic development since the 1920s; it had become traditional military behavior.[133] Also in 1964, Colombia's controversial General Alberto Ruiz Novoa, a staunch and articulate advocate of the military's developmental role and a man whose political pronouncements finally led to his retirement, would tell the Conference of Latin American Armies meeting in the Canal Zone that military organizational skills should encompass the totality of a country's activities. Armies had trained and disciplined work forces capable of taking on large-scale developmental projects, led as they were by physical and intellectual elites—disciplined professionals with technological expertise applicable to "many civilian situations."[134] Internal security, whether challenged by outright insurgency, as in Colombia, or ideological subversion, as elsewhere in the region (Argentina, say) was the army's business.

Late in 1965, Juan Enrique Guglialmelli told an attentive audience of staff and high command officers that "the armed forces, owing to their peculiar characteristics, are active in all fields. They take part in all community activities, and in each they have a tendency to create both a feeling and a reality of sovereignty."[135] Wishful thinking or thoughtful wishing, Guglialmelli's statement was a good summing-up of Argentine officer corps thought and self-perception just before the 1966 *golpe* headed by Juan Carlos Onganía. As usual, such thought extended to the Malvinas question.[136] Argentina's powerful geopolitical problem would be always on the mind, no matter the theme or topic of an essay or speech.

Argentina's traditionally fecund publishing industry and the country's generally high level of intellectual activity doubtless have been responsible for the attention paid by officers to translated works and works by officers from other Spanish-speaking countries. Ruiz Novoa, Mercado Jarrín, Couto e Silva, and Russians, Germans, and Frenchmen—all have been made accessible to Argentine officers in official journals. The widely read (and already cited) September 1973 address by Mercado Jarrín to the Conference of Latin American Armies would appear soon after its delivery in Guglialmelli's *Estrategia*. In it the Peruvian proclaimed most eloquently a historical, traditional *razón de ser* of Latin America's armed forces.[137] Mercado Jarrín's words were welcome ones to Argentines facing a new Perón government and learning more each day about what was transpiring across the Andes in Chile.

A pseudonymous "Juan Ramón Muñoz Grande," a "distinguished high-ranking army general, who, owing to the high position he occupies, has chosen not to make his name known," would tell *Estrategia* readers later that same decade that the role of the army "will not be limited exclusively to classical warfare, always possible within a regional context, but will also be one of fighting against the deceitful intervention of subversion in the internal context, as already manifest in many countries of Latin America. To think of the army of the future is to link it to the nation we want for tomorrow."[138] The active, internal role contemplated by this Argentine was a timeless one. This would be food for thought in the 1980s and 1990s.

As amply demonstrated, soon after the end of World War II Peruvians had resumed with verve their own march toward the future. "The army has always been considered a mute institution characterized by the silence of obedience, which is the synchronized force of its actions," wrote one officer. Those who portrayed the army as "a devourer of millions in order to respond to its personnel needs," or who thought that military service "reduces the number of workers and peasants necessary for progress," were all wrong, he went on.[139] Peruvians were honing the self-perception necessary for a very sophisticated self-image.

Comparable examples range in the region. "The welfare of the people," wrote one Bolivian officer in 1961, "must be the first concern of all governments, therefore of the armed forces who are the representatives of that people."[140] Paraguayans would read that they and their civilian countrymen should learn Guaraní—in much the same way Peruvians had been told for decades they should be learning Quechua: "He who hates Guaraní hates his own land, his people, and their national traditions."[141] He who opposed the military could expect the same opprobrium.

"The Brazilian army is proud to be the American precursor of all this activity," editorialized the *Revista do Clube Militar* in 1969. Five years into Brazil's very own time of the generals, 1964–1985, few Brazilian officers would challenge this assertion. "Our traditions can be traced to the earliest times of our history as an independent nation, even to colonial times, for our engineers were being trained by the Portuguese then."[142] The first army to undertake "all this activity" did so selectively using history, colonial, early national, and recent, as justification for a role expanded to proportions never dreamed of in earlier times.

And up north in the Caribbean, where professionalism was barely theoretical but where words were plentiful and constructive action imperceptible, officers would say most of the same things. "The defense of democracy is consubstantiated(!) with internal peace, and the army has provided us with the proper tools to assure this role,"[143] wrote a Cuban in 1950. In Somoza's Nicaragua the National Guard could be portrayed again and again as a guarantor of national security, a bulwark of the state, an economic benefit, an educator, a source of vocational training, a civilizer. Without the *Guardia,* opined its members, Nicaragua would be anarchic.[144] Symbols would never become substance there.

Guatemalans were no less nobly committed to tranquility and democracy. "In the files," one officer observed in 1951, "the rich and the poor fraternize, blending themselves with one idea and with one simple objective, working together."[145] Guatemalan *ladino* aristocrats, one might assume, were to derive pleasure and gratification in obligatory service, rubbing shoulders with members of the more modest sectors of society. Guatemalans would also be put on notice in the 1960s that their army was not a drag on the economy—by now a theme common enough all over Latin America. Above and beyond its role as guarantor of liberty, etc., the army was also portrayed as doing many things for its short-term members that prepared them for return to a productive, civilian life.[146] Across the border in tiny El Salvador the drill was much the same for military writers. Colonel Fidel Sánchez Hernández echoed current Guatemalan sentiments in a 1967 discussion of his homeland's "firm and lasting cement of society."[147] Salvadoran and Guatemalan civilians probably just did not realize their good fortune.

In the 1970s things would remain much the same. Dominicans read about the same things their Isthmian colleagues did. Their army had a "sacred mission of defense," and civic action was as much a part of it as was conventional warfare.[148] Guatemalans were told that their army was a key factor of "development and incorporation of indigenes."[149] This 1976 pronouncement briefly discussed the sad situation of Guatemala's Indians, questioning whether or not they were "ready" to be citizen-soldiers, and tendered suggestions on who was to blame for such a waste of manpower. Nicaraguans were still hearing that the *Guardia* protected them all from any number of threats, and that its members were—who dared deny it—"the brothers of the people."[150]

"The Mexican army constitutes much more than a sector of the citizenry," General Juan Gastelum had written back in 1966.[151] Part of a work already cited, his claim was surely more legitimate than those of Central Americans or Caribbeans. The Mexican Revolution, whatever its manifest or latent shortcomings, already had brought peasants, labor, and popular sectors closer to integration than many other social movements in Latin America. The blending of the military into the popular sector achieved under Lázaro Cárdenas (1934–1940) made the Mexican army distinguishable from all others. If it fell short of being a school of democracy or a temple of civic virtue, it fell no shorter than the armies of the Southern Cone. If its role in civic action merited criticism, it merited no more than any other, and less than many. If it was to play no major counterinsurgency role, it was because there was none yet to be played. Mexico's army was a far cry, professionally, from that of any Central American or Caribbean country and far less militaristically inclined than the professional armies of South America.

Gastelum continued his discussion of revolutionary military doctrine, saying that the army's mission "within the national brotherhood is to keep vigil over the security of the state, over the internal and external security of the federation." A civilian colleague, writing some years later, would update this very "traditional revolutionary" role definition. Mexico's "bulwark of national sovereignty," he wrote, "was animated not by aggression, but by construction." Rural literacy, school building, hygiene and nutrition campaigns, and efforts to do away with banditry and drug trafficking all revivified and reinforced the army's role as a bulwark of *La Revolución*.[152] The army was now fulfilling "an endless number of tasks to the benefit of the civilian population that have earned it the affection and respect of the people from whom it comes, and who find in their army the support and backing necessary to carry out their labors in peace, knowing themselves to be protected by [men] who stand vigil over their security."[153] Circumlocutory as this passage may strike the reader (and the most circumlocutory military pronouncements in these pages are yet to come), it conveys vigor and feeling characteristic of most Mexican and many Latin American paeans to the military as peacetime servant, protector, and timeless symbol of national identity.

Some Europeans would end up blurring tradition and action, the old and the new, in similar ways with similar results. If it was not politic to invent new metaphors—or use, ad nauseam, old ones—it would be necessary to plead the army's case and assert its legitimacy. This is best demonstrated by having a look at the French and German cases.

French military authors continued a long-standing tradition of love-hate relationships with former allies and disdain for neighbors. Complicating French relations with the rest of the North Atlantic community were the changing times of the pre– and post–de Gaulle years, the ambivalent attitude toward NATO, the *force de frappe* policy, and decisions to retire the armed forces from the old empire to metropolitan France itself. France became an ex–colonial power but only a reluctant continental one. None of this would reduce the intensity of French military thought or its influence in Latin America. It made the French army look more like a Latin American one, and it may even have encouraged Latin Americans to think more seriously about their own situations.

The defense of France, wrote sociologist Marcel Clément in 1960, was the duty of all Frenchmen, and true citizens were those who could put personal ambition and wishes aside to cooperate for the benefit of the commonweal. Military traditions, Colonel Suire would state several years later, were based on historical need for defense of the nation. To Suire, esprit de corps had become equivalent to national identity.[154] The need for national defense, thus, was now a positive force of integration, on a plane above that of simple obligatory service. This would obtain as well out there in what remained of the French Empire.[155] There, as seen, the military had always been regarded as an integrating force. The old colonial traditions were adaptable to the new metropolitan reality.

For there were still areas of France where the peacetime presence of the army could bring Frenchmen—peasants, bourgeoisie, soldiers, professionals—together better than any other national force. Provincial garrisons were now being described as artificially isolated from garrison towns, and town societies as unnecessarily closed, cautious of outsiders. Owing to this, one writer opined, officers and their men felt isolated themselves, *apart from* those in whose units they served. Therefore, garrisons should be striving to do all they could in the field of public works, local fetes, concerts, snow plowing, athletic competitions, and other projects to show how much they belonged and were *a part of* the community.[156] Such an argument indicates that late in this very century, in one of Western Europe's powers, there were still serious, perceived military-civilian conflicts. If the argument is not strictly comparable with those made in Latin America, it certainly strikes a familiar note. Civic action, by any other name, was entirely compatible with traditional roles, even in France.

The nostalgic ring of "Pour un nouveau rôle social de l'armée" struck a note as familiar as the 1973 call for more community involvement and public relations.[157] Here, Lyautey's old arguments were again employed to urge French officers and soldiers to strive to overcome that "disaffection" for the profession felt by civilian society, which had always accompanied long periods of peace. France, according to this writer, had forgotten her soldiers, forgotten how ex post facto mobilization had failed to keep Germans from taking advantage of the remilitarization of the Rhineland, after all. In order to bring civilian and soldier closer together the army should be getting involved in disaster relief activities, construction projects, historic preservation, public works in poor villages, and environmental protection. *Le rôle social* itself had also become plain civic action in France. France's army had accomplished much in Algeria (only to see it come to naught) and could accomplish much at home.

The defense of France in the mid 1970s had become very much a practical occupation, communism and nuclear threats notwithstanding. Still sensitive to allegations of being a drag on the economy, French military authors strove to link disaster relief efforts to the defense of

French culture, environmental protection to mobilization potential, physical well-being to combat readiness.[158] Such arguments were virtually interchangeable with those being proposed in Latin America. So, too, was one made in a 1982 book on French military reorganization.[159] Here J. Vernet wrote that owing to World War II and its aftermath, the army now had a fourfold mission. France needed an intervention force for use in Europe and Francophone Africa to preclude both another Rhineland disaster and Marxist aggression in Africa. France needed an army to guarantee territorial sovereignty and one to maintain order in overseas possessions. French soldiers should play a role in European collective security as well, for "the army is the guarantee, along with the civil administrative structure, of national sovereignty." This had always been the case, according to the author.

In Germany, obvious complications of postwar military-civilian relations did not preclude discussions like those ongoing in France. Peacetime defense meant primarily the protection of Western Europe, but not simply from the Warsaw Pact nations: from other *Germans* as well. It depended upon adherence to the principles of *Innere Führung*. Arguments would have to be made, and were, that the *Bundeswehr* was "closer" to social realities than had been any other version of the army in German history.[160] Germany's defense role now made "the nation" somewhat subservient to "the West." Discipline had become more than an ideal; it was now a prerequisite to democracy's survival throughout the entire Western world.[161] *Innere Führung* was seen more and more as a blessing, for it had brought democracy into the army and had made a "democratic army" an even more powerful defense against antidemocratic forces.[162] Germany's *Staatsbürger in Uniform* would defend his fellow-citizens, the West, democracy. France's officers need not have worried about a *re*-reoccupation of the Rhineland. Their former foes would now cooperate with them. Germany's army was still necessary if democracy were to survive and its enemies to be held at bay. Even Italians had spokesmen for a "militant peacetime" role. General Andrea Viglione's 1977 essays, for example, would evince arguments for internal and external roles quite comparable to those of French and German writers.[163] Surely advocacy for an internal peacetime defense and security role was not a monopoly of Latin American generals and subalterns seeking to justify their existence. Western Europeans, like Latin Americans, consistently perceived a common foe. Until the late 1980s, at least, the Soviet Union, the Warsaw Pact, or Marxist-Leninist ideological penetration, the "Red Menace," threatened Western ideals and values—some of which officers themselves even questioned. Western professionals' attempts to cling to old ways by adapting old arguments to the circumstances of the times attest to this.

Surveying the myriad ways in which traditional miliary roles were blurring with new perceptions of reality, one is at times reminded of the argument that helped condemn Arthur Koestler's unfortunate Rubashov in *Darkness at Noon*: that to eschew civil war as a form of opposition to dictatorship is to eschew opposition itself. This is indeed the case with an argument like that of Soviet Colonel A. Milovidov in an essay of 1969.[164] "In the Soviet armed forces," he wrote, "unconditional fulfillment of orders as an important aspect of conscious military discipline does not enchain the serviceman's freedom of will but, on the contrary, provides broad scope for its rational manifestation." Discipline, then, bred fulfillment, which indicated commitment to the Revolution, which led to freedom. Unconditional fulfillment of orders meant total freedom: an unconditional totality bordering on tautology of Orwellian dimension as well as on Koestlerian logic. In their own way the uniformed agents of the ideology and the power most hated and feared by Western officers were very much like their counterparts when it came to adapting (on paper) the old to the new.

But in the strict sense of internal role, argued Colonel A. Timorin, the Red Army had none.[165] Fulfillment of one's duty and aspiring to revolutionary perfection were simply parts of every citizen's socialist destiny. Only armies of capitalist countries played an internal role, to be sure, for they opposed the goals of socialism, i.e., freedom and justice. The Red Army and the Soviet Union were one, blessed by representing together the people of the Motherland. Some Western imperialist countries and their armies could not be true representatives of any people. The only external function of the Red Army was to safeguard revolutionary gains of the past and goals of the future; that of Western armies was to keep inevitable revolution from spreading. Like other officers, Soviets might utilize both objective and subjective conditions to show their indispensability.

The intriguing relationship between liberty and discipline that forms a part, explicitly or implicitly, of so many cases made by officer-authors is limitless. It is comparable across ideological frontiers, across regional and cultural boundaries. It is timeless. It is at once self-serving and credible: the fabric of a society and a polity cannot withstand total liberty; discipline must be based on an acceptance of its legitimacy and necessity. "It is only discipline that enables us to live in a community and yet retain individual liberty," Field Marshal Slim had said back in 1950.[166] To Slim, and to officers everywhere and whenever, one could not exist without the other. The dual roles of the army, those of internal and external imperative, of peace and war, of recognizing *autres temps, autres moeurs,* would also prove comparable across dividing lines of time and space.[167] In the later twentieth century the workings of the military mind would indicate, both in Latin America and elsewhere, the presence of a consensus mentality based on both the traditional and the contemporary.

As apparent as a general consensus may appear to have been throughout Europe, there was a Latin European variation on this theme that bears mention. Italians, Portuguese, and Spaniards have never influenced Latin American military thought traditionally, but, in short-term, "post–Cold War" retrospect, comparability of both sociocultural background and recent democratization processes may lead to some new perspectives. At present this must remain tame surmise.

Like the French, the Portuguese played a role in Africa in the postwar years. Until the decolonization of Angola and Mozambique in the mid 1970s most Portuguese officers would have agreed with Captain Leandro Sandoval, who wrote in 1963 that "it is indispensable that the military mission, in the secular as well as the religious field, continue to expand."[168] Portugal's mission in Africa was spiritual, therefore, as well as modernizing, but the attendant "culture shock" was palpable. In the last years of imperial activity these Iberians saw their extra-European efforts in much the same way that their contemporaries in Latin America did their domestic activities: as part of a civilizing and integrating mission to less-developed regions and sectors.

Italians were viewing peacetime internal defense in ways comparable to both Latin Americans and other Europeans. Civil defense, "abnegation and enthusiastic defense of democracy," and participation in all facets of national life were now the essential lot of the Italian soldier. Military service made citizens complete, for it was a "sacred duty" and made society cohesive.[169] Defense of the West was not the only role of the Italian army. Spaniards, especially after the passing of Franco, would begin to see the army's internal role in similar terms. "To be a Spaniard," asserted Captain Gerardo Torres Bados, "is one of the few things worth being in this world." Of course, to be a Spaniard *and a soldier* was even better, for soldiers, "thanks to their vigil, make possible the dawn of Spain's every new day."[170] No matter the specific situation, European armies, conscious of peacetime anomalies and traditions to be maintained or forgotten, were determined to preserve their status and their prestige, however modest that may have been. All the while they insisted on a visible peacetime domestic identity.

This also obtained among the new colonial armies and among those French who still served in Africa. There would be no end to the use of Lyautey and Psichari as examples for colonial officers and their men either.[171] Military strength and the upgrading of all aspects of training and education would always be seen as critically important for the preservation of the new nations.[172] In most parts of the globe, it could have been asserted, the "purely professional officer seems to be the one who [makes] his value commitments explicit."[173] Explicit value commitments would determine much of the content of professional militarism; the form that it took would depend greatly on the milieu in which the military existed and on the conditions under which it adapted past to present.

Of all the roles assigned to, or assumed by, officers for themselves and their armies, then, those of educator and civilizer would be most consistently and universally written about. These roles had always made them *a part of* society. The education and training allegedly imparted in barracks and on parade grounds provided recruits and draftees with the finishing touches on the education they had received from family, religion, and formal schooling. Boys became men, citizens, contributors to the rest of society—at least in theory they did. These same roles, however, also forced army officers to perceive themselves as *apart from* society, especially in the face of so much and so many different kinds of change. No amount of practice ever convinced Latin American officers that they should not cling to their basic attributes; no amount of "outreach" ever convinced officers in Western Europe and the U.S. that they were appreciated or understood enough. Between these two extremes were thousands of officers whose dilemmas resembled both.

Because officers and armies still stood for so many of the ways that were challenged by time's passage, being *apart from* society would always be more beneficial than having to be *a part of* it, especially in those countries where steadfast clinging to military tradition and militant confronting of perceived change were most pronounced. In South America change and tradition both abetted the metamorphosis of professionalism into militarism.

The gulf between theory and practice, often simplistically thought of by officers as the difference between old and new, was widest where obligatory military service did not result in successful inculcation of traditional ideals and values, where civilian society did not respond the way officers thought it should. In most places the idea that time in the ranks would channel individualism toward service to the whole of society, for example, proved to be no more than illusion. Convictions that civic action and national security were the logical offspring of so many traditions and time-tested programs, and that the army was the factor common and indispensable to them all, appealed to officers in many countries for obvious reasons. In Latin America testimony to this effect was all the more vivid and consistent, for there change had occurred in ways distinct from the rest of the world. The conviction that an army was the purest image of the nation and constituted the nation in arms would never cease to figure boldly in military literature. In Latin America this conviction figured, increasingly, under new rubrics.

Emphasis on symbols, metaphors, and similes, and retention of tradition for its own sake belies emphasis on social synthesis, civilizing agency, and schooling for democracy. For all their insistence on being *a part of* society, officers had always depicted themselves and continued to depict their armies, as being just as much *apart from* it. Given attitudes toward the new world paradigm in all its dimensions, officers in some countries were able to convince themselves that to them had fallen the burden of saving national societies and western culture from the mistakes of civilians who had abetted the destabilization of polities and economies. Where conditions permitted, such convictions led to professional militarism. The potential for hostile military-civilian relationships would be enhanced, if not fulfilled, where officers could convince themselves and others that they and their men were indeed more *apart from* than *a part of* the world of unpleasant change surrounding them on all sides.

Grudging acquiescence would continue to characterize those who acknowledged being but part of a more important whole. Politics and ideologies often became the targets of officer-authors convinced of their apartness. If they could not influence politics and ideologies, they would think themselves justified in acting politically in order to reshape society in their own image. They would strive all the while to keep their charges free from pernicious civilian and alien influences—a paradox of ingenuousness, not ingenuity, that was very much a sign of the time of the generals.

FIVE

Politics and Ideologies: Struggling with Military Separateness and Civilian Primacy

Of course, government in general, any government anywhere, is a thing of exquisite comicality to a discerning mind; but really we Spanish Americans do overstep the bounds. No man of ordinary intelligence can take part in the intrigues of *une farce macabre*.

—Joseph Conrad, *Nostromo* (1904)

—Don't ever get mixed up in politics, because it's no place for decent men.

....

—But if you leave politics to indecent men, you hand them the country on a platter.—Arturo Von Vacano, *Morder el silencio* (1980)

Latin American political behavior has been subjected to intense scrutiny since the time of independence. The most consistent targets of disgust and disdain by intellectuals and political "outs" have been men in uniform. Army officers have always thought a great deal about politics. Because they have never considered themselves men of just "ordinary intelligence" and because they have traditionally perceived most politicians to be "indecent men," their own actions should be viewed in the context of their thought and self-perceptions.

Perceiving themselves to be not only *a part of* but *apart from* the societies around them probably made it impossible for professional militarists, once officers became such, to avoid political action. It may have justified their actions in the eyes of fellow officers who did not share their militancy owing to their own ideas on politics and ideology. At this stage of the book few eyebrows should be raised upon reading what officers thought about politics and ideology. Many of them, after all, were trying to bring the present into line with the past. They were confronting, reconciling, maintaining, and adapting, not embracing or yielding. This study shows how they also struggled with separateness and the concept of civilian political primacy.

In South America this struggle served to intensify feelings of uniqueness. Elsewhere in Latin America and beyond the region it helped define military-civilian relationships in keeping with the changes characteristic of the new world paradigm. Variations of intensity of perception aid in differentiating between manifest and latent militarism within Latin America, and in demonstrating that professional militarism is a contextual phenomenon.

Political change and ideological challenges added greatly to the discomfort of military men who strove to hold on to selective pasts while also striving to survive their unsettling present. The more they saw themselves as *apart from* the rest of society, the more they found civilian primacy unacceptable; the more they could understand the advantages of seeing themselves *a part of* society, the more they could tolerate civilian leadership. It was often a question of institutional survival. In Latin America discussions of ideology were often lamentations of democracy's weakness or condemnations of communism. Politics was dealt with delicately, often in the form of admonitions and remonstrations against officers becoming involved in partisan issues and civilian manipulation of the military. Politics and ideology would be perceived by Latin Americans as divisive to civilians and military alike.

Here, two case studies of European military thought on politics and ideology show how uniqueness could underlie superficial typicality. West German *Innere Führung,* unique to that country's historical experience, emerges from the literature as a near ideology, a corollary of democracy, at least. It would be as unique to the *Bundeswehr* as would *don (dom) de mando* to Latin Americans. Soviet Marxist-Leninist military thought takes on the aspect of vocation as described, sans ideological prerequisites, by most non-Marxist officer-authors. Both democracy and communism needed professional protection from ideological competition, then, and military might was supposed to assure this protection.

Anticommunism and the vulnerabilities and excesses of democracy would figure in western military literature, more boldly in Latin American sources than anywhere else. Discussions here indicate that politics and ideology were used to validate professional qualities and assigned or assumed roles. Democracy, unlike communism, needed a defense against itself. The perceived degree to which it needed to be defended helped draw the line between professionalism and militarism. Military writing on politics and ideology, in fine, served primarily to perpetuate already-held thought and self-perceptions and to solidify military-civilian relationships already in the making since the dawn of the postwar era.

"The army, the armed forces, gentlemen, are above all the guardian of the permanent," wrote Uruguay's commander in chief, Lieutenant General Luis V. Queirolo in 1981.[1] His immediate concerns were subversion and insurgency, but he neglected to state the obvious: in his country partisan politics was also part of *lo permanente,* part of national tradition. Queirolo railed against communism and championed the army's role as a protector of the nation, but he showed no inclination toward democracy, nor toward any other kind of politics for that matter. His struggle—how to rationalize a *patria política* with *lo permanente* was a common one in late-twentieth-century Latin America. The fact that it was not unrecognized elsewhere indicates still further that uniqueness and typicality are not mutually exclusive. It also provides one more ingredient to the world perspective within which professional militarism should be placed.

General Sir Roy Bucher (KBE, CB, MC) had stated back in 1948 that "no army which concerns itself with politics is ever of any value. Its discipline is poor, its morale is rotten, and its reliability and efficiency is [sic] bound to be of the lowest order. You have only to look at certain foreign armies which are constantly mixed up in politics to realize the truth of what I say."[2] Bucher made no reference to Latin America, of course, but his allusion was clear. A quarter century later Argentina's Omar Parada would seem to have confirmed Bucher's opinion when he advocated "immersing" the armed forces in the government.[3] Total avoidance of politics, said some, total immersion preached others. Background differences aside, the direct cause of military involvement, as many would observe, was civilian incompetence.[4] Somewhere betwixt and between lay the truth in every case. André Maurois presciently wrote just after the war that "there have been . . . more coups d'état and more military dictators in Latin America than we have been used to for some time, at least in Western Europe; but on the whole these may have been less destructive to the general cultural and economic lives of these republics than our own large-scale international wars. The Latin American politicians have, on the whole, failed either to transform their countries or destroy them."[5] Maurois was, for his time, quite perceptive.

Forty years later it could be written that Latin American military leaders had failed in the same way civilians had, for they had remained tragically bound to politics. Officer corps continued to resemble "political battle grounds" where ongoing struggles raged between strictly defined professionalism and politically oriented militarism.[6] Officers continued to "serve two masters by combining political and military duties." They often became what Major General Albert Kwesi Ocran warned fellow Ghanaians and other Africans against becoming: both a bad soldier and a bad politician. "Many eminent generals and politicians on both sides of the world's ideological camp have come to the inevitable conclusion that military supremacy over civilian authorities ruins both the nation and the whole military," he said.[7] Would that this African view had obtained there, and in Argentina, Brazil, Chile, and Peru; in Bolivia, Paraguay, Uruguay, and Ecuador; in the Caribbean and Central America.

Uniformly, as it were, officers ultimately blamed politics for most national ills, and politicians for the military's shortcomings. The fact that civilians made politics what they were was taken for granted. Denials of anticivilian feelings would often be buttressed by disclaimers that not all civilians were bad, just the politicians who led them astray. The Guatemalans who overthrew Jorge Ubico in 1944 had so argued.[8] Peruvians concurred.[9] The postwar glow of democracy and reform in countries like Guatemala, Peru, and Bolivia—Indian countries all—prompted officers to attempt to erase their countries' dictatorial or oligarchic past. Never mind that what passed for democracy was far from it, civilian politics now prevailed, if only briefly. The Bolivian restorationist movement that toppled the controversial regime of Major Gualberto Villarroel in 1946 caused one general to blame the 1943–1946 political experience for all the army's recent problems: personalism, cliques, corruption.[10] Brazilians, still recovering from the authoritarian rule of Getúlio Vargas, read in 1948 that military discipline was again in jeopardy, given renewed civilian political activity. That same year Peruvian officers were told that the October putsch that had removed President José Luis Bustamante from office was totally justified. The president's incompetence had obliged the military to act, not out of personal ambitions, nor at the behest of cliques or camaraillas, but for "love of country"—and dislike of politics, especially when *Apristas* participated.[11] Just a year prior to the great Bolivian upheaval of 1952, the *altiplano*'s uniformed servants would be told that the army must be forever subordinate to the government.[12] But a few months later their new president would tell them essentially the same things they had read back in 1946 about the preceding regime.[13] Same message, different sender. Official military professions of post–World War II democratic zeal often appeared in essays dealing specifically with themes discussed in the first four chapters. That is to say they often appeared out of, as well as in, context.

Quiescent in most respects until the 1970s, Chileans nevertheless would think and write about politics after the war. In a trenchant 1953 piece, "Ningún cuerpo armado puede deliberar" (a constitutional proscription), Captain (attorney) Fernando Montaldo Bustos argued that the army's "principles of discipline and instruction oblige us to think carefully, reflecting and examining all ideas, discussing, approaching from different angles. *Eso es deliberar.*"[14] The army had to deliberate in order to fully understand things, its own role, for example. Back up on the *altiplano,* Bolivia's new military leaders and their civilian counterparts were still lashing out at the 1946–1952 *sexenio*. Masons, *La Rosca,* and communists, all playing at politics, had ruined Bolivia and undermined her army.[15] As noted earlier, the post-1952 army would reassert traditional roles and claim new ones, all in the name of revolution. Back down on the coast, Chileans still luxuriated in their comparatively demilitarized country. But army leaders feared full demilitarization, disarmament, and pacifism. In 1958 the imminent election of Jorge Alessandri Rodríguez (son of the *bête noire* of Chilean soldiers of the pre–World War II era, Arturo Alessandri Palma) compelled one editorialist to warn his fellow officers of "well-intentioned men and idealists who, basing their thought on the erroneous assumption that traditional armaments are now useless, favor disarmament as a viable economic step."[16] Politicians and propagandists were not to be believed if Chileans were to remain free.

Far up the coast in Colombia, officers would read after 1957 that they were free from the *politiquería* of the Rojas Pinilla years, *apart* again from politicians, back in barracks, on parade grounds, and in the field where they should be.[17] Nearer the end of the decade, Guatemalans were being kept aware of the disastrous effects of Colonel Jacobo Arbenz's leftist politics on the military profession during his 1951–1954 administration.[18] Depending on local conditions, previous systems, parties, and military-civilian relationships were potential targets for attack. Where tradition kept the military separate (not necessarily equal) there was no lack of wariness about contemporary politics either. So, too, where the military remained on "alert." General Pedro Aramburu wrote in 1961 that it was more necessary now than ever before for the army to remain impervious to all political influences and to all issues that divided public opinion.[19] Even though Perón had been elected democratically, he had become a divisive dictator. Military action to restore a proper balance had been necessary. Action to maintain a proper balance might still be necessary.

Politicians, after all, were ever goading officers to take action in order to reap the benefits themselves. They had done so in Guatemala time and again. They tried to do it in Peru, Venezuela, and Argentina. "Some say," wrote Chaplain Major José Manzanares, "that Venezuelan history is comparable to those modern recordplayers that have up to 78 revolutions a minute."[20] By the 1970s, continued goading and repeated intervention had created an atmosphere characterized by a hostile separateness. One Argentine would go so far as to cite one of Leopoldo Lugones' prewar authoritarian bromides. Nineteenth-century liberalism was dead, its offspring, constitutional government, was decrepit, and "the army is the last aristocracy . . . the only possible defense against demagogic dissolution. Only military virtues provide, in these historic times, a superior blend of beauty, hope and force."[21] Soon after Lugones was so quoted, Juan Perón would return to the Casa Rosada. Action to maintain proper balance would appeal yet again. Argentines could now write about politics the way Peruvians wrote about APRA, the way Brazilians wrote about their pre-1964 experiences, and the way Chileans would soon describe their pre-1973 situation. There had to be a better way, a way to avoid individualism, subversion, rampant materialism, Marxist outrages, foreign influences—change. Perhaps a "fundamental organic" kind of regime would do the trick.[22] Such alternatives still appealed to generals in many countries.

"Today's political systems have been left behind by new ideological conceptions that are based fundamentally on humanism and that organize and make use of new systems emphasizing individual man as the supreme entity of society."[23] Neither democracy nor totalitarianism, continued Peru's Mercado Jarrín, served the interests of humanism: "of man as an end in and of himself." The army now did, by virtue of its participation in the movement of 1968. It had done the same in Brazil in 1964, claimed writers from that country.[24] Separate and hostile, Latin American officers disdained politics and politicians—even when they knew they did so hypocritically. "Politicians tend to use the various organizations that exist to further their own ends," Brigadier J. Nazareth told his Indian readers in 1972.[25] Even though the same case was made in Latin America, officers there found it difficult if not impossible to eschew political contacts from the end of World War II forward.

"No matter how authoritarian the power may be, it still emanates, directly or indirectly, from the sovereignty that resides in the people. . . . We shall always adhere to the popular will. . . . The moment the people demand that this movement, this enterprise, this experiment be dismantled, it shall be dismantled."[26] So President Ferdinand Marcos would claim in 1973. Such sophistry was worthy of many a Latin American politician or general of the time. It evinced the same confused conception of military-political separation and masked an addiction to power based on feigned selfless service to the fatherland in the name of ridding the land of unscrupulous manipulators.

In much of the world the principle of civilian primacy in politics received some cautious attention from officers. The fact that there is no massive corpus of official military literature specifically devoted to civilian politics attests to wide toleration or grudging acceptance of the principles of military separateness and civilian primacy. Their presence in literature devoted to other themes, though, testifies to the depth of military feelings and motives, thought and self-perception vis-à-vis politics. One of Marcos' own countrymen wrote in 1956 that "a government that is wanting in integrity is one that is least able to enforce the necessary national discipline for preparedness against a situation that we may face."[27] His unintentional foresight aside, the implication of the claim is quite significant. The primacy of politics over military interests prevails only where civilian governments allow the military no room to claim an unfulfilled role, social, political, cultural, or ideological.

"Politics and soldiering do not mix," one Indian officer insisted in 1961.[28] Nor, officers from around the world believed, did other significant traits of civilians and soldiers. "We of the military are perhaps more conscious than our civilian brothers of other ways of life—of how other people live, of other political regimes," an American officer asserted.[29] Familiarity with other regimes was insulation; it assured security for Americans as long as civilian political primacy obtained—and as long as military men and women voted and fulfilled other civic duties. Security of place for *Bundeswehr* officers was assured through both *Innere Führung* and the primacy of politics, inseparable principles in the new Germany. "Without the principle of command and obedience there can be no guarantee of political primacy," wrote one general in 1979.[30] Frenchmen would read that systemic primacy was more important than personal or military leadership of national affairs.[31]

There were, as well, arguments raised against the quality of political primacy, if not that of primacy itself. A Spanish officer would opine in 1979 that "partisan struggles are a waste of time and of energy that work to the detriment of decision and carrying out of one's orders, and that brazenly undermine hierarchy."[32] Lyautey could have written that and, in essence, he had. This Spaniard's specific example of "partisan struggle" was that of ideological and generational confrontation encouraged by a crisis of civilization—the result of "consumer societies"—i.e., change. A North American officer would observe the inner tensions of the U.S. political system in a 1978 essay quite similar both to that just cited and the Chilean Montaldo's mentioned above.[33] Such essays emphasized the potential divisiveness of all civilian political systems. They also reflected perpetual consternation over sociocultural change.

Throughout these pages the military soul searching that has occurred following the overthrow of dictatorial governments in Latin America is evident. Mexico, Guatemala, and Bolivia; Peru, Argentina, Venezuela, Colombia, and El Salvador have already served as examples. These Latin American armies suddenly became reluctant guardians of civilian-led democracy, liberty, of political and social justice. Some would soon revert to type. Democracy for some military writers suddenly became the best way to bring people together, the best integrative force, but their arguments often sounded hollow.[34] Politics might achieve primacy, but where democracy did prevail in late-twentieth-century Latin America it would do so because of consistent economic growth, social programs, good political sense, and the military's realization that it could provide no better for the *patria.* In order for this to obtain there had to be a past worth repudiating. It is highly improbable that this can ever be applicable to Latin America in toto. But it is even possible that strict observance of the primacy of civilian politics may obtain in other countries where the military historically wielded considerable influence over civilian affairs. *Innere Führung* is a case in point.

Essential to Federal Germany's rearmament, to the creation of the *Bundeswehr,* and to its participation in the defense of the West, *Innere Führung* would serve as a binding agent, a force for depoliticization of the military, a guarantee to civilians of military abstinence from open deliberation and dictatorship, military or otherwise. It brought democracy—hitherto only a memory to most living Germans—into the army. German officers generally accepted it as something more than a necessary evil, something less than ideal. It repudiated the past.

"We must build not *again,* but *anew* . . . an army is not democratic by virtue of democratic organization, but only when its officer corps stands firmly on a democratic foundation and is ready to fight for it; human values—freedom and dignity of the individual soldier—are protected; the armed forces are not suspended in a vacuum, but draw their strength and morale from the fact that they consider themselves to be that part of the nation which is serving under arms."[35] Democracy was thus linked by a German officer of the 1950s to the concept of the military as *a part of* the whole—with the primacy of politics assured.

The official definition of this German invention provided by the *Schule der Bundeswehr für Innere Führung,* the army's training center for the doctrinal orientation of officers, portrayed it as "the duty of all military superiors to educate soldiers for the protection of the rights and freedoms of Germans."[36] The use of the plural "Germans" was not incidental, for German unity would be an oft-discussed topic. Other discussions of *Innere Führung* amplified but did not alter either its definition or intent. Officers were bound by rules prohibiting the violation of fundamental rights and freedoms guaranteed by the constitution. Unless war became a reality, conscripts had to enjoy everything in uniform that they did as civilians. The army could not involve itself in partisan politics. The officer was a "functionary of the state."[37] The army's role in society was a restricted one. Civilian morale was more important than traditional officer corps esprit. Major Heinz Karst wrote in 1958 that the army should only be viewed as a collection of "citizens in uniform." His use of such a term in such a context was literal, not figurative.[38] Karst did insist, though, that strict discipline, responsibility, and dedication to national defense prevail within the ranks.

Captain Karlheinz Schubert, a contemporary of Karst, subscribed to *Innere Führung,* seeing it as a doctrine for the upholding of western values, not just German democracy.[39] Officers and soldiers needed to be reminded of exactly what they were defending Germany against. Citizens who put on a uniform to defend both their new democracy and the values of western civilization retained their rights and freedoms, well and good, argued another of *Innere Führung's* senior champions, General Wolf Graf von Baudissin. A soldier certainly had the right to refuse an order, indeed the duty to refuse, "when it violated the law or called upon him to do so."[40] Baudissin stoutly defended *Bundestag* fiscal and administrative control of the military but, as would others, allowed as how certain military traditions should be subject to no control beyond that of the officer corps.[41] *Innere Führung,* then, was construed as a doctrine of military-democratic fusion, compatible with western values, a kind of political education tool and legal code, but not restrictive of tradition. These essential characteristics would dominate its discussion during the 1970s and 1980s.

Some did fear, though, that *Innere Führung*'s political education function made it in essence a propaganda tool, and that this would occasion attacks from the left. The response was that officers from the *Schule* were exposed to a spectrum of political thought (a little like the argument for including social science content in the CAEM curriculum, this) but were not turned into partisans. Democracy, not Christian Democracy or Social Democracy, reigned supreme in the BRD.[42]

Tradition would only become an acceptable subject for officer-authors a quarter century after the collapse of the Third Reich and the *Wehrmacht,* coincidentally when generals who revered the past ruled in Latin America. It became once again fashionable to display symbols used in the past—no *Hakenkreuze* (hooked or twisted cross, swastika) or *Totenkopfe* (death's head, a favorite SS emblem) of course, just military symbols and regalia—and to take pride in idealized military prowess. Tradition, argued one general, ought not be confused with fantasy or fanaticism. The *Bundeswehr,* he wrote, identified neither with the fanaticism of the *Wehr-*

macht nor with the elitism of the *Reichswehr,* only with the truly honorable defense of German democracy.[43] This 1977 essay was pitched to the younger generation, those Germans who had no actual memory of the horrors of Germany's military heritage but who might be swayed by selective portrayals of past pomp, ceremony, and nationalist zeal. These arguments were akin to those employed by Latin Americans embarrassed by their institutions' past, often repeat, performances.

Once the time was ripe, others would argue that defense capabilities must not be limited by *Innere Führung* and its literal definition of *Staatsbürger in Uniform*. Military efficiency must not be compromised by exaggerated definitions of rights and freedoms. But, ideally, this would never happen, for the *Staatsbürger* now understood this. Civilian supremacy and the primacy of politics must take this all into account, went the argument.[44] For this to happen, *Innere Führung* had to become part of an ideology for all Germans.

This ideology would have as its tenets the primacy of civilian political activity over military activities, the confinement of military influence and deliberation to matters under the control of the defense ministry, integration of defense forces into all facets of community life, the integrity of the soldier as citizen first and foremost, and respect for his individuality: the true meaning of *Staatsbürger in Uniform*.[45] Put another way, the army should be the purest image of the state, a *Volk in Waffen*; but these terms had long since become passé. Despite disclaimers, *Innere Führung* would always be viewed by skeptics as a strengthening of military ideals both through constant redefinition and emphasis on their compatibility with "western spiritual values."[46] Latin Americans would use similar argumentation to justify their political roles.

By the 1980s it would become possible to discuss openly the *Bundeswehr* and its doctrine as *eine Schule der Nation*.[47] The army provided employment and vocational training, it brought together Germans from all walks of life, and it was of economic benefit to the Federal Republic. The army could once again be portrayed as a German asset as well as a symbol of the East-West struggle. Arguments utilized for decades in Latin America might now be used in a country where militarism of classic proportions had once led to tragic national, continental, and global consequences and where some would come to doubt the necessity for the presence of armed foreigners—western foreigners.

Innere Führung came close to becoming an ideology of its own, for it incorporated so much beyond a citizen-soldier's rights and freedoms. "In the *Bundeswehr,*" after all, "men with different educational backgrounds come together," and in such a crucible their commitment to democracy, to western spiritual values, to Germany, to each other, was reinforced.[48] In measured tones, well within the confines of *Innere Führung,* officers might inculcate military tradition, close ties to the state, and the concept of citizen in uniform in the minds of young Germans. The primacy of civilian politics was still linked to the army's capability for defense against both ideological and political threats. The similarities with Latin America ought to be obvious.

So the threats that made *Innere Führung* most of what it was capable of becoming, until 1989 at least, came precisely from outside West Germany's borders, from the East and the left simultaneously, in the form of Marxism and the Warsaw Pact presence. But to hear Marxists tell the same story was to hear of socialist peoples forced to take up arms only because of armed capitalist, imperialist military powers. They stated all this in a different context, but in terms fascinatingly comparable to those used both by champions of democratic *Innere Führung* and Latin American professional militarists. Along with family, school, party, and workplace, a socialist army helped to combine education for life with desire for peace—for war only if needs be.[49] A number of pieces in the *Soviet Military Review* would specifically address the army's relationship with communism. "The realization by the officers and men that they are serving the just cause of the revolution boosts the army morale, strengthens discipline, and improves the training of personnel,"[50] boasted one ideologue in 1967: no separation of army and politics here, rather an undiluted primacy of ideology. To Major General P. Zhilin, "socialism was the army's secret of invincibility,"[51] and had been since Lenin's (not Trotsky's) "founding" of the Red Army.

Military successes following World War II were consistently seen as the result, not the cause of, socialist success, of the inevitability of the revolution rather than as the guarantor of communist domination of, say, Eastern Europe. Indeed, as Marshal Matvei Zakharov put it, "the army of a socialist state has qualities that are inherent only in the military organization of the new social and state system. For the first time," he continued, "an army has been turned from a weapon of class enslavement and aggression into a weapon for the consolidation and defense of the power of the working people. For the first time it came into possession of sources of strength like a close-knit rear characterized by a progressive economic and political system, moral and political unity, and cooperation between working classes and nations."[52] Who could have asked for more?

Considerations of the Red Army as image of the state, molder of unity and (inter)nationalist solidarity resembled, to a degree, those made by westerners—with nationalist solidarity more the latter's priority, of course. "While men are in the army," opined Colonel S. Vovk, "their world outlook is molded, and they enrich themselves spiritually. An important part in this is played by the system of ideological and theoretical education conducted during service time."[53] Red Army soldiers spent time in evening schools studying Marxism-Leninism; enrolled in "people's universities" and culture schools; took part in amateur theater, cinema, orchestra, and artistic projects; and joined "literature lovers" associations. The Red Army would consistently champion its own role as inculcator of ideology; it did not feign neutrality, as it claimed western armies did, rather it served the interests of the entire motherland.

Defense Minister Andrei Grechko, writing in the early 1970s, viewed the Soviet armed forces (why stop with the army?) as owing "all its successes and victories over the enemies of the revolution to the firm leadership of the Party and its Central Committee."[54] World outlooks, spiritual enrichment, education, moral and political cohesion—these were things common to all armies, or so officers everywhere insisted. The essential difference always lay in the definition of terms. In the Marxist view the army *owed* a debt and was not allowed to forget it. Unlike the armies of the West, the Red Army was truly of the people, its leaders had always claimed. Its officers had never represented one class, its men another, for socialism opened the ranks to all.[55] Marxist military men were to be considered socialists first and foremost. Only a true socialist could be a professional. Contrasts with the thinking of western officers on this ideological point were stark.

So were contrasting definitions of and justifications for leadership and discipline. In discussions designed to legitimize unity of command—in opposition to soviet-style leadership, say—Red Army officers often fell back on their own version of vocation, "party-mindedness."[56] An officer led and commanded based on party policy, and his devotion to party principle was his most desirable professional quality. This assured "unbreakable unity" of peoples and classes; it assured morale, preparedness, discipline, rationale, order, and political correctness. The majority of officers, according to one colonel, faithfully attended their Marxism-Leninism classes, and there they "learned to cope scientifically with the complex tasks of training and educating their men." They gained a "scientific world outlook."[57] No "gift," no *Innere Führung,* no religious convictions could possibly lead to such results, could they?

It was a "scientific world outlook" that enabled Red Army officers to defend their source of inspiration and ensure its continuity against the counterrevolutionaries, revisionists, imperialists, and fascists who constantly sought ways to destroy socialism. "The record of history," said one general, in 1973, "teaches that peace will not be gotten out of imperialists—it should be reliably defended."[58] Despite its alleged inevitability, then, socialism did need a professional army the same way democracy needed armed force to defend its own manifest superiority.

In fact, if arguments of Red Army officers were analyzed for content and form and with certain catch phrases extracted, they would be consistently as comparable to those made by Latin Americans as were those of *Innere Führung*'s advocates. One Russian general would argue in the 1980s that officers must always display "an objective approach toward facts and phenomena."[59] An objective approach was, of course, "a military one," but based on "party-mindedness." "The Communist Party," he wrote, "is the vanguard of the Soviet people." Because the army was a reflection of the party, it was part of the vanguard, a position not altogether different, really, from all those Latin "vanguards."

To balance and complement arguments for a scientific military/socialist approach to facts and phenomena, Red Army officers would continue to point out that the Communist Party also provided the officer corps with a justification for centralized command through the presence of political officers. These did not command, they merely provided necessary ideological input to assure officers full knowledge of all official positions.[60] Elimination of class interests and inseparability of party and people facilitated this. If commands were given and decisions taken according to Marxist-Leninist teachings, centralized command posed no threat to the collective. Justifications of *Innere Führung* and *don (dom) de mando* were couched in similar terms, of course.

Marxists frequently offered views on other armies, too, some of which already have been made apparent. It is proper to specify them in this context as well. Imperialist armies, Colonel E. Sulimov wrote back in 1966, served their state-monopoly economic combines in the interests of world domination.[61] Workers (peasants were rarely identified discretely) had no stake in militarist-imperialist ventures, in Malaysia and Vietnam, for example. Military service out there in the developing world only further divided classes that by rights should be uniting across national boundaries.

The *Bundeswehr* regularly came under attack from Red Army officers and others as a pawn of NATO-capitalist-imperialism, German industrial-militarist dreams of lost glory, and *Drang nach Osten*.[62] Especially in the 1970s Marxists, focusing on Western Europe or Latin America, produced variations along the capitalist-imperialist, industrialist-militarist lines. One extremely naive and condescending western Marxist anthology, for example, insisted that no military organization was capable of becoming a revolutionary one unless it was led by the masses.[63] This was tantamount to asserting that military organizations per se ought to be, and had the inclination to be, revolutionary; or that the Soviet Union itself was led by the masses (or that it was not). Most Marxist comments on the military in Latin America strove above all to strike down professional arguments that extraprofessional functions of the military dated from the independence era.

Another western Marxist work would argue, with a lack of originality characteristic of all ideologically driven literature but in precise and clear terminology, that since the state was only a mechanism for the control of one class by another (with no reference to the Soviet variant), it was only natural that its agent, the army, served the same purpose.[64] Armies might acquire the traits of corporations and castes, all right, but could not act independently of the interests of elites, this source claimed. This was a clear and purposeful misreading of reality. Marxists agreed consistently that all western military organizations were "class enemies," remnants of feudalism.[65]

Western views of Europe's most pretentious and dangerous Marxist fighting force were no less stern. The *Nationalvolksarmee* of "Democratic Germany" would be described as thoroughly politicized, Soviet-manipulated, and ideologically fanatic, a transmogrification of Prussian-style militarism.[66] Western views of the Chinese Red Army were similar.[67] Internationalization of military thought and self-perception did nothing to draw military men together politically, but it did allow them to share many professional ideals and values. Internalization of ideology and political action by Marxists, on the other hand, reinforced western professional military convictions that Marxism threatened all they held sacred. The breakdown of parties and systems of Eastern Europe in 1989—coincidental to the ebbing of military involvement in South American politics and government—would make dramatically new conditions for ideological-military relations in both places. But until that time westerners would not let up on the greatest ideological foe of their profession.

Cold warriors' views of Marxism's international machinations always made it clear that any party or organization that sympathized with Marxists or coalesced with socialist or communist parties was likely to be considered antipatriotic. "Political groups with international tendencies are highly pernicious," wrote Lieutenant Rafael Angarita Trujillo in a 1951 essay on politics and the Venezuelan army.[68] A Peruvian captain put it slightly differently only four years later. In an argument for "national spirit" he stated that "the internationalization of morals, laws, and religion is a world conspiracy."[69] Nationalism, he was convinced, did not set nation against nation. International antagonisms were historical, not nationalistic: a weak argument, but his only one.

"The dream of world dominion within a few years is a constant of those who follow the stated doctrines of Marx and Lenin, and whom [the forces of] Colombian democracy must defeat," proclaimed an editorial of 1959.[70] Another western hemispheric military author wrote that "the massive size, global scope, versatile capability, and unmistakable menace of the communist threat viewed against a background of our military situation pose the greatest danger which the United States has ever had to face throughout its history."[71] General Lyman Lemnitzer's statement was not altogether unlike those of Latin Americans. His audience, the politico-military implications of his words, and the national context within which they were published differed significantly, of course.

Communists and their ilk were nefarious by all western military accounts. General Somoza Debayle pointed out the difficulties of fighting communists in an already cited 1960 speech in which he emphasized their ability to hide among the peasants, hit and run, plant bombs, and carry out terrorist acts.[72] Soon thereafter, another Nicaraguan would allude to the military's participation in what amounted to the "third world war": "In reality, if armies should disappear, the ideological conflict, and with it the decisive campaign of the third world war, will be won by the enemy."[73] Somoza, in the very same issue of *Guardia Nacional,* damned communism again and claimed that Nicaragua was a free country with full civil liberties for all. There was no censorship, either. *Selecciones del Reader's Digest,* he boasted, circulated quite freely within the national borders.[74] With assurances like this, who would have predicted the events of 1979? Other Latin Americans of the 1960s discussed brainwashing and communism's known inroads into the British Labor Party and African politics.[75] From a European standpoint, *Revue de Défense Nationale* warned in 1962 of communism's inroads into Latin American politics owing to Castro's recent triumph in Cuba.[76] The victory over Batista would trigger Latin American responses and helped, doubtless, to sharpen them. Argentina's Colonel Tomás Sánchez Bustamante would call communism, Cuban or no, "intrinsically perverse" in 1962. Ticking off communism's advances since 1945, he discounted any thaw in the Cold War—ever. "The fact that any sincere cooperation on their part with the . . . western world is impossible *must be beyond doubt*."[77] For Latin Americans the Cold War had heated up the years of changing times, and the Cuban debacle merely reinforced extant professional military anticommunism. Other developments, especially those discussed in the first two chapters, would refine it to a point where it became a fundamental part of professional militarism. The world-changing events of 1989 were never contemplated.

The fact that communism had gained control of British geopolitician Halford Mackinder's Eurasian "heartland" was touted as confirmation of Clausewitz's famous dictum in reverse; "Peace was a prolongation of war by other means," averred a Guatemalan officer in 1962.[78] He was referring to the Cold War as a false peace. Peaceful coexistence, stated an Argentine the next year, was merely a cloaking device for Soviet designs on the democracies. Both China and Russia, Major José A. Vaquero soon assured his readers, had the same goals; their differences were in the long run minimal.[79] Communism's international behavior made it appear monolithic, all the more so because military writers could find no effective argument against it or method to combat it, other than seizing power in order to hold it themselves.

Venezuela's General García Villasmil once depicted communism as an "armed international coalition" struggling to defeat nationalism and national integration.[80] New countries, he believed, must have armies if they expected to survive this peril. Following the Tlatelolco tumult of 1968, one Mexican would lash out at "professional agitators, intellectuals, foreigners, and students who tried to subvert order, guided as they were by "exotic doctrines."[81] Their anarchic behavior was counterrevolutionary, for it had sought to destroy Mexico's own revolution, "which, after all, preceded by seven years the Russian Revolution." In the same vein, an Argentine officer attempted to point out the great differences between Marxist theory and Leninist practice, claiming the two were wholly contradictory.[82] And a German essay of this same time would confirm the allegations made by Latin Americans of the hopelessness of peaceful coexistence with communism. Popular fronts, coalitions, and allusions to working "within the system" constituted nothing more than the tactics of the *Trojanisches Pferd*.[83] Did communists really think they were fooling military professionals?

By the 1970s Latin Americans would be viewing the communist menace as global with hemispheric as well as local implications. The internal enemy's strength was now being more closely linked to the external foe's. A good number of articles ostensibly limited to geopolitics would deal extensively with international communism, pointing out Moscow's (and Peking's) current designs on Africa. The weakness of democracy there was making the continent ripe for the picking. Its position on the eastern flank of the South Atlantic had already alarmed Brazilians, who believed they had successfully averted a communist takeover in their own country by inaugurating the time of the generals there in 1964.[84] One Brazilian would proudly argue a few years before he and his colleagues turned the reins of government over to civilians that communism had become stagnant owing to its failures and was resorting to force to maintain itself, while democracy had become more dialectical. In the democratic world "there is daily manifested the mechanism of conciliation between capital and labor, between owners and workers."[85] This constituted a whitewash of "democracy," as supervised by the Brazilian military between 1964 and 1985. As such it should not be considered particularly enlightened for its findings on communism's problems, especially given what would soon transpire in Eastern Europe and the Soviet Union.

Latin Americans had read for years that the international struggle between communism and democracy was indeed being lost by the United States owing to that country's obsession with conventional warfare and weaponry.[86] Democracy still needed protection to survive, but "the best way of combating communist ideas," wrote a Colombian in the 1980s, "is up to the developed countries to make it possible, with their technology and their ideals, for the countries of Latin America to shake off their sociocultural and economic lethargy, thus ceasing to be easy prey to Marxist ideas and activities."[87] Armies could do only so much, especially when democracy continued to allow the *Trojanisches Pferd* within the walls of free countries, where conventional strategies and tactics were useless.

"Democracy demands," a Brazilian major would say in 1984, "that the political process be carried out by leadership legitimated through the vote. Frequently there exists in politics and among many politicians an inconsistency of wanting, but not appreciating, a democratic regime."[88] Consistency, stability, solidarity, and consensus, not easily achieved in a pluralistic ambience, were necessary, he argued, for the assurance of national security. Democracy by inference was not conducive to their flowering. Was not military tutelage necessarily conducive to the inculcation of the necessary democratic values? Such a question had been raised many times, and many western military professionals would respond in the affirmative. Most would continue to see liberal democracy as vulnerable, undermined from within, attacked from without, and in danger of being imminently destroyed—despite its preferability to communism. That democracy's excesses could be blamed for communism's successes would be at the core of much professional military thought worldwide, and indeed had been long before World War II.

"One tends to forget that an army is really a negation of democracy since its success in battle depends upon its discipline, which in turn requires implicit and immediate obedience to orders."[89] Major J. D. Lunt's admonition of 1945 was indicative, even back then, of the dichotomous relationship between democracy and organizations sworn to defend it against its enemies. Forty years later debate raged on over democracy as a legitimate political form and as an unwitting progenitor of Red victory, even as Red victory began to look impossible. Inherent weaknesses in the democratic system, thought some officers, made democracy its own worst enemy—and the army's. Democracy's dependence on legitimation through voting allowed its enemies to participate in deliberation of all issues. Party politics, essential to pluralism, allowed "revolutionary and anti-Christian Marxism" to influence the evolution of democracy, one Bolivian officer had written in 1949.[90] One balks at the labeling of Bolivia as a particularly democratic country in that era, and the linking of communism to the fragility of democracy may have been intended for another purpose, but the imagery would become standard in Latin America and elsewhere.

Democracy allowed for too many differences of opinion and permitted situations to exist in which opponents of military power might become opponents of all forms of "national expression": "A fatherland without soldiers is unimaginable"[91] (something like a "house without doors," perhaps). Those who showed anything but whole-hearted support for the military might just be considered "internationalists," because "the world of today has polarized itself in two camps: one that pays homage to materialism, another that pays tribute to spiritual values."[92] Bipolarity was creating a situation in which human dignity was under constant attack. "The drawback to democracy—one party to the now global struggle—was "that it forces the democrat to think. The beauty about communism," this Australian author went on, "is that individual cogs which compose the machine do not have to be autonomous in any way."[93] And ignorance of purpose among the democratic peoples deprived citizens of the ability to stand united against the foe. Lack of individualism in the Eastern Bloc provided for unity of purpose: a strength of communism juxtaposed with a weakness of democracy. Between the two, it struck many Latin Americans, stood only the army, capable of acting with unity to defend the individual and liberty.

"Our soldiers," wrote Captain J. J. Donohoe for his Australian mates in 1963, "must also have a thorough grounding in the basic principles of freedom and democracy, because only with this as his armor and truth as his weapon will the advances of communism be halted."[94] Knowledge, the right kind of knowledge, could make and keep men free. Y. A. Mande, the Indian, posited a decade later that "today we accept democracy and trade unions, majority votes, and collective bargaining. Obviously, the social and political conditions affect the man in the armed forces. The impact is discernible in day to day life and we call it indiscipline."[95] Mande insisted that democracy could not prevail within an army if that army was to remain a disciplined, orderly machine, one capable of protecting a democratic government.

Democracy's inherent weaknesses and the effects these had on military discipline were seen by some as allowing communism to infiltrate the West by utilizing democratic institutions. Abuse of press freedom, manipulation of unions, and demoralization of the forces of order were all helping to undermine the military, asserted one Brazilian general in the 1970s. The USSR waged war at little risk to its own security throughout Latin America. And the last bastion in this struggle was the army. Marxism-Leninism, that *tóxico mental do século XX,* must not be allowed to advance further. But if the military maintained its position as unifier of civilian and soldier, its discipline would produce a higher comprehension of civic duties, and *participation of all in a common effort,* then democracy could be saved.[96] In fine, if the military were allowed to remain essentially undemocratic, democracy would survive. Irony fairly leaps from these pages. Clear-cut attacks on Marxism-Leninism would be de rigueur in the time of the generals. Chileans read yet again, in the last 1982 issue of *Política y Geostrategia,* of an army that was the spinal column of the fatherland (hardly a new metaphor) and of a situation in which three forces contested control of their country: Marxism, liberalism, and soldiers.[97] This kind of argument repeatedly presented little choice for true patriots in Chile, or elsewhere for that matter. Repetition of absolutes was intended to legitimize them.

According to what French Battalion Chief Yemeniz had written back in 1950, for example, liberal democracy did not have to grant everyone rights to speak on an issue. Many, he reasoned, knew nothing about that of which they spoke. Soldiers did not debate commands, did they? They knew their duty because they understood leadership and discipline. Conscientious objection was equivalent to antidemocratic thinking, and so was pacifism, for both weakened a democracy's ability to defend itself.[98] Political leaders, he went on, did not take all this into account. The officer corps did.

Democracy was just too individualistic, Bolivians were told again and again after the altiplano uprising of 1952.[99] Social disorder had been rampant ever since the decline of feudalism (of course) and the rise of capitalism. The French Revolution had exacerbated social unrest far beyond France. Democratic political activity allowed the bourgeoisie to exploit and mobilize the lower classes and allowed socialists to manipulate both. This source argued for the application of *Rerum Novarum* (1891) and its teachings on the conditions of working classes to Bolivia's social problems, lest the current revolution fail. The evolutionary chain of man's tragedy from feudalism to the Protestant Reformation to the French Revolution to liberal democracy to Marxism was by no means limited to "revolutionary" Bolivia. Emphasis on individual components, as already shown, would differ from country to country, but the purpose would always be the same: democracy was the fatal retribution of historical error.

Some would see the chain of tragedy extend to the present because of democracy's exaggeration of liberties of the individual. Urbanization, immigration, juvenile delinquency (stock themes all), and the euphoria of freedom following the ouster of Pérez Jiménez, one Venezuelan believed, had led many to equate democracy with freedom from all restraint.[100] Rejection of the past in the name of democracy was cutting man off from tradition, destroying continuity, and alienating humans from each other. Tradition, "the soul of an army," must not be subverted in the name of democracy. Democracy, in turn, must not be permitted to destroy man's sense of mutual obligation, thereby becoming fertile ground for subversives and demagogues.[101] The Brazilian who wrote this in 1973 believed his army was doing precisely what it should to protect and preserve the right kind of democracy for Brazilians. He combined, as others frequently did during this era, most themes discussed in these chapters—sure evidence that the time of professional militarism in theory and practice had come. The increased combination (and confusion) of themes also indicates that those that served the interest of the profession first, last, and always were the most important themes.

Citizens had an obligation to defend what they enjoyed and should be corrected if they did not; democracy, true democracy, was based on natural law and order; egalitarianism debased democracy, for it leveled society and ignored the natural differences between human beings; communism perverted egalitarianism and destroyed humanity.[102] This Argentine argument of 1979 was a shameless defense of the 1976 *golpe de estado* and its violent aftermath.

In another country, one untouched y manifest professional militarism, an officer could say that "domestic and international travails of the past decade . . . testify to the bankruptcy of liberalism's attempts to engineer a 'great society' or a congenial world order. Furthermore, presumably benevolent liberalism in its old age has revealed a hitherto unsuspected character: it is rigid, arrogant, and universalistic."[103] That 1979 North American swipe at "liberalism" was more than reminiscent of contemporary Latin American criticisms of both democracy and communism. It was as bold a statement on civilian ways as that made in another country whose officers were convinced it was locked in the battle between East and West. There the chief of state denounced his civilian foes as "pseudo-democrats who falsely preach of respect for human rights and who are vulgar instruments of communism."[104] There just was no fooling the likes of Alfredo Stroessner. Contextual differences notwithstanding, military professionals did think alike.

Had it not been for the Cold War and the perceived communist threat on the home front, it is conceivable that democracy's failings in many parts of the world might have been overlooked rather than highlighted in military literature. In the few Latin American countries where civilian political systems either posed no threat to men in uniform (in Colombia, say), or provided them with all they needed, as in Venezuela, or buffered them from pressing problems of a socioeconomic nature (Mexico, say), this might have conceivably been so. But how many countries like these were there in the world?

"Communism in action," according to Australia's early postwar military leadership, "is a living example of the lesson of history that arbitrary power in the hands of a small group is always absurd."[105] Pluralistic democracy would continue to be seen as communism's last major foe in the West; and, of course, disciplined armies were democracy's last resort in the struggle to stave off the red menace. Communists must never be allowed to destroy the vital, organic relationship between democracy, the people, and their army, a postrevolutionary Bolivian would argue.[106] Bolivia's was a national, not an international revolution, and no alien should ever be permitted to infiltrate the affairs of the fatherland. The comparability of antipodal and *altiplano* arguments on the relationship of the military to democracy is coincidental, to be sure, yet all the more representative of transnational, professional concurrence.

A Cuban editorial essay of 1956 would score those "antidemocratic" individuals who had attempted to destroy democracy in the "unjustified insult" of 26 July 1953.[107] Between the Moncada assault and Castro's 1959 entry into Havana there would be more pieces in military literature tying the 26th of July Movement to international communism. From the 1950s forward military authors viewed most Latin American insurgency movements as first and foremost communist-inspired.[108] It soon became *la hora de llamar al pan, pan y al vino, vino,* i.e., a time "to call a spade a spade."[109] It would be time for the generals to strike back at the perfidious, hypocritical, atheistic monster they all saw taking advantage of liberal democracy's manifest incapacity to come to its own defense. That which could not defend itself might, after all, not be fit to survive. To the very brink of the collapse of Marxism-Leninism in 1989, 1990, and 1991, military professionals in the West were thinking alike about communism. What direction their thought will take in times to come will make stimulating reading.

It was accepted everywhere following World War II that the nature of war had changed. Ideology had replaced dynastic and diplomatic alliances as the determining factor in the composition of opposing camps. Military leaders everywhere concerned with changing times understood this. So did those more concerned with specific kinds of change. Some argued that standing *apart* from society was the only way armies could save civilians from subversion. "By a gradual process of infiltration and propaganda a number of 'isms' like socialism, communism, and atheism have already been injected into the minds of our youth," Major Syed Shahid Abbas Naqvi would opine, in 1973.[110] This Pakistani argued that Islam provided all the ideology his countrymen needed. Inspired with the "Spirit of Jehad" by "noncontroversial scholars" Pakistan's army and citizens could withstand any alien ideological subversion. His argument, stripped of specifics, was comparable to those of anticommunist officers the world over. The struggle could be won if only soldiers and civilians were not encumbered by the wrong sort of secular and democratic baggage.

One Peruvian, writing in 1956, pressed for action against subversives based on French theories—largely ineffective, as results would show. There should be no meddling by politicians once the army took the field, in order that unity of purpose guarantee victory.[111] A few contemporary Argentine sources of the same epoch concurred with this argument,[112] but a German source warned that nearly all forceful responses to communist subversion ran the risk of being labeled fascist by democracy's red foes.[113] *Kommunistenhysterie* served no one who sought to save democracy; responses to subversion needed to be temperate, measured, and supported by a consensus. This was not always easy. In 1959 a Portuguese officer presented his country and its African army as defenders of the West and Christianity against communism, presciently cautioning fellow Europeans to expect subversion throughout the developing world and at home in times to come.[114] Argentines would discuss this problem in writings of the late 1950s and early 1960s,[115] and as the decade of the sixties moved on, military anticommunists everywhere would analyze with more precision the threat of subversion.

One Salvadoran officer would note that a national consensus against subversion had to be formed through both civic action and counterinsurgency. Without a sense of security, the civilian population could not be expected to withstand the blandishments of subversives.[116] A Brazilian general, writing in 1966, likened the 1964 overthrow of João Goulart to the rooting out of all those subversive elements that had tried to destroy Brazil's traditional values, to the casting out of atheism, communism, tyranny, and the salvation of the fatherland and army. He justified the military's retention of power following Goulart's ouster as a guarantee against Castroite subversion of Brazil's rekindled national spirit.[117] If civic action and counterinsurgency could not do the trick, a *golpe de estado* would. If that were not enough, long-term military supervision of national affairs would be.

Another anticommunist observer of the 1960s, the Venezuelan Colonel Antonio López Salas, sharpened the focus on subversion of national spirit even more. Treason and subversion, he thought, were illnesses of the mind: "the grandchild of a traitor is a traitor." Treason, like other forms of mental illness, could be genetically transmitted. One could always pick out traitors and subversives from a crowd of citizens. They were silent, furtively moving people; they were secretive, sullen, introverted, pessimistic, and dour; restless, owing to the sickness of their souls; cowardly, resentful, ambitious, and envious.[118] They were not very pleasant people at all.

If all citizens knew their place, and if all citizens behaved in a principled way, there would be no traitors or subversives. But somehow, thought yet another Venezuelan, the people had lost their cultural bearings. There was need of a "national mystique," a feeling of group action, community spirit, tradition, willingness to sacrifice, compassion, respect, honesty, generosity, warrior spirit, resolution. There was a reason, therefore, to instill military values in the rest of society. "The shepherd who keeps his flock together is far wiser than the one whose vision is blurred by the illusions of alternative paths," he wrote.[119] Venezuela's recently won democracy had still not passed muster with everyone in uniform. "National mystique" was essentially the same thing military writers were writing about elsewhere, different contexts notwithstanding.

In the 1970s these same arguments showed up over and again in military journals and reviews. Knowledge of the enemy, familiarity with the countryside, cooperation with the people, judicious use of force, firmness and resolve by the government—these well served a counterinsurgency, antisubversive campaign and those who led it.[120] But by this time the enemy had adjusted and learned new ways to undermine western culture. They now used rock and roll music[121] and had stooped to the enlistment of animals (animals rights movement) and nature (environmentalism) in their determination to rule mankind. Was there no end to perversity? Was there no end to sociocultural change?

However successful the communists were, their own ideology remained a compilation of "false doctrines, which were utilized with great ability to exploit the mistakes of those societies they strive to enslave."[122] Despite its hollowness, subversion was now turning the West against itself, turning man against that sublime and noble object of his devotion, his fatherland.[123] Early in the 1980s, one Brazilian would write that soldiers and their officers needed to strengthen their anticommunism with something more positive: prodemocratic conviction.[124] This was all very well and good, for now Brazilian officers were making ready to abandon the ship of state and return to barracks and bases. Subversion had come to naught there and in most of the rest of the hemisphere, they told themselves, because of what had been accomplished between 1964 and 1985. Democracy would now be on safe ground, thanks to reordering of the economy, and creation of a new political system by professional militarists and their civilian allies.

Steeped in tradition as they were, army officers feared communism not only because it was subversive, geopolitically driven, atheistic, totalitarian, internationalist, and so many other unpleasant things, but because it represented so much that the army did not. Family, religion, home life, traditional gender and social relationships, hierarchy—these were all fair game for subversives. Communists subverted morals more militantly than liberals. They did not even respect the national flag, unless it was that of the Soviet Union.[125] They had allies, too: all socialists, liberals, pacifists, Seventh Day Adventists, Jehovah's Witnesses, Masons, the press.[126] Anyone who was not promilitary, in fact, might be considered suspect—somewhere, sometime.

Some officers would show far more concern for communism's subversion of faith than democracy. They would write of the struggle against communism in terms of red and white, seeing communism as above all atheistic.[127] As such, it was anathema in the literal sense. Religious convictions frequently blended with nationalist zeal in the minds of officers, and the alleged national character of religion would be sharply contrasted with the international, revolutionary character of exotic, atheistic communism.[128] "Our national unity was sealed with the blood of the sons of this land," wrote an Argentine lieutenant colonel in 1962, "and foreign ideologies must not, nor will we permit them to, threaten that unity. . . . In order to further their communist agenda any means are licit to the party leadership. Crime ceases to be crime. Treason is not dishonorable. To mutilate an old person or sacrifice a child or violate a maiden is considered a glorious achievement. Ask Spain if this is an exaggerated assertion."[129] Would that the Argentine readers of these lines had been able to reflect upon them twenty years later.

In countries where national integration had not begun, army officers perpetually fretted that it would take place at their expense, if not by those who represented liberal, Europeanized culture, then by those who served Moscow. "If the army does not participate actively, the communists will," the Guatemalan Luis Sieckavizza would write in 1967.[130] Communists, it was plain to officers nearly everywhere, would destroy them, given half a chance.[131] If they succeeded in the Americas, warned General Alejandro Lanusse, they would be destroying "the vanguard of national unity . . . in which many of those who have done the most for our countries . . . have served."[132] In Europe, cautioned General Ulrich de Maizière, communism's "aim was always the same: to isolate, to drive a wedge between superiors and subordinates, leadership and institution, soldier and constitution, army and citizenry, Germany and her allies." Moreover, communism sought to break a bond between army and state, one best cemented by religion. Ever since the Reformation, he believed, devotion to Christ and military duty had been reconcilable.[133] Defense of a faith and all it stood for was no monopoly of Catholics or Muslims. Western armies, whatever their relationship to the state, nation, and society, were thought of as defenders of religion and targets of its enemies.[134] It is readily understandable just how views expressed on politics and ideology could become confused with those on religion per se. Such confusion, discussed in the following chapter, would contribute much to the final forging of a Latin American military ideology: professional militarism.

No matter the subject and regardless of theme, fear of change and reaction to current situations characterize most official military literature examined in these chapters. If all officers did not share these fears and reactions, those who wrote about them did. Western officers' views on politics and ideology compounded the dilemma of being both *a part of* and *apart from* the society that surrounded the military profession.

Democracy and communism in their post–World War II guises at times almost seem afterthoughts, even incidental to the entire new world paradigm rather than essential characteristics of it. This may explain why professional militarism was so easily dependent on tradition, and why the aftermath of its 1964–1989 heyday may be construed as another era of change. In Latin America commitments to democratic values were variable and inconsistent in contrast with adherence to military tradition, whereas democratic commitments ranged from the expedient to the enthusiastic elsewhere. In Latin America, democracy was often seen as a necessary evil, something to put up with in search of the right kind of military-civilian cooperation. Latin Americans saw communism as a wholly unacceptable evil, one that directly threatened the establishment of military-civilian cooperation for the good of the entire nation, and even western civilization. Soviets, of course, saw things as diametrically, if not dialectically, opposite.

The intensity with which communism was perceived by Latin Americans as an immediate threat to democracy and the military profession alike, let alone to economic development and orderly social change, partly explains why the metamorphosis of professionalism into militarism took place in that region only. So does the vehemence expressed toward communism's subversive threat to religious faith and nationalist traditions. That these could be placed on a higher plane than democracy itself was only natural to military men in countries where democracy's record was so blemished. That Marxism-Leninism could be placed above military professionalism was equally natural to officers of the Red Army.

It is the quality of writings on politics and ideology that makes the difference, not the quantity. By now it should be easy to understand that the steady increase in the blurring of main themes in military literature during most of the postwar era lends an aura of confusion to much officer corps thought and self-perception. This becomes all the easier to discern in the following chapter.

Faith, Wisdom, and Nationalism: Confusing Each with Professionalism

But when one spends too much time travelling, one becomes eventually a stranger in one's own country; and when one is too interested in what went on in past centuries, one usually remains extremely ignorant of what is happening in this century.—René Descartes, *Discourse on the Method of Properly Conducting One's Reason and of Seeking the Truth in the Sciences* (1637)

Let them have their German, abstract ideology passed through a sieve of Slavic Cesareopapism for a people whose Counter-Reformation authoritarianism is enough and more than enough.—Carlos Fuentes, *Cristóbal Nonato* (1987)

The confusion of military views on politics and ideology with religious fervor, convictions of intellectual superiority, and nationalist zeal made it easier for military men of the later twentieth century to draw lines between the profession and civilians. Throughout Latin America the specific proportions of each element would vary, but it takes little effort to see where the final mix was most volatile. The time of the generals occurred when and where the mix resulted in manifest professional militarism and generals sought to solve national problems, not when historical and political factors tempered the military mentality and allowed civilians to prevail politically.

This chapter deals with thought on religious faith, wisdom as the result of education, and nationalism born of tradition in that order. Its purpose is to show that there was yet more to thought and self-perception that could be interwoven with convictions about the dangers of change and role definition. It adds some essentials to the metamorphosis of military professionalism into professional militarism, manifest and latent, to be further explained in chapter 7.

Military writers will call on the good Christian (Protestant and Catholic) and Muslim to practice his faith in confronting the new paradigm, maintaining traditions, leading and following, and coming to his nation's defense. What this often meant, of course, was that officers confused national defense with defense of their religious beliefs. Officers lauded their own military education for the wisdom it imparted, while often criticizing civilian school experiences as resulting in mere knowledge. Faith, wisdom, and nationalism were portrayed in ways comparable to those in which officers wrote about the steadfastness of officers and men. Politics and ideology were depicted in tones more comparable to those in which changing times and socioculture were written about. Military writers may very well have been veritable strangers in their own countries, so steeped were they in their past, so unyielding were they to their present. But nowhere would estrangement produce what it did in South America.

Military education was routinely seen as superior to its civilian equivalent. There were exceptions, but by and large the most officers would be willing to concede was that uniformed and civilian educators might learn from each other, for armies were the natural guardians of those traditions, the wisdom and the spirit that had shaped nationalism. Nationalism would become, in military parlance, synonymous with national security, and when it did officers would justify anything in its name.

This chapter further confirms the existence and strength of a late-twentieth-century military mentality shared to a degree by officers everywhere. Its definition and applicability to national problems was unique; its general contours, though, were typical.

Faith knew no boundaries; its influence on officer corps thought and self-perception was limited, however. An Anglo-Saxon Protestant, for example, might possibly view communism in terms as absolute as those of a Latin Catholic. Writing back in 1952, an Australian lieutenant colonel labeled communists "pagan patriots." His countrymen and others of the West he called "Christian patriots." Christianity, he argued, was in danger of fading from everyday life, and it was up to politicians to make sure the trend was reversed. "Our national leaders must avert this drift by infusing Christianity into government,"[1] for, he thought, Christian values were plainly compatible with constructive patriotism. A U.S. chaplain writing later in the same decade called upon his army to provide the inspiration to make "free men worthy of their freedom."[2] As in Australia, excessive individualism and materialism were seen as corruptive of religious values and humankind in general. A military commitment to traditional, national values would be of great comfort, this source claimed, "to those who hold with authority, to those who yearn for gratification in the proper performance of duty, to those who do believe in One nation under God."

On a few occasions Germans would allude to the Protestant Reformation (often cited by Latin officers as evidence of the decline of western civilization) as evidence of the need for armies to defend a just cause. The enemy might no longer be the Holy Roman Emperor; he might be the leader of the USSR. The career of arms, instead of being associated with sectarianism, as it had been centuries before, had become an obligation of the modern era.[3] Chaplains often voiced their concerns in discussions of their own specific tasks. One Canadian padre recalled Lyautey's model officer when he discussed the essential close relationships between chaplain and flock in 1969.[4] A pseudonymous British author noted that "even Christ seemed to have a soft spot for soldiers," citing Jesus' meeting with the faithful centurion (Matthew 8:5–13). "In terms of charity to one's neighbor," he added, "the charity of comradeship on the battlefield is an experience the Christian may not refuse."[5] This was an argument against the behavior of conscientious objectors, who betrayed their neighbors by not performing the Christian duty of defending a just cause.

This argument also formed the core of retired General Ralph E. Hines's lecture-cum-essay of 1984, "Christian Leadership in the Armed Forces." Hines, an Episcopalian, considered himself both a "Calvary man and a cavalry man" and argued that the officer should be a Christian role model to his men. Soldiers must have faith, he said, and "where that faith is lacking they should seek actively to develop it through fellowship with believers, study of Holy Scripture, and opening of communications channels to God." Officers should follow Christ's examples in all ways possible, he insisted. "They must be plugged into the power source of God's love and grace, manifested in his son, Jesus Christ, and made available to them through the Holy Spirit. It is from God that all authority on this earth, both temporal and spiritual, derives, as we are told specifically in St. Paul's letters to the Christians in Rome (Romans 13:1)."[6] This was, it bears repeating, no fervent Latin Catholic exhorting fellow officers to stamp out Marxists or Protestant missionaries.

The 1975 Catholic Holy Year prompted a military pilgrimage to Rome by the uniformed faithful. Fully 24,000 Catholic military personnel, along with 250,000 civilians, showed up in St. Peter's Square on 23 November to hear Pope Paul VI. The Holy Father did not disappoint those in uniform, for they were, he said, "more able than most others to understand the significance of the Holy Year. . . . None more than you can speak for peace. . . . You defend it, justice, and order. . . . You more than all others know how great a thing, at the national and international level, is peace."[7] His Holiness confirmed the close bond between the true Christian and the man of arms—to the point of governing their own countries by force if necessary.

Most Catholic military writers at one point or another reconfirmed long-held arguments on the compatibility of religion, vocation, and arms. Some would do it with remarkable originality, despite the familiarity of the theme. "Remember, Soldier, to God you are not unknown!" began one inspirational message to Paraguayans in 1983.[8] Officers were instructed to remind their men that their helmets were analogous to a crown of thorns, their shouldered arms to a cross, a forced march to Christ's preaching the length and breadth of the Holy Land, and that almost everything they did every day of their lives, and every night too, was analogous to something Jesus had done.[9] There were frequent references to scripture, construed as justifying, honoring, or sanctifying the military way.[10] One could find a passage from scripture to justify nearly all ends.

In discussing the role of the officer it had long been a custom to liken officers to priests in terms of vocation or calling, but there were stronger arguments than those already mentioned in these pages. One Peruvian noted that officers were bound by both their loyalty to the fatherland and their faith to fulfill their military duties, making no attempt to separate the sources of inspiration.[11] "The unity of purpose that binds the priest and the soldier is well understood by all enemies of the Christian West," claimed one Argentine. When these attacked the army publicly, he maintained, they also attacked Christianity itself.[12] This was a transparent tactic designed to solicit support for the military during the troubled sixties.

At about this same time, when South Americans were fusing religion with rule, the Portuguese army still struggled in Africa against "enemies of the West." Although exaggerated in its absoluteness, one outsider's observation of 1969 bears mention. Colin Beer, a former police officer in British Africa and the Congo, claimed that he had not met in Angola "a soldier—of any rank—who expressed the slightest doubt about the justice of their cause. Of course they are largely Roman Catholic, and this gives them an additional zeal when fighting insurgents who have the logistic support of the Communist world."[13] Catholics were ready to perceive an army as a "religion of armed men."[14] So doing, could they not argue any point in defense of a faith?

Conscientious objection, volunteer-service armies, permissive civilian ways, pacifism, and antimilitarism were often tied to faith, and this could endanger lives, it was repeated, for they denied to nation, state, and society the military as their protector. "To believe that Christians have no place in the army," insisted one Argentine, "is to leave the manifest responsibility for defense and resort to force to those men who have little reason to behave like human beings." This was something akin to leaving politics to "indecent men." The value placed on life by the true Christian obliged him to don the uniform when called upon to do so, for "the values we wish to defend justify the price in human suffering and life."[15] This kind of argument was cold comfort to those who paid the price in Latin America for voicing even slight objections to the way some officers defended their Christian values.

But it was a popular argument. "The similarity of rigid conservative principles, of structures based on hierarchy and discipline, of ceremonies, of the catechistic and integrative missions, of the cult of values and ethics," wrote several French officers, "confirms the old aphorism 'military life is that of a priesthood.' "[16] And it was religion, argued a German, as if to confirm all to the more than occasional German-reading Latin American, that guaranteed that soldiers would have the criteria, sensitivity, and sophistication to understand the synthesis of national security and military power.[17]

That synthesis also provided the true Christian and the good citizen a way to justify his participation in the defense of his fatherland. It made him more appreciative of the preservation of national spirit. In other words, the preservation of the proper morals, ethics, and virtues could be assured through a religiously based harmonious association of nation, state, and society, the catalytic agent being the armed forces. Religion and military service or career could, and did, assume levels of militancy just as the combination of military service and Marxism-Leninism did.

Like their Portuguese counterparts, French officers often saw African struggles of the postwar years as stages of a war to defend Christian frontiers established centuries before.[18] Geopolitical concerns had abetted this, and so had opportunism. Germans naturally related *Innere Führung* to the clash between atheistic and Christian values.[19] Many others (including non-Christians) considered Marxism a menace to their faith.[20] Officers with backgrounds as different as Taiwanese and Paraguayans surely might, asserted one Paraguayan editorial, for were these not two "countries where spiritual values superimposed themselves over purely materialist ones, and which are capable of defeating atheistic Communism relying solely on the love of God and the fatherland?"[21] The absurdity of a spiritual kinship between Paraguay and Nationalist China notwithstanding, the potential for confusion of faith with military roles was common to Christian officers worldwide.

It was common to Muslims too. The blending of faith and nationalism by Pakistanis is comparable to that of Latin Americans. "Soldiers need courage," Lieutenant Colonel Shaukat Riza had written in 1961. And he believed that two things, more than any other, inspired that courage: "Religion is one. Discipline is another. Discipline is easy to obtain in our men. Our religion and family environment make the average Pakistani naturally amenable to service discipline."[22] "God . . . rewards those who died in his name," Captain Sondha Khan Malik would note two years later,[23] for the Koran indeed promised eternal life to those who served Allah. Islam thus provided Pakistanis with a way to foster and sustain "a sublime state of moral strength" in the armed forces and in the rest of the population too.[24] Still another officer writing in the 1960s called on "mothers, mosques, and mullahs" to keep the faith and bring up Pakistani youth along Islamic lines in order that "this wonderful heritage will remain evergreen in our blood, and our soldiers, though uneducated in the modern sense of the word, will keep on getting . . . invaluable indoctrination."[25] Islam provided officers and men with everything they needed to succeed in this life and the one to follow.

"In a nutshell," wrote still another officer of that decade, "Islam preaches peace under normal circumstances. But being a realistic way of life it realizes that constant maintenance of peace may not be possible under all circumstances. Because those who do not believe in peace may endanger it, compelling true believers to restore peace by force." The enemy, as in Latin America and Europe, was ever-menacing, the same author continued, urging his readers to "make preparations . . . to strike terror into God's enemy and your enemy. . . . God knows them. Whatever you spend in the cause of God will be repaid to you in full measure, and you shall not be wronged." He also told his readers that "Muslims must use force to compel the oppressors to let humanity live in peace."[26] The good Muslim, like the good Christian (and like the good Marxist) would never, ever, be the aggressor. That was the enemy's way.

"A state based on an ideology must of necessity make sure . . . its armed forces reflect the basic principles of the ideology which has brought into existence the state," Brigadier Gulzar Ahmad summed up cumbersomely, citing the French and Russian Revolutions as fusions of ideology, state, and army.[27] To him the only true army was the army in which there was a union of heart and mind. Colonel Tanwiral Haq thought about the heart in a more literal way. "God has given us a beautiful figure," he wrote, "and it is up to us to develop and maintain it. Grace of form is therefore much more desirable in service personnel."[28] The true believer must cut a good figure if he expected to be a proper soldier, one could infer.

In the 1970s Pakistani military literature directly concerned with Islam also dealt with the need for reinvigoration of Islamic teachings among civilians. Secularization of society had been leading toward excessive individualism and corruption. Major General Shirin Dil Khan Niazi, writing on the need for a civil service code of ethics, opined that "adherence to Islamic precepts is the only way out of this quagmire of moral degeneration."[29] He believed what all Pakistanis needed was more emphasis on honesty, courtesy, truthfulness, responsibility, modesty, trust, fairness, generosity, cooperation, and unity: in short qualities lauded in the Koran and endemic to army officer corps—as clear a fusion of faith and role as any found in Latin America.

Another Pakistani essay of 1970 agreed, lamenting that "Islam as an ideology has not permeated our social, economic, and political spheres of life."[30] The author asserted further that any consideration of Pakistan as an ideological state was folly until it did. Islam once had served the faithful well, but no longer was this the case. In his 1971 essay "The Soldier, the Battlefield, and Leadership," Lieutenant Colonel Ijaz Ahmad would claim that "the success obtained by the modern armies beginning with the holy wars under the guidance of Prophet Muhammad, and later during their conquests, starting in early 600, were founded mainly upon higher standards of morality, firm discipline, and above all on religious belief."[31] The past lived on in yet another way for army officers. And late in that same decade a Pakistani general reiterated arguments for an Islamic renaissance, claiming that "alien powers" had kept Moslems historically divided against themselves. The glory of Islam and military strength, he believed, were inseparable. "Islam remains the only salvation power clearly visible in the Muslim world. The mind cannot be conquered by the weapons of war."[32] Mind made right.

"Islam has a . . . conceptual superiority over all philosophies of life and cannot as such be driven to total oblivion, even under the most forceful onslaught, like the one it has undergone over a period of about 400 years," concluded a lieutenant colonel in 1980.[33] This source would go on to criticize "westernized Muslims," but allow as how even some of these had finally seen the light and realized the hypocrisies of the West: racism, atheism, the "spiritual suicide" of the western "crusader mentality." Islamic renaissance was only a matter of time, and Pakistan, with its proud army, was the natural country to lead it to victory.

Pakistanis believed theirs was the best army in the Muslim world, based as it was on willing discipline and obedience of citizens under arms. Islam and military service would be portrayed as providing an ambience in which "obedience is not submission to 'authority' but rather a social necessity in the interest of the community, closely associated with leadership, which is also a social necessity in the interest of the community."[34] This was a neat summing-up of professional militarism, comparable in every respect to those traditionally provided by Catholic Latin Americans. In the mid 1980s the retired General E. H. Dar would even go so far as to compare Pakistan with Israel. The latter's success, he claimed, was based on the unique blend of religion, ideology, and military strength created by the Jews. Israel, like Pakistan, was more than a geopolitical entity, it was an ideological state, and Pakistanis, like Israelis, should use ideology and religion as catalysts for national greatness, lest "a vague and ill defined search for identity . . . lead nowhere."[35] Dar blamed Pakistan's slowness in becoming a true ideological state on the British and their favorites, the Hindus. His work evinced a tactic similar to that employed by Latin Americans in their military literature: blaming outsiders for the fatherland's ills, all the while ignoring home-grown reasons.

Exploitation of the external menace would lead to more than one manifestation of fanaticism in military literature. Examples abound in these pages of rock and roll music, television, perfidious "alien influences," hair styles, women's liberation, and the like being seen as dire threats to civilization, eastern or western. In Spain, where Catholicism exceeded that of Latin America in its military expression, there was more than a touch of fanaticism during the Franco years and shortly after. The journals *Reconquista* and *Ejército* carried more than ample amounts of material devoted to Spain's historic role of saving the West (from both Islam and Communism), of expanding Christianity's frontiers in the New World and Asia, of halting the spread of the Protestant Reformation, and of stopping Napoleon, all forms of the Antichrist.

"The light from the beacon of the Roman Church is that which should . . . serve as sure guide in the development of the geopolitics, geostrategy, and geopsychology of Christian civilization. But said beacon does not always show up in navigational charts of the Occident."[36] "Nuestra cruzada," the essay from which that quote is taken, was an oft-used title and slogan in Spanish military sources of the postwar years. Under Franco the external menace was regularly and increasingly identified as communism, the means to defeat it a kind of military-religious fusion.[37] A brief *Reconquista* piece of 1965 bluntly argued à la *Pakistan Army Journal* that nationalism devoid of religious (Catholic here, of course) conviction could not exist, for "spiritual vinculation of man to his native land" was the essence of all nationalism.[38] There was no either/or. The tendency to fantasize and fanaticize was no one's monopoly.

In Latin America's time of the generals it assumed its grossest dimensions in Argentina. Most of the disorder in the modern world, military chaplain Roberto A. Wilkinson had argued back in 1953, was the result of sixteenth-century occurrences. Until then, allegedly, man had always lived in peace with his neighbor. Barbarians had eventually converted to Christianity, Attila's conversion being the Church's most noteworthy triumph over the sign of the pagan. But then the world fell apart when the Protestant Reformation, with its motto *no más iglesia,* introduced the virulent germ of individualism, emancipated individuals from spiritual authority, and encouraged the tendency toward "autonomy and independence."[39] Then the eighteenth-century "enlightenment" ("No more God"), the Age of Reason, and nineteenth-century liberalism had carried mankind still further away from God. Individual consciousness and permissiveness had led to Marxism. Now, in the twentieth century, the motto of the day was "no more man." Catholicism was the world's last hope, certainly Argentina's. Authority, all authority, flowed from God; this was in the natural order of things, and Argentines would fall from grace if they forgot it.

That gem from the Perón years was soon followed by a translation from the French that argued for a perfect harmony of religious and military vocation. "There can be no true vocation other than that which comes from He who knows our innermost thoughts, and who has the power to reach our hearts: God." Vocation was individual, with its own characteristics, and did not have to be strictly clerical. It could be that of the "career of arms, that of he who sacrifice[s] the comfort and material well-being of other ways of life in order to give himself over to the defense of his fatherland and fellow citizens."[40] That which is done in the name of national defense—national security—could arguably be done out of faith.

In the early 1960s one general would tell Argentine officers that, "inspired by the Divine Master, it is the hour to expel energetically all those unworthy government functionaries, just as Jesus drove the moneychangers from the temple."[41] Long before the classical time of the generals, then, political action had a mystical tinge. In 1972 a colonel would urge fellow Argentines to stand firm in the defense of western, Christian humanism. Argentina's, and indeed the world's, future citizens deserved to enjoy the spiritual values of the past.[42] The Reformation, another writer of that decade would claim, had created all the conditions favorable to the rise of atheism.[43] Politics, this source also noted, really meant observation of that which was of concern to the *polis,* the city, and its hinterland. An elaborate, wholly contrived etymology appeared in this piece, purporting to show that *política* was an object of study, not an activity.

General Ramón Camps spoke up for humanism—his own brand—in

1979.[44] The humanist, he thought, was ethical, not opportunistic, a man who would never employ humanism (as opposed to individualism, which many called it) to justify nefarious political acts. Humanism was something that "comes from no place other than our hearts and our consciences." In sum, Argentines could be every bit as fanatic and fantastic in their blending of faith with professionalism as were Spaniards or Pakistanis, every bit as willing to bend military thought to the interests of religious or ideological zeal as were Muslims—or, say, officers of the ideologically controlled Red Army. Argentine actions between 1976 and 1982 proved it. Everywhere faith could be construed as a bulwark against the unpleasant and unacceptable, and so could wisdom, the end result of military education.

In fact what was occurring was the forging of military ideology. "A state without ideology is like a temple without God or a liturgy without faith" (as meaningless as a nation without heroes, a house without doors?), asserted a Venezuelan editorialist of the 1980s.[45] Militarism—military spirit, not "externalization" of values and ideals—was an effective ingredient of democracy's struggle to defend itself against communism, this source concluded. This, obviously, was not an uncommon belief among officers, but "military spirit," as an ingredient of democracy's liturgy, could mean many things, including reactionary thinking.

"The soldier is a conservative brute; he hates new ideas, not because he is necessarily a congenital idiot, but because the ideas are new. This may be because all new ideas are accompanied by a stream of books and manuals which have to be read and discussed, but whatever the reason may be, he does not like change."[46] Major Lunt's cogent observation of 1944 would be confirmed over and again in the decades following the war. Surely his comment on the aversion to reading books and manuals struck home, for if an idea could not be fathomed at the outset, what useful purpose could it serve? What was the purpose of knowledge? Could ideas and knowledge serve the interests of militarists? Was knowledge the same as wisdom?

Officers from various backgrounds would plump for what can only be called militarism as the purest expression of national ideals, conservative or innovative. "Military service molds the character of our youth." It led to the physical and spiritual perfection of males. In the barracks the young Argentine "breathed in an atmosphere of healthy *argentinidad*, which comes to be the ideal inspiration of his actions."[47] Militarism was national spirit, timeless, enduring.

"I am convinced," said one North American writing in 1960, "that the strong and the wise of our country must 'carry on' if we are not to commit national suicide. I feel that forthright men of letters, science, the cloth, and the sword, from the very nature of their work and their temperament, are most likely to know the 'doer' types—and surely the most virile, the most daring, and the most selfless of this group are the latter—the soldier."[48] Militarism was elitist and dynamic.

Preservationist, nationalistic, elitist, and dynamic, both the latent and the manifest professional militarism of the later twentieth century would ultimately draw from the past and react to the present in the name of the future. It would be transcendental to its adherents, folly to its detractors, of great concern to all who would experience its political forms. "Rightist" officers could be "revolutionaries" when the times called upon them to be.[49] They could interpret right and wrong. They acted in the name of the people. They could, if the situation demanded it, be champions of tradition and revolution all at once, all in the name of nationalism.[50] Militarism could be all things to all citizens for all time. The value of knowledge depended on its utility as well as its compatibility with tradition. This made it wisdom.

Traditional learning, wrote one German in 1959, was a healthy ingredient of the progressive democracy, for it anchored the present and legitimized social, economic, and political development. An army, a traditional institution, might also be revolutionary, for it readily accepted new technology (no mention of new ideas here). It was progressive as well, for it retained tried and tested concepts of tactics and strategy. It was above all consistent, for it was living proof that certain military values never changed. *Ritterlichkeit* (chivalry) had not faded with the past.[51] *Innere Führung* might not be everything to Germans, for in the 1960s and 1970s, as noted in these pages, tradition found its way back into the *Bundeswehr.*

One of the prolific Major Lunt's fellow Indian Army officers would argue years later that military conservatism was a positive feature of the institution. "It is natural for the military mind . . . to rely on facts and what is known, on the lessons of history and experience, rather than on experimentation and theory."[52] Officers could learn a lot from civilians, this source admitted, but civilians ought to be as ready to learn from the military. There had to be a meeting of minds. The mind, after all, was "the atomic pile in which ideas are born, bred, and burned. They often start a chain reaction. . . . Ideas are the ammunition of thought-force. . . . Ideas, like bullets, must be collected in a magazine."[53] Education, lots of it, wrote an Australian, made both citizen-soldiers and soldier-citizens.[54]

Ideas could be seen as positive influences—if they were the right kind of ideas and if they were properly conveyed from instructor to pupil.

Education, and military education especially, made for better officers, ones capable of dealing with the ideas and problems of the late twentieth century: ideological conflict, social change, geopolitical problems, technological advances. Where properly conceived, though, civilian institutions might still serve an army's educational purpose. According to Colonel Jackson Shirley, following World War II, the United States Army had forseen that "military and technical training alone would not give officers the means to cope effectively with the coming problems at home and abroad."[55] Education had become "standard equipment for the officers of the future," worldwide. Knowledge gained could be put to good use if it were properly channeled.

In Latin America, renewed emphasis on continuing education—professional *and* "secular"—would lead to the creation of institutions like Brazil's *Escola Superior de Guerra* (ESG), the CAEM, where most of the professional military solutions to Peruvian problems came from, the Argentine *Instituto de Altos Estudios,* and Chile's *Academia Nacional de Estudios Polítcos y Estratégicos,* (ANEPE)—places where high-ranking officers and civilians exchanged ideas on national security and a number of other timely topics, learned from each other, and united for the common good. As noted, these were patterned to a varying extent on the old French *Centre des Hautes Études Militaires*. Italy, Spain, Portugal, Germany, Great Britain, the United States, and Canada also purportedly had such high-level institutes.[56] After all, as General Hans Speidel asked Argentines in a 1969 translation, "who, nowadays, dares draw lines between chemistry, physics, and biology?"[57] He went on to say, not surprisingly, that "one can say something comparable about the links between military and political leadership." The argument for military-civilian cooperation would never end.

Ideas, troublesome to some, invigorating to others, buffeted military men (and civilians too), but they nevertheless led some officers to greater achievements. "Without them man would remain frozen and incapable of evolution, but ideas must not clash with reality," wrote one French general in 1979.[58] "Those of us who do not cultivate their literary tastes find it difficult to express their ideas intelligently or elegantly, dedicated as we are to anticipating . . . action."[59] The action-oriented man, opined the Venezuelan author of these last words on advanced studies, needed to know more than logistics, tactics, and strategy to defend his country. He needed wisdom gained through experience.

If military authors agreed that they and their fellows should pursue and expand their educational interests, they still believed that education per se should be other than it was. Civilians did not always know what was best. Education, as it were, might be too important to be left to educators. One Bolivian officer, writing back in 1947, had gone so far as to suggest that all university curricula be shaped with military needs in mind.[60] A French officer suggested just a few years later that an education was incomplete if military experience were omitted. Officers were superb educators and had been since the days of Lyautey, and "the government should not forget it."[61] A British observer would lament the jaundiced views of his countrymen toward the intellectual capabilities of officers. The "grooving" of the brightest boys in public schools toward law and business had led to the remainder being diverted to the clergy and the military.[62] This was a civilian-made situation that went unremedied at the risk of national security. An Argentine writing in the late 1950s argued that the army and the government should work more closely for a number of reasons, one of them being so that their two educational systems would be as one. Circumscription of the army's educational mission, or the clergy's for that matter, he considered tantamount to treason.[63]

In the 1960s, the ROTC became controversial on many U.S. campuses, and there was a cautious recognition and criticism of the delicate relationship between military and university educational traditions. A professor of history, Captain James Smith observed, "Who is sympathetic toward the goals of the ROTC, may have a tremendous effect upon the student in his decision to enter upon the advanced course. The antipathetic professor may have an opposite effect."[64] What Smith was incapable of concluding, of course, was precisely what any "right-thinking" Latin American officer could have: *that the antipathetic historian was a traitor.* Nor did Smith lament the lack of influence that an ROTC professor might have on student-cadets with regard to their decisions to pursue a given major.

Defense *and* education and education *for* defense often blurred in the minds of some military writers of the postwar decades, leading some to believe that the two were inseparable. Advanced military-civilian educational experiences like those just noted were one result of this confusion. National security doctrines were another, especially in countries where democracy still did not have the adherence of a consensus.[65]

An Indian major saw education as the medium for inculcation of traditional values and national spirit, as well as more immediately practical knowledge. "Education," he wrote, "should bring home to our men our glorious heritage, our ancient culture, and our noble traditions. It should imbibe (sic) in the men the spirit of loyalty and devotion to the country." Because civilians did not do the job properly, responsibility for education lay primarily with the officer corps; the Indian government ought to be doing much more, especially "to keep the threat of external aggression alive."[66] This was an argument for manipulation of education and acquired knowledge to create an ideological state, and nothing less.

A British veteran of the Indian army would agree with the Indian major (without making explicit reference to his article) in his 1974 review of a work on the United States Army. Here, the reliable J. D. Lunt feared that modern educational systems were too permissive. "Indeed there is nothing more frightening for the future of the western democracies than the apparent reluctance of those responsible for educating youth to impose any measure of discipline on those who lack both the experience and the inclination to discipline themselves."[67] Education was both a reflection of society and a shaper of values, and in both senses it was found wanting, he believed. A North American military academic would counter this argument in 1977 by stating that "the relatively broad scope of civilian-type education systems, their stress on conceptualizing, and their relatively free range of intellectual inquiry makes them more attuned to the kinds of educational necessities required for military professionals than the educational system in the military establishment."[68] At least some military educators—but not many Latin Americans—believed they needed some additional lessons from civilian counterparts.

Should there, perhaps be broad-based educational schemes that included discipline? Some officers thought so. "On more than one occasion the lack of attention to education in a world marked by violence and the countercultural activity of Marxism-Leninism has been equivalent to the undermining of the security of the democratic way of life . . . the citizen must be educated civically, therefore, in order to reject the totalitarianism, paternalism, demagogy, permissiveness, and dogmatism of politics."[69] Democracy with discipline, "protected" democracy—the terms vary over time—should be a result of sound education, or so thought one Argentine of the early 1980s. There is little guesswork involved in coming up with just what kind of education they and their counterparts in comparable settings had in mind during the time of the generals. Knowledge should serve a greater interest. It should result in the kind of wisdom officers and their men allegedly shared.

Referring to Mortimer Adler's *The Paidea Proposal* (1982) and *A Nation at Risk* (1983), Colonel Robert Miscow Filho would argue in an *Arielista* tone that democracy was in peril unless citizens were educated in a way that led them to understand the true meaning of equality of opportunity. Democracy must not mean "mediocracy," he insisted. Opportunity and ability must not be synonymous. Education should lead to the perfection of man.[70] In short, both education and democracy must be hierarchical and oriented toward specific goals. This was true in both general and specifically practical terms.

There would be recurrent interest, throughout the decades in question, in the study of foreign languages by officers (and by all citizens, in fact), as a way of maintaining currency in world affairs, of "knowing one's enemy" and providing quality intelligence. As early as the Normandy invasion, military journals were linking language study to contemporary affairs. Indians, Australians, and Italians would soon see it as necessary for an appreciation of geopolitical realities.[71] South Americans would read of language study in even more specific terms: as a way to combat communism.

In 1963 retired General Giovanelli urged his Argentine readers to learn at least one foreign language. The Soviets used 63 languages to disseminate their vicious propaganda, he noted, and the influence over human beings around the world thereby adumbrated was considerable.[72] Brazil's Captain Manoel Lima Assis was even more to the point: "In combat we would better understand the enemy."[73] These ever-practical, nonintellectual arguments for language study exemplify military attitudes toward advanced, practical education and training in nonprofessional fields. So did a 1975 British opinion. "Reading Greek mythology may be fine, and learning a language may be interesting. They will certainly broaden the mind, but they should not be attempted without a thorough grounding in regimental soldiering."[74] So much for the expansion of intellectual horizons. So much for the underlying meaning of wisdom.

More than once it was asserted that civilians and military should learn from each other how to improve their respective educational functions. Emphasis on who could learn most from whom varied according to time and place, but everywhere political systems, national security, and ways of life could be the beneficiaries of military-civilian cooperation, and the diffusion of knowledge was no exception to the formula. Values and traditions could be preserved, and necessary and beneficial progress made in orderly fashion if only the right kind of education received the right kind of attention. That many civilians would be saying the same things (usually with different ends in mind) encouraged officers everywhere to think and write on the subject.

"The army of today has a number of different functions involving specific activities. A goal-oriented education is necessary in order that these be performed," wrote a German major in 1972.[75] Officers had to absorb so much to defend their country and its allies. If they were to do this their education had to be highly structured *and* broadly based. Officers also had to be educated to deal with attendant problems like apathy and pacifism, or what one Italian called *amilitarismo*.[76] The end result of any kind of education had to be reinforcement of extant opinions on the historical, educational, civic, and social roles of the army. It is hard to believe there could have been any other conclusion; education should result in knowledge and wisdom as weapons for the defense of national (sometimes western) traditions.

Armies, after all, were "guardians of national tradition, which [is] constantly menaced by doctrines and ideas designed to destroy the concept of the fatherland."[77] That this role should be undertaken by educators as well was a long-standing belief of officer-authors. The long-term educational role of the army helped to drive professional officers in Latin America further toward professional militarism. That the educational role was quite important elsewhere during these same years makes it obvious that as professionals, Latin Americans were "in step."

From the end of World War II, the conviction that the army guaranteed the continuity and quality of national traditions reinforced the assumption in more than one country that nationalism should be defined in terms of the values and ideals of the officer corps. Citizens of a given country, according to most military writers, shared a common culture, no matter what their class or status. This was as true in Peru as it was in Argentina or Cuba; as true for France as it was for Francophone Africa or Italy. National security demanded a concerted effort by all if the common culture, the nation, were to survive ideological subversion. So claimed Argentine, Peruvian, Cuban, and British writers.[78] Peruvians, Venezuelans, French, Italians, Mexicans, and Nicaraguans all argued that normal historical evolution had always depended on a military presence.[79] Such sources, as well as those cited in other contexts, claimed that the professional officer corps—not politicians—had primary responsiblity for the preservation of tradition and national culture; nationalism depended on militarism, or at least military professionalism.

"The actual imperative demands that officers understand national problems and participate in the development and progress of the life of the nation; and this cannot occur," wrote Lieutenant Colonel Cayo Jiménez Mendoza in 1966, "without a solid basis and deep understanding of all the variables that influence Colombia's future."[80] A colleague averred that it was the army's job to create a "national consciousness" for Colombia. With a "Venezuelanist mystique," one of that country's officers would write a few years later, "and evident efficiency the armed forces have energetically and decisively fought against the irregular groups that persist in their abominable objectives of provoking the distortion of public order in both rural and urban areas."[81] In so doing, the armed forces defined the *mística venezolanista* for all citizens.

After all, no one else was stepping forward to define tradition or national culture, what with individualism and pluralism rampant. For all their lip service and opportunistic adherence to democracy, some officer corps were still chary in their judgments of civilian government. Brazilians certainly were, believing that the prime responsibility of government was to combat "exotic and subversive ideas of communism . . . as well as their antithesis . . . markedly rightist tendencies." Somewhere in between those extremes, thought General Afonso de Albuquerque Lima, there existed nationalism.[82] One German writing in 1970 had thought *Entspannung*—détente[83]—might inspire civilians to nationalistic fervor. Few Latin American officers would have placed much credence in such an argument by that time.

Rather, they were now pushing for total preparedness; utilization of their wisdom for the maintenance of national security and democracy. "To want peace because of incapacity for war, to want peace because of a feeling of one's own weakness, out of fear of foreign superiority, is the miserable condition of those peoples who do not have within themselves a supreme commitment to persistence and their own dignity," stated a Venezuelan in 1971.[84] Needless to say, it was in the army where commitment and dignity (tradition and nationalism) flourished, ready for civilians to observe, experience, and retain.

"The political trajectory of the Brazilian army cannot be separated from its efforts to become an efficient, disciplined, and professional organization," stated a civilian friend in 1973.[85] The trajectory and efforts of the army and its sister institutions had now blended so felicitously for many Brazilian officers that they would forget where traditional professionalism left off and political action began. They had, by this time, marched Brazil into the era of professional militarism.

Such ideas were obviously never unique to South Americans. In his 1973 argument for eternal vigilance against France's foes, France's General François Maurin would state that "a society, like all living systems, in order to assure its development and further its evolution must have . . . 'antibodies.' The fact that the crisis of civilization that we are experiencing is characterized by a near total abandonment of traditional values, by an explosion of liberty in which anything is permissible and restraints are lacking, necessitates as counterpoise the strengthening of the nation's traditional structures."[86] The antibodies were, of course, the armed forces, and it was up to them to restore national health through proper doses of nationalism. A contemporary agreed that the army was an agent of "national reconciliation,"[87] but military service as well as respect for the uniform from all citizens were necessary for this to be a reality, he was convinced.

A North American officer, also writing in the 1970s, believed that a national spirit was the sine qua non of survival. "If I had to pinpoint one problem that concerns me most about this country," he would say, "it is not the army, it is the element of faith and confidence we have in ourselves. I am positive that we do have the intellectual and the material and the moral strength to do whatever has to be done. We can indeed afford to do the right thing. As a matter of fact, as we embark on a third century as a free nation, we cannot afford *not* to afford it."[88] General Fred Weyand's bicentennial exuberance was designed to depict antimilitarism, pacifism, and isolationism as menaces to national security, to nationalism defined any way. "Men without ideals are creatures of impulses," offered Squadron Leader N. K. Parik that same year. "With ideals and causes to guide them before, men go ahead to attain them with fire and determination."[89] Patriotic zeal, traditional values, and national culture, often lacking or ill-defined by civilians, were omnipresent in the military profession.

The profession, it was obvious to its members, was all things. It was at once militaristic and humanistic. In Colombia, for example the profession might be described as "based on a dual structure: one, military, in which high levels of technical excellence and firmness of thought and behavior must be attained; and humanist, the other, in order to provide the officer with a broad complement of wisdom that permits him to fathom those issues that in a given moment and facing a specific problem aid in reaching the appropriate solution."[90] A combination of technological expertise and wisdom made members of the profession ideal problem solvers, at least according to that Colombian.

Elsewhere the military profession had become an "efficient and indispensable way to assure the security of our population through the proper use of power however and whenever necessary."[91] The profession existed above all to maintain national values, insisted this Brazilian officer. In other places this was not so easy. As Major James Narel, writing in *Parameters* five years after Weyand's bicentennial exhortation, put it: "Like so many other social institutions, the military profession suffers today from a spiritual malaise that undercuts our collective confidence, saps our energy, and produces a cynicism that seems to feed on itself."[92] The juxtaposition of these two comments from the early 1980s suggests that there were military writers to be found everywhere who believed a malaise had enveloped the entire West.[93]

"In modern society," a Brazilian general would assert in 1982, "man has lost the right to live as a human being . . . the state is a machine that enslaves . . . the man of the twentieth century lives in moral solitude. He has no faith in himself, nor similarly in a civilization dominated by materialism . . . and he finds no solace for his spirit. We suffer from one of the gravest illnesses of mankind: man no longer believes in freedom."[94] That was real *malestar,* and it was not unique to Latin American military literature by the 1980s.

Military men worldwide were now seeing themselves as leaders of a profession that either suffered the same problems civilian institutions suffered or remained immune owing solely to institutional superiority. Latin Americans had convinced themselves they were doing something about all the "problems." In some cases they believed they had been doing so for decades. In Mexico, for example, the profession continued to guarantee traditional values and nationalist ideals by being part of *La Revolución.* And in Peru and Chile army officers would attempt to demolish civilian institutions they believed were fomenting or abetting alien influences and internal enemies of tradition and national culture. Mexico, Peru, and Chile provide a comparative case study in the blending of traditional nationalism (or its lack) with professionalism.

Because the army was a creation, not a creator, of Mexico's great national revolutionary movement, its defense of tradition and nationalism would always be a defense of the living revolution. "The origin of our army is the Mexican Revolution. . . . Mexican soldiers being part of the people itself, they and their families have a right to expect the government to assure that they receive the social benefits necessary to raise their standard of living [just like other citizens]."[95] So said President Adolfo López Mateos on 9 February 1961, Army Day in Mexico. López Mateos was hewing to government lines established in the 1920s and 1930s: the military, like any other part of the "revolutionary family," deserved no more, no less from *La Revolución.*

That same decade, just two years prior to the tragedy of Tlatelolco, General Juan José Gastelum would repeat the old argument that "our army is revolutionary; risen from the revolution in arms, it is the bulwark and maximum guarantee of national institutions created by that revolution and, being a creation of our people, is at their service."[96] Revolution, *pueblo,* state, and army were one. Colonel Arnulfo Aguirre, writing on "El pasado y el presente," opined that the Mexican Revolution had transformed political life. The engine of this transformation, he believed, was progress: "the goals of the revolutionary movement are varied, mutual, and as changeable as life itself."[97] As *La Revolución* matured, so would all its institutions, including the army, in a steady, coordinated, progressive evolution.

Commemoration of *20 de Noviembre* means as much to Mexicans as any independence or revolutionary anniversary to any country. In 1967 one Mexican general remembered it by asserting that the people had resorted to a military movement in 1910 in order to achieve, political, social, and economic change. Arms had broken the "state machinery of an oligarchy, vindicated the peasants and workers." Arms had enabled men to write a new constitution, then had defended that document. The army had maintained the Mexican Revolution, assuring Mexicans that they would never again have to live like strangers in their own land.[98] The army was everything to Mexico. The army was *nacido de La Revolución,* as much through principles as through its leaders. "The revolutionary army was of the people and guaranteed national sovereignty, maintained the peace, and safeguarded all that which was "most genuinely Mexican."[99] Following the tension of 1968, army writers would urge young officers, soldiers, and civilians to be wary of Mexico's enemies: communism and "other exotic doctrines and systems that do not go with our idiosyncracy, our history, and our traditions."[100] The army would go on defending Mexico's historical tradition against all attacks from right and left, insisted General Marcelino García Barragán in 1970, for that tradition was revolutionary, and to fail it would be to fail Mexico and her people. The people stood ready to assist the army in every revolutionary duty; their common defense of the nation provided "an unlimited field of action, in which we may develop our initiative, exchange ideas with our leaders, with the result that [the army] becomes more effective and renders even greater service."[101] Revolutionary nationalism and the army were synonymous in Mexico.

According to its own criteria, the Peruvian army had outpaced civilian institutions by the 1960s. In a process beginning early in the century, Peruvians developed French colonial military theories into an elaborate *misión civilizadora.* The culmination of the process, thought-become-action through professional militarism, came between 1968 and 1980, during the years of the "Revolutionary Government of the Armed Forces," Peru's time of the generals. Like their French mentors, Peruvians had convinced themselves that they had a mission to civilize—not Algeria or Morocco, of course, but the Andes. The hinterland became as much a crucible for the Peruvian army as Africa was for the French and the Portuguese.[102] It became their nationalist inspiration, at least for institutional purposes.

Peruvians had become used to concentrating on joint command and unity of action—guiding principles of the *golpe institucional* of 1968—by the time they began to voice their opinions on such specific topics as agrarian reform and economic development.[103] In the 1950s they well knew about counterinsurgency, Marxism's menace to western civilization and culture, and about the need to make each citizen into a willing collaborator with government and army.[104] The concepts of mission and responsibility were well developed. As Lieutenant Colonel Víctor Sánchez Marín put it just a year before the *golpe* of 1962, "the famous statement of the ex-president [Batista] of Cuba, 'my army failed because it was not prepared to wage a revolutionary war,' must not be repeated here in Peru."[105] Peruvians prepared themselves so militantly for an internal war that their successes convinced them by the mid-1960s that their talents for problem solving knew no limits, no frontiers. The army would save Peru even if Peru would not do right by the army.

"Our frontiers are not on the coasts of this continent, but where a threat is encountered, and, therefore, it is necessary to confront a threat before a threat is present in our own home,"[106] was General Juan Mendoza Rodríguez's admonition of 1964. It was testimony to the army's confidence in its ability to identify all foes and deal with them. Never before had a Latin American army developed such an elaborate blend of nationalist thought over such a long period of time.[107] Not even in Argentina, where ideological extremism usually dominated actions, would there occur such an unrestrained and simplistic application of military ideals, values, structures, and practices to the solution of civilian problems. In no other Latin American country would officers, to recall the Cartesian comment at the beginning of this chapter, come so close to understanding their own century and yet fail so miserably to deal with the problems of their own country.

According to General José Vásquez, in a 1972 *Revista Militar del Perú* piece, Peruvian history had demonstrated vividly that "material wealth, unless accompanied by austerity and civic virtues, is not sufficient to maintain territorial integrity and a healthy state."[108] Vásquez went on to say that Peru's tortuous geography, multiplicity of dialects, and her racial differences made military involvement in education and national development necessary. Peru needed the army. Unlike Mexico, but like her South American neighbors, Peru had neither a revolutionary nor a traditional agent to bind military to civilian institutions, which helps explain how the disjunctive nature of Peruvian military-civilian relations contributed mightily to Latin America's most full-blown elaboration of professional militarism.

In Chile's case, a functional, but nevertheless tension-filled, military-civilian relationship would be shattered in 1973, when the armed forces overthrew the government of President Salvador Allende Gossens. Latin America's bloodiest *golpe de estado* of the century took place, ironically, in a country with a long-standing but superficial tradition of civilian political primacy and separation of politics from the military. The *golpe* was followed by the harshest professional military-governmental experiment in Latin American history.

"We are the depository of a pure and brave tradition," wrote Chaplain Florencio Infante Durán just before the 1973 rising.[109] The army had resisted political action as long as it could, holding to its tradition of "deliberation" but nonintervention, wrote colonel Raúl Toro Arriagada in 1975.[110] "No one pretends that errors have not been made," editorialized the *Memorial del Ejército de Chile* in 1979, six years after the rising; "no one claims there is total agreement among Chileans on current political matters. What has been achieved is neither infallibility nor perfect unity, but [there is] a consensus that the armed forces lead this country with patriotic criteria and that [it was] a lack of open debate that facilitated the concentration of their energy in this productive work."[111] Chile, in the eyes of military professionals, had nearly permitted the destruction of her national culture and her army. The army had, in turn, saved civilians from themselves. The army would now impose new rules, and in doing so attempt to remold a nationalist tradition partially destroyed by excessive political pluralism and Marxist subversion, infiltration of the universities, and "dissolution of the family through, for example, pornography and the exacerbation of generational conflict."[112] That Argentine contribution to Chilean military literature indicated the lengths Chileans were planning to go in order to take care of their responsibilities. To confront their future Peruvians would seek to modernize, and Mexicans to preserve. Chileans wanted to restore a past, but which one?

By 1980 they had hardened their stand against the recent past, and had settled in to their time of the *general*. That year officers would read a brief essay by a Uruguayan lieutenant colonel, an adjunct professor at the *Academia de Guerra,* the army staff school. Lieutenant Colonel Ricardo Díaz Herreyra reiterated for his readers ideas every bit as extreme as those propounded by his Argentine neighbors. Pluralism, he claimed, was the destroyer of liberty, for it was "permissive beyond belief." The western world had gone mad, he claimed. "Homosexuals band together, and succeed in having others consider them normal . . . freedom of religion has led to devil worship. Alcohol . . . and drug addiction expand crazily. . . . Abortion, that crime against the most innocent and defenseless of beings, also has become readily accepted. Tomorrow it will be euthanasia, and then (why not?) the handicapped and retarded will take their turn."[113] Only through an "integral" society, Díaz thought, would his countrymen and his hosts be able to save themselves from destruction. The institution most capable of setting the tone for integration everywhere was, of course, the army.

Colonel Humberto Calderón agreed in 1981. People everywhere had become sheep to be led to the slaughter, "egged on by utopian promises."[114] He specifically blamed liberation theology for leading Chileans away from the road to eternal salvation. Lieutenant Colonel Jorge Catanzaro Corradi blamed Marxism for destroying Chile's social harmony.[115] Then, in 1985, Lieutenant Colonel Miguel Krassnoff Martchenko brought the anti-Marxist thrust of Chile's uniformed defenders into the sharpest focus ever. Because the armed forces had defeated Chile's atheists and Marxists, Moscow was now supporting the attempts of Chilean exiles to subvert and discredit the armed forces. What occurred in 1970, he wrote, was the real break with Chile's past; what had happened since had led to the reestablishment of national culture, dignity, tradition, faith, and legitimacy.[116] By the late 1980s Chileans were as militant as Argentines had been in the previous decade, as convinced of their purposes as Peruvians and Brazilians, as devoted to their own nationalist-traditionalist cause as were Mexicans to theirs. Like other South Americans they had lost touch with time and place as their militancy increased.[117] Nationalism could mean anything to army officers, for it was both unique and typical.

Throughout Latin America and worldwide, the fifth and sixth chapters have shown, there was a distinct comparability of ideas expressed in military journals on politics and ideology; on religion, wisdom, and nationalism. Confusion of these ideas with others traditionally held by officers was critical to the directions taken by military professionals in addressing institutional and national problems.

In Europe, the lands of the Commonwealth, and the United States politics was either separated from the military or the primacy of civilian politics was acknowledged. In Latin America the emphasis was on separation, not primacy. In the West communism was universally acclaimed a menace, an insidious threat to an often idealized "way of life." Traditional values—and national cultures—had to be defended.

In Catholic and Islamic countries, as faith blended more easily with militaristic thinking, religious militancy became an important ingredient of both professionalism and militarism in both thought and action. In South America, religion and ideological orientation were confused as nowhere else, except possibly Pakistan, and all aspects of professionalism, including technical expertise (not to be confused with wisdom, despite the protestations of military leaders), were brought to bear on the definition and fulfillment of self-assigned military roles. It now becomes possible to show how the confusion described in this chapter and the struggle to reconcile military separateness and civilian primacy with reality, depicted in chapter 5, aided in the metamorphosis of professionalism into militarism, thus producing the time of the generals.

SEVEN

Professional Militarism Manifest and Latent: Hearing Different Drummers, Going Separate Ways

Do you know what I think? These are shadows cast upon their minds by some half-shaped images which they cannot disentangle and clear up inwardly, and therefore are unable to express outwardly; they do not yet understand themselves.—Michel de Montaigne, "On the Education of Children" (1580)

Neither past nor future, neither development nor progress, neither history nor science, neither light nor darkness: only fable and shadow.—José Donoso, *Casa de campo* (1978)

What occurred in South America between 1964 and 1989 did not constitute a sudden veering away from typicality by Argentine, Brazilian, Chilean, and Peruvian militarists. Their uniqueness had been there all along the historical road to the time of the generals. In their countries the idealized past created by officer-authors from the 1890s forward clashed most dramatically with the new world paradigm brought into being by World War II and the hemispheric and global rise of the United States as a military power.

All typicality and world perspective aside, uniqueness has been pointed out throughout the preceding chapters where it has manifested itself most significantly: *Innere Führung,* Soviet Marxist-Leninist orthodoxy, Pakistani Islamic militancy, and the "gift." Typicality and uniqueness both, then, fostered professional militarism in countries where past and present, despite numerous efforts, could not be reconciled, where the military profession perceived change over time to be a threat to its very existence. All factors considered, the difference between manifest and latent professional militarism is stark.

Manifest professional militarism was an extremely complex and confused set of ideas. The latent militarism associated with other countries and regions was comparable in form and content, to be sure, but neither so intensely nor so continuously expressed. Where professionalism prevailed it was always more transparently, less mystically formulated and presented to readers. The importance of national context, already mentioned in these pages, and evinced by the amount of social science literature devoted to recent relations between military and civilian sectors, is difficult to overstate.

In this chapter some of the more intense expressions of thought and self-perceptions of Argentines, Brazilians, Chileans, and Peruvians must be practically parsed in order to understand them. There are some "half-shaped images" here that are hard to disentangle. But it would be a mistake to dismiss such writings as inconsequential owing to their turgidness or prolixity. The more intense or emotional an assertion of professional militarism, the more unlikely its clear expression. This was primarily the result of officers being historically so far *apart from* the rest of society while having to be *a part of* it. It was also a sign of great frustration, professional development, and strength of conviction. And it was evidence of idealization of times gone by, alienation from times at hand, and concern for those to come. It was peculiar to four countries, but even there not all officers would commit themselves to mystical and arcane essaying of the great issues at hand.

The constantly self-enriching mixture of thought and self-perception that characterized the writings of military professionals everywhere carried with it into the later years of the century all, not just most, past influences on professional development. National security schemes, participatory roles, and geopolitical foci in Latin America, thus, should be viewed in historical terms as much as or more than contemporary ones. Indeed, in much of the world the events of 1989–1992 show, these factors have diachronic as well as synchronic importance. They are just as significant across time as they are during specifically delineated epochs. This is admittedly more the case where the profession has had a long history, a tradition. For this reason this chapter must not be limited solely to the literature produced during the 1964–1989 quarter century.

Much of Latin America would not suffer manifest professional militarism, of course. Mexico, Central America, the Caribbean, and Venezuela, Colombia, and a few other South American countries, as their military literature shows, experienced forms of professional development and military-civilian relations that engendered only a degree of latent professional militarism. Change in its various forms would not occur at the same pace everywhere in Latin America; nor would it in the rest of the world. National and international influences varied. So did the domestic and foreign roles of armies. Domino theories applied to cause and effect of institutional *golpes* are at the outset moot, and so far debates have not proved very fruitful.

This chapter illustrates the ways in which typicality and uniqueness can be fundamental parts of the same contextual phenomenon, for despite so many similarities in their thought and self-perceptions, officers would not, indeed could not, transform them into action in uniform ways. Metamorphosis of professionalism into militarism did not have to take place everywhere in some ineluctable process, neither in Latin America nor elsewhere in the world. Instead of insisting on the eternal qualities of the "gift," for example, many officers early on in the postwar era accepted psychological factors and management techniques as a matter of course. Few of these were Latin Americans, to be sure. Many recognized they were citizens first, soldiers second. Many had no choice. The uniqueness of both manifest and latent professional militarism, and of military professionalism, should be obvious, but so should their typicality.

The earliest, clearest expressions of professional militarism as defined herein occured not in Brazil, site of the first institutional *golpe* (1964), but in Peru, where, since the founding of CAEM, once Latin America's premier higher military studies center, in the 1950s and the literal institutionalization of themes fixed in military thinking fully a half century earlier, military literature had come to include a defined set of priorities. Military government in 1962–1963, the counterinsurgency campaigns of the 1960s, and then the *golpe* of 1968 would put into action ideas long popular among army officers. It is significant that Latin America's only true military *regime* (as opposed to *government* or *administration*) was an abject failure; it is equally significant that in the long run this may not dissuade another cohort from doing it all over again. Some lessons are never fully learned; some, when learned, are soon forgotten.

In 1967, just a year before the Peruvian *golpe,* a United States lieutenant colonel, John J. Saalberg, wrote that "the simplistic nature of military activity often encourages army leaders to oversimplify the complexities involved in modernizing a society. . . . All problems," he summarized, "can be overcome if someone will only give the correct order."[1] Seizure of power, he added, was often followed by a call for civilian expertise when officers found they could not deal with the realities of national leadership.

In Peru this call would be minimal by the standards of the era. Whether because of their penchant for oversimplification or because of their disdain for a civilian polity that had failed miserably to push the modernization process as far as they thought possible, Peruvian officers would attempt to direct national affairs and to both formulate and implement all aspects of a centralized national policy. Saalberg also argued, it should be pointed out, that military leadership could contribute to national development, but that it could not produce it alone. His argument would have convinced few Peruvians of the 1960s.

It would never have appealed to the prolific Mercado Jarrín. His most memorable contribution to military literature, one of the region's most widely read essays, is the oft-cited "El ejército de hoy y su proyección en nuestra sociedad en período de transición (1940–1965)."[2] Therein he demonstrated at once the boundless optimism of the officer, a simplistic approach to national-level problem solving, and an utter conviction that only the armed forces could save Peru from chaos.

Two principal reasons made this the case in his mind. First was his conviction that the establishment of a Peruvian general staff system had already endowed the military with the ability to both devise and execute policy. This had occurred over a period of time, he noted, but already had flourished before the process of industrialization had commenced in Peru.[3] In short, the expertise was there, but only men in uniform could apply it. Second, a revolutionary change in officialdom had "permitted the formation of a nucleus of officers with modern attitudes, new techniques, renovating spirit, social consciousness, [who were] inclined to maintain peace and order." The last words should not be ignored, for true structural change would never be a significant goal of professional militarists anywhere.

Peru's army, Mercado Jarrín insisted, long before other state agencies and most private enterprises, "began to exercise influence on the progress and modernization of the country." He continued, discussing a number of specific ways in which the army shared, or ought to share, in the development, progress, and modernization—the terms being synonymous to Mercado Jarrín—of the country. Military technology was so advanced, organization so modern, and experiences so varied; recruitment policy was so well coordinated nationwide; and military education was so superior that the army provided a perfect base upon which to establish a new Peru. The military, "molded in the image of an industrial enterprise," provided jobs and vocational training for the future and did more to foment economic development than any other government agency. The army was an agent of social mobility (as opposed to structural change, let it be clear). It was the only sector where equality of opportunity and objective merit prevailed, where *cholos, campesinos, indios, andinos, costeños*—where all citizens, in short—became true Peruvians. In effect, the army *was* Peru, he was arguing. That Peru should be more like the army was the less-than-veiled suggestion. In a Mexican setting such an essay would have borne copious references to *La Revolución,* but this was Peru.

Mercado Jarrín's point of view was merely the iceberg's tip, to strike an un-Peruvian metaphor, but probably the most eloquent and comprehensive of a number of pre- and post-1968 exhortations to Peruvian officers. And it did not stand alone. In fact, to some Peruvian *uniformados* it merely confirmed what foreigners had already told them.

Three years before Mercado Jarrín's seminal work appeared, the Peruvian *Revista de la Escuela Superior de Guerra* had published a controversial report by Arthur D. Little, Inc.[4] This report to the second administration (1956–1962) of Manuel Prado y Ugarteche stated that "the Peruvian national effort toward economic development should be comparable in swiftness and efficiency to a military mobilization, along the lines of a war effort." The report advised the mobilization of all sectors of society, workers and employers, landowners and miners, all classes and parties. It called for a significant state role in the process, new labor legislation, technology transfer, internal and external capitalization, massive investment in the transportation and communications infrastructures, and economic diversification in the areas of agriculture, mining, and industry. It called for penetration of the interior, the opening of untapped areas beyond the mountains. It called for what military writers had long been advocating in Peru.

Officers took this all very seriously, of course, and they did not forget that most civilians wanted nothing to do with a military role in any kind of development for Peru. They took it seriously when they overthrew Prado in 1962 in order to nullify inconclusive presidential elections, and while they ran the country through a junta until 1963, then for five more years, while Fernando Belaúnde Terry attempted to turn his own ideas on modernization into realities, only to be overthrown himself in 1968.

Officers took it so seriously that when they attempted to simplify the modernization process and gear all conceivable aspects of the economy to national security and defense they found they were unable to accomplish their goals.[5] Since the mid 1950s, Peruvians had been refining lessons once learned from French mentors who had often wishfully insisted on a national scheme to integrate social, economic, and political activities into military affairs in order to insure rapid military mobilization. In Peru, the concept of mobilization had long been considered a panacea for both underdevelopment and its inevitable result, subversion.

Mobilization would crop up in essays dealing with all aspects of economic and social development. Geopolitics inwardly directed, a long-popular Peruvian topic, also influenced thought on mobilization. "Our country," Major Víctor Sánchez Marín said in 1955, "has lost opportunities for power owing to lack of political vision and administrative incapacity."[6] He referred directly to Peru's loss of territory to Chile in the past century as evidence that bad (civilian) government and lack of (civilian) foresight were long-standing problems.

National security had now become a popular concept. As evolved at CAEM, it would become inseparable from mobilization and geopolitics, justifying the former, legitimizing continual reference to the latter. "Today more than ever," one colonel would write in 1957, "*national security* depends on the coordinated efforts of the entire nation, for the problems of a national dimension that have led to military conflict impose upon social conflicts modalities and activities that affect all citizens of a country, be they individuals or the population as a whole."[7] *Retranslation*: "Conflict, be it internal or external, has an effect on the entire country; therefore the efforts of the entire country must be brought to bear in order to avoid damaging circumstances. Planning for national security through mobilization based on geopolitical realities—the Peruvian military mind readily grasped the linkages—would assure development. It had to." To then-Colonel Francisco Morales Bermúdez this was all too obvious. His "Planeamiento estratégico" had linked planning and mobilization together, but it was not expressed clearly.[8] If ever there was an example of the influence of Saalberg's "simplistic military activity," this was it. There would be others.

Things followed along the lines of "simplistic activity" in the 1960s.[9] In 1963 Lieutenant Gastón Ibáñez O'Brien even did his colleague Morales Bermúdez one better. In an essay on command and delegation of authority and responsibility he outlined a way in which all (national) activities should lead to desired results. Three kinds of policy-oriented activity assured this. Determinative activity resulted in the issuing of orders. Executive authority resulted in the carrying out of the orders. Evaluative activity resulted in the monitoring of executive authority and produced recommendations for further deliberation and action.[10] Ibáñez had created, five years before the 1968 movement, a scheme for the organization of the regime of General Juan Velasco Alvarado. The president, the Junta, and the cabinet all determined; the ministries and the *Sistema Nacional de Apoyo a la Movilización Social* (SINAMOS) carried out; and the CAEM, SINAMOS, the *Comite de Asesoramiento a la Presidencia* (COAP), and local agencies would evaluate all policies and action resulting from them. This is in essence how the military would attempt to apply professional militarism. It was all very simple.

At about the time Mercado Jarrín was putting the finishing touches on "El ejército de hoy . . ." he published another essay, and several colleagues published still other treatises dealing with state responsibility for development. In "La política de la seguridad integral," Mercado Jarrín wrote that "the goals of the state must be decisively manifest in objectives to be realized by the nation."[11] *Retranslation*: "The entire population must be made aware—through Ibáñez's determinative, executive, and interpretive dialectic—of their responsibilities to the state and to each other."

Just prior to the 1968 movement other officers were refining the arguments made by Mercado Jarrín, Ibáñez, Sánchez, Morales Bermúdez, and others. The army should be put in complete charge of penetration and colonization of the interior, opined a lieutenant colonel in 1966.[12] All regional planning should be placed under the army's supervision, said another.[13] Mercado Jarrín even took his case to the business community, telling them that their army educated and trained men better than any other single agency. This was an old argument, but Mercado now took it a step further. Lack of planning (as always) by civilians, and their failure to recognize the army's potential services on behalf of the labor pool, virtually constituted criminal action. The lack of jobs available to ex-conscripts made for a waste both of human talent and of money invested in their technical and vocational preparation.[14] This essay, "El ejército y la empresa," constituted the last of the outspoken "what-the-army-can-do-for-Peru" pieces, for beginning in late 1968 the emphasis of military literature was shifting to what was already going on.

When General Angel Valdivia Morriberón spoke out publicly on 5 November 1968, he made it clear that the military, i.e., the army, was now in charge, already taking steps to mobilize, develop, make secure, and apply geopolitical theories.[15] The job long wished for became a crusade. Army officers who had studied at CAEM (and some who had not, it must be said), began to call themselves *revolucionarios*. They were hardly that, but in the end most could subscribe to General Jorge Chávez Quelopana's 1973 dictum that CAEM was based on the premise "that the state has as its supreme end the common good defined as the social means through which man achieves his destiny."[16] *Retranslation*: "CAEM-trained and CAEM-influenced officers were doing their utmost to create a state that would provide the means to avoid class conflict and instability." They were doing this, so they thought, by nationalizing all possible socioeconomic activities and cultural organizations, redefining *peruanidad*, and eliminating traditional political practices. However revolutionary this may have sounded, it was clear from the inception of the 1968 movement that it hardly constituted a revolution. It was too steeped in the professional military past. Nothing experienced by Peruvians since the return to civilian government in 1980 has served to change this essential fact of Peruvian professional militarism.

Across the continent, Brazilian officers were by now into a fifth year with professional militarism as the guiding principle(s) of government. There, it is clear, they did not seek to nationalize, à la Peru, for Brazil had endured two shaky experiments with economic nationalism. Thus, military economic remedies that were applied contrasted sharply with those used in Peru. But this did not mean that Brazilians were not equally ambitious. Theirs was a huge land with staggering problems. Geopolitics had long influenced them as much as it did Peruvians, and there was certainly a role for the state to play, especially in the development of the interior. The industrial and urban sectors were seen as places where "neoliberal" economics (as both monetarist and supply-side economics came to be called in the region) would develop, modernize, and create progress—with *order*. Like Peruvians, Brazilians would show little interest in structural change.

Writing back in 1950, a French captain had stated that "the exigencies of national defense determine the structure of an army; this structure determines in turn the directions of military education and the role for the army within the nation in peacetime. To define *a priori* that role . . . is to cut off dangerously [the army] from its major mission and relegate it to secondary activities."[17] Brazil's French heritage, despite the United States' influence, would be a heavy influence on the founders of the *Escola Superior de Guerra* following the war. Brazilian officers would strive to beat back any attempts by civilians to define *a priori* their peacetime role and relegate them to "secondary activities."

Barely a year after Peruvians had sent President Belaúnde off to exile, Brazilians saw a new constitution come into being. The *poder moderador* had come to fruition. In Chapter VII, Section VI, Articles 90–93, there appeared the essence of a military-civilian relationship that would prevail into the 1980s—and perhaps beyond. The armed forces were charged with the defense of the fatherland, with guaranteeing law and order and the proper function of government. Control of the armed forces was placed in the hands of the chief executive. All this and more was done because it was "essential" to the "execution of national security policy."[18] In short, the armed forces, led by the army, had achieved the desired end imagined by their French mentors: the power to define their own role. Like the French-influenced Peruvians, Brazilians achieved it by enacting legislation that would outlast their control of the government. This, of course, was something the French had never even dared attempt. The Brazilian military seized control of the government and began to convert professional militarism from theory into praxis.

The ambition of Brazilians—as great as the country's problems, surely—was no more a recent thing than that of Peruvians. Like their brethren far beyond the *sertão, mato,* and *fronteira,* they had a rich history of thought and self-perception to fall back on. They had not forgotten the teachings of their own soldiers of yesterday. Only a few years after the second world war, Brazilians were beginning to see (again) that theirs was still *a terra de amanhã*. In essays dealing with the need to exert more control over petroleum production (as opposed to eminent domain) and penetration of the interior, professional military writers were intellectually setting the stage for the *golpe* of 1964 as early as 1950.[19] If most of these earlier writings do not compare in tone with those of Peruvians, it is because the successful World War II record of the *Força Expedicionária Brasileira (*FEB), the founding of *Escola Superior de Guerra* (ESG), and exercise of the constitutionally mandated *poder moderador* made it unnecessary for Brazilians to have to assert themselves too much. The flowering of a sort of democracy upon the demise of the *Estado Novo* of Getúlio Vargas and the lack of immediate Peruvian-type pressures also helped render Brazilian professional writings less hostile toward civilian institutions.

As is evident from much of the literature studied, Brazilians would not have pretexts for action identical to those of Peruvians. But once they were in power their writings did take on a comparable tone of self-justification and self-legitimation. Brazilians like the widely read General Carlos de Meira Mattos would always link educational reforms within the military to the ability to better defend and develop, just as Peruvians did.[20] They would see development and defense as a vital function of military-led colonization schemes. Such schemes, according to Major Levy Ribeiro Bittencourt Junior, were nothing less than national security measures in accordance with the law of 29 September 1969. This decree legislation codified national security as essentially the ability and obligation of a state to attain national objectives without opposition, either internal or external. "Internal security," the major confirmed, was "a vital part of national security and should be maintained in the face of threats of "any origin, form, or nature that produce an effect in the country."[21] Frontier colonization, linking of the far interior with populous areas of Brazil, and control of all that lay in between was absolutely necessary for both internal and external security. Peru and Bolivia might not have been seen as significant threats to Brazilian security, but they were limitrophe states in the throes of development. Being similarly dependent on national security, their own development out there in the continental heartland might conceivably impinge upon Brazil's plans for the future.

"Unless the political power is 'prepared,' though, the conditions necessary for the realization of any and all mobilization" could not obtain.[22] National mobilization, according to the essay from which that passage comes, was based on permanent preparedness. This was decidedly not a new assertion; it was, however, one made under a military government, one that was striving to realize the intentions of the officers who had created it. Needless to say, these officers believed they represented Brazil better than any other group; therefore their vision of Brazil had to be the most realistic. After all, the army had always been the vanguard in the "struggle for attainment and maintenance of permanent national objectives of nationality."[23] *Retranslation*: "The army had always striven to do what it was doing when this was written, that is, in 1973. Independence, nationhood, territorial integrity, and sovereignty had always been the army's business." The 1964 "revolution" was, thus, merely a natural result of activities of the likes of Pedro I, the Duke of Caxias, and General Cândido da Silva Rondon, the "great *bandeirante* of this century."[24] But the vanguard was not alone in all this.

Chile's Lieutenant Colonel Herbert Orellana Herrera, writing in 1974—with a definite purpose in mind, let there be no doubt—emphasized Brazilian claims that the founding of the ESG and its subsequent history revealed "the cohesion of civilians and military in the search for solutions to national problems."[25] The unity of purpose that Latin American and other officers had so long advocated had been achieved, or so Brazilians and other South Americans might have thought, but this was only through force, not mutual agreement.

Fully fifteen years after the 1964 *golpe,* Brazilians would still find it necessary to tie strong executive leadership to national security. One writer would assert in 1979 that recent developmental strides made by France, Germany, Mexico, and Brazil had been possible because of forceful executive leadership. Forceful individuals (Charles de Gaulle, for example), unlike "compromise candidates," could create consensus, enforce national security doctrines, avoid sectoral conflicts, and lead impartially through the use of technology.[26] Some sort of technocratic elite, it seems, was necessary for the achievement of national goals. No politicians, "swing men," or compromise candidates, need apply. The achievement of economic goals was incompatible with disorder but not with personal liberty. A directed economy was compatible with a directed form of democracy; both were necessary for true liberty.[27] *Retranslation*: "Authoritarian decisions in the economic realm ought not be seen as detrimental to anyone's interest, but as leading to meaningful progress for all."

In the late 1970s and early 1980s, Brazilians were still fretting about the far frontiers. None of Brazil's far-flung areas were well enough integrated into the whole, and they all were still too much influenced by adjacent states.[28] The fact that Venezuelans, Colombians, Peruvians, and Bolivians (not to mention Brazil's other neighbors) all thought pretty much the same about Brazil's influence on their own hinterlands was cold comfort to Brazilian geopoliticians and professional militarists.

One of the great failures of Brazil's professional militarists was their grandiose plans for *interiorização,* "interiorization," the taming of frontier areas. Geopolitics driven inward, as already noted, had turned out to be no more a doctrine of development than any other set of ideas. But such ideas did provide in relatively simplistic terms solutions for national problems, and these solutions appealed to officers far more than most of those proffered by civilian leaders. Unity of command, purpose, and effort were what Brazilian generals would offer in reply to participatory democracy, open debate, and pluralism. Like Peruvians, their reasoning became ever more self-reinforcing, ever more simplistic, more fatuous, and more fanciful. As it did, it also became expressible only in terms equally confusing. When it became no longer possible for generals to blame civilians for economic stagnation and social discontent, for political ineptitude and cultural degeneration, their time would be up. Once they understood this, Brazilian professional militarists would feel constrained to relinquish control of national affairs. They accordingly did so in 1985.

"Once the state and the nation have chosen their path," Lieutenant Colonel William L. Hauser quoted Charles de Gaulle, "military duty is spelled out once and for all. Outside its guidelines there can be—there are—only lost soldiers." Hauser was citing de Gaulle's 1972 essay on the French army in the wake of the Algerian crisis.[29] He could easily have been thinking about Argentine officers even before the Malvinas crisis, for they were already lost.

Their de Gaulle had been Perón, and this pale shadow of France's leader had personalized and divided the army just as much. Until the advent of Augusto Pinochet Ugarte, no twentieth-century Latin American military leader has come close to doing that to a truly professional officer corps. Perón's 1955–1973 years were as significant as de Gaulle's and Pinochet's political careers owing to the long-term effects each had on their profession. France was probably the better for de Gaulle; Argentina has yet to recover from Perón. By striking down governments in 1966 and again in 1976, Argentina's lost soldiers would find themselves deeply involved in politics and government. Doing so, they also evinced one characteristic that distinguished them from strident, confident Peruvians and hypernationalistic Brazilians. Argentines were the most outspoken antipopulists of the South American professional militarists, at least until Chileans in the 1980s began to face a revived civilian opposition.

Argentines had good reason to be antipopulists, for nowhere else during the 1964–1989 time of the generals or before it was there anything quite like *peronismo*. Neither *getulismo* in Brazil, *aprismo* in Peru, nor Chilean Marxism could boast both the recent impact and personalized content of *peronismo*. Whereas Peruvians were able to vent their spleens fairly freely at all times without much fear of civilian recrimination, and whereas Brazilians had a World War II heritage to buoy their historical image, Argentines had tacitly supported the losing side in the global conflict and had been politicized from both within and without long before their first institutional *golpe* in 1966.

National security as conveyed in Argentine military literature was much the same as it was in Peruvian and Brazilian journals. It would find its way into most of the essays germane to professional militarism. It consistently carried with it criticism of, and threats to, populist political organizations. The tragic consequences of *la guerra sucia* and the Malvinas fiasco had their roots in both antipopulism and hypernationalism. "The Argentine revolution has taken on the responsibility of leading the country, without deviation, toward a future of grandeur. The most viable way in which citizens can become the artificers of their own destiny is through development, and this cannot be realized without adequate provisions for national security."[30] *Retranslation*: "Progress and development will only come through assurance of Argentine national security."

The well-published author of that passage, General Osiris Villegas, would go on to discuss the need to integrate the marginal sectors of the population—be they political, social, cultural, racial, or religious; be they class-based or of an economic nature—into the mainstream of Argentine life. All this he asserted in an essay ostensibly devoted simply to the need for hydroelectric development in the La Plata basin. His compatriot, General Juan Guglialmelli, founder of *Estrategia*, Argentina's own *Zeitschrift für Geopolitik*, would later argue that the responsibility for development, integration, and national security—again, the self-justifying circularity of the logic is crystal-clear—rightfully belonged in the hands of the officer corps. "The armed forces," he said, "have a specific and essential mission: the defense of the fatherland, the safeguarding of its honor; the inviolability of its frontiers, the maintenance of internal order against all subversive tendencies that threaten the national being."[31] *Retranslation*: "The military is responsible for Argentina's future and all that may affect it."

Their writings showed that Argentines had few doubts about their responsibilities from the beginning of the Perón era forward. They would emphasize nationalism and economic development until Perón's fall in 1955, then antipopulism until the *golpe* of 1966 and beyond, all the while blending both with national security and geopolitics. Economic development had been tied to national defense since the early postwar years, as in most Latin American countries.[32]

As early as 1951, Lieutenant Colonel Jorge E. Atencio was rejecting classical *Lebensraum* as incompatible to Argentina but applying its essence domestically. Argentina had no need for external vital space, he insisted, for there was still all that "empty" national space to be exploited.[33] Atencio's argument would prove applicable to most Latin American countries, and most underdeveloped countries, of course. It would also contribute greatly to the geopolitics-development-national security relationship still forming in the minds of military leaders.

Like Peruvians and Brazilians, Argentines would also consistently stress that national defense must be coordinated by both civilian and military authorities. This was most easily done, one officer argued back in 1955, by strengthening the ability of the executive branch of government.[34] Another officer argued two years later that national defense depended upon the strengthening of civilian morale and national spirit.[35] By the 1960s, in the wake of the first Perón government (1946–1955), Jorge Giovanelli would continue the discussion by asserting that coordinated national defense and improved national spirit should be influenced more heavily by the military than by civilians. "Like it or not," he wrote, "Argentine history is principally military history, to the point where it appears that destiny wants it to continue to be so."[36] *Retranslation*: "Military force created Argentina, and thus should continue to direct affairs of state."

By the mid 1950s Atencio, now a colonel, had adjusted his geopolitical emphasis to make it more compatible with the non-Perón interregnum. Contradicting his earlier dismissal of geopolitics as Haushoferian and Hitlerian, he now allowed as how officers and civilians ought to become more familiar with the ideas behind geopolitics if only to better understand how geography had influenced Argentina's historical development.[37] Soon Lieutenant Colonel Mario Orsolini would write without concern for the stigma of German geopolitical fanaticism that it was up to the state to promote progress and development through national planning and direction of the "national will." This planning and direction should take into account all factors, including geography, and should be based on fixed objectives and ends.[38] The former he saw as tactical stages, the latter as elements of a national strategy. Direction of the national will toward Argentina's destiny should brook no opposition was the oft-repeated argument.

Although Argentina, as developed as it was, did not provide a fertile ground for the kind of colonization programs discussed by Peruvian and Brazilian officers, Argentines did show an interest in something they called "civic action." Far from being seen as an adjunct of counterinsurgency, it would become a rubric for suppression of populist opposition following the 1966 movement led by General Juan Carlos Onganía and preceding that of 1976, finally resulting in the institutionalized violence known as *la guerra sucia*. Because it was the army's job to "safeguard the nation's highest interests," it was only natural for it to be included in all developmental projects. "We all know the enemy's procedures and the places where he is active; because of this we must be present in the same places and exert our will, our own procedures, in order to contest his actions."[39] *Retranslation*: "Civic action is a way to stamp out dissidence and do it in the name of development." With the right rationale anything could be done. Osiris Villegas would write in 1969 that "*the development and security of the Argentine Republic will be* unswervingly associated with, and dependent upon, the capability attained through fissionable material, as well as participation in the technological revolution, whose epicenter must be the exploitation of nuclear energy by the civilian sector."[40] Villegas' faith in nuclear energy was, no doubt, strengthened by Brazil's interest in it as well as his realization that Argentina was a chronically energy-poor country.

Throughout the evolution of professional militarism Argentine geopoliticians would continue their established interest in Patagonia and the South Atlantic. There is an unbroken chain of military literature on the subject, but the tone used in dealing with the subject did vary over the years. Manifest professional militarism encouraged Argentines of the 1964–1989 quarter century to see Patagonia as a potential danger to national security, sovereignty, and integrity: a source of insidious opposition to all things Argentine. The main problem, as seen by one source writing in the early 1970s, was that Patagonia, while geographically part of the national domain, still was not "Argentine" enough.[41] Now important for even more complex national security reasons, Patagonia had to be further nationalized, and thus made free from anything that proved a variation of the military-defined "national will": a simplistic solution to a major problem. At no time prior to the 1960s was Patagonia treated in such exaggerated terms.

Colonel Máximo Garro's important essay of 1970 pointed out that the farther south one went, the less Argentine the land and its people appeared, the fewer real Argentines there were. The size of the mixed population increased, the percentage of Argentines *de raza blanca* decreased. Moreover, the further toward Magellan's Strait one proceeded, the greater the influence originating from beyond the Andes (*proveniente de allende Los Andes*) an apt way of putting it, given concerns about Chile's upcoming electoral exercise and the possibilities of an Allende, Marxist victory. Chileans, after all, were "spiritually isolated" from Argentines. They did not think like Argentines. National security dictated, Garro insisted, that non-Argentines, including Anglophone Patagonians (but excluding those of Irish descent) be better incorporated into the national spirit of *argentinidad*. Needless to say, his remedy for any and all menaces to the very existence of the Argentine nation was to turn things over to the armed forces. This way, he argued, Argentina's claims to sovereignty over the Malvinas—what all good Argentines called those islands—and the Beagle Channel—which Chileans insisted on calling their own—would one day go uncontested owing to the armed forces' (alleged) abilities to defend them.

The often desperate search for consensus has been an Argentine historical theme ever since large numbers of immigrants and large amounts of foreign capital began entering the country in the last century. Various "Old Argentinas," those of the 1943–1955 golden age of Peronism, of *La Concordancia*, of *La Bella Época*, for example, had passed into history at great expense to, and to the great discomfort of, many. Because there had been so many Argentinas, so many pasts, there would be continued concern in military literature for *argentinidad* and for possible futures.

At the same time they were thinking of their own kind of civic action in Patagonia as both opportunity and challenge, Argentines continued to urge it as the way to stamp out subversion—and to confront both Brazil and Chile to boot. National objectives were equated with protection against all forms of extremism repugnant to Argentina's national "vocation." Efforts to assure conformity with their own objectives should begin with education itself, believed Colonel Carlos Landaburu. In 1970 he would state that "the objectives of education should be guided by close consonance with the policy objectives of the country. . . . That is to say education is directly connected to national planning [of that] ideal country we want to shape for the greater good of our generation."[42] *Retranslation*: "A truly Argentine *mentalidad* was still lacking, and someone had to create one." This was, needless to say, a job for the armed forces, for a revolution led by the military. General Guglialmelli would put it this way in 1972: "For the peripheral countries the concept of nation and its sovereign reality has been revived, but to make it definitively real is a primary and fundamental necessity."[43] Without military leadership, a colleague insisted, nationalism would simply revert to theory. The army, certainly, would lead under any conditions, "without bread, tobacco, and equipment," if needs be, "but with a duty to obey,"[44] just as it always had.

In blending past and present so much, Argentine (and other) army officers continued to acknowledge only certain parts of their history, idealized or acceptable pasts, not the entire background to their current situation(s). In the late 1970s, as the excesses of professional military rule were becoming tragically obvious in many places, goals and strategies still justified tactics employed, and the future was becoming more and more threatening.[45] By the mid 1980s, under a fledgling civilian administration doing its utmost to resolve military-civilian differences, reestablish Argentina's place in hemispheric and world communities, and still the voices of hypernationalism, an officer would still be able to ask his fellows, "who can now deny that non-Argentine voices encourage our people to forget your great triumph, there in the Malvinas?"[46] Dissent, populism, foreigners—they still threatened the generals' view of what Argentina might one day represent. The time of the generals had not changed the way Argentine officers thought or perceived themselves very much at all by the time they left power in 1983.

When General Augusto Pinochet and his fellows overthrew Salvador Allende in 1973, they ended forty years of professional military subservience to civilian government. Chile's heritage had once stood in stark contrast to those of her neighbors. Despite frequent grumbling in the years after 1945, Chilean *uniformados* had not had the opportunity to respond to either a crisis situation or the appeal of a civilian support group, until the early 1970s. Not since the 1924–1932 years had they sought to exercise governmental authority. Chilean civilian institutions had held firm until Allende became the first freely elected Marxist president in the history of the hemisphere—by a razor-thin margin. Three years later he was dead, La Moneda was gutted by an artillery and air strike, and civilian political institutions had been recessed.

In terms of its theoretical base, the Chilean example of professional militarism was no exception to patterns and themes being discussed herein. Chile's civilian institutional contrasts to her neighbors must not have counted for too much, for democracy was just as much an exercise in formality there as anywhere else. Like too many bad novels, form dictated content; as with military thought and self-perception, conviction was more important than substance. Chile's professional militarists would turn to technocrats to denationalize where they thought it would help the economy and to depoliticize in order to undermine populism and partisan politics. In bold contrast to Peru, they halted state direction of economic affairs where they thought it smacked of socialism—and of Chile's immediate Marxist past. As in Peru and Brazil, an increasing number of officers moved into government positions hitherto reserved for civilians, but not for identical purposes. As in Argentina, antipopulism would appeal to officers.

Describing a 1980s' viewpoint of Greece's army, General V. Kourfakis wrote that "we think it better not to disturb the economy in the country with our defensive efforts."[47] Noting that the army had many internal roles to play years after the restoration of civilian government, Kourfakis acknowledged the preferability of a *laissez-faire* attitude toward economic development. Chile's military leaders, at the outset of their campaign to radically alter the nature of civilian affairs, acknowledged essentially the same thing. Despite their resort to more state direction after the recession of the early 1980s, Chile's professional militarists found both socialist ideology and democratic politics so distasteful that they encouraged drastic shifts in economic policy in their desire to eradicate both. In their repression of dissent, they exceeded at times that which had characterized Greece's 1970s military-political experience, to the point where transition to civilian rule begun as a result of the plebiscite of 5 October 1988 would not be as easy as it appeared on the surface between then and early 1992.

Midway through the 1980s General Herbert Orellana Herrera stated in *Política y Geoestrategia* that the uprising of 11 September 1973 had created "a stable regime that guarantees the fullest and finest realization of mankind, associated in this Chilean community and living in harmony and peace here in this continent and in this world."[48] *Retranslation*: "The Pinochet regime, owing to its hardline policies, imposes order on Chile;

order is beneficial; that which occurs because of disorder is by definition wrong."

Much of what was done by Chilean officers was done in the name of national security and "guided democracy." By whatever name, national security would provide a justification for any economic, political, and social policy the Pinochet government adopted. According to one Chilean regime figure, "national security is a vital necessity of the nation-state, whose satisfaction is achieved by bringing about a combination of conditions that guarantees to the community the achievement of its legitimate aspirations and permanent interests in accordance with the dictates of the common good, utilizing in the final analysis political potential. In the same way [national security] determines that such conditions enable the state to prevent, detect, confront, or overcome those vulnerabilities, interferences, menaces, or aggressions that significantly affect its historic-cultural identity, the bases of its institutionality, or its territorial integrity."[49] *Retranslation*: "In the name of national security the state may do whatever it pleases." Taken to extremes, belief in stability and order—i.e., permanence—and other ideals that fall under the national security rubric, became a cult in Chile as much or even more than it did in Argentina, Brazil, or Peru. What was done in the name of national security in Chile was every bit as all-encompassing as it was anywhere else. Some of this was not really new.

Despite their apparently traditional apolitical stance, Chile's military authors had long expressed their concerns over economic shortcomings and the need for some form of coordinated development—this in the country that founded a state development corporation before World War II. Long before 1973, then, they had specified that national security was something more than simply mobilization and preparedness in anticipation of attack by a foreign power.[50] In 1957 there had appeared a clear-cut statement in favor of broad national security doctrine and an organic state-society construct within which it could operate.[51] There followed a period of time during which Chileans channeled their expressions of professional militarism along ways already described.[52] Chilean arguments would not be as consistently strident as those made in Peruvian journals, nor as varied as those gleaned from Argentine, Brazilian, or other Latin American sources. Nor were they as plentiful. But they did exist, and they were no less serious in quality.

Chile's time of the generals (1973–1989, strictly speaking) brought with it an initial period of quiescence based on a need for unity during regime consolidation comparable to that which had obtained elsewhere.

But by 1976, secure in their national leadership and desirous of justifying it ex post facto, Chilean officers began to elaborate on the numerous public statements and decrees issued following the 1973 *golpe*. They began to refine their commitment to national security and the organic state as if to explain their deviation from historical acceptance of a subservient role. No government, argued Colonel Elio Bacigalupo Soracco, had either the luxury or the right to avoid confrontation with threats to its security.[53] The 1970–1973 Allende administration had avoided confrontation to its peril; the present government would not. Based on the structure of an extended family, Chilean society should be hierarchically organized to increase exercise of authority at either end of the chain, this is to say, at the family and national-government levels. This was all very well, one presumes, provided there was no difference of opinion as to who should have authority over what.

National security and hierarchical social organization—not so very much different in their Chilean mix from forms advocated by other South Americans—enabled man to realize his full potential, to share in authority, for man was "a synthesis of wisdom and madness, and [his] history was consequently a result of these two essential features."[54] National security assured by a strong state guaranteed an order in which wisdom would dominate madness, in which reason would prevail over emotion. National security also assured Chileans of protection against that which had threatened their existence as a nation: Marxism. "By not being anti-Marxists we see ourselves subjugated to the doctrines of the Antichrist, and to oriental culture, which may be a good culture but not our own."[55] This source also called for a national legislative chamber, one third of which would be named by the president and two thirds by other members of the junta and regional authorities. (The Constitution of 1980 would provide for something akin to this.)

Geopolitics had long been an integral part of Chilean national security thinking.[56] By 1979 General Rigoberto Rubio Ramírez could argue its importance to the "humane essence" of national security doctrine as well as to the authority of the state. "National security," he said " . . . could by no means constitute an official ideology imposed by force of arms."[57] In other words, the results of national security were so manifestly beneficial they could not be construed as anything but the will of a majority. "Without national security," he predictably added, "there is no development, and without development there is no security, for they are totally interdependent concepts." *Retranslation*: "Ends are naturally the results of justifiable means."

An up-and-coming major, Juan Cheyre Espinosa, would also fuse geopolitics and national security in an essay of the early 1980s addressing the restructuring of regional administration. He saw national security as "a permanent political responsibility of the state devoted to the motivation, coordination, orientation, and control of specific processes . . . in all fields of action (internal, external, economic, military), with the goal of preventing actions or threats against the national being."[58] National security would be enhanced, he believed, by a well-structured regionalism, not a "separatist regionalism," but one that streamlined and stabilized administration of local affairs. Such an administration would naturally be hierarchical, coordinated, and specific in purpose. Cheyre's argument sounded very much like that made earlier by Peruvians. The fact that he was serving as a regional administrator in the late 1980s attests to the acceptability of his thesis in Chilean government circles. Lieutenant Colonel Nelson Gaudiño Benavides argued in 1980 that what Chile had experienced since 1973 was very much in the historical and geopolitical tradition of smaller nations. Switzerland and Vatican City had a world influence disproportionate to their size, he thought; the glories of the Renaissance were, moreover, those of city-states, not large nations.[59] In all ways, therefore, well-administered small countries had made history. So could Chile, one infers. Gaudiño made no mention of Uruguay here.[60]

Argentines, Brazilians, Peruvians, and Chileans, the professional militarists par excellence, were brazenly resorting to circular reasoning, conceits, and exaggerated self-justification to legitimize what they wanted to do or what they convinced themselves had already been done. That their ideas became harder to grasp as they neared *golpe* time and even more convoluted after assuming a practical leadership role, follows naturally the fact that their responses had always been so simplistic in theory. Once pressed to play the role they had long championed, South America's professional militarists would be unable to respond cogently or eloquently. They were bearing out Montaigne's notion of self-understanding, and so proving that many of their cherished ideas were indeed based on "half-shaped images."

North of the Cone and the South American midcontinent, Colombia and Venezuela would pass through the "golden age" of institutional *golpes de estado* unscathed by professional militarism. Having rid themselves of particularly unpleasant military-backed governments in the late 1950s, citizens of both countries had proceeded to establish fragile but expedient military-civilian relationships based on mutually beneficial role definition, commitment to civilian-run formal democracy as preferable to both military rule or rampant populism, and a civic-action military imperative. By the mid 1980s, however, it was apparent that the future might not be all that easy for the northern republics. Nor, as the economic crash of the early 1980s indicated, might things prove quite so predictable in Mexico.

Colombia and Venezuela, as seen, had armies that professed a determination to see democratic "revolution" to the end. But such professions beg questions; these in turn beg answers. Could Mexico's revolutionary military-civilian balance withstand the heavy pressures brought to bear on state, official party, and economic model by the events of the 1980s? Would Mexico continue to become more like other Latin American countries each year? Would Venezuela's petroleum-fueled prosperity survive the era of price fluctuation and continue to support a democratic political system? Could Colombia, like Venezuela, maintain the military-civilian balance established in the late 1950s? Could she survive the centrifugal pressures created by convenient political party compacts and exacerbated by the power of drug lords? Until it can be shown that armies can provide viable alternatives to whatever civilian-dominated governmental structures provide, the answer to each of these questions should continue to be "yes." Sources most comparable to those from the more southerly countries do indicate that the military mind in northern South America and Mexico has functioned in much the same way. The same essential ideas have prevailed. Thus, professional militarism there must be considered at least latent. As such, it could be expressed in more traditional ways. This may not mean that any of these countries is on the brink of a *golpe de estado,* but the brink may be nearer than some are willing to either consider or contemplate.

Juan Carlos, King of Spain, told the armed forces of his realm in January 1978 that they should demonstrate to the world that "we are capable of living in peace and in democracy and in liberty. But we must do it with the power necessary to duly influence, direct, and control events, in order that these do not control us and disturb us to the extent that they lead us to excesses or exaggerations as extreme as stagnation or retrocession."[61] The Bourbon monarch could have lent copies of his Epiphany address to the presidents of either Mexico, Venezuela, or Colombia, for there the issues were much the same: both military and civilian leaders were aware that they had to work hard to assure that extremes should not influence unduly the status quo. Times must not change too much. *El Rey* told his uniformed colleagues in 1980 that "in my heart, throughout my entire being, my love for the fatherland exists side by side with a military spirit, and I feel eternally identified with my companions of the armed forces."[62] The sentiments of *El Rey* were very much like those of Venezuelan presidents of the post-1958 years.

Rafael Caldera, for example, claimed in an address of 31 December 1970 that "the Republic is proud of its armed forces, and these sally forth at this time to enjoy the full appreciation, the respect, and the esteem of their compatriots."[63] Another Venezuelan, a general, noted in the same issue of *Revista de las Fuerzas Armadas* that "we have nurtured in the fertile ground of the armed forces the seed of love and respect for the nation's constitution, and of a total adherence to the sovereign popular will."[64] Mutually reinforced attention and cooperation maintained military-civilian relations at an intensive level in both Venezuela and Colombia.

Just before the fall of Rojas Pinilla in 1957, a Colombian lieutenant colonel claimed that "in our country the government of the armed forces has begun to address the greatest national problems with the idea of continuing [under civilian direction] to do so in the future."[65] He went on to emphasize civic action and military colonization of remote areas as means of pacifying and developing his country. A few years later a Venezuelan colonel would argue that in the event mobilization became a necessity, Venezuela would have a hard time accomplishing it. The national railroad network was a disgrace; "the circulatory system" of the national economy "did not function well even under normal conditions."[66] Such arguments were quite in keeping with discussions of mobilization, interior colonization, and development appearing in the professional journals of countries either on the brink of, or already experiencing manifest professional militarism.

Venezuelans would continue to discuss in understandable forms the circular relationships between national security, economic and social development, geopolitics, civic action, mobilization, and planning into the 1980s.[67] That they did so indicates the rapid development of a mentality similar to that found to the south, a grappling with the same problems at roughly the same time, under different circumstances. The fact that Venezuelan sources do not exude the same vehemence as those from further south indicates that, until the early 1990s, at least, balanced military-civilian relationships still constituted a most important circumstance, and that the need for an acutely distinct military ideology was not yet necessarily of circumstantial significance.

Over in Colombia, national security, as defined in Venezuela and elsewhere, would figure in military literature from the Rojas Pinilla years forward.[68] Statements such as this one characterized discussions: "It is necessary that the politically or administratively responsible civilian have a clear understanding of national defense; and at the same time the officer charged with provision of national defense be grounded in economics, sociology, etc."[69] The author of this statement, a colonel, did not see his way clear to specify just what other field officers should be familiar with, but he did make it clear that defense was a two-way operation. Colombians were no less concerned than their neighbors to the east with the complexities of defense, internal security, and development, "etc."

It was the military, "the basis and the structure of civicism, that had brought peace [such as it was] to Colombia in the twentieth century—after a nineteenth century in which civilians had succeeded in keeping the nation weak and internally divided."[70] But, it seemed, the effort had not been enough. Peace (such as it was) notwithstanding, one of Colombia's leading military figures would have to argue in 1967 that the country was still woefully disunited, underdeveloped, and, consequently, incapable of defending itself against internal or external enemies. In a neat turn, General Alvaro Valencia Tovar called Colombia a "Mediterranean country."[71] Centralism and poor peripheral development still prevented the country from exploiting either its Caribbean or Pacific littorals; centripetal politics and loyalties still denied Colombia a coordinated, stable government. This was all tantamount to labeling Colombia the "sick man of South America."

In a similar vein, Colombians would be told again in 1976 that "the army is perhaps the only institution with sufficient cohesion, capable of furthering certain social processes."[72] This apparently forceful assertion of a military role (originally made in 1973) was, in context, merely a call for participation in infrastructual development projects. It was entirely in keeping with most Colombian literature on the role of the armed forces published in the 1960s and 1970s.[73] Colombians were striving hard to maintain a balance. By the 1980s that balance came under greater pressure, as both ideological and narcotics-based challenges to the authority of the Colombian state drew the army ever further into national affairs. Accordingly, two officers would warn their colleagues that drug traffickers now were virtually sovereign in parts of the country and were threatening to establish a parallel economy over which the central government would have no control.[74] This fact would revive interest in national security and the army's internal role in maintaining it against all foes. It also rekindled speculation as to just how great that role ought to be.

Major Gustavo A. Flórez Valeriano, a Honduran, wrote for Colombians in 1981 that "when the armed forces decide to take over the government of a nation it is not because of ambition or a desire for the enormous responsibility of directing the nation's destiny; if they do [take power] it is because of situations in which those discontented with the traditional system of democracy want to violently and radically replace its structure with a communist one."[75] Flórez went on to state that constitutional obligations could compel the armed forces to seize power in order to preserve sovereignty and preclude anarchy. This was very close in tone and content to the pre-*golpe* utterances of officers in countries to the south. Colombia's shaky Conservative-Liberal consensus had found little recent favor in military circles, but little would be done to express disfavor beyond guarded expressions of professional opinion. Some of these took the form of geopolitical browsings or found their way into the odd essay on mobilization.[76] A basis certainly existed for professional militarism in Colombia, but the sociopolitical and economic challenges were too great, and the capabilities of the armed forces too limited for military professionals to transform themselves. How long this could continue only time would tell.

This was probably true for Mexico also. Based principally on what went on after the 1968 bloodbath of Tlatelolco, some would begin to view Mexico's military as being in the process of forming a mentality comparable to that of Colombia's *uniformados*. Greater emphasis would be placed on the army's internal imperative role after 1968 than at any time before. Civic action, counterinsurgency campaigns, and the *apertura democrática* of the Luis Echeverría administration (1970–76), would affect the army's outlook on the steady crumbling of the great revolutionary edifice.[77] So would the economic collapse of the early 1980s and the electoral contest of 1988.

Despite all the revolutionary rhetoric, the Mexican army represented *el pueblo* no more than the groups who made up the political and economic elites did, and Mexican officers continued to represent a lower-middle-class sector far better than most of their Latin American colleagues did. Theirs had been a steady diet of revolutionary propaganda,[78] but acceptance of this propaganda was no longer assured by the incremental successes of revolutionary programs. It may depend, in times to come, on how well the state and its guiding power, the Institutional Revolutionary Party, cope with a Mexico that looked in the late 1980s and early 1990s like just another Latin American country with overwhelming problems, rather than like an exceptional case of national development.

There is, as it were, a manifest difference between the recent writings of Argentines, Brazilians, Chileans, and Peruvians and comparable material produced by Colombians, Mexicans, and Venezuelans. It is more than one of quantity. It is contextual. It is one facet of the difference between armies, on the one hand, whose pre–World War II European heritage linked them to an imaginary past that never was and to political traditions and continental-style power relationships with long histories, and, on the other, armies whose professional development was either indigenous or more recent. Despite being Latin Americans, the second group had not yet endured experiences conducive to the flourishing of manifest professional militarism.

The armies of Mexico, Colombia, and Venezuela had not yet developed institutionally to a point where they could have offered anything but short-term theoretical responses to perceived collapses of polities. They had neither the experience nor the support to act like southern South Americans. Nor had their thought and self-perception yet evolved to the point where they would lose the ability to understand themselves and know their limitations. This may have enabled them to forecast the possible results of institutional political action. The fact remains, of course, that most of the immediate social and economic causes of institutional *golpes de estado* showed no signs of abating in Mexico, Colombia, and Venezuela. Because professional militarism is a contextual phenomenon, the apparent end of the time of the generals in the late 1980s might still, therefore, be viewed with a cautious eye.

Even further from the point where professional militarism became viable were countries of the Caribbean and Central America, and Bolivia, Ecuador, and Paraguay. Despite a few superficial similarities, these armies were not nearly as professionally advanced as those of Mexico or the South American countries mentioned above. There are several reasons for this, principal among which is the role of the United States. Neither through military nor civilian influence did the "Latin American policy" of the United States achieve the stated goals of each: professionalism and democratic consensus. Quite the contrary. Inconsistent and short-sighted policies regularly encouraged military leaders to act according to their professional beliefs or lack thereof. In the political arena some—both the least and most rigidly professional—found themselves exposed to the greatest temptation of politics: personalism. Wherever the United States had the initial responsibility for professionalization of an officer corps, a principal result was the early personalization of the profession. Where an earlier outside influence faded and where the United States then exerted other forms of influence on weak polities, much the same occurred. It makes little sense to ask "what if the United States had been involved in southern South America, and France and Germany had been active in the Caribbean?" The fact is that this was not the case. Guatemala, El Salvador, Honduras, Nicaragua, Haiti, and Santo Domingo stand as examples of the disastrous results of half-hearted U.S. involvement in the development of professionalism. So did Cuba (before 1959). Where personalism dominated a political-military fusion over decades, as in Paraguay, it was much the same. In Bolivia, where a revolutionary-military fusion failed miserably, a similar situation resulted. Despite (increasingly fading) memories of its birth under German tutelage, associations with social reform movements of the 1930s and 1940s, and its rebirth after 1952 as a revolutionary partner à la Mexico, the Bolivian officer corps remained a parody of professionalism throughout the time of the generals.

Bolivians had once written very much like Peruvians and Mexicans. In the 1950s they had been devoted revolutionaries—like Mexicans had been for years, and like Peruvians of the 1960s and 1970s would be.[79] But by the 1970s little remained in Bolivian military literature that indicated a continuation of professional development toward anything resembling professional militarism. The same must be said for El Salvador and Guatemala.[80] Paraguayan literature of a type comparable to expressions of professional militarism might kindly be called mimetic, unkindly scandalously hypocritical.[81] "With General Stroessner as the soul of its people and as its civic consciousness," after all, "Paraguay is and will be forever the heart of the free world."[82] With generals like Alfredo Stroessner and the Bolivians, Ecuadorans, Central Americans, and Caribbeans who figured so destructively in their countries' affairs, professional militarism per se was unthinkable.

Although general conditions favorable to latent professional militarism did prevail in much of Latin America, then, its ultimate manifestation was limited to four countries. Despite so much comparability of thought and self-perception, it took much more to turn these into action. Despite so many readily available comparisons, there was a significant parting of the ways between them, their Latin American neighbors, and other parts of the world.

In other parts of the world the military profession changed more over the post–World War II decades than it did in Latin America. This is owing partially to the fact that much of the world changed more than Latin America did. Less-developed and politically inexperienced parts of the world—in Africa and Asia—did resemble Latin America, but in most of

Europe and the English-speaking world a civilian consensus dominated within the polity in the post–World War II years. In Latin Europe, military-backed regimes came to an end in Iberia and democracy tottered on in Italy. These were times of change rather than simply changing times. Change itself had become as important as the passage of time, and the military profession in most parts of the world remained reactive both to recent and historical variables. This reactive quality and the exigency of political action marked manifest South American professional militarism. It influenced the latent variety characteristic of the rest of the region too. This was not the case where change over time was fundamental, rather than partial or superficial.

For example, there is no body of Latin American military literature comparable in tone to that of European countries and the United States dealing with psychology and human factors, leadership and man-management, and the preeminence of the profession as a place where official careerism could lead to a skill or vocation of practical value upon demobilization or retirement. Most Latin American officer corps of the post–World War II decades can be said to have served in "different times," and this confirms it. In André Maurois' remarkably perceptive *Captains and Kings*, his "Philosopher" asks: "Why, in such pacific and favorable conditions, should we submit to a discipline which is only useful in exceptional circumstances?"[83] Why, indeed, should soldiers and officers behave in times of peace as if they were momentarily on their way to the battlefield? Answers to this question necessarily varied according to time and place.

Much was being written everywhere in the decades after the war about the social and developmental roles of armies, about the vocational benefits of service stints. Latin Americans would continue to champion the profession as molder of citizens and men, builder of nations, and maker of men out of boys, but never (in print) as a way to retire early and pursue a second, civilian career under peaceful conditions the way others did routinely. This constitutes a dramatic contrast with wide-reaching ramifications.

Peace and its benefits, it was believed, had given the military new prestige in the United States, until Vietnam, at least. In peacetime the United States could more readily achieve its national purposes,[84] and individuals, by extension, could realize the American dream better when open conflict was avoided. "After a history of peacetime neglect," wrote one officer in 1971, "the military establishment has enjoyed twenty years of prestige unknown before in American history. We owe this status to the threat of communism, and the complex apparatus constructed to wage this peace."[85] But waging peace was not all that easy. Politics, intra–executive branch struggles, and funding disputes all weighed upon the professional mind.

And what if the communist menace should prove less than frightful someday? What if a war be lost? In the decades following World War II the United States would be passing through a cultural revolution in which generations of youthful and inexperienced Americans challenged the status quo as never before. Traditional values fared poorly with younger Americans. From the 1960s forward, social causes took precedence over ideological ones. Rising expectations, more often associated with developing societies, influenced young men. Better opportunities for education and advancement in the civilian sector rivaled military service as a way to get a start or get ahead. Conscription became socially and culturally unacceptable to many with access to another way of life, especially during the Vietnam era. Changing times and social change now had an impact on the U.S. military mind quite comparable to that which they had on Latin American thought.[86] The entire second half of the twentieth century might be perceived as the most dynamic period of change of all time by a military man. But proximity to events clouded the vision of even the most perceptive uniformed observers everywhere.

One consistently perceived change—everywhere but in Latin America—was that involving the proper relationship of officers to men, so it was not unusual for it to concern U.S. officers. A 1971 essay in *Parameters,* for example, dealt with leadership skills of U.S. army officers as if they were essentially managers.[87] No Latin American officer would ever have taken this sort of argument seriously; management was for bureaucrats, not "leaders." Many characteristics traditionally associated (ad nauseam) with leadership were now discussed in U.S. sources as simply "management skills": technical expertise, communications ability, and interpersonal relations.[88] Technology and its mastery was becoming as important as mastery of men.

But there were occasional exceptions. General Edward C. Meyer would write in 1980 that management was in fact not the same as leadership; technocrats were not leaders of men, cost analysis not the result of a true vocation. In an obvious response to numerous changes affecting the Department of Defense during and shortly after the Kennedy and Johnson presidencies, Meyer wrote, "Forgotten [is] the fact that employees of Sears Roebuck and Company or General Motors Corporation were not asked to give up their lives for corporate cost-effectiveness. Leaders cannot, must not, bind themselves to a one-answer, one-method scientology."[89] Meyer's argument was akin to some made by Latin Americans. Its allusions to old-style leadership techniques, especially the use of psychology, made it comparable, as well, to some European sources.

A 1981 argument made by Lieutenant Colonel (chaplain) Malcolm J. Brummit likewise alluded to such techniques. Acknowledging that a volunteer-based army brought with it problems of command and leadership, Brummit cited "management" as a major difficulty. Depersonalization of leadership and human relations had made it more difficult for leaders to lead. The army should not be just another job for officers and men, he believed, for the military profession was still "a principled, rigid, disciplined, often undemocratic institution entrusted with the mission of serving the defense needs of the country."[90] Army life was one of sacrifice, dedication; without these qualities defense was quite impossible. As shown in these pages, army chaplains could often write in a way that made them *más militares que los militares,* no matter what their origin.

Tentative resistance to cold, cost-analytical management (evidence of its perceived threat) continued well into the 1980s. The best officers, one author would claim, were those who could lead, manage, and command, and do all equally well.[91] No matter how many officers wrote about the need to maintain the old ways in the face of change, though, young men in decreasing numbers saw the army as much of a career.

The decline of career appeal, some reasoned, even as the tide appeared to turn during the Reagan years, was a result of too much "management," lack of opportunity for rapid advancement, too heterogeneous an officer corps, and a surfeit of better opportunities to "lead and achieve" in civilian life.[92] This, of course, did not apply to Latin Americans and others from the developing world, for in these areas theories of traditional leadership still prevailed over flow charts for modern management. So did opportunities. Postretirement careers might appeal to officers everywhere, of course, but few would ever be candid on the subject. One U.S. officer, writing back in the 1950s, had opined that retired officers might make excellent teachers, experienced as they were with training, managing, and leading. Teaching would also be a way, he thought, to continue active service to the nation, "furthering its educational aims, creating responsible citizens, enriching their lives, and providing for future defense needs."[93] Like military service, education was a field where leadership (and management) skills could benefit all. Latin Americans might have concurred with this.

U.S. officers had long realized that relationships to their men and to the civilian sector were changing,[94] but the army of the 1980s evinced none of the essential ingredients of even latent professional militarism. It had suffered consequences of peacetime apathy (and support), social upheavals accompanying civil rights and student movements of the 1960s, and the Vietnam tragedy. The army had weathered the storms swirling around man-management, cost analysis, and depersonalization. But it would never be sufficiently affected by anything that would deter it from a traditional role. Nothing would threaten its existence or persuade it that there was a lack of consensus for continuation of the sociopolitical order within which it had been so buffeted.[95] However badly U.S. officers might think they were faring in the 1970s and 1980s, there was no internal enemy. Leadership, that essential of both professionalism and militarism, would never be the catch-all it had become in Latin America. National security had quite a different meaning for the military professionals of the United States than it did for the professional militarists of Latin America.

The separate ways were slightly less distinguishable between Latin America and Europe. As seen in discussions of military service and *Innere Führung,* Germans also had adapted to changing times. From the 1960s well into the 1980s, Germans would discuss leadership in a context focusing on clashes between the individualism of modern society and the organic qualities of military life.[96] Italians would recognize grudgingly that vocational and technical training were often the only things that attracted men to the army.[97] Germans, Italians, and Frenchmen all showed interest in human-factors psychology and management techniques as essentials of leadership.[98] A military career was often discussed as merely a "springboard to a civilian career."[99] Even Spaniards, once *El Caudillo*'s time had passed and Spain's NATO era had begun, showed themselves able to make some adjustments—all the while expressing great concerns.[100] Amid the ultramodernity of Western Europe, the present would not triumph entirely over the past. European authors, while recognizing the necessity for adjustment to change, still had misgivings about directions being taken by their profession.

To the east, Soviet officers, hewing to the party line, at least until 1991, would indicate that they, too, understood change was a permanent (possibly a dialectical) thing. They would make many cases for a military-socialist partnership in progress. They also would see this as a feature of Third World sociopolitical evolution. Out there change was imminent, "but what kind of change it will be—progressive or reactionary, contributing to social progress or hampering it—depends, in each concrete case, on what forces have authority over the army, who gives it its program of action."[101] Red Army officers could agree in principle with the most outspoken Latin American anti-Marxists on this issue. Collapse of their government in 1991 made it possible that they might just agree more than in principle.

They might, for example, find it institutionally convenient to think along the same lines Chileans were supposed to think in the early 1990s. "The armed forces and *carabineros,* being armed corps, are naturally obedient and not deliberative. The forces dependent upon the ministry charged with national defense are moreover professional, hierarchical, and disciplined."[102] Or so the Chilean Constitution of 1980 would have had Chileans believe. In the time of the generals Chilean *uniformados* had decided on their own "program of action." They intended to see it through too.

In much of Latin America, professionalism still had no place for the likes of man-management or political determination of "programs of action." Whereas in other parts of the world officers were doing their best to adapt leadership to man-management and human-factors psychology (or vice versa), or to hold on to the old ways by giving them new civilian-approved labels, Latin Americans barely mentioned the new-fangled ways. When they did, it would be well within the context of established themes of public affairs, contributions to socioeconomic progress, national security, and the internal enemy.[103] Specific references were few and far between.

In Latin America officers remained convinced, as was one French officer, that "the military must function as the image of the nation. It must reflect a coherent and realistic policy. It must evince traditional virtues adapted and refined according to the exigencies of our times. It must, in fine, be motivated by a permanent devotion to duty."[104] If this sort of traditional argument could still find its way into French military literature of the 1970s, it should not be a surprise that Latin Americans, still so fond of the pre-1939 French military tradition, would find it so conveniently applicable to their own situations.

The unique finishing touches that Argentines, Brazilians, Chileans, and Peruvians put on their literary definitions of professionalism would help transform it into militarism every bit as much as would seizures of power. Contemporary refinements of thought and self-perception by Colombians, Mexicans, and Venezuelans showed that many of the same ideas could become popular among them even if, perforce, civilian political systems still enjoyed their support. Elsewhere in Latin America the comparisons remained incidental and fragmentary: different drummers and different ways for different armies.

Europeans, North Americans, and even some Latin Americans recognized these times of change and their meaning by acquiescing to the fundamental shifts in military-civilian relationships that altered the ways in which soldiers served their country. But Argentines, Brazilians, Chileans, and Peruvians, so up-to-date in many ways, unfortunately represented their present as dramatically different from that of Europe and North America. Their writings considered in this chapter show that their own present confused them. So they would defy it by seeking either to reestablish the past or shape the future. When they did so they became lost in the shadows of their own era. It is now necessary to study professional militarism as an aspect of recent times of change, as distinguished from changing times, that is, when change itself is the prime characteristic of the epoch, not time's passage.

EIGHT

"Invertebrate America": Contemplating the Future in Times of Change

The present lack of solidarity produces a phenomenon which is very characteristic of our public life—*anyone has strength enough to undo*—the soldier, the workman, this or that politician, this group or that of newspapers—*but no one has strength enough to do anything, not even to make sure of his own rights.*
—José Ortega y Gasset, *Invertebrate Spain* (1921)

I have a feeling that the *hablador* not only brings current news but also speaks of the past. He is probably also the memory of the community, fulfilling a function similar to that of the jongleurs and troubadors of the Middle Ages.—Mario Vargas Llosa, *El hablador* (1988)

The time of the generals drew to a close late in 1989 with the election of Patricio Aylwin Azócar to the presidency of Chile. Or did it? Such a question suggests that professional militarism now be studied briefly from a present-future perspective, and that new themes and contexts might be considered. Such is the purpose of this chapter. The past-present orientation of the previous seven chapters has helped to elucidate the intense pressures exerted by changing times and a new world paradigm on traditional role definitions and world views. As earlier pages have shown, military professionalism was a shared experience to varying degrees, and its metamorphosis into manifest professional militarism was a contextual phenomenon, based heavily on the clash between idealized past and unpleasant present. Standing out from the rest of Latin America and the rest of the world because of this clash, Argentines, Brazilians, Chileans, and Peruvians would attest to both the typicality and (ultimately) the uniqueness of officer-class thought and self-perceptions in the decades since World War II.

Seen in this light, professional militarism, especially in its manifest sense, might be considered as simply an inability or unwillingness to adjust to change. In the "times of change" with which this chapter concerns itself, change appears to be more substantive than ever before; typicality and uniqueness of thought and self-perception exist, but in new settings. Change is the prime factor in futures being projected from the tumultuous events of late 1989 forward: culturally, diplomatically, economically, ideologically, and socially, not just politically. Europe and Asia are the scenes of ideological and imperial breakdowns, the USSR has indeed dissolved, the international Communist apparatus no longer functions, "redemocratization" (a concept fraught with definitional problems) staggers on in Eastern Europe and Latin America. The Middle East has been engulfed in war.

Through it all, certainly in the eyes of Latin Americans, the stance of the United States is still unclear. To many Latin American army leaders this is not surprising. Events of the late 1980s and early 1990s make their perception of change and all it entails as important as ever, especially within a shifting geopolitical framework. And it is perception that shapes responses. The thought and self-perception of professional militarists perpetuate almost with a vengeance a "memory of the community" that sustains the past. Might this perpetuate as well their propensity and willingness to act, to again "undo" what civilians may have done in some future time?

Most studies of the Latin American military have, consciously or unconsciously, compared and contrasted officers there with Europeans or North Americans. As social scientists carry on the study of military-civilian relations, the use of Western Europe or the U.S. as the most appropriate points of comparison and contrast for Latin America may prove invalid. The reformation of Eastern Europe, in which armies formerly influenced by Communist Party lines will play major roles, portends military-civilian adjustments there. This may happen in the West too, but it is too early to even tentatively forecast military roles with something other than a Warsaw Pact or a NATO to shape them. In Latin America the resurgence of personalism and *cuartelazo* (barrack revolt) activities in the countries where professional militarism had ostensibly raised military political action to a high level of sophistication may also be a portent. Augusto Pinochet's *caudillo*-like manipulation of the Chilean army, the Salvadoran *tanda* (graduating class) system of warlord politics, the persistence of hardline antipolitics officers like Argentina's Colonel Mohamed Alí Seineldín—are these the shadows of things to come as well?

Such examples make one wonder if Africa may be a more enlightening point of comparison for Latin America than Western Europe or the United States. Post-independence Africans were just beginning to attempt to make sense of their history when the time of the generals began in the 1960s. Well before Eastern Europeans would begin to do the same (again) in the 1980s, neocolonial African civilian systems had proved inappropriate, and the military had become an integral part of the political process. Should Africa become a more useful point of comparison, Latin America might in future decades be the standard by which both African and European (especially Eastern European) military-civilian relations are assessed.

The seventh chapter drew some sharp distinctions between Latin America and the rest of the world in the same way discussion of the "gift" did in the third chapter. And here, for example, selected geopolitical assertions and discussions of military attitudes toward women, appropriate to "times of change," indicate still other ways in which uniqueness can prevail over typicality, not only in Latin America, but elsewhere. Latin American geopoliticians never ceased to rely on outmoded theories to justify both actions at home and attitudes toward the United States. For the most part ignored in military literature until mid-century, women in the military and in civilian society became objects of attention everywhere soon thereafter. The contrasting views presented in this chapter also make it plain that Latin American resistance to change transcends changing times and traditional themes to remain strong in times of change. If this continues, might not the time of the generals repeat itself in Latin America—or come to pass in other parts of the world where democratic institutions prove weak and unable to respone to social and economic exigencies?

Transmittal of tradition across generations has lasting effects, and the exact nature of the transmitter(s) is significant. At about the same time Latin American generals began trying to provide solutions to their countries' dilemmas and Africans began to struggle with their heritage, Latin Americans were experiencing the great literary movement known as *El Boom*. Coincidence of *El Boom* with the time of the generals from the early 1960s to the 1970s, would result in a number of efforts by novelists to make sense out of their country's and their region's history at the same time militarists convinced themselves that they could. The "new novel," the subgenre to which recent prose efforts belong, is evidence of what may be a process of an intellectual vertebration in Latin America that transcends national boundaries. Central American cooperation (however tenuous) for regional peace, like-mindedness on matters of transnational debt obligations and U.S. policies, and dialogues involving intellectuals and writers all contributed to a heightened consciousness of *latinoamericanidad* (Latin Americanness, regional identity). "Times of change" bring new themes to the fore. Old themes may, in the long run, prove just as important in Latin America, for in "times of change," just as in "changing times," past, present, and future can become indistinguishable to men in uniform. This blurring of time is as essential to regional identity as is any meeting of minds. It is not unique to Latin America.

A Soviet colonel wrote in 1976 that "by strengthening its armed forces the Soviet Union does not threaten anybody, it proceeds exclusively from peaceful motives and due regard for the past and for the necessity to secure favorable conditions for the successful fulfillment of the grandiose plans of economic aid and cultural construction."[1] The future, in short, demanded that the Red Army continue all those roles it had been playing for decades. It is doubtful at present that a Russian army looks to the past with much regard now, but it may again. A U.S. general, writing in the following year, would state that the army officer "sees the present as a burden imposed by yesterday's ideas to be borne until tomorrow comes. . . . He tends to view the past as a time of intellectual opportunity, which if usefully exploited, will yield a sounder environment of action on the morrow."[2] Officers of the Cold War's principal adversaries could perceive their roles comparably as projections of the best of the past onto the future. U.S. officers still do. *Bundeswehr* officers would too,[3] and late in the 1980s French officers shifted ever so gradually away from the traditional Gaullist notion of military independence in favor of tighter cooperation with West Germany, Britain, and other North Atlantic Treaty Organization allies. In South America, Brazilians showed signs of rejecting much of the ESG national security–development doctrine that had sustained them since mid-century and which was an underpinning of the 1964 movement; Peruvians had reason to doubt the teachings of CAEM leaders who had led the 1968 movement. Change was continuity; continuity was change. Each was timeless. If this be true during the time of the generals, why not after it?

Past (idealized or not) and future (feared or not) met headlong in the contested present in Latin America and much of the developed world. Do they also meet one another likewise in less-developed areas? Is it conceivable that, say, Africa, especially Black Africa, provides anything like a reprise of Latin American military-civilian relations?

Africa suffered from the injustices of colonialism and from the intellectual baggage engendered by it far into the twentieth century. Though it did not endure as long as Ibero-American colonialism—from the early sixteenth century to the early nineteenth—it has lasted longer into modern history. African "nationalists" such as Ali Mazrui have argued that the impact of the West there was largely negative. Though not a new argument, the debate naturally rages on over the historical significance of the "westernized," "professional" military in neocolonial Africa. Africans and Africanists have dealt with the subject in ways similar to Latin Americans and Latin Americanists, giving substance to the idea that methodology and politics have as great an influence on the writing of history as history does on them.

One Nigerian scholar viewed African military disengagements from politics as signs of failure, rather than indications of tasks completed.[4] A French observer wrote in 1976 that African armies acted politically to protect their interests as much as for any other reason.[5] Both Ghanaian and Nigerian officers involved in 1966 overthrows would describe military political participation in terms of stabilization, purging, national redemption, and salvation.[6] Such arguments had become generic to militarism, professional or not, regardless of continent.

French and British sources cited in these pages attest to the fact that Europeans were greatly concerned with their former charges after independence.[7] They would point out, as would Africans themselves, that tribalism, factionalism, regional rivalries, generational differences, and antipolitical attitudes had all motivated army officers to overthrow civilian governments.[8] And, just as in Latin America, personalism was another motivating factor, there being no better example of it than former Sergeant Major of the African Rifles, Idi Amin Dada, "President for Life" of Uganda (1971–79). "Tell me, Mr. President," Queen Elizabeth II is reputed to have asked her Ugandan luncheon guest, one day in 1971 (after he arrived in London unexpectedly), "to what do we owe the honor of your visit?" "In Kampala," he replied, in his slow, deep voice, "[It is] very difficult to buy good pair size 14 brown shoes. So now I am President, I come to London."[9] So much for military professionalism and its attendant responsibilities in that part of British East Africa. So much for Latin America's monopoly on *outré* military bosses, patriarchs, and tyrants.

Views of the heritage left by the French in their part of Africa were generally more rosy.[10] But the fact remains that neither the neocolonial states of French, nor those of British, Africa would be free of a scourge that resembled more closely the personalism of nineteenth-century Spanish America than it did the professionalism and militarism of a century later. Not even Egypt compares very favorably with twentieth-century Latin America in terms of professional militarism. "Nasserism," in theory, was nothing very new. One day, though, might not Africa's twentieth-century personalism be studied alongside that of a Batista, a Pérez Jiménez, a Stroessner, a Trujillo—or even a Pinochet? Will African military leaders and civilians ever, as Léopold Sédar Senghor, Senegal's soldier-poet-president, asked, "see paradise beyond the horizon of legendary times?"[11] Will postcolonial Africa have to endure a "Latin American period" too? Is personalism really dead in Latin America, for that matter? By 1989 Paraguayan military authors had spent as much or more space and time lauding Alfredo Stroessner (president 1954–1989) and wars of the past as they had contemplating the present or the future. Up to the end of his rule Stroessner, that "strategist of peace and warrior of national grandeur," had had far more impact on his country than any true professional. This is true for the Somozas (in power from 1933 to 1979), whose *alabadas* (praises) were every bit as slavish.[12] Nicaragua and Paraguay resembled African military despotisms far more than Latin American countries where professional militarists held power. In the late 1980s and early 1990s, Chile, like Argentina (where the likes of Lieutenant Colonel Aldo Rico and Colonel Mohamed Alí Seineldín could still run amok), briefly teetered on the brink of personalism. Thus professional militarism in at least one case was by no means immune to the megalomaniacal personalism of the past. Time alone will tell how resilient are professionalism and militarism.

This is also the case for geopolitical thought and U.S.–Latin American military relations. By the last decade of the twentieth century, professional militarists had proved to all but themselves that there was no firm foundation on which to base most of their aspirations and theories. By the same time the United States had failed (depending on one's viewpoint) to either inhibit Latin American attempts to turn militaristic theory into practice or support the efforts of militarists to "save the West." The Cold War thawed, froze over, and then thawed again, but most Latin American officers still perceive it as simply a conflict to be lost on the local levels, especially after the West led on by the United States began to establish new ties to states of the former USSR and Eastern Europe. The United States could or would do no right; Marxism was still winning by default, despite so much change.

José Maria Eça de Queiroz, Portugal's great nineteenth-century *pensador,* once wrote that "Russia will continue to be Russia—that is, an immense empire."[13] Eça was thinking of the imperial Russia of Nicholas II, of course. Latin American officers eight decades later would still be saying much the same about the Marxist-Leninist Soviet Union and its satellite empire, then (they were convinced) with a foothold in Latin America. The Eastern European and Soviet events of 1989–1992 would not erase thirty years of Cuban revolutionary existence. Nor would they immediately cause either professionals or militarists to change their thinking about communists. Because of this they would continue to view dimly much of what the United States would do to facilitate accomodation with the USSR under Mikhail Gorbachev, and with Russia under Boris Yeltsin. Some *uniformados* might convince themselves that they had rolled back the "red tide," but their civilian counterparts saw little substance to their arguments. Very few officers took the collapse of communist regimes to be evidence of liberal democracy's or pluralism's triumph, especially when they surveyed its state in their own countries and considered the continued ambivalence of the United States in world and hemispheric affairs.

Admiral Chester Nimitz had correctly claimed back in 1948 that the United States controlled the world's oceans.[14] Thirty years later a Chilean colonel, Víctor Chaves Dailhe, could rightly assert that the United States' naval power no longer dominated any ocean, much less the Pacific.[15] Between these two opinions, woven into both traditional and inward-directed geopolitical thinking, there was hard evidence of sustained, even reinvigorated professional military disdain for the United States. Some of this disdain was expressed in discussions of the growing power of the Red Navy, some in reactions to a perceived lack of concern shown by the United States of America, especially under President Jimmy Carter, for its Latin neighbors. Until the early 1990s *glasnost* and *perestroika* meant much less to Latin American officers than they did to others. The tone of their traditional hostility changed very little.

North American concentration on post-Vietnam changes, the search for new service military roles, man-management, and other seemingly parochial problems of the 1980s indicated serious debate in civilian as well as military circles over the decision-making and war-making capabilities of what had been briefly considered the world's foremost defense establishment. So did reassessment of defense needs in 1991 after the cessation of hostilities in the Persian Gulf. North Americans had rarely been viewed as good leaders by Latin Americans, for leadership, intelligence, planning, initiative—all these and more—were seen as being in short supply north of the Río Bravo. Latin Americans would assert often over the decades that only the United States' numerical, logistical, and economic superiority had won the century's major war. The victors even debated this themselves, which was therefore all the more reason for professional militarists to keep proclaiming their own world views, doctrines (however vapid) of security and defense, and their definitions of defense, leadership, and planning. What North Americans had appeared unwilling or incapable of doing in the name of national security in their own "backyard," Latin Americans still wanted to do, either genuinely believing in it or using it as a justification for abuses and excesses. Geopolitics dictated it. So did patriotism, regionalism, and anti-U.S. feelings.

Often regionalism and geopolitics were used to assert *latinoamericanidad* as much as professional militarism. Argentina's 1966 military rising, for example, was referred to as "an act in accordance with the great majority of Argentines . . . the most genuine expression of national being and feeling, its most perfect, its most sensitive and effective interpreter."[16] General Villegas had emphasized domestic regional development in this 1968 essay, but he also hinted at an international type of regionalism. It was just one more thing that a "great majority of Argentines" wanted, hence the *golpe* of 1966. Other officers from other countries also linked international and regional development. An Ecuadoran lieutenant colonel reminded his fellows of their country's precarious position between Brazil, Colombia, and Peru in a 1969 essay.[17] Another Argentine called for a greater international role for his country just a few years later.[18] Villegas by this time had developed a scheme for Argentine-Brazilian hydroelectric cooperation in a lengthy RESGA piece.[19] Ecuador will most probably never improve her territorial situation vis-à-vis Brazil, Colombia, and Peru, and Argentina's international role beyond South America will probably continue to be peripheral, but a cooperative hydroelectric effort with Brazil did result in growth of energy output in the La Plata basin during the 1980s. At about this same time Brazilians were thinking more about their need for water and land routes to the Pacific: river navigation, cooperative railroad ventures, and the use of Pacific ports.[20] They had also increased their writing output on Brazil's role in the South Atlantic and the La Plata region.[21] Brazilians, by the 1980s, were also ready to indicate that they had less than total confidence in the United States' ability to defend the hemisphere from communism. Both Brazil and Argentina showed considerable, consistent independent-mindedness when referring to relations with the United States well into the 1980s, partly for political purposes, and partly for genuine and traditional reasons. Professional militarists were never surrogates or "proconsuls." They show few signs of changing, even in the aftermath of political failure.

As they had during the changing times discussed in chapter 1, "democratically inclined" Colombians and Venezuelans continued to show an awareness of their own regional status in essays of the mid-1980s that treated the circum-Caribbean region. The Panamanian Isthmus and Central America would be discussed as "problem zones" with which powers in the vicinity should be perpetually concerned.[22] In 1968 a Guatemalan had shrewdly dissected the Western Hemisphere into blocs, each with identity other than that of just "hemispheric" nations. Citing (of course) Karl Ritter, Friedrich Ratzel, Rudolf Kjellen, Halford Mackinder, Alfred Mahan, Karl Haushofer, and Lord Curzon, he broke down the hemisphere into several blocs: the United States and Canada, the Caribbean and the Central American isthmus, the Andes, Brazil, and the Platine region. Colombia and Venezuela, he noted (and he was not alone) were associated with the Caribbean and Central America. Chile and Argentina could be tied together in the Southern Cone. Brazil was a subregion in and of itself.[23] America had become "invertebrate," disconnected, divided against itself, he averred, and the Kremlin was even then taking advantage of the development. Most geopolitical writing since that time guides one toward an "Invertebrate America" conclusion, as if other themes do not, despite assertions of regionalism.

It has already been pointed out that Argentines and Brazilians have had a long-term vital interest in the South Atlantic. Already, in the early years of the century, a power rivalry existed between them that could be traced back to the nineteenth century and even to the colonial period. It would show up in print in various ways before and during the 1964–1989 quarter century, contributing further to the concept of "Invertebrate America." Professional militarists blamed the U.S. as well as the USSR for the region's woes. In a 1977 essay Peru's Mercado Jarrín recognized Brazil's continental importance by arguing that South Americans, and Brazilians specifically, should avoid involvement in conflicts between the United States and the USSR.[24] Brazilians themselves would evince a kind of concern for the rest of the world different from the Peruvian geopolitician's. Carlos de Meira Mattos' 1977 book envisioned a Nigerian-Angolan-Brazilian triangle as a stabilizing element for the region—and as front against the white African south.[25] He was not the only Brazilian who would see the west coast of Africa as a sphere of influence for a new South American "subregion."[26] Attention was also paid to the South Atlantic–Southern Cone–Antarctic as a grander sphere of activity for the two regional rivals,[27] owing, often, to a perceived lack of influence by the United States—at least until the end of the 1980s.

By the time Chileans had begun to project geopolitics outward their own wariness of the United States had been increased by the hardening of relations between the two hemispheric rivals. Captain Luis Bravo Bravo's 1979 claim that the United States was "sounding retreat" in the postwar years was a clear challenge to U.S. leadership.[28] Chile's Pacific location allowed her little possibility to construct triangles like the fanciful Brazil–Nigeria–Angola structure; there could be no feasible Chile–Korea–Taiwan Pacific defense arrangement,[29] and the tenuous Chile–New Zealand–Australia economic relationship of the 1980s was no substitute, for Chile was not the leading economic partner. However, Chileans did continue until the late 1980s fancifully to see their role as blocking any

Soviet incursion in the eastern margins of the Pacific.[30] The fact that no evidence existed to support the ideology-based geopolitical claims of Southern Cone professional militarists failed to deter their model-building. Nor did European events of 1989–1992. But this did not mitigate their hostility toward the United States.

Over on the other side of the continent, interest in Africa would go beyond the possible strategic advantages for Brazil owing to color or language affinity. "Luso-tropicalism," that ingenious term devised by Gilberto Freyre to connote Portugal's successes beyond Europe, served to encourage Brazilians to theorize to their heart's content—and beyond. "The Soviet Union quietly takes over in the South Atlantic in direct proportion to the withdrawal of the United States from that area,"[31] a Brazilian navy captain wrote in 1976. Another, writing in that year, believed that Argentina could not be trusted because of its fixation on the Malvinas and its Antarctic territorial disputes with Chile. Its ties with white South Africa precluded endorsement of any joint African policy that would constructively serve the interests of Brazil and Black Africa as well.[32] Some policy toward Africa was needed, continued this source, for the (perceived) inability of Africans to withstand either Soviet penetration or irresponsible military political action now made it appear that they were headed into an age of militarism.[33] By the end of the 1980s the issue of Soviet penetration had ceased to attract much attention, but Brazilians still were interested in African ties.

The world of the 1970s and 1980s appeared far more dangerous to Latin American geopoliticians than it had two decades earlier. As they continued to look outward, one wonders if they were overlooking or just misunderstanding what was going on at home. Their long-term interest in geopolitics now buttressed their resistance to influences from the north. It had become a vehicle for excessively convoluted, self-reinforcing, overlapping currents of thought: shadows on the mind. It may be the single most pervasive element of Latin American professional militarism, that which perpetuates and gives substance to it. For all the attention paid to change, roles, leadership, politics, ideology, and religion, the use of geopolitics to frame domestic and foreign policy would prevail. Years after it became unfashionable to discuss global or regional strategy in Haushoferian terms, many Latin Americans nevertheless continued to do so, and by the end of the 1980s nothing indicated that they would do otherwise. There were few indications that they really understood themselves or their countries, but there were many signs that they ignored real causes and effects. How much this affects their responses to times of change in the rest of the world will determine their professional attitudes on numerous national issues in coming years.

Whenever the subject of male-female relations (and the impact of sociocultural change on them) has come up, for example, Latin Americans have betrayed a propensity for ignoring causes and effects unacceptable, in their opinion, to maintenance of tradition. Latin American women, whether in uniform or in civilian life, remained second-class citizens, whereas in the military literature of other parts of the world there were significant attitudinal shifts. Both male and female officers worldwide have written with great care in recent decades about the increasing numbers of women in career service, about "officers and ladies." Because traditional male-female relationships changed less in Latin America, women in the military there fared poorly in comparison to Europe and the United States, where there would be a far greater emphasis on women as participants in the process of socioeconomic change. In Latin America, for all the interest in national security, modernization, development, and regional geopolitical adjustments, internal social change per se would be consistently seen as a threat to national interests.

By the early 1960s, women could vote at the national level in all countries of the Organization of American States, the United States being the first and Paraguay being the last to extend suffrage. Women were liable for obligatory military service by the early 1980s in Chile, Ecuador, Peru, and Venezuela, and for some form of national service in half the hemisphere's countries. One Latin American author claimed that ten percent of West Point's cadet corps was composed of women and that, whereas general and admiral ranks could be attained by women in the United States, the highest rank yet attained in Latin America was that by one Uruguayan female colonel.[34] Political and economic improvements, the author went on to argue, were not accompanied by social or cultural change (defying the process of change as experienced in the United States and Europe). Latin American women were still women, nothing more, neither as voters nor as officers, than they ever had been.

With rare exception, Latin American military literature confirms this. The odd paean to Eva Duarte de Perón notwithstanding,[35] Argentine military writers, when they deigned to consider women, did so in tones that can be described as patronizing only by stretching both one's tolerance and objectivity. In a 1971 book, for example, one Argentine colonel delivered a twenty-seven-page discourse on the "biological subalternity" of the fairer sex.[36] Women talked too much, complained about their husbands, and resorted to *el tuteo,* the use of familiar verb forms, much too quickly. Colonel Luis Gozzoli thought that too much idle time spent under hair dryers induced women to bare all in "verbal hemorrhages." His was the most blatant attack on women, but it was not the only one of the postwar era. In most sources women fared about as well as did Indians and peasants in discussions devoted to internal security, the social role, development, and the like. Examples from Chile and Mexico, two apparently dissimilar professional settings, lead to such a conclusion and confirm this kind of resistance to change.

In Chile the Pinochet regime consistently claimed to be the liberator of womankind, and in some economic ways this was true. In the land of the living revolution, Mexican military literature bound women to *La Revolución* in a way that implied certain types of behavior were truly revolutionary but others were not. In both countries the reality was that civilian women and those in uniform were expected to stay in their place socially and culturally. Neither professional militarists nor military revolutionists would argue otherwise.

Women's place, according to Chile's *primera dama,* was as a participant in the various activist organizations established by the regime following the *golpe* of 1973. Chilean women, she claimed, were now totally included in the responsibility for specific national projects.[37] Yet all the while they were expected to maintain their traditional femininity, added one *uniformada.*[38] Numerous historical examples would be given of patriotic, feminine Chileans, ranging from Pedro de Valdivia's conquest companion, Inez de Suárez, to women who had served gallantly in the War of the Pacific, in order to convince *chilenas* that they had always played "national-military" roles. Gabriela Mistral even received an occasional mention as a woman of accomplishment, but these were merely public relations arguments. When it came down to national security, the Cold War, Chile's (geopolitical) place in the world, development, et cetera, women were relegated to the all-important role of childbearers. Whatever else they might do, argued one expert on national security, *chilenas* should have at least four children in order that the state have enough people to carry on the developmental tasks assigned it.[39] Family planning (which, along with matrimony, was considered a matter of national security) did not mean birth control to the "liberated" women of post-1973 Chile. Family planning was an essential of national security, "not in its simple instinctual form, but within the domain of reason or what has been termed 'responsible parenthood.'"[40] The rising birthrate among lower-income groups and an alarming number of abortions among the higher were seen as detrimental to the maintenance of all that was good in hierarchical Chilean family life. Official claims that women enjoyed greater economic and decision-making leeway in professionally militarized Chile—their own cadet corps and academy, for example—did not indicate much real change in social or cultural status. In the home, *chilenas* would continue to have primary responsibility for child rearing no matter what their career or social activities.

So, too, in Mexico. Those "modern-day *adelitas,* the wives of officers . . . must make the greatest of efforts and plan their activities so as not to neglect their own homes."[41] So were all Mexican women, by extrapolation, supposed to sacrifice and serve their men. If not out there on the field of battle anymore, they could still show their worth in the home—all in the name of *La Revolución*. Another Mexican source would claim that, "leaving aside the term 'feminism,' which never should appear in the form in which it is used, it is necessary to point out that man, having the position of leadership, will beckon the most appropriate woman to aid him in the improvement of the condition of our people."[42] Invoking historical figures from Malinche and Sor Juana Inés de la Cruz to the *adelitas* and *juanitas* of revolutionary days, Mexican army officers made cases for women as a revolutionary force responsive to men, but never threatening the dominant role of males.[43] Women might stand to attention in military service, well and good, and they might be vital to civilian professional and labor forces, but in the home they obeyed the commands of their husbands.

In Latin America there is no substance to arguments that military professionalism has ever provided significant opportunities for women, and thereby encouraged social change. Nor is there justification for any argument that feminization of the military profession leads to a more democratically inclined profession. Latin American military organizations successfully withstood changing times, when youth and labor were perceived as threats to an orderly society, after all; and they yielded not one centimeter of ground to women during the time of the generals.

How does this contrast with other examples of "military-feminine relations"? In the English-speaking world a colorful mix of attitudes and positions characterizes military literature, ranging from "old boy," Blimpish male superiority to strident feminism and commitment to social activism. This literature's richness of tone and argument makes up for the lack of numerous examples. Early on after the war, for example, Chief Commander S. M. Crowley strongly advocated a women's role in the British Army, but allowed as how women, no matter their career, would always consider home and hearth their first responsibility. Crowley also soundly criticized wives, especially those "charmers" who tried to keep their husbands home and safe during times of war. Such women should be objects of "horror and contempt," and husbands who tried to keep their wives at home were just as contemptible.[44] Despite this potentially auspicious beginning, it would be years before any distinct body of literature dealt specifically with women in English-speaking armies.

In her 1973 "Open Letter to the Female Officers of the Australian Army," Captain L. J. Gregson would refer to the army as a "mirror of its social environment." She would warn her fellow female officers that to seek to displace males by using feminist reasoning would be counterproductive, for Australian military males, chauvinists all, and their allies, "Sheilas," would have none of the feminists' arguments.[45] Gregson advocated easing males off their "thrones," rather than any brusque confrontations, and devoting their time to duty as ways for female officers to achieve equality. Two years later the U.S. General Mildred Bailey published an essay in the same journal that had carried Gregson's. Bailey responded to Gregson by arguing that the army was a promoter of social causes—integration, education, opportunity—and that women's liberation was indeed a worthy cause as long as it did not become partisan or politicized.[46] In the United States, the difference between political liberation and liberation in pursuit of professional equality would become a major point for discussion. Major Marcia Thompson recognized the need for superiors to make more scrupulous efforts in officer evaluation, lest women be patronized and given breaks they did not deserve.[47] So did Lieutenant Colonel Suzanne Boening, who charged in 1983 that "army leadership has been pressured to please ardent feminists demanding the right of women to be treated the same way that men are treated, and at the same time not offend more conservative brothers and sisters who want women out of fatigues and back behind their typewriters."[48] Delicate relationships between feminism and professionalism like these never crossed the minds of Latin Americans, male or female. Professional militarism would indeed represent a "mirror of its social environment."

Continental European military literature dealing with women falls somewhere between *machismo*-influenced attitudes of Latin Americans and feminist-traditionalist debates of the Anglo-Saxon world. There "the army as agent of change" would be the principal vehicle for discussions of woman's role. French authors used historical figures like Latin Americans did—Joan of Arc and French Revolution and *Résistance* leaders. They also acknowledged that in the new France, law had established equality in ranks for women. This was seen as evidence of "the abandonment of an anachronistic regime,"[49] and as a sign of economic change, for the armed forces was the largest employer of French women.[50] The French were on the whole quite proud of their role as employers and social progressives, but they said little about the presence of female officers constituting an improvement of defense capability. This was pretty much the case in Federal Germany and Italy as well. Social action justified a women's role in the *Bundeswehr,* and *Innere Führung* certainly condoned this if it could be shown to be democratic and progressive.[51] Neither German nor Italian defense capabilities rated mention, but in the Soviet Union they did. Women in Marxist countries were "provided with all kinds of allowances and pay," just like men, and the Red Army purportedly did not discriminate between the sexes.[52] The fact that Slavic male-female relationships under Marxist regimes were in reality about as egalitarian as those in Latin American societies belies the claims made in Soviet military literature as much as it reveals the hollowness of Latin American claims.

Perhaps a Spaniard, María del Carmen González Ribas, best summed up the situation of all Latin women with professional ambitions by stating in 1981 that the army ought to open up to women in order that a "significant number of persons who want to serve" be allowed to bring their talents and skills to the service of the fatherland.[53] Auxiliary service and second-class citizenship were simply not enough for many women in Europe, even Spain, or in English-speaking countries either. That they remained the best Latin American females could expect testifies to the perduration of old ways. In a way military-civilian relations are analogous to male-female relationships. Placing women at a sociocultural level close to that of Indians, workers, and peasants testified further to the steadfastness of Latin American military organizations within the flow of western history, during times of change.

It may also lend substance to the concept of *latinoamericanidad.* If one of the distinguishing characteristics of the region has been its own internal divisions and the invertebrateness of the societies, politics, economic bases, and, until recently, cultures of its individual parts, it is conceivable that the 1964–1989 quarter century represents at least an attempt to arrest the disastrous process that began with the shattering of the Iberian empires in the early nineteenth century. Abetted by caudillism, regionalism, outside interference, ethnic and linguistic exclusivism, elitism, and a lack of constructive nationalism, Latin America's invertebrateness was analogous, but not identical, to what Ortega y Gassett wrote about in

España invertebrada. Spain, in the early twentieth century, was divided against herself (as was Portugal); there was no political consensus, no unifying force, not even a sense of nationalism. Spain's (and Portugal's) New World heirs were not much better off near century's end. Professional militarists understood this.

In his 1971 essay on leadership, for example, Venezuela's Colonel Antonio López Salas emphasized fundamental differences between national cultures. "Latin countries, characterized by an excessive individualism," he wrote, "have had success in individual efforts, in which they have shown a good deal of initiative, and have failed principally when it has been necessary to act together; Anglo-Saxons have been able to lead based on distance and silence; North Americans have led principally because of ease and favorable economic conditions; Russians by making ample use of their autocratic character."[54] Rarely since independence, was his point, had the concept of "Latin America" meant much to Latin Americans, beyond those who resided in the the realms of rhetoric or letters, that is.

Mercado Jarrín's 1973 treatment of security doctrines can be used to support this assertion. In what he called a "critical period" for U.S.–Latin American relations, the Peruvian claimed that security meant different things to different Americans. In Latin America it was not simply the ability to withstand attack; security was "the right to exploit natural resources, raw materials, and the acquisition of the financial and technological capacity to achieve the integrated development of the population through the implementation of policies independent of the world power center."[55] Security predated a U.S. presence, hence was not dependent on it. It was internally motivated and directed, and attempts to attain it would always include those "declarations of independence" discussed in preceding chapters.

Ecuador's Admiral Nelson G. Baidal, writing in the 1970s, blamed independence for the political dissolution of Spanish America into its constituent parts. He blamed outside manipulation for the further disintegration of the region.[56] Another South American wrote that in his country "there is no unity based on fatherland. There is no human solidarity. There are no rules of social conduct that guide by consensus. Degraded by its exercise of power, public authority has degraded itself as well by its moral conduct; each the consequence of the other. The evils of political life, in fine, have corrupted society. . . . The country needs to establish an order, a true national order, the order of a new and stable society."[57] That 1976 description of Colombia applied in greater or lesser degree to most of the region during most of the time of the generals. Despite ludicrous claims that Latin American countries behaved *bolivarianamente* when Argentina suffered her hard-earned 1982 defeat, Latin America, until quite recently, has never shown signs of being anything other than less than the sum of its parts.[58] Professionals and militarists both bear responsibility for this, especially those who saw professional militarism as the only way to avert social revolution. Generals and admirals determined to make their countries over in a professional image would forget in the 1960s, 1970s, and 1980s that such an image was more identifiable with the past than the present. They refused to acknowledge the legitimacy of sociocultural changes that they had striven to comprehend back in the 1950s.

Early in the sixteenth century Francesco Guicciardini wrote that "the men of this country . . . are proud and think that no other country is comparable to their own . . . they are inclined toward arms, perhaps more than any other Christian country, and capable in their use."[59] Machiavelli's follower was referring, of course, to Spaniards, especially Castilians. Nearly half a millennium later these words might apply to the generals and officers of any of Latin America's constituent parts. In that part of the world, Count Hermann Keyserling would muse, lived those humans "most strongly attached to their native country."[60] Keyserling referred to South America only, but the writings of most Latin American officers would expose them all as being so attached. Their profession demanded it. To create a viable "native country" was no mean feat; to hold one together no less a feat. Both imperatives would ultimately propel some officers onward toward professional militarism. Past, present, and future would blur in the time of the generals, for it was not so long a historical time from the days of Guicciardini to those of Bolívar, from those of Bolívar to Lyautey's, and from Lyautey's to those of Gugliamelli, Meira Mattos, Mercado Jarrín, and Pinochet. Nation-building, begun in the early nineteenth century, was still incomplete. Professional militarists understood this too.

Abundant examples of *latinoamericanidad,* ranging from use of historic myths and expressions of Cold War concerns to Central American peace initiatives and perceived decline of the United States as a world military power, lend support to the hypothesis that Latin Americans may finally be thinking of themselves as more than citizens of their native lands. That actions resulting from this thought are carried out in an inchoate fashion ought not signify that substance and form have no chance of becoming manifest coevally. Latin America is exceptional. Professional militarism's existence proves that.

By the late 1980s a synchronous relationship had developed between professional militarism and the emergence of the "new novel." The novel and other prose of Latin American novelists ought to be considered analogous to professional militarism and the prose of officers. The Latin American novel of the second half of the twentieth century forms as bold a collective declaration of cultural independence as does the corpus of Latin American military literature. Politics, history, society, the economy, ideology, the role of the military, women, Indians, peasants, workers, politicians, students, education, religion, urbanization, rural life, foreign relations—all these are treated perceptively and vividly by "new novelists." That they are often treated differently than they are in a turgid essay on national security or in a prolix one on leadership must not surprise. Nor must the fact that occasionally treatments are similar. That intercalation, stream of consciousness, frequent time and tense changes, and magical realism achieve so much more in terms of enduring historical quality than do "shadows on the mind" characterizing the writings of professional militarists is consistent with recognized Ibero-American cultural dualism: Miguel de Cervantes and the Pizarro brothers, Sor Juana Inés de la Cruz and the *fuero militar*, Joaquim Maria Machado de Assis and Mariano Melgarejo, José Enrique Rodó and Juan Vicente Gómez, Jorge Luis Borges and Augusto Pinochet Ugarte.

Are not the "alternative realities" and "parallel histories" concocted by "new novelists" as valid as the pasts, presents, and futures perceived by professional militarists? They are equally part of the inchoate responses to dilemmas posed by "Invertebrate America" to date. The time of the generals and the "new novel" are contemporary contextual phenomenona of historical proportions. "Time and time again," wrote David Craig about Gyorg Lukacs, "in literary studies, historical explanations so cry out to be invoked as a help with cruxes of interpretation that the scholar committed to preserving the 'purity' of the literary has to deny the relevance of the historical."[61] Not so with the "new novel," and treatment of literature as historical documentation need not be Marxist at all. The "new novel" is as relevant to the study of Latin American history as is any other printed source, any other genre. Officers in those countries most heavily affected by professional militarism did indeed heed Baldesar Castiglione's advice that "the practice of arms pertains to both the soul and the body . . . and I hold that to no one is learning more suited than to a warrior."[62] Despite Marshal MacMahon's oft-repeated admonition against military writing,[63] officers have written, professionally or not, on a variety of topics in modern times. They have spoken out often on the importance of education, though their definition of it may be at odds with civilian definitions. They have advised their fellows to read widely. They have fancied themselves men of ideas. There may be no deeper historical relationship between letters and arms than there is in Latin America.

Do professional militarists read novels? It appears generals did not in Argentina, Brazil, Chile, and Peru between 1964 and 1989. Many authors were exiled, and books were banned and burned. Elsewhere a few officers would note the importance of literature. Referring specifically to Latin America, U.S. Major Kenneth Taggart advised his fellow officers that "novels provide us an access to the historical and contemporary reality of a nation which may not be gained in any other way."[64] In his 1972 book Spain's General Manuel Díaz Alegría opined that the modern novel was an excellent way to gain a sociological and historical perspective on a country and its people.[65] But most late-twentieth-century Latin American men of arms and men of letters would not find common cause. No, their relationship was of another kind.

Milan Kundera claimed that "the path of the novel emerges as a parallel history of the modern era."[66] In Latin America—and in all countries where reality remains a relative concept—this is the case. Those who write novels there sometimes resort to the essay to explain what they are trying to do, just as officers have done, thus the commentary of a novelist, often directed to the "outside world," is analogous to the officer's essay.

"Only in an act of the present can we make present the past as well as the future,"[67] wrote Carlos Fuentes in 1987. These could have been the words of a zealous professional militarist seeking to "modernize traditionally"; for he too would be concerned with history and time, change and continuity. In Mario Vargas Llosa's *The War of the End of the World* one of the characters states that "there is no such thing as chance in history, that however fortuitous its course may seem, there is always a rationality lying hidden behind even the most puzzling of outward experiences."[68] Officers time and time again have offered rational explanations for what they perceived to be going on around them. Cuba's Reinaldo Arenas once wrote that historians see time's infinity as linear. "What proofs have they that time moves in that way?" he asked. "Before the ingenuousness of a man who tries to scale Time or put it on the scales, file it away with progressive or even 'progressivist' intentions, Time quite simply bristles, digs in its heels, and will not budge."[69] Generals have continually refused to budge; time remains immobile to the novelist.

But might not an officer, like Alejo Capentier's "Head of State" in *El recurso del método* (1974), praise the organization and discipline of a society from which young men of modest means can by their own efforts rise to the topmost ranks of the army? Professional militarists continually asserted that their armies provided this kind of opportunity, closed ranks or not. And they continually repeated, when the occasion merited it, that they were "revolutionaries." "Blessed are the armed forces, for they shall call themselves Children of the Revolution," asserted kidnapper-terrorist Carlos Esquerdo in Christopher Hampton's drama, *Savages*.[70]

Novelists also displayed a wariness about the United States, about its military prowess—or lack thereof. Manlio Argueta, a Salvadoran, lashes out at the United States and its military advisers through the mouth of a peasant in one of his novels: "The advisers don't know anything about us. That's the problem. They come to our country in big airplanes. They tour the countryside in their helicopters. They wear dark glasses so they can't see our light. They drive bullet-proof Chevrolets. They don't speak Spanish. How are they going to understand us like that?"[71] Military men, when they spoke of U.S. advisers, used terms less harsh, but nonetheless critical.

In his Harvard University commencement address of 1983, Carlos Fuentes warned the United States of the willingness of the Soviet Union to take advantage of turmoil in Latin America, echoing in many senses what military men had been saying for years. Fuentes pleaded for a wiser policy, one that would reflect something more than that evinced by Argueta's gringos: "But if power with historical memory and diplomacy with historical imagination came into play, we, the United States and Latin America, might end up with something very different: a Latin America of independent states building institutions of stability, renewing the culture of national identity, diversifying our economic interdependence, and wearing down the dogmas of too many nineteenth-century philosophies. And a United States giving the example of a tone in relations that is present, active, cooperative, respectful, aware of cultural differences, and truly proper for a great power."[72] That Fuentes and other intellectuals still do not agree with their uniformed *conciudadanos* about the specifics of what U.S.–Latin American relations should be is evidence both of *latinoamericanidad* and of invertebrateness.

Officers have often hinted at a "third way" for Latin America, something between socialism and capitalism, East and West. Even the most reactionary officers have recognized the need for modifications of "free-enterprise" capitalism. Writing in 1984 (partly in response to a Nicaraguan interview with Günter Grass), Mario Vargas Llosa recognized that many European and North American intellectuals, while demanding democracy for themselves, advocated revolution for Latin America, in some cases even subordination to the Soviet Union.[73] Like those officers whose definitions of democracy differed sharply from his own, the Peruvian writer challenged such views. While he excoriates *uniformados* in most of his works, then, he also champions a Latin American solution to the region's manifest problems: typicality and uniqueness, *latinoamericanidad* and invertebrateness.

What future can Latin Americans hope for? Officers, as emphasized, have consistently feared it and have striven to use their power to control it, for they also fear the present. In Ariel Dorfman's *The Last Song of Manuel Sendero* it is an unborn child who asks about the military and the future: "Who's going to assure me, including all the ones who haven't even been conceived and whose interests we can legitimately represent in their absence, they won't be in control for a millennium? And who's going to guarantee us that when they finally depart, you'll be able to get your act together so they'll never come back?"[74] Both Dorfman and his fellow countryman José Donoso would write from and about exile, the latter's masterwork of exile being as replete with poignant scenes of those deported and relegated to internal exile as Dorfman's.[75] Both have forced readers to contemplate the awful results of actions taken by generals who sought to perpetuate the past through displacement, relegation, exile, prison, and torture. Their words and those of others gave civilian and military leaders alike cause to ponder what the future of military-civilian relations will be like.

Dictatorship of one form or another may be the professional military response to a given situation, but in times of change it is risky business. It is never, as one of the Nigerian intellectuals in Wole Soyinka's *The Interpreters* (1965) would have his associates believe, the most sensible form of government for any nation. May it never be again. What will a future bring if professional militarists believe, like Ernest Renan, "that the future will judge us as we have judged the past."[76] Alternatives to the past still frighten intellectuals and officers alike. Might they ever see eye to eye in some as yet unthought-of future? Or will they continue to judge each other as they judge the past?

In his fictive future history, *And Still the Earth: An Archival Narration,*

Ignácio de Loyola Brandão has a character state: "For centuries and centuries historical and social coordinates functioned as expected. But for the last thirty years everything has been out of synch. The acceleration of history has changed everything, the dynamics are totally different now, the dynamics are everything, total conception—or else transforming constantly minute by minute."[77] Will there ever be time enough for intellectuals and officers to see eye to eye? They both achieved distinction and originality in the late twentieth century, but *apart from* each other, not in concert. What will it take to bring these two vital sectors together?

Why, as Gabriel García Márquez asked in his Nobel Prize address of 1982, should "the originality so readily granted us in literature be so mistrustfully denied us in our different attempts at social change? Why think that the social justice sought by progressive Europeans for their own countries cannot be also a goal for Latin America, with different methods for dissimilar conditions?"[78] Is it because those who dwell too much in the past are condemned to relive it and those who fear the future so much are doomed to perpetuate the present? What if militarists and writers, *uniformados* and *políticos* could find ways to use their talents with the same goals in mind? What if they could leave history behind and give substance to *latinoamericanidad*? "To live only for history," said Octavio Paz, "is not really to live. History is a search for totality, a hunger for what lies beyond. This is history's greatest paradox: its eternities flicker, and its only absolute is change itself."[79]

Change over time, however imperceptible to some and exaggerated to others, was a major influence on professional military thought and self-perception in the decades following World War II. Change over time influenced perceptions of history, of professional roles, of institutional missions; it shaped thought on politics, society, ideology, and religion. In "Invertebrate America" it led to professional militarism, the time of the generals; and it propels all Latin Americans toward their future(s),[80] now with many of their intellectual and ideological convictions rendered moot. At present there is no way of telling whether this future will be a continuation of their invertebrate status, some form of Ortegan solidarity based on military-civilian consensus, a future characterized by "different methods for dissimilar conditions," or just another time of the generals in which one profession's resistance to change and reliance on memories isolates all Latin Americans in another world paradigm not of their own making.

POSTSCRIPT

Because of the comparative and thematic approaches used in this book, most conclusions have already been stated or are so obvious as to need no iteration or amplification. Nevertheless, a few points do need refining, especially given the sequential relationship of the book to *Yesterday's Soldiers*. In that chronicle of the development of the military profession in Latin America I pointed out that by the time professionalism was a reality, militarism was in a gestational stage. In its own postscript I wrote: "In fine, the legacy of yesterday's soldiers, that which I term professional militarism, has not been dissipated. If anything a search for the idealized past, motivated by pre–World II reactions to the present and concerns for the future, and set forth in relevant terminology, still figures boldly in the South American professional military mind."[1] I well remember the day I reached such a preliminary conclusion. It was in the spring of 1978, in London, just as I finished working with the French and German documentary material for *Yesterday's Soldiers*. Five years later, when the book appeared, professional militarism was a reality in both manifest and latent forms.

That officer-authors continued to search for idealized pasts, that their reactions and concerns have remained much the same, and that they would be set forth in terminology relevant to the late twentieth century reinforces the position I took for South America, and for Latin America as a whole. It is the reason for these eight chapters. Pasts and presents would remain irreconcilable, the literature shows, no matter the type and level of professionalism or militarism. Futures remained problematic, eternally subjects of great concern to men in uniform. And the overall comparability of what Latin Americans thought and wrote with the opinions of officers from other continents indicates the limits to which uniqueness and typicality can be affected by national context.

That there was so much agreement among military writers might be construed as evidence that officers thought and wrote certain things simply because they were ordered to, that they meant little of what they said, that they continued to maintain an official line because they were expected to do so, that they knew no better. I think there is more to it than that. Beyond doubt is the fact that sociocultural forces external to the military profession have such an impact historically and politically on the profession that thought and self-perception do not always lead to political action. This validates the argument that while professional militarism is both manifest and latent, a contextual phenomenon, a "military spirit," or military mentality, does exist everywhere.

Only in South America did professional militarism rise to the level of ideology, for nowhere else would it become so compatible with other social and political phenomena of the post–World War II decades. There values and ideals of a bygone era—so important to military men everywhere—defied sociocultural change more consistently and perhaps with less competition (although it has not always seemed so to those involved) than anywhere else in the world. They may continue to do so.

Nothing can change and still be the same, appearances notwithstanding, but the more fundamental the change, the greater the amount of time and effort necessary to effect it. To many professional officers of the late twentieth century so much appeared to be changing. Where change did not appear to threaten, it still provided challenges to the very existence of the bases of the military profession. All else failing in certain circumstances, some professionals became militarists, and some militarists became political officers. Where they did, their actions reflected their thought and self-perception on the range of subjects considered herein.

Their actions also changed the profession. Ultimately, in each case, the venerable Barros Ortiz's admonition about extended political involvement was proven: "If the armed forces prolong more than is strictly necessary the function of arbitrating and ordering, they run the risk of passing, without realizing it, from the role of judge to that of party."[2] Once a "party," i.e., a participant or accessory, a professional officer is never quite the same, and an army rarely ever as it was before.

Struggle against change over time—all men being "soldiers in the war of time," according to Lope de Vega—can be seen as a vain attempt to impose idealized pasts on presents. In the attempt all qualities of all officers, all roles of all armies, must be adjusted, refined, brought up to code, as it were. But the basic attributes of all officers and all armies remain timeless. Superficial changes, certain accommodations to the times, some flexibility, are good things, but too much newness is dangerous. The world over, professional officers have attempted to hold on to those things that had made them both *a part of* and *apart from* the rest of society. In so doing, they have not been able to avoid dealing directly with change itself.

There being no such thing as a pattern of change over time that is orderly enough for military men, their writings in Latin America, and elsewhere too, would more often than not reflect consistency of theme and argument. This also meant that the same old ideas found their way over and over into essays, speeches, and papers ostensibly devoted to a variety of topics. An aura of timelessness about professional literature coincides, in Latin America, with that which characterizes recent prose fiction, concerned as it is with place as much as with passage of time. All this suggests that in military literature verb tense remained less important than adjective or noun form.

Something in the professional military makeup, something in the ethos of those in uniform, I am convinced, led them to confuse and simplify as they looked increasingly inward for inspiration in the face of perceived imminent threats to their profession and the world surrounding it. When they prolonged "functions of arbitrating and ordering," professional militarists really did become "party" to the process. By trying to do so much, they may have undone even more and can no longer feign objectivity or impartiality, much less achieve either. Their ideas became shadowy, their intellectual tradition suspect. Their thought processes jumbled; they confused beads with rosary. Application of solutions based on a military ethos proved to be as dangerous to the health of the profession as it was to the health of civilian institutions under stress. The ability to reason, to select the most logical solution, became ever more limited, so that proximity to a situation really did inhibit effective response capable of providing long-term benefits to all affected.

It is significant that retranslation and paraphrase were not necessary to analyze and interpret writings of officers from countries where professional militarism was a latent phenomenon or where personalism still prevailed. Years of harping on a particular theme did result in some fairly vapid repetitions worldwide of traditional ("old" is often the more appropriate modifier) ideas and it often resulted in blatant plagiarism. The Churrigueresque incantations and exhortations of South Americans still stand by themselves as examples of extremity, but it is not inconceivable that others, Soviets, Eastern Europeans, Asians, and Africans, say, find themselves in situations of comparable complexity someday. This suggests that the South American experience may have more relevance to other regions where past, present, and future appear to clash so much than the world perspective portrayed herein now indicates.

Most themes and issues discussed in the first seven chapters remain comparable and consistent despite obvious contrasts in context and political culture. And this is why comments like those of Edward Luttwak, in his review of Paul Kennedy's *The Rise and Fall of the Great Powers: Economic Change and Military Conflict from 1500 to 2000*,[3] come to mind in connection with a book about Latin America. Luttwak cautioned against the "perils of writing history so broadly that secondary sources must be accepted at face value without even a glimpse of the documents." Documentation is sufficiently comparable throughout these chapters to support findings that the basic ingredients of professional militarism are widespread indeed. It was Admiral (ret.) Gene LaRocque, USN, after all, not some developing-world professional militarist, who could say with all candor, "We have institutionalized militarism. . . . Everybody's for defense. Otherwise you're considered unpatriotic."[4] If a North American can make such a comment about military-civilian relations in the great bastion of military subservience to civilian authority, is it any wonder that officers in other countries should ponder the implications of the same problem?

Early in the 1990s there still appeared some prospects for a "time" *after* that of the generals. Despite signs of regional identity, or *latinoamericanidad*, noted in chapter 8, *fin de siècle* Latin America still demonstrates a lack of consensus among those groups critical to the maintenance of political stability, social development, and economic growth along capitalist-democratic lines. That is why I think the term "Invertebrate America" is appropriate. It is not yet clear how literary sophistication and professional militarism are historically related in Latin America, but this does not diminish my conviction that the simultaneous flowering of the "new novel" and professional militarism's flourish of trumpets is no historical accident. Nor do I think it odd that the ebb of U.S. influence and a surge of military professionals to national leadership posts should have coincided historically.

The future is awfully hard to write about, but if the novel "represents change, adds to and interprets reality," as Edward Said claimed, then the conclusion of one of the characters in Paraguayan novelist Augusto Roa Bastos' classic study of dictatorship are probably worth remembering: "There is always time to have more time."[5] The time of the generals may have generated only short-term urges by civilians to compromise and reach consensus.

What went on in Argentina, Brazil, and Peru in the first few years following the restoration of civilian rule hardly augured well for a definitive end to militarism in those countries. Elected chiefs of state were forced to struggle against bullying, frustrated military leaders, tough political opponents, and terrorism. Theirs were not fulfilling terms of office. Guatemalans, Salvadorans, and Panamanians watched while military men ran wild. Dominicans, Ecuadorans, and Bolivians all continued to feel the heavy influence of their armed forces. Uruguayans continued to grapple dramatically with amnesty for those involved in the most unattractive side of military rule. Mexicans, Colombians, and Venezuelans watched their countries being torn apart by economic distress, violence, and narcotics traffic. Chileans tiptoed into the post-Pinochet era. Paraguayans found themselves in the post-Stroessner era without a viable civilian system to rely on.

Conclusions often take the form of further questions. If manifest professional militarism failed where it was strongest, can it ever be taken seriously elsewhere? Or will *narcotraficantes uniformados,* personalists, opportunists, and *gorilas* prevail in the Latin American future? What will the United States' role be, that of committed ally in wars against subversives and drug traffickers, or that of inconsistent military titan and declining economic power in a multipolar world? What roles will interest groups excluded from deliberation during the time of the generals in Latin America play to forestall professional militarism's revival? Are there manifest and latent characteristics of democracy that need to be considered in relation to professional militarism? Historical, religious, and sociocultural experiences created a Latin American heritage within which the twentieth-century political experiences could be both unique and typical. It is impossible at present to tell what the shape of twentieth-century Latin military-civilian relations would have been if the United States had not become the dominant, and unwelcome, external force in the region. Bearing in mind the U.S. response to Iraq's August 1990 invasion of Kuwait, a codicil to the foregoing assertion presents itself in the form of a question: what would the Middle East have been like had it not been for the two world wars and the United States' massive retaliation against Iraq in early 1991?

Further, might the Persian Gulf War somehow make this book's findings more applicable to military-civilan relations in the countries involved? Will the armed forces of the powers who fought against Iraq see the war as further justification of their continued existence—despite the collapse of the Soviet Union and the weakened position of the Red Army? Increased reliance (with or without choice) on military solutions to major national problems, it is clear, boosted the confidence of generals and their like in Latin America. Problems of worldwide dimensions may do the same elsewhere, in the United States, say, encouraging professional officers to take the term "just war" quite seriously, perhaps even to react against political dissent and deviation from military norms of behavior in the form of pacifism, feminism, gay liberation—indeed to identify dissent and deviation with antimilitarism. Will the Vietnam debacle be erased from U.S. military memory by the "liberations" of Grenada, Panama, and Kuwait, and the associated thought and self-perception? Will Latin American professional militarists "take heart"? It is too soon to even consider adequate responses, but such questions beg asking.

Answers to these questions may be easier to come by, though, if it can be remembered that the now-apparent demise of manifest professional militarism is not the equivalent of the perceived triumph of liberal democracy and capitalism over Marxism-Leninism or any other form of authoritarianism in the times that follow 1989. The Latin American experience of 1964–1989 must neither be equated with, nor isolated from, that of other parts of the world between 1945 and 1990. To do either would be to deny both the possibility of *latinoamericanidad* and the existence of professional militarism itself.

A possible new world economic order, population growth, *guerrilla,* inflation, hunger, new foreign menaces, the brief age of *perestroika* and *glasnost* (and of a labor union inside the army itself), new dimensions to relations between the U.S. and the USSR (in its new form), at what many believe is the end of the Cold War (not to mention possible new dimensions of U.S. military activities worldwide), Islamic renaissance, Protestant fundamentalism and Catholic reactions to it in Latin America, a delicate position for *Innere Führung* in the new East-West relationship, Eastern Europe's new configuration (and changes in its military-civilian relationships)—these are some of the serious challenges that confront military professionals everywhere. They may induce perception of another new paradigm, or they may not.

Decades from now it may fall to another to look back on the time of the generals with such a perspective in mind. Future observers would do well to bear in mind that most Latin American armies have assigned (sometimes self-assigned) national security roles that now fairly oblige them to act internally. Will they allow themselves the luxury of running out of enemies to fear, or will democracy's inherent instabilities and inconsistencies take the place of discredited Marxism-Leninism?[6] Will sociocultural change, say in the form of women's movements, harden official military views? Will hostility to the United States and its selectively applied hemispheric "get-tough" military image—Grenada, Nicaragua, Panama, Peru, Bolivia—assume new, more ominous dimensions? Will dilemmas comparable to those that brought armies to the brink of power in Venezuela and Peru in early 1992 confront military men elsewhere? They might. I think there will always be "time to have more generals."

BIBLIOGRAPHICAL NOTES

These bibliographic citations make no pretense to being definitive. Nor do they represent every possible source of information. Most secondary sources cited in the text contain ample bibliographies on aspects of military-civilian relations and institutional development not treated herein. Many deal with military political action. Because it has not been my aim to duplicate existing studies of the military profession in Latin America, much less elsewhere, I have provided references to a degree consistent with sound scholarship and sufficient to indicate appropriate, alternative views. Omission of a work from the following notes is no indication of a negative qualitative evaluation on my part; it indicates that in my judgment further documentation is redundant, that the work is of such a nature that it does not sufficiently apply to the subjects of these chapters, or that the work is cited in one of the secondary sources already mentioned.

I have used abbreviations in the multiple citation of most military journals, especially those with multi-word titles. Minimal title changes are not normally indicated unless format and content also change, or unless library or archival locations might be affected. I have cited journals by date rather than volume number, owing to changes in publication intervals, numbering, errors, and omissions by publishers. Original orthography; diacriticals and punctuation have been retained unless confusion might result owing to pronunciation or alternate definition. The following list should aid the reader in identifying the most frequently cited journals.

AA	*Armées d'Aujourd'hui*	France
AAJ	*Australian Army Journal*	Australia
ACE	*An Cosantoir*	Eire
ACN	*Acción Cívica*	Nicaragua
AD, AID	*Army (Information) Digest*	USA
ADJ	*Asian Defence Journal*	Malaysia
ADN	*A Defesa Nacional*	Brazil
AFS	*Armed Forces and Society*	USA
ASEC	*Armas y Servicios del Ejército de Chile*	Chile
BAR	*British Army Review*	Great Britain
BEC	*Boletín del Ejército*	Cuba
BEES	*Boletín del Ejército*	El Salvador
BMBC	*Bulletin Militaire du Congo Belge*	Belgian Congo
CAJ	*Canadian Army/Military Journal*	Canada

CFS	*Canadian Forces Sentinel*	Canada
DFJ	*Defence Force Journal*	Australia
EL	*El Legionario*	Mexico
EW	*Europäische Wehrkunde*	W. Germany
FA	*Frères d'Armes*	France (French Africa)
FAF	*Forces Armées Françaises*	France
GN	*Guardia Nacional*	Nicaragua
IT	*Information für die Truppe*	W. Germany
JUSII	*Journal of the United Service Institution of India*	India
MECH	*Memorial del Ejército de Chile*	Chile
MR	*Military Review*	USA
PAD	*Philippine Army Digest*	Philippines
PAFJ	*Philippine Armed Forces Journal*	Philippines
PAJ	*Pakistan Army Journal*	Pakistan
PG	*Política y Geoestrategia*	Chile
RCID	*Revista del Colegio Interamericano de Defensa*	USA
RCMA	*Revista del Círculo Militar*	Argentina
RCMB	*Revista do Clube Militar*	Brazil
RDN	*Revue de Défense Nationale*	France
REC	*Revista del Ejército*	Colombia
RECEMMEA	*Revista de la Escuela de Comando y Estado Mayor Manuel Enrique Araujo*	El Salvador
REFAM	*Revista del Ejército y Fuerza Aérea*	Mexico
REM	*Revista del Ejército*	Mexico
RESGA	*Revista de la Escuela Superior de Guerra*	Argentina
RESGP	*Revista de la Escuela Superior de Guerra*	Peru
REV	*Revista del Ejército*	Venezuela
RFAC	*Revista de las Fuerzas Armadas*	Colombia
RFADR	*Revista de las Fuerzas Armadas*	Dominican Republic
RFAE	*Revista de las Fuerzas Armadas*	Ecuador
RFAES	*Revista de las Fuerzas Armadas*	El Salvador
RFAP	*Revista de las Fuerzas Armadas de la Nación*	Paraguay
RFAV	*Revista de las Fuerzas Armadas*	Venezuela
RIA	*Revista de Informaciones*	Argentina
RMA	*Revista Militar*	Argentina
RMB	*Revista Militar Brasileira*	Brazil
RMBO	*Revista Militar de Bolivia*	Bolivia
RMC	*Revista Militar*	Colombia
RMDR	*Revista Militar de la República Dominicana*	Dominican Republic
RMG	*Revue Militaire Générale*	France
RMGU	*Revista Militar*	Guatemala
RMI	*Revue Militaire d'Information*	France
RMIT	*Rivista Militare d'Italia*	Italy
RMNU	*Revista Militar y Naval*	Uruguay
RMP	*Revista Militar del Perú*	Peru
RMPO	*Revista Militar*	Portugal

RUSI	*Journal of the Royal United Services Institute for Defence Studies*	Great Britain
SMR	*Soviet Military Review*	USSR
SN	*Seguridad Nacional*	Chile
TAQDJ	*The Army Quarterly and Defence Journal*	Great Britain
WR	*Wehrwissenschaftliche Rundschau*	W. Germany

Introduction

1 The best examples of scholarly multi-country studies of the relationships between the professional military and civilian interest groups appropriate to the time of the generals are Edwin Lieuwen, *Arms and Politics in Latin America,* rev. ed. (New York: Frederick A. Praeger, 1961); John J. Johnson, *The Military and Society in Latin America* (Stanford: Stanford University Press, 1964); Lyle N. McAlister, Anthony P. Maingot, and Robert A. Potash, *The Military in Latin American Socio-political Evolution: Four Case Studies* (Washington, D.C.: Center for Research on Social Systems, 1970); and Brian Loveman and Thomas M. Davies, Jr., eds., *The Politics of Antipolitics: The Military in Latin America,* 2d ed. (Lincoln: University of Nebraska Press, 1989). Johnson's edited work, *The Role of the Military in Underdeveloped Countries* (Princeton: Princeton University Press, 1962), is a good example of multi-regional comparative analysis. Some of the work on this subject during the years in question is discussed in Frederick M. Nunn, "Arms and Politics in South America and Mexico: Observations on a Quarter Century of Research and Publication" (paper presented to the Latin American Studies Association, Albuquerque, April 1985).

Recent comparative works dealing with consequences of the Latin American military in power most worthy of note are Philip O'Brien and Paul Cammack, eds., *Generals in Retreat: The Crisis of Military Rule in Latin America* (Manchester, Eng.: Manchester University Press, 1985); George Philip, *The Military in South American Politics* (London: Croom Helm, 1985); Genaro Arriagada Herrera, *El pensamiento político de los militares: Estudios sobre Chile, Argentina, Brasil, y Uruguay,* 2d ed. (Santiago: Editorial Aconcagua, 1986); and Alfred Stepan, *Rethinking Military Politics: Brazil and the Southern Cone* (Princeton: Princeton University Press, 1988). For a pre-*glasnost* Soviet view, see *El ejército y la sociedad: América Latina* (*Estudios de Científicos Soviéticos,* No. 13) (Moscow: Soviet Academy of Sciences, 1982).

2 The military-civilian genesis of the 1973 Uruguayan military *pronunciamiento* marks off the ensuing twelve-year experience from institutional movements elsewhere in the Southern Cone. The April 1989 vote to retain the amnesty arrangements provided to the military following the restoration of civilian leadership, however, did not indicate that Uruguayans found themselves in a situation much different from that of Argentines, Brazilians, Chileans, or Peruvians in the early stages of a post-military era. It is the first reason that prompts exclusion of Uruguay from being dealt with in depth in this book. Be this as it may, Uruguayans are scrutinizing military-civilian relations and what they portend for their future as well as for those of their neighbors. See, for example, Carina Perelli, *Los militares y la gestión política,* and Juan Rial, *Las fuerzas armadas en los años 90: Una agenda de discusión,* both published in Montevideo by PEITHO, 1990.

3 Several non–Latin American countries that might be expected to figure in this book do not. There is no treatment of the Union of South Africa, for example, although

source material is readily available. The military-security establishment there became so wrapped up with the apartheid question that professionalism no longer governed military thinking to the degree that it did in those other countries of the British-influenced world included here—Australia and India, for example. From a Latin American perspective, Africa has for years meant principally the Sub Sahara. The Union of South Africa figures most prominently in geopolitical studies, and these are examined herein. Linguistic limitations preclude exploitation of primary source material from other obvious places. A few secondary sources are merely suggestive and are not intended to be considered comparable in a definitive sense.

A sufficient quantity of work has been done on the Middle East—Egypt and Israel obviously come to mind in this context—to make the region's inclusion in this book unnecessary. The intensity of intra-regional conflict draws the armies of the two principal powers, not to mention the others, apart from others considered. Pakistan serves as a better example of a situation in which military professionalism and religion relate intensely and in a balanced way.

This is because Pakistan's "military spirit" is more traditionally European-oriented, hence more comparable, than that of Middle Eastern countries involved in recent conflicts, notably the Persian Gulf War that broke out in 1991. Persistent military relations between Islam, nationalism, and jihad preclude the metamorphosis of professionalism into militarism in ways comparable only to the Soviet experience. The ongoing state-of-war mentality in the Middle East has been unparalleled in intensity and complexity. Ba'ath politics are incomparable with those of Latin America and the rest of the Judeo-Christian world in that they provide a unique linkage between religion, socialism, and the military, hence an effective cultural counterpoise against Marxism.

Exclusions are based, moreover, on the fact that the book is, after all, one dealing with Latin America first and foremost. The non–Latin American examples selected are appropriate to the end in mind.

4 Hilaire Belloc, *The Crisis of Civilization* (New York: Fordham University Press, 1937), esp. chap. 3, "The Reformation and Its Immediate Consequences," 108–32.

A far greater number of officers around the world would cite, paraphrase, and refer to one or more of the following works and authors, either having read them, read about them in works of their superiors and instructors, or having heard their ideas repeated by instructors. What may at first appear to be plagiarism, therefore, is often the result of militarylore's permeation of literature. These works have all gone through various editions and translations. In chronological order they are: Karl Maria von Clausewitz, *Vom Kriege*, 3 vols. (1833); Alfred de Vigny, *Servitude et grandeurs militaires* (1835); Colmar Freiherr von der Goltz, *Das Volk in Waffen: Ein Buch über Heerwesen und Kriegsführung* (Berlin, 1883); Louis Hubert Gonzalve Lyautey, "Du rôle social de l'officier," *Revue des Deux Mondes* (15 March 1891): 443–59; Charles de Gaulle, *Le Fil de l'épée* (1932); and Hans von Seeckt, *Gedanken eines Soldaten*, rev. ed. (1935).

Chapter One

1 "Palabras del director de la Escuela Superior de Guerra, general de brigada d. Joaquín A. Aguilar Pinedo, en el acto de iniciación de cursos (1. III. 1966)," *Revista de*

la Escuela Superior de Guerra (Argentina) (March–April 1966): 5–14. Hereafter RESGA.

2 "O Problema da Formação do Corpo de Oficiais e os Nossos Institutos de Ensino Militar," *Revista Militar Brasileira* (January–June 1943): 5–16. Hereafter RMB.

3 See "Anotações Para a História da F.E.B.," RMB (January–December 1945): 19–79; also see Lieutenant Colonel Augusto Maggessi Pereira, "Participação do Brasil na Guerra e Ação do Exército Nacional na Itália," ibid.: 110–19.

4 "El ministerio único para las fuerzas armadas," *Revista Militar* (Argentina) (May 1946): 923–28. Hereafter RMA.

5 "Hacia la creación de una futura academia militar," *Revista Militar de Bolivia* (July–October 1946): 465–73; (November–December 1946): 588–97. Hereafter RMBO.

6 "Defensa continental," *Revista Militar del Perú* (January 1947): 5. Hereafter RMP. See also the editorial, "La transición," RMP (February 1946): i–ii.

7 "Día del ejército," *Armas* (Mexico) (January–February 1976): 79.

8 Santiago F. Baigorria, "Fuerza moral del frente único," RMA (May–June 1952): 301–8; (July–August 1952): 463–69; (September–October 1952): 613–16; (November–December 1952): 765–68. Also see Lieutenant Colonel Julio César Salvadores, "Defensa nacional: La reestructuración del poder ejecutivo y la existencia del consejo de la defensa nacional," RESGA (January–March 1955): 18–26.

9 "Ideario de la defensa nacional para la guerra moderna," RMP (May 1956): 9–18.

10 General Jorge A. Giovanelli, "La unidad moral: Nación-fuerzas armadas," RMA (May–June 1956): iv–ix.

11 Colonel Matías Laborde Ibarra and Dr. José Manuel Astigueta, "Consideraciones en torno a una ley de defensa nacional," RESGA (October–December 1962): 358–99.

12 "Subdesarrollo es un reto: Decisión y voluntad, la respuesta," RMP (January–February 1969): 58–61.

13 "Reflexiones sobre la seguridad y el desarrollo en América Latina," *Estrategia* (September–October 1973): 29–40. The quoted material appears on p. 30.

14 Ibid., 41–48.

15 Ibid., 20–29. The citation is from p. 21.

16 "Um Estranho Novo Mundo," *A Defesa Nacional* (January–February 1978): 109–17. Hereafter ADN.

17 Major Júlio Agostini, "Aspectos Económicos do Problema Siderúrgico Nacional," RMB (July–September 1941): 209–16.

18 Major Leoncio Colina R., "La industria y la defensa nacional," RMP (January 1945): 37–59. See also Lieutenant Colonel Luis Bustos G., "La industrialización y la guerra," RMP (October 1953): 74–79.

19 "Reflexões da Guerra no Brasil," RMB (January–June 1946): 221–30.

20 Captain Jaime Eduardo Ruiz, "La movilización industrial," RMA (August 1946): 247–54; (September 1946): 463–70. The citation comes from p. 253. See also Colonel Pablo Beretta, "Defensa civil," RMA (May 1946): 929–42; (June 1946): 1125–51; and Lieutenant Colonel Salviano R. Herrera, "El elemento primordial en la guerra," RMA (February 1946): 309–14.

21 Major Víctor Sánchez Marín, "El departamento de movilización integral de la nación: Elemento básico del ministerio de la defensa nacional," *Revista de la Escuela Superior de Guerra* (Peru) (July–September 1955): 30–53. The cited passage appears on p. 33. Hereafter RESGP.

22 Major D. Lunt, "The Training of the Young Officer Cadet After the War," *The Army Quarterly and Defence Journal* (April 1944): 115–22. The quotation is from p. 115. Hereafter TAQDJ.

23 "Matters of Moment," *Journal of The United Service Institution of India* (April 1946): 151–56. Hereafter JUSII.

24 "Regards sur l'année 1949," *Revue Militaire d'Information* (10 January 1950): 4–5. Hereafter RMI.

25 Lieutenant Colonel F. E. Anderson, "Arms for Warriors," *Canadian Army Journal* (March 1951): 32–44. Hereafter CAJ.

26 "The German Armed Forces and Democracy," tr. and reprinted by permission of *Wehrkunde, Australian Army Journal* (December 1953): 19–22. Author's own italics. Hereafter AAJ. See also "A Shortage of Militants," *The Economist*, 7 July 1957; and "De la nouvelle armée allemande," *Revue Militaire Suisse* (September 1960): 447–51.

27 See General André Zeller, "L'armée de terre liée à la nation," *Revue de Défense Nationale* (June 1959): 957–66. The quoted passage comes from p. 960. Hereafter RDN. See also Colonel J. Nemo, "La formation des cadres de défense nationale," RDN (March 1958): 471–86.

28 "The American Soldier," *Army Information Digest* (July 1963): 50–53. Hereafter AID. This text was delivered as a commencement address to the U.S. Military Academy, 1963.

29 "Some Comments on the Rebuilding of the German Bundeswehr," *Journal of the Royal United Services Institute for Defense Studies* (August 1965): 271–77. The citation is from pp. 276–77. Hereafter RUSI.

30 Ibid., 274.

31 "What is America?" AID (July 1968): ii.

32 "Der alte Soldat und die Bundeswehr," *Wehrwissenschaftliche Rundschau* (November 1968): 602–15, esp. 605–6, 611. Hereafter WR.

33 *Der Primat militärisches Denkens: Die Bundeswehr und das Problem der Okkupierten Öffentlichkeit* (Köln: Pahl Rugenstein Verlag, 1969), p. 51. See also his *Die unbewältigte Bundeswehr: Zur Perfektionierung eines Anachronismus* (Frankfurt am Main: Fischer Taschenbuch Verlag, 1973).

34 General André Beaufré, "Le malaise de l'armée," *Le Figaro*, 13 February 1969. See also his "Die Entwicklung der Französischen Armee," *Österreichische Militär Zeitschrift* (April 1970): 279–84.

35 General William C. Westmoreland, "On Professional Competence and Integrity," *Army Digest* (January 1970): 36–37. Hereafter AD.

36 Jean-Paul Moreigne, "Officiers, pour quel office?" RDN (May 1971): 718–27.

37 Colonel Adolf Reinicke, "Sorgen des Staatsbürgers um die Bundeswehr," *Wehrkunde* (October 1972): 515–18.

38 Stuart Drummond, "The Role of the Indonesian Army in Society and Its Attitude towards the Use of Force," TAQDJ (October 1977): 423–32.

39 Colonel A. Korkeshkin, "With the Party, with the People," *Soviet Military Review* (February 1976): 4–6. Hereafter SMR.

40 Squadron Leader A. K. Robertson, "Theirs Not to Reason Why . . . ?" *Defence Force Journal* (December 1976): 35–44. Hereafter DFJ.

41 Captain P. L. Cameron, "The Military and Political Involvement," DFJ (September 1977): 26–30.

42 General Eugenio Rambaldi, "Esercito e società," *Rivista Militare d'Italia* (January–February 1978): 2–6. Hereafter RMIT.

43 See Colonel William S. Hollis, "On the Growth of the American Economy: The Role of the U. S. Army," *Military Review* (December 1978): 10–18. Hereafter MR. See also Lieutenant Colonel (ret.) Sam Sarkesian, "Changing Dimensions of Military Professionalism," MR (March 1979): 41–56; and Ronald Atwell Zoll, "A Crisis in Self-Image: The Role of the Military in American Culture," *Parameters* (December 1982): 24–31.

44 See, for example, Lieutenant Colonel Gustav Lünenborg, "Elf Thesen zur Sicherheitspolitik," *Information für die Truppe* (March 1985): 5–7. Hereafter IT.

45 Lieutenant Colonel Eugenio Volpe, "Seguridad nacional," *Revista Militar y Naval* (Uruguay) (December 1951–April 1952): 66–69. Hereafter RMNU.

46 General Felipe de la Barra, "Factores primarios de la defensa nacional," RMP (August–September 1954): 1–16.

47 See Colonel Víctor Odicio T., "Ensayo sobre lo que podría ser una ley de seguridad o de defensa nacional," RMP (January–February 1957): 23–31; and Major Enrique Gallegos V., "Organización y métodos de la escuela de estado mayor de Francia," RESGP (April–June 1958): 36–40.

48 Lieutenant Colonel (ret.) Arturo S. Pasqualis Politi, "El problema marxista y su incidencia en nuestra resolución de estrategia cordial," RMA (July–September 1968): 45–79; and Colonel Osiris Guillermo Villegas, "Guerra revolucionaria comunista," RMA (January–March 1960): 3–26.

49 "Introducción al estudio de la guerra revolucionaria," RMP (March–April 1961): 132–51.

50 General Giorgio Liuzzi, "Caratteristiche ed esigenze di un esercito moderno," RMIT (May 1961): 561–67. The quoted material appears on p. 563. See also General Andrea Viglione, "Le forze armate e le sfide del nostro tempo," RMIT (November–December, 1977): 2–8.

51 See "Momento de Ação," RMB (July–September 1941): 163–66.

52 See "El panamericanismo: Escudo de la humanidad del presente y del futuro," RMBO (March–April 1948): 9–11.

53 "El Perú y la defensa hemisférica," RMP (June 1955): 110–20. The cited passage appears on pp. 110–111. See also Colonel César A. Pando Egusquiza, "La junta interamericana de defensa como garantía de la paz en el continente," RMP (April 1956): ix–xxix.

54 "La guerra psicológica entre oriente y occidente," RMA (November–December 1957): 5–10.

55 "La escuela de comando y estado mayor de Fort Leavenworth y algunas diferencias con la nuestra," RESGP (April–June 1958): 15–35.

56 "La situación mundial: El cerco estratégico," RESGA (January–March 1962): 1–12. The cited material appears on p. 5.

57 RMP (March–April 1963): 132–36.

58 "El movimiento moderno de las ideas: Algunas reflexiones destinadas a los jóvenes oficiales de nuestro ejército," *Revista del Círculo Militar* (October–December 1963): 9–18. Hereafter RCMA.

59 General Edgardo Mercado Jarrín, "La política y la estrategia militar en el sistema interamericano," RMP (September–October 1968): 5–19. The cited term appears on p. 16.

60 "El perfeccionamiento del sistema militar interamericano: Análisis de la situación actual, orientación para su mejoramiento," RESGA (September–October 1968): 5–15. The citation is from p. 14.

61 See his "Dos ejemplos, una conclusión," RCMA (April–June 1969): 63–66. See also his "Reflexiones," RCMA (January–March 1970): 81–86.

62 Cited in Lieutenant Colonel Luis Mericq Seoane, ed., *Edgardo Mercado Jarrín: Seguridad-Política-Estrategia* (Santiago: Estado Mayor General del Ejército de Chile, 1975), 63.

63 "Responsabilidade de Gerações," RMB (January–April 1979): 26–29.

64 "O Militar e o Momento Atual," ADN (May–June 1980): 41–53.

65 Colonel Víctor Chaves Dailhe, "El poderío naval soviético: La seguridad del occidente y Pacífico Sur," *Memorial del Ejército de Chile* (January–April 1981): 109–18. Hereafter MECH.

66 "La guerra que el mundo libre está perdiendo," *Revista de las Fuerzas Armadas* (Colombia) (July–September 1984): 357–79. The citation is from p. 378. Hereafter RFAC.

67 "L'Allemagne et le destin du soldat," RMI (25 February 1955): 23–25; and his "La future armée allemande et sa place dans l'état," RMI (10 June 1955): 21–26.

68 *Soldiers and Scholars: Military Education and National Policy* (Princeton: Princeton University Press, 1957), 96, 100.

69 "Cuba, 1962," TAQDJ (April 1963): 28–32.

70 Colonel Reginald Hargreaves (MC), "The Abiding Flaw," TAQDJ (January 1969): 203–17. The citation is from p. 217. Author's own italics.

71 General Baron Leo Geyer von Schweppenburg, "Notes on Nato," *Defence* (January 1972): 41–43.

72 Colonel Arturo Baldini, "Strategia indiretta e forze morale," RMIT (September 1970): 1350–58.

73 "The Military Profession in the 1970's," in J. N. Wolfe and John Erickson, eds., *The Armed Services and Society: Alienation, Management, and Integration* (Edinburgh: Edinburgh University Press, 1970), 5–17. The citation is from p. 8.

74 See Jean Larteguy, *L'adieu à Saigon* (Paris: Presses de la Cité, 1975).

75 See Ali A. Mazrui, *Soldiers and Kinsmen in Uganda: The Making of a Military Ethnocracy* (Beverly Hills: Sage Publications, 1975), 133.

76 See Denis Martin, Alain Rouquié, Tatiana Yannapolous, and Philippe Decraene, *Os Militares e o Poder na América Latina e na Africa* (Lisboa: Publicações Dom Quixote, 1975).

77 See General José Perrou, "O Rio São Francisco: seus Problemas, suas Soluções," RMB (October–December 1942): 545–53; Joseph J. Thorndyke, Jr., "Geopolítica: La fantástica carrera de un sistema científico que un británico inventó, los alemanes usaron, y los americanos necesitan estudiar," MECH (September–December 1943): 881–901; Major Luis Vargas Feliú, "Chile y Argentina," MECH (March–April 1944): 305–6; Emilio Castañón Pasquel, "Geopolítica," RMP (December 1946): 53–63; (January 1947): 25–38; (February 1947): 127–35; Colonel Armando de Castro Uchoa (tr.), "Karl Haushofer e a sua Influência nos Estudos Geopolíticos," RMB

(January–June 1947): 81–103; and Lieutenant Colonel Jorge E. Atencio, "Influencia geopolítica del mar," RMA (December 1951): 1445–56.

78 "Bolivia: Una experiencia geopolítica," RMA (March–April 1951): 361–67. Cited material is from p. 361.

79 "El mayor general profesor dr. Carl Haushofer y su influencia en los estudios geopolíticos," RMBO (April–June 1951): 49–55. See also "Salida al mar," ibid., 75–82.

80 "La junta interamericana de defensa como una garantía de paz en el continente," RMP (April 1956): ix–xxix.

81 See, for example, Colonel Enrique Rottjer, "Oriente y Occidente," RMA (July–August 1956): 53–65; (May–June 1957): 31–40; (July–August 1957): 33–46; Major W. Contreras A. "La teoría geopolítica de Mackinder y la apreciación político-estratégica de las potencias aliadas y de Alemania en las guerras mundiales," RMP (March–April 1959): 24–29; and Contreras, "Geopolítica," RMP (May–June 1960): 65–81.

82 See RESGA (July–September 1960): 401–8; also see his "América del sur: Protección de los Estados Unidos de Norteamérica," RMBO (April–June 1961): 88–92.

83 See Captain Agustín P. De Elía, "La política mundial y su repercusión en América del Sur," RMA (January 1951): 51–54; and Lieutenant Colonel Jorge E. Atencio, "¿Cuál debe ser nuestra posición en geopolítica?" RMA (October 1950): 1339–43. See also Atencio, "Geopolítica y geografía militar," RMA (February 1950): 153–55; and "'Geopolítica': ¿Cómo debemos estudiar geopolítica?" RMA (July 1950): 898–900; Colonel J. B. Magalhães, "Fundamentales para el estudio de los aspectos militares de la Cuenca del Plata," RMA (April 1950): 426–33; and Lieutenant Emilio Radamés Isola, "Las influencias geopolíticas en la formación de nuestro estado," RMA (January 1950): 41–50.

84 See "A Posição do Brasil na Cojuntura Económica Mundial," RMB (July–September 1966): 33–50.

85 RMB (October–December 1972): 11–19. See also Everal do Backheuser, *A Geopolítica do Brasil* (Rio de Janeiro: Biblioteca do Exército, 1952); General Golbery do Couto e Silva, *Geopolítica do Brasil* (Rio de Janeiro; Editôra José Olympio, n.d.) and *Aspectos Geopolíticos do Brasil* (Rio de Janeiro: José Olympio, 1957); and General Carlos de Meira Mattos, *Projeção Mundial do Brasil* (São Paulo: Gráfica Leal, 1960) and *A Geopolítica e as Projeções do Poder* (Rio de Janeiro: José Olympio, 1977).

86 Major Agnaldo del Nero Augusto, "A Política Militar Francesa," ADN (July–August 1976): 3–24; and Meira Mattos, "A Evolução do Conceito de Poder e Sua Avaliação," *Revista del Colegio Interamericano de Defensa* (June 1976): 3–12. Hereafter RCID.

87 See their works cited in notes 85 and 86. Also see General Juan E. Guglialmelli's *Estrategia* essays, "Argentina: Política nacional y política de fronteras" (December 1975–January 1976): 5–21; and "Golbery do Couto e Silva, el 'destino manifiesto' brasileño y el Atlántico Sur" (March–April 1976): 5–24.

88 Captain Luiz Sanctos Döring, "Algumas Lições de Angola," ADN (March–April 1978): 139–47.

89 ADN (July–August 1979): 5–25. The citation is from p. 25. See also her "América Central-Caribe: Area Vulnerável do Hemisfério Occidental," ADN (March–April 1981): 77–86; and "Uruguai: Polígono Geopolítico do Cone Sul," ADN (March–

April 1982): 37–40; and "O Caribe em Ritmo de Guerra Fria," ADN (November–December 1983): 35–54. See also Captain (navy) Ricardo Ramos Ormeño, "Pensamento Político de Mercado Jarrín," ADN (March–April 1981): 89–110; Eurípides Cardoso de Menezes, "Africa do Sul e ONU: Dois Pesos e Duas Medidas," ADN (March–April 1982): 73–77; ibid., "A Antártica e os Desafios da Era Oceânica," ADN (May–June 1981): 121–29; Admiral Múcio Piragibe Ribeiro de Bakker, "Antártica: Uma Nova Perspectiva para o Brasil," ADN (May–June 1982): 5–56; and Captain (navy) Wintecas Villacas Barbosa de Godois, "Considerações Geopolíticas," ADN (July–August 1981).

90 RCID (April 1977): 12–21.

91 Colonel Florencio Zambrano, "Oriente y Occidente: Posibles objetivos," ibid., 22–30.

92 See "Visión geopolítica mundial," *Seguridad Nacional* (July–August 1979): 21–44. Hereafter SN. Also see Bravo's "Teorías geopolíticas para lograr un dominio mundial," SN (September, December 1981): 39–50; and his "Visión geopolítica de Chile en el Pacífico Sur," SN (January–April 1981): 75–89. See also Colonel Julio César von Chrismar Escuti, "Algunas definiciones y alcance de geopolítica," SN (May–August 1981); General Ramón Cañas Montalva, "Reflexiones geopolíticas sobre el presente y el futuro de América y de Chile," SN (July–September 1979): 59–88, and "Chile, el más antártico de los países del orbe y su responsabilidad continental en el Sur-Pacífico," SN (July–September 1979): 89–118. Recent writing on this subject by Chileans has been heavily influenced by Chrismar Escuti's *Geopolítica: Leyes que se deducen del estudio de la expansión de los estados* (Santiago: Estado Mayor General del Ejército de Chile, 1968) and by Colonel Augusto Pinochet Ugarte's *Geopolítica: Diferentes etapas para el estudio geopolítico de los estados* (Santiago: Estado Mayor General del Ejército de Chile, 1968). Both works, like most others written by South Americans, are highly derivative of European geopolitical theory. The Pinochet work was republished following the 1973 rising (Santiago: Editorial Andrés Bello, 1974).

93 SN (April–June 1983): 13–35. See also Admiral José Toribio Merino Castro, "Geopolítica oceánica de Chile," ibid., 5–12.

94 Ricardo Caillet Bois, "Las Islas Malvinas," *Revista de Informaciones* (September–October 1948): 641–727. Hereafter RIA.

95 RMA (January 1949): 12–28.

96 General Felipe N. Viscarra C., "Geopolítica boliviana: Bolivia en el continente sudamericano," RMBO (April–May 1952): 28–34. The cited passages are from pp. 30–32. See also Major Roberto González Polar, "La geopolítica y el ingeniero," RMBO (April–May 1952): 35–40.

97 See Captain Arturo Castilla Pizarro, "El Perú como nación: Nacionalismo y conciencia nacional: Sus factores formativos," RMP (January–March 1955): 89–101; Editorial, "El potencial nacional y la industria siderúrgica," RMP (April–May 1955): 1–4; and Castilla's "Geopolítica," RMP (August 1955): 51–62.

98 RESGP (April–June 1956): 67–72.

99 "El censo y los aborígenes selvícolas de nuestra Amazonia," RESGP (July–August 1956): 149–62.

100 RMP (November–December 1956): 19–43. In this context, see also the Meira Mattos RESGP reprints: "Conciencia geopolítica brasileña" (July–September 1961): 14–16; and "Proyección mundial del Brasil," ibid., 17–50.

101 Colonel Ronant Monje Roca, "Navegación fluvial y soberanía," ibid., 58–61.

102 "Geopolítica de la región amazónica de Bolivia," RMBO (April–June 1961): 27–31. See also Major Jesús Vía Soliz, "Por que inicialmente la navegación fluvial en Bolivia debe estar bajo el control del ejército," RMBO (April–June 1961): 51–55; and Captain Yves de Alarcón Romero, "¿Un batallón fluvial?" ibid., 75–80.

103 Lieutenant Colonel Hugo Antezana, "El camino al Ichilo: El ejército y la Corporación Boliviana de Fomento," ibid., 81–85.

104 "Iniciación de los cursos de 1965 en el Centro de Altos Estudios Militares y en la Escuela Superior de Guerra," RESGA (March–April 1965): 5–13. The citation is from p. 9.

105 RMP (July–August 1972): 2–8. See also Colonel (ret.) Armando Cueto Zevallos, "La independencia política y la independencia económica," RMP (September–October 1972): 8–15.

106 Editorial, "El nuevo régimen gubernamental," RMBO (April–May 1972): 1–2.

107 RMP (September–October 1973): 2–19. The quotation is from p. 6.

108 RMI (10 January 1950): 15–18.

109 S. P. Sharma, "Geopolitics of the Indian Ocean," AAJ (October 1951): 37–41.

110 RMI (25 November 1952): 30–35.

111 See "Le voyage du général Perón au Chili," RMI (25 March 1953): 30–36.

112 von Burkhart Mueller-Hillebrand, "Nationale Armee oder Europarmee?" WR (April 1953): 165–67.

113 "Deutsche Sicherheitspolitik und Atlantische Verteidigung," *Wehrkunde* (July 1963): 346–48.

114 See Major Walter P. Jacobs, "The East German Wehrmacht," *Army* (July 1957): 39–43.

115 "La défense atlantique: Remparte de l'Europe," RMI (November 1960): 39–47. The quotation comes from p. 43.

116 RDN (May 1966): 777–92.

117 See Ferdinand Otto Mischke, "Que devient être l'armée allemande?" RDN (December 1967): 1994–2001.

118 See TAQDJ supplements, General C. H. Stanforth, ed., *The Defence Forces of Switzerland* (1974); *Finland* (1974); *Austria* (1975); and *Sweden* (1975) (Devon: West of England Publishers).

119 Staff Sergeant P. G. Gittin, "Australia, Asia, and Ignorance," AAJ (May 1961): 50–52. See also his "A Catechism of Communism," AAJ (December 1962): 32–38.

120 See General Saiyud Kerdphol, "The Communist Threat in S. E. Asia," *Asian Defence Journal* (January–February 1978): 12–19. Hereafter ADJ.

121 Lieutenant Colonel P. G. Skelton, "Indian Ocean's Longest Coastline," DFJ (July–August 1979): 16–30.

122 Zara Dian, "Armed Insurgency and National Political Stability in the Southeast Asian States," ADJ (November–December 1979): 14–21. See also Major A. Weaver, "Japan's Reluctant Return to Military Power," DFJ (March–April 1984): 52–60.

123 "Interview with General Mohammed Zia-ul-Haq," ADJ (October 1981): 64–67.

124 "Interview with General Yaakov Even," *Israeli Defence Journal* (December 1984): 33–37.

125 See Franco A. Casadio, "La conflittualità mondiale nel periodo 1954–63," RMIT (January–February 1983): 13–32.

Chapter Two

1 General H. E. N. Bredin (CBO, DSO, MC), "The First Job of an Officer," AAJ (February 1975): 29–35. The cited passage is from p. 35.

2 Editorial, NA (November 1939): 1.

3 General (ret.) Indalicio Téllez Cárcamo, "La profesión militar," MECH (March–April 1942): 1135–40.

4 Nini Miranda, et al., "A Vida do Marechal Hermes Rodrigues da Fonseca: Sua Ação no Exército e na Política," RMB (July–September 1942): 351–430. Also see Lima Figueiredo, "Hermes e O Clube Militar," RMB (July–December 1955): 191–205; Lieutenant Colonel Luiz Gonzaga Valença de Mesquita, "Os Fonsecas," ibid., 255–79; and General Felicíssimo de Azevedo Aveline, "Rui Barbosa e Hermes da Fonseca," RMB (December 1973): 97–108.

5 "A História Militar Brasileira," RMB (July–December 1944): 356–66. See also Lieutenant Colonel Jorge Antezana Villagrán, "Bolivia y la junta interamericana de defensa," RMBO (November–December 1947): 26–31; (January–February 1948): 47–58; and an excerpt from the work of *Reichswehr* champion General Hans von Seeckt, Major José Joaquín Jiménez, tr., "El ejército en el estado," RMBO (November–December 1947): 32–37.

6 *El problema del vestuario y equipo del soldado en el altiplano* (La Paz: Editorial Trabajo, 1944), 5.

7 Lic. Arturo Logroño, "El ejército: Ayer y hoy," *Revista Militar de la República Dominicana* (October 1945): 4–5. Hereafter RMDR.

8 G. Pope Atkins, *Arms and Politics in the Dominican Republic* (Boulder: Westview Press, 1981), 33.

9 RMP (November 1946): xvii + 1–164.

10 Colonel J. H. Garcia, "A França de Ontem e Hoje: Semelhanças que Atormentam," RMB (January–June 1952): 67–76; General Paula de Cidade, "Da Missão Militar Franceza aos Nossos Dias," RMB (July–December 1954): 181–86.

11 See, for example, Major Miguel A. Peña B., "Un instituto militar orgullo de la América del Sur," *Revista Militar* (Colombia) (July 1955): 84–86 (hereafter RMC); Colonel Manuel Guillermo Martínez Pachón, "Efemérides de la Escuela Superior de Guerra, RMC (April–June 1960): 109–16, and "La reforma militar de 1909," RFAC (April–June 1984): 173–98; and Colonel (ret.) Leonidas Flórez Alvarez, "La Escuela Superior de Guerra: Reseña histórica," RMC (May 1959): 25–30.

12 See Lieutenant Colonel Montaigne, "El sentimiento del deber," RMP (September–October 1957): 87–88.

13 General José Venturelli Sobrinho, "Bilac, O Exército e a Pátria," RMB (January–June 1959): 84–98. See also Carlos Maúl, "A Glória de Bilac no Seu Centenário," RMB (January–March 1966): 7–30.

14 General (ret.) Enrique Indacochea Galarreta, "El Centro de Altos Estudios Militares de Francia," RMP (November–December 1960): 29–34; Major Oscar de Barros Falcão, "A Revolução de 5 de Janeiro de 1924," RMB (July–December 1961): 71–152; General Tristão de Alencar Araripe, "Ideias Fundamentais sobre a História Militar do Brasil," RMB (January–June 1963): 7–23.

15 General Juan José Gastelum Salcedo, "Doctrina filosófica de la revolución mexicana," *El Legionario* (August 1966): 7–13. The citation is from p. 7. Hereafter EL.

See also Lieutenant Colonel Jesús Ponce de León Rodríguez, "Esbozo de la educación militar en México," *Revista del Ejército* (Mexico) (April 1969): 3–10. Hereafter REM.

16 "Sesenta años después: La Escuela Militar de Cadetes marca el final de las guerras civiles y el principio de civilismo," *Revista del Ejército* (Colombia) (June 1967): 263–66. Hereafter REC.

17 Colonel Víctor José Fernández Bolívar, "La academia de defensa nacional," *Revista de las Fuerzas Armadas* (Venezuela) (January–December 1967): 76–80. Hereafter RFAV.

18 "Breve reseña histórica del ejército peruano," RMP (March–April 1967): 32–41.

19 See the address of 14 March 1948 by Lieutenant Colonel Aníbal Palma Guzmán commemorating the seventeenth anniversary of the establishment of El Salvador's Escuela de Comando y Estado Mayor Manuel Enrique Araujo, in *Revista de la Escuela de Comando y Estado Mayor Manuel Enrique Araujo* (June 1968): 75–80. Hereafter RECEMMEA. See also addresses in which Chileans received praise for their efforts in El Salvador, RECEMMEA (December 1968): 142–48.

20 See especially General Luis Rivas López, "Unidad pro encima del partidarismo: Cárdenas," EL (November–December 1968): 34–35. On Kundt's resurrection as a founding father of the Bolivian war machine, see "Homenaje al general Hans Kundt," RMBO (February–March 1969): 45–51. On Paraguay's successful campaign against Kundt's pupils in the War of the Gran Chaco, see "A nuestros lectores," *Revista de las Fuerzas Armadas de la Nación* (Paraguay) (July–November 1982): 76 (hereafter RFAP), and "Una arenga al batallón 40," RFAP (June 1983): 77–80.

21 See General Marcial Romero Pardo, "Bodas de plata del Colegio Militar Leoncio Prado," RESGP (January–March 1969): 56–60.

22 "Consideraciones sobre la historia integral del ejército peruano," RMP (January–February 1969): 48–57.

23 See, for example, M. R. Henry, "Colección de máximas militares," RFAV (January 1971): 14–18 (February 1971): 40–43; and Angel Ziems, "¿Quién fue Samuel McGill?" RFAV (October–December 1980): 43–44. McGill's still questionable contributions are placed in historical context by Holger R. Herwig, *Germany's Vision of Empire in Venezuela, 1871–1914* (Princeton: Princeton University Press, 1986), esp. 124–25.

24 Emerson Santos Parente, "A FEB: Primeira Manifestação do Brasil Potência," RMB (1973 special issue): 77–81. See also Major José Felipe Sampaio Barbosa, "Regresso e Desmobilização da FEB: Problemas e Consequências," ADN (May–June 1985): 27–44; "Força Expedicionária Brasileira: 40 Anos da Glória Perene," ibid., 5–26; and Colonel José Pedro de Mello, "Origens Sociais dos Quadros do Exército Brasileiro," ADN (April–June 1977): 51–62.

25 General Aurélio de Lyra Tavares, "Tradições Militares Franco-Brasileiras," RMB (July–December 1974): 7–14; Colonel Cláudio Moreira Bento, "Centenário do General Bertholdo Klinger, Co-fundador de *A Defesa Nacional* (1884–1969)," ADN (January–February 1984): 5–16; and Marshal Odylio Denys, "Revolução do Exército: A Missão Indígena," ADN (March–April 1985): 5–18.

26 "Síntesis histórica de la Escuela Superior de Guerra," *Revista del Ejército y Fuerza Aérea* (Mexico) (October 1975): 24–36. Hereafter REFAM.

27 Colonel Alejandro Medina Lois, "Teoría de seguridad nacional," SN (September–October, 1976): 33–42.

28 See Juan Rafael Llerena Amadeo, "La política al servicio del hombre," RESGA (March–April 1978): 47–56.

29 "The Shortage of Officers," TAQDJ (January 1949): 205–11.

30 "Army Officer: Mercenary or Missionary," AAJ (September 1956): 20–28. Cited material appears on p. 22.

31 Werner Hallweg, "Die neue Silhouette des Deutschen Soldaten," WR (May 1956): 142–50.

32 General Marcel Boucherie, "Les causes politiques et morales d'un désastre: 1940," RDN (March 1958): 409–16. See also S.E.I.T.C., "Mangin et l'armée noire," *Tropiques* (May 1954): 16–19.

33 Hans Doerr, "Gedanken über Jean Jaurès' Buch, *La nouvelle armée*," *Wehrkunde* (September 1959): 467–71.

34 General Baillif, "Les forces armées dans la nation," RDN (February 1960): 217–23.

35 See Colonel Fernand Schneider, "Après le transfert des cendres: Hommage à Lyautey," *Tropiques* (November 1961): 5–13; General de Boisboissel, "Lyautey parle," *Tropiques* (April 1951): 34–37; General Jean Charbonneau, "Joffre colonial," *Tropiques* (August–September 1952): 3–11.

36 See Lieutenant Colonel Flament, "La force publique au service du Congo," *Bulletin Militaire* (Belgian Congo) (June 1960): 341–53. Hereafter BMBC.

37 Hans-Joachim von Merkatz, "Vom Sinn der Tradition," WR (November 1961): 609–16. Cited passages appear on pp. 614, 616.

38 See Karlheinz Schubert, "Wahrung der Tradition," WR (May 1962): 288–89.

39 Martin Blumenson, "Some Thoughts on Professionalism," AAJ (September 1964): 44–48.

40 "Brothers in Arms," RUSI (August 1967): 261–64.

41 General W. A. B. Anderson, "The Military Profession," *Canadian Forces Sentinel* (February 1968): 1–5. Hereafter CFS.

42 "Die Bundeswehr und die Tradition," *Allgemeine Militärische Rundschau* (*Revue Militaire Générale;* RMG) (January 1970): 84–103. See also Siegfried Grimm, *Bundesrepublik treu zu dienen: Die geistige Rüstung der Bundeswehr* (Düsseldorf: Droste Verlag, 1970), 214–19.

43 "The Wind of Change," JUSII (October–December 1977): 317–23. The citation is from p. 321. See also Sri Nandon, "The Military Tradition," JUSII (October–December 1970): 350–56.

44 "The Value of a Commission," TAQDJ (April 1971): 330–41. The quoted passage comes from p. 339.

45 See Pierre Demeron, *Les 400 coups de Massu* (Paris: Jean Jacques Pouvert, 1972; Marie Madeleine Martin, *Charles de Gaulle cité au tribunal de l'histoire en l'année de Saint-Louis* (Paris: Éditions Reconquista, 1972); "*Le fil de l'épée*: Un entretien avec Michelle Michel," *Armées d'Aujourd'hui* (April 1973): 4–5 (hereafter AA); and Raoul Salan, *Memoires: Fin d'un empire: L'Algérie, De Gaulle et moi* (Paris: Presses de la Cité, 1974).

46 "Trends in Modern Society," *British Army Review* (April 1975): 11–21. Hereafter BAR.

47 "The New African Officer Corps," TAQDJ (October 1975): 433–39.
48 "Bessere Führung: eine Analyse des Gesammtproblems," WR (January–February 1976): 9–13.
49 "Le forze armate: Analise di una realità: Problemi e prospettive," RMIT (January–February 1977): 2–7.
50 "The Falling Pillars of Professionalism," *Pakistan Army Journal* (March 1971): 89–96. Hereafter PAJ. See also Major Abdul Qayyum's overdrawn appeal to Pakistanis to remember great leaders of the past, "Changes Khan and Timur Lang: A Study in Personality and Generalship," PAJ (January 1964): 47–69.
51 "Demain et hier," *Forces Armées Françaises* (December 1974); 13–17. Hereafter FAF.
52 "Bundeswehr und Tradition," *Europäische Wehrkunde* (June 1978): 286–87. Hereafter EW.
53 "Bundeswehr und Tradition," *Truppenpraxis* (September 1978): 715.
54 "The Crisis of Obedience," JUSII (October–December 1979): 336–47. The citation is from p. 345.
55 PAJ (March 1980): 81–105.
56 "Herausforderung Wehrdienst: Der Mensch im Mittelpunkt?" WR (July–August 1980): 111–12.
57 "The Pride and the Privilege," PAJ (March 1981): 42–48. The quotation appears on p. 45. See Captain Tobías Barros Ortiz, *Vigilia de armas: Charlas sobre la vida militar destinadas a un joven teniente* (Santiago: Estador Mayor General del Ejército de Chile, 1920). This seminal work was reprinted in 1973.
58 "Soldatentum in unserer Zeit," IT (January 1984): 27–41. Details on the forming of the *Bundeswehr* can be found in the well-presented *A Military History of Germany from the Eighteenth Century to the Present Day,* by Martin Kitchen (London: Weidenfeld and Nicholson, 1975). An excellent, recent work on the importance of both tradition and reform in the *Bundeswehr* is Donald Abenheim's *Reforging the Iron Cross: The Search for Tradition in the West German Armed Forces* (Princeton: Princeton University Press, 1988).
59 See Michael King, *New Zealanders at War* (Auckland: Heineman Publishers, 1981), p. 1. See also Ian Bellany, *Australia in the Nuclear Age: National Defence and National Development* (Sydney: Sydney University Press, 1972); Brigadier D. S. Thompson, "The Australian Army Today," AAJ (September 1972): 3–24; Ross Babbage, *Rethinking Australia's Defence* (St. Lucia: University of Queensland Press, 1980); and Thomas Durrell Young, "The New Zealand Army: How Is It Structured, What Is Its Role?" TAQDJ (July 1985): 272–76.
60 *Tristes tropiques* (Paris: Plon, 1955). The allusion is to remarks made in Part Two, Chapter Nine, "Guanabara," best rendered into English in the Charles and Doreen Wightman translation (New York: Atheneum, 1974).
61 See, for example, Isaac Sandoval Rodríguez, *Las crisis políticas latinoamericanas y el militarismo* (México, D. F.: Siglo Veintiuno Editores, 1976).
62 Louis A. Pérez, Jr., *Army Politics in Cuba, 1898–1958* (Pittsburgh: University of Pittsburgh Press, 1976), 170.
63 On difficulties encountered by military organizations struggling to preserve a semblance of tradition, see Gerhard Weiher, *Militär und Entwicklung in der Türkei, 1945–1973: Ein Beitrag zur Untersuchung der Rolle des Militärs in der Entwicklung der Dritten Welt* (Opladen: Leske Verlag, 1978); Lieutenant Commander William F. Hickman,

"Ravaged and Reborn: the Iranian Army, 1982," staff paper, The Brookings Institution (Washington, D.C., 1982); and Sam C. Ukpabi, *Military Involvement in African Politics* (London: Conch Magazine, 1972).

64 "The Army's Profile in Changing Times," MR (October 1960): 19–36. Quotations are from pp. 35 and 19, respectively.

65 "La ética frente al materialismo," RMA (March–April 1953): 155–61. The citation is from p. 161.

66 "Psicología del mando," RIA (September–October 1953): 552–75.

67 See Lieutenant Colonel Federico Gentilhuomo, "Guerra total y nación en armas," RMA (January–February 1954): 11–13. See also General Adolfo S. Espindola, "Las fuerzas morales son las que en definitiva conquistan la victoria," RMA (September 1948): 1047–56; (December 1948): 1465–74.

68 "Nuevas ideas sobre la educación moral," RMP (January–February 1956): 310–36.

69 "Los militares estudiantes," REM (October 1956): 62–65.

70 See Lieutenant (ret.) Domingo I. de Jesús López, "Educación civil y educación militar," RMA (October–December 1959): 65–68.

71 "Amor, fidelidad y servicio," RFAV (January 1960): 4–5.

72 General (ret.) Raúl A. González, "Panorama económico, político, y social argentino," RCMA (July–September 1962): 8–25. The quotation is from p. 12. See also Lieutenant Colonel Luis Alberto Leoni, "Homo militar," RCMA (April–June 1964): 103–8.

73 See Captain Enrique Blas Gómez Saa, "El orden público y la acción psicológica," RCMA (October–December 1969): 41–46.

74 "Aula Magna na Escola Superior de Guerra pelo Excmo. Presidente da República," ADN (March–April 1970): 11–26. The cited passage is from p. 12.

75 Colonel Carlos A. Landaburu, "Reflexiones sobre la situación argentina y la obtención de los objetivos políticos nacionales," RESGA (July–October 1970): 41–46.

76 Captain Carlos Francisco Sicardi, "El sentido de la milicia en el mundo de hoy," RESGA (November–December 1971): 123–32. The quotation is from p. 129.

77 João Paulo dos Reis Velloso, "Novas Dimensões da Sociedade Brasileira: Integração Social e Estratégia Externa," RMB (January–June 1972): 7–22. The cited material is found on p. 9.

78 José Fernandes Dantas, "A Família e seu Reflexo na Posição de Juventude Perante a Seguridade Nacional," ADN (July–August 1973): 15–28.

79 "Como afrontar el cambio," RESGA (January–February 1974): 9–12. See also Colonel (ret.) Emilio Bolón Varela, "El ideal de perfección," RESGA (November–December 1973): 73–80.

80 "Psicopolítica e Contrapsicopolítica," ADN (November–December 1975): 3–40. The cited passage is from p. 32.

81 SN (August 1976): 71–78. The quotation is from p. 75.

82 Majors (*carabineros*) Ramiro Rosales and Adrián Figueroa L., "Las drogas y su incidencia en la seguridad nacional," SN (April–June 1978): 103–17.

83 "Comunicação e Cultura de Massa," RMB (April–June 1978): 73–83. The quotation appears on p. 77.

84 "El humanismo," RESGA (January–February 1979): 91–95. Camps served as police chief of Buenos Aires during the most violent phase of the "dirty war" against opposition to military rule in the late 1970s and early 1980s. He was convicted, along

with a number of his professional colleagues, of kidnapping, torture, and murder in 1986. He served less than five years of a twenty-five-year sentence and was pardoned by President Carlos Menem in December 1990.

85 "O Papel dos Elites no Contexto da Segurança Nacional," ADN (January–February 1980): 31–43. Cited material appears on pp. 35, 36, 42.

86 See Lieutenant Colonel (ret.) Caio Augusto do Amaral, "A Força da Opinião Pública," ADN (July–August 1980): 87–93.

87 General Antônio de Brito Júnior, "A Violência: Causas e Medidas," ADN (September–October 1980): 133–38.

88 See Philippe Faucher, *Le Brésil des militaires* (Montréal: Les Presses de l'Université de Montréal, 1981), esp. 45–53.

89 See General Taunay Drummond Coelho Reis, "Deveres e Direitos dos Ouvintes e Telespectadores," ADN (March–April 1982): 87–90; and Captain Adão Pantoja de Maria, "Comunicação de Massa: Espelhos da Sociedade ou Criadores Modelos," ADN (July–August 1984): 125–38.

90 See Colonel Daniel Oviedo Uzcátegui, "Las funciones específicas de las fuerzas armadas," RFAV (1968): 18–26.

91 "Pax" and "Internal security," JUSII (January 1946): 87–93. The citation is from p. 93.

92 "Soldier," "What Makes a Good Unit," AAJ (June–July 1948): 36–37.

93 Editorial, "Soldier, Where Do You Stand?" AAJ (October–November 1949): 3–5.

94 Lieutenant Colonel A. Green, "Revolution in the Military Profession," AAJ (June 1954): 5–9.

95 Of a number of responses, the best was that of General S. F. Legge, "Soldier, Scientist, or Socialite," AAJ (October 1954): 5–12.

96 Walter Hildebrandt, "Politik und Kriegführung in neuer Sicht: Probleme und Aufgaben der Streitkräfte im Zeitalter des Weltanschauungskriegs," WR (March 1955): 106–17. The citation is from p. 117.

97 See, for example, Warrant Officer K. L. Hanrahan, "The Soldier's Place in Modern Society," AAJ (July 1955): 10–14.

98 "Is Money All They Want?" TAQDJ (July 1958): 228–34. The quoted passage appears on p. 229.

99 Rolf Elble, "Die Situation des Soldaten in unserer Zeit," *Wehrkunde* (September 1958): 472–82.

100 See "The Officer's Career," BAR (March 1959): 17–25. See also J. R. Tournoux, "A Praetorian Army," *The Reporter* (2 February 1960): 18–21.

101 "Man: The Essential Ingredient," AID (May 1960): 4–13. The quotation is from p. 12.

102 "La relazione attitudinale nell'esercito," RMIT (November 1962): 1323–28. See also General Raffaele Binetti, "La preparazione spirituale delle forze armate," RMIT (June 1965): 846–57.

103 See Major Marcello Eydalin, "Opinioni: Gli opposti blocchi ideoligici di fronte alla propaganda," RMIT (November 1963): 1337–44.

104 Edgard Pisani, "Agriculture et défense nationale," RDN (November 1963): 1605–17.

105 Lieutenant Colonel Howard Green, "Hardship," TAQDJ (July 1965): 231–41. The citation appears on p. 239.

106 "Man and the Army," JUSII (October–December 1965): 253–59, 265. The quoted passage is from pp. 253–54. And see Lieutenant Colonel R. D. Palsoka, "Officers for the Twentieth Century," JUSII (October–December 1966): 333–39.

107 "Gespräch in der Bundeswehr: Offizier und Ehe," *Truppenpraxis* (July 1967): 84–85. See also for comparison on this matter J. Garrido, "Liberación sexual;" N. de Córdoba, "No politizar el divorcio;" and "Rodrigo," "La familia unida es lo normal;" all in *Reconquista* (January 1981): 60–63.

108 Lieutenant Christian Kunz, "Jugend und Wehrgedanke," *Wehrkunde* (August 1967), 422–26.

109 Dr. B. Chakravarty, "Is Political Indoctrination of Our Armed Forces Necessary?" JUSII (October–December 1968): 410–14.

110 Cadet Paul O'Donnell, "Preparing for an Educated Army," *An Cosantoir* (Eire) (July 1969): 236–37. Hereafter ACE.

111 "Die Ehre der Soldaten," *Wehrkunde* (August 1969): 409–11.

112 "Vocación y selección en la carrera militar," *Ejército* (February 1970): 37–40.

113 See William Coulet, "Armée, nation, et discipline," RDN (3 parts) (March 1970): 433–41; (April 1970): 610–24; (May 1970): 793–801.

114 "East is East and West is West," AAJ (May 1970): 41–46.

115 "Gedanken zu antikem und modernem Feldherrentum," *Wehrkunde* (June 1970): 281–84.

116 JUSII (October 1970): 347–49.

117 "Erziehung zum Gemeinschaftsgeist," *Truppenpraxis* (February 1971): 87–89.

118 "Officiers, pour quel office," RDN (May 1971): 718–27.

119 "The Soldier, the Battlefield, and Leadership," PAJ (September 1971): 15–23.

120 "The Impact of Science and Technology on Society in the 1980s," AAJ (February 1972): 19–32. The citation is from p. 31.

121 Captain Julius T. Crouch, "The Black Officer in Today's Army," MR (May 1972): 61–67. The quoted material is from pp. 64–66.

122 Brigadier J. Nazareth, "If We Rest We Rust," JUSII (July–September 1972): 213–35. The cited passages are from pp. 225–26.

123 *Parameters* (December 1972): 9–17.

124 Captain D. S. Knapp, "Leadership," CFS (January 1973): 13–18.

125 General (ret.) T. N. R. Nayar, "Reflections on the Generation Gap in Our Times," JUSII (October–December 1973): 353–60. The quotation is from p. 354.

126 Ugo Sciascia, "Evoluzione sociale in atto e ripercussione sulla organizazione militare," RMIT (January–February 1974): 60–64.

127 "Technology and National Military Potential," PAJ (December 1974): 12–16. See also his "Science and Technology for Development," PAJ (June 1978): 39–43.

128 Lieutenant Colonel G. D. Johnson (MBE, MC), "The Thinking Soldier," TAQDJ (July 1975): 290–303. The citation is from p. 300. See also Colonel Peter J. Dietz and Lieutenant Colonel J. F. Stone, "The British All-Volunteer Army," *Armed Forces and Society* (Winter 1975): 159–90; and M. D. Feld, "Military Professionalism and the Mass Army," ibid., 191–214. Hereafter AFS. And see Lieutenant Werner Breindl, "Führung aus sozialpsychologischer Sicht," *Truppenpraxis* (August 1976): 529–33.

129 Brigadier (ret.) N. B. Grant, "An Officer and a Gentleman," JUSII (October–December 1978): 317–23.

130 Brigadier (ret.) P. H. C. Hayward (CBE), "Behind the Times," BAR (April, 1979): 13–16.

131 Commander Rafael Gravalos Guzmán, "Ejército, juventud, participación," *Ejército* (August 1979): 44–45.

132 General Walter F. Ulmer, Jr., "Notes on Leadership for the 1980's," MR (July 1980): 10–12.

133 Martin Kutz, "Kontinuität von Reform und Gegenreform in der Offizierausbildung der Bundeswehr," in Karl-Ernst Schultz, ed., *Die Neuordnung von Bildung und Ausbildung in der Bundeswehr: Ein Zwischenbilanz nach zehn Jahren* (Baden-Baden: Nomos Verlagsgesellschaft, 1982), 25–48.

134 General Manuel Cabeza Calahorra, "La socialización militar," *Ejército* (January 1983): 3–14. The quotation is from p. 5.

135 Indira Awasty, "Alienated Leadership," JUSII (October–December 1983): 325–28.

136 Admiral (ret.) Henry Eccles, *Military Power in a Free Society* (Newport, R. I.: Naval War College Press, 1979), 15, 29–30.

137 *The Condor and the Cows: A South American Travel-Diary* (New York: Random House, 1949).

138 André Maurois, *My Latin American Diary*, tr. Frank Jackson, fwd., G. S. Fraser (London: The Falcon Press, 1953), 23.

139 *South American Meditations: On Hell and Heaven in Man's Soul*, tr. Therese Duerr (London: Jonathan Cape, 1932), 103. Author's own italics.

140 RMP (November–December 1964): 1–20. The cited material is from p. 7.

141 MECH (July–August 1970): 11–51.

142 General Jorge A. Giovanelli, "El verdadero y amplio significado que la defensa nacional tiene en los tiempos modernos," RESGA (August–October 1964): 47–57; Colonel Tomás A. Sánchez Bustamante, "Seguridad nacional," RESGA (November–December 1964): 5–18.

143 ADN (September–October 1975): 29–62.

144 See Pierre Chouleur, "Le rôle de l'armée en Afrique Noire," RMG (April 1965): 10–18; Mariano Baptista Gumucio, *De las guerrillas a la escalada nuclear* (Montevideo: Editorial Alfa, 1970); Samuel Decalo, *Coups and Army Rule in Africa: Studies in Military Style* (New Haven: Yale University Press, 1976); General Albert Kwesi Ocran, *Politics of the Sword: A Personal Memoir on Military Involvement in Ghana and of Problems of Military Government* (London: Rex Collings, 1977); Theophilus Olatunde Odetola, *Military Politics in Nigeria: Economic Development and Stability* (New Brunswick, N. J.: Transaction Books, 1978); J. 'Bayo Adekson, *Nigeria in Search of a Stable Civil-Military System* (Aldershot, Hants.: Gower Publishing Company, 1989); and Odetola, *Military Regimes and Development: A Comparative Analysis of African States* (London: George Allen and Unwin, 1982) for pertinent treatment of military-civilian relations in Africa.

145 Adekson, *Nigeria*, 141.

146 S. E. Finer, "The Man on Horseback—1974," AFS (Fall 1974): 5–27. The cited passage is from p. 6.

147 See Kenneth W. Grundy's *The Rise of the South African Military Establishment: An Essay on the Changing Locus of State Power* (Capetown: South African Institute of International Affairs, 1983) and *The Militarization of South African Politics* (Bloomington: Indiana University Press, 1986); Jonathan Kapstein, "Armed Confrontation

Builds in South Africa," *Proceedings of the U.S. Naval Institute* (December 1981): 7–38; Philip H. Frankel, *Pretoria's Praetorians: Civil-Military Relations in South Africa* (Cambridge: Cambridge University Press, 1984); and the July 1983 issue of *South Africa International* for material on intensification of South African military-civilian relationships.

148 "On Development and Security," ADJ (September 1981): 16–17. On intensification of relationships in Asia and the Middle East, see Ulf Sundhausen, *The Road to Power: Indonesian Military Politics, 1945–1967* (Kuala Lumpur: Oxford University Press, 1982); Mohammad A. Tarbush, *The Role of the Military in Politics: A Case Study of Iraq to 1941* (London: Kegan Paul International, 1982); Amos Perlmutter, *Politics and the Military in Israel, 1967–1977* (London: Frank Cass, 1978); Perlmutter, *Political Roles and Military Rulers* (London: Frank Cass, 1981); Onkar Marwah and Jonathan D. Pollack, *Military Power and Policy in Asian States: China, India, and Japan* (Boulder: Westview Press, 1980); Stephen P. Cohen, *The Indian Army: Its Contribution to the Development of a Nation* (Berkeley: University of California Press, 1971); Cohen, *The Pakistan Army* (Berkeley: University of California Press, 1984); Lieutenant Thomas A. Marks, "Professionalism in the Royal Thai Army," *Proceedings of the U.S. Naval Institute* (January 1973): 47–53; Gavin Kennedy, *The Military in the Third World* (London: Gerald Duckworth & Co., 1974); George M. Haddad, *Revolutions and Military Rule in the Middle East: The Northern Tier* (New York: Robert Speller and Sons, 1965); Anouar Abdel-Malik, *Egypt: Military Society*, tr. Charles Lam Markmann (New York: Random House, 1968); P. J. Vatikiotis, *The Egyptian Army in Politics: Pattern for New Nations* (Bloomington: Indiana University Press, 1961). This is a mere sampling of representative works dealing with themes developed in these pages.

149 Arthur Conte, *Sans De Gaulle* (Paris: Plon, 1970); General Paul Stehlin, *La France désarmée* (Paris: Colmann-Levy, 1974) should be consulted for insights into military-civilian relations of that epoch.

150 See Stanley G. Payne, *Politics and the Military in Modern Spain* (Stanford: Stanford University Press, 1968).

151 Joe Gray Taylor, Jr., "The Bundeswehr and German Society," *Parameters* (September 1983): 68–75. The citation is from p. 69. See also David Eshol, "Bundeswehr: The New German Army," *Defence Update No. 57* (1985): 28–63; Alfred Grosser, *Geschichte Deutschlands seit 1945: Eine Bilanz* (München: Deutscher Taschenbuch Verlag, 1974); Eric Waldman, *The Goose Step is Verboten: The German Army Today* (New York: The Free Press of Glencoe, 1964); Hans Karst, *Das Bild des Soldaten: Versuch eines Umreises* (Boppard am Rhein: H. Bolt, 1969); and General Harald Wust, "Tradition in der Bundeswehr," EW (August 1978). All are useful sources on the intensification of German military-civilian relationships.

Chapter Three

1 Count Hermann Keyserling, *South American Meditations: On Hell and Heaven in Man's Soul*, tr. Therese Duerr (London: Jonathan Cape, 1932), 77.

2 See Lieutenant Oscar Bueno Tovar, "Dirección de tropas," RMP (July 1947): 219–21; Lieutenant Rodolfo I. Pedeflous, "Lirismo y realismo en el militar," RMA (November 1949): 1425; "Despedida de la Escuela Superior de Guerra a los jefes y

oficiales del curso de e. m. de 1948," RIA (July–August 1948): 467–71 and (November–December 1948): 733–37.

3 Lieutenant Colonel Manuel Abel Arce, "Deberes del oficial en el ejército," RMP (October 1949): 41–43.

4 Lieutenant Roberto Wayar Aníbaro, "La instrucción individual en el ejército," RMBO (September–November 1950): 42–46.

5 Lieutenant (chaplain) Cayetano del Duca O., "El carácter en el militar," RMBO (January–February 1954): 55–59.

6 Sergeant Andrés Mercedes Jerez, "Cortesía y disciplina militar," *Revista de las Fuerzas Armadas* (Dominican Republic) (May 1954): 17. Hereafter RFADR.

7 "El comandante y el mando," RMC (September 1956): 39–54.

8 "Honor de sus armas," RMC (June 1959): 15–19.

9 See "Palabras del director de la Escuela Superior de Guerra, Coronel D. José Luis D'Andrea Mohr, en el acto de entrega de diplomas de oficiales de estado mayor a los jefes y oficiales egresados del 3. curso de 1958," RESGA (October–December 1958): n.p.; Cadete Erasmo Pinzón Rodríguez, "El arte del buen mando," RMC (June 1959): 20–21; Captain (navy) Gabriel Roberto Reyes C., "La ética de la profesión militar," RMC (March–April 1965): 37–45.

10 Coronel Osiris Guillermo Villegas, "El valor," RMA (January–March 1959): 27–36. The citation is from p. 29. Prera, "El carácter," *Guardia Nacional* (November–December 1961): 64–66. Hereafter GN. See also "Moral militar: Virtud," RFADR (March–April 1962): 21–22; and Lieutenant Héctor E. Lachapelle Díaz, "El don de mando," RFADR (May–July 1962): 13–15; Sergeant Rubén Darío Bustillos R. "El jefe y el arte de mandar," *Revista del Ejército* (Venezuela) (January–February 1965): n.p. Hereafter REV. Lieutenant Colonel Juan Manuel Sucre Figarella, "Las fuerzas morales del jefe," REV (September–October 1965): 815; Sucre's "Las cualidades del jefe," REV (January–February 1966): 53–57; and Colonel Jacinto Pérez Arcay, "El honor militar," REV (December 1976): 15–20.

11 "Cualidades del oficial de estado mayor," RFAC (June 1963): 283–88.

12 Colonel Ricardo Benza Carreras, "Importancia de la eduación moral militar," RFAP (January–May 1967): 7–11.

13 "El poderío nacional y su contenido," *Revista Militar* (Guatemala) (October–December 1967): 16–29. Hereafter RMGU.

14 "Condiciones del oficial educador," RMP (May–June 1969): 31–34.

15 "Etica del jefe," RECEMMEA (June 1969): 95–102.

16 "¿Está usted listo?" RECEMMEA (January–June 1970): 35–43.

17 Lieutenant Colonel Federico Castillo Yanes, "La Guardia Nacional de la República de Panamá: Una institución al servicio de su pueblo," RECEMMEA (January–June 1971): 39–42.

18 See, for example, Captain Rodrigo Otálora Bueno, "La eterna disciplina," RFAC (July–September 1970): 43–49; Captain Roberto Badillo Martínez, "La discreción en el ejército," REM (August 1970): 29–31; Captain Felix Zárate Monges, "El poder de la voluntad," RFAP (June–December 1975): 16–20.

19 RMB (January–April 1979): 2–25. See also General Sebastião José Ramos de Castro, "O Comandante," ADN (September–October 1984): 5–14; General Jonas de Morais Correia Neto, "O Capitão: Chefe e Lider," ADN (September–October

1984): 15–27; and Major Miguel Tapia de la Puente, "La dirección de un organismo civil," MECH (May–August 1979): 116–22.

20 *Reconquista* (July–August 1955): 108–17.

21 De Mattos, *Revista Militar* (Portugal) (April 1955): 262–73. Hereafter RMPO. Suire, RMI (January 1964): 22–31. See also Canon Dr. Antônio dos Reis Rodrigues, "A Fisonomia Espiritual do Chefe Militar," RMPO (August–September 1956): 539–54; and Captain Henrique A. Nascimento Garcia, "Velhos Princípios, Princípios de Sempre," RMPO (February–March 1957): 143–52.

22 PAJ (December 1964): 34–36.

23 Captain (navy) Olaf Preuschoft, "Vom Stil des Offiziers," *Truppenpraxis* (June 1964): 411–12.

24 See Lieutenant Colonel Núñez Maturana, "Sine qua non," *Reconquista* (February 1966): 24–26; Lieutenant Colonel Martínez Bande, "Don Quixote, no," *Reconquista* (April 1966): 8–11; Colonel Delgado Pinar, "Quijotes, sí . . . , y a mucha honra," *Reconquista* (June 1966): 15–18; and Lieutenant Sáez Bayo, "Quijotes, sí, Quijotes, no," *Reconquista* (September 1966): 9–11.

25 "Nôtre enthousiasme," RDN (May 1970): 763–68.

26 V. V. Shelyag, A. Glotochkin, and K. K. Platonov, *Military Psychology: A Soviet View* (Moscow: Military Publishing House, Ministry of Defense, 1972; Washington, D. C.: GPO, 1975), 309.

27 Prada Canillas, *Ejército* (April 1973): 22–26; Pamplona, *Ejército* (January 1978): 11–16.

28 Commander Jean Serge Longy, "Commander en homme libre," AA (November 1980): 70–73, 75.

29 Rolf Elble, "Die Situation des Soldaten in unserer Zeit," *Wehrkunde* (September 1958): 472–82.

30 General Enrico Ramella, "I graduati di truppa," RMIT (January 1963): 54–71; Colonel Guglielmo Petri, "La formazione del soldato e del commandante," RMIT (May–June 1981): 9–16.

31 "The Training of the Young Officer Cadet After the War," TAQDJ (April 1944): 118.

32 "Statesmen and Commandos," TAQDJ (October 1951): 33–43. The cited passage appears on pp. 35–36.

33 "The Good Officer," CAJ (May 1950): 13–23.

34 "The Military Profession," CFS (February 1968): 1–5.

35 See "Leadership," AAJ (February 1951): 3–10; and "The Qualities of a Good Officer," AAJ (August 1952): 19–20.

36 Major W. F. Burnard, "The Leader and the Led," AAJ (April 1964): 11–13; Warrant Officer R. Burns, "The Good Leader," AAJ (April 1966): 46–53; and Major (ret.) Reginald Hargreaves, "The Leader and the Led," MR (September 1960): 3–10. See also Captain Luciano I. Gunabe, "Leadership Training of the Present," *Philippine Armed Forces Journal* (January 1951): 22–24. Hereafter PAFJ. And General Mateo Capinpin, "On Leadership," PAFJ (February–March 1955): 52–66.

37 Lieutenant Colonel B. L. Raina, "Leadership," JUSII (January–April 1950): 7–20. The citation is from p. 18. See also, for example, the treatment of human factors and environmental stress in Lieutenant Colonel J. O. Langtry's "Man the Weapon: Neglected Aspects of Leader Training," AAJ (March 1966): 3–13. See also Major

Hargoolal, "Leadership," JUSII (January–March 1966): 61–70; and Major D. H. Ralls (USA), "Excellence in the Military Profession," AAJ (June 1968): 26–28.

38 "Reflections on Leadership," MR (October 1961): 2–13.

39 "The Officer as a Model of Ethical Conduct," MR (July 1978): 56–65.

40 "Thoughts on Leadership," MR (May 1983): 46–50. See also Lieutenant Colonel Boyd M. Harris, "A New Army Emphasis on Leadership: Be, Know, Do," MR (February 1983): 46–50; and Colonel Dandridge M. Malone, "The Essence of Army Leadership," MR (August 1980): 30–36.

41 "El actual soldado boliviano," RMBO (November–December 1947): 38–45. The quotation is from p. 39.

42 "El jefe," REM (December 1948): 4–12; "El hombre y las fuerzas morales," REM (January 1949): 10–17; and (February 1949): 16–20. See also these REM editorials: "Disciplina," (March 1949): 1–3; "La moral militar" (April 1949): 1–2; "Mando" (May 1949): 1–4; "El servicio nacional" (June 1949): 1–3; "El sentido de la responsabilidad" (August 1949): 1–3; and "Pueblo y ejército" (November 1949): 1–3.

43 "El ejercicio del comando," RMP (June 1949): 1–5.

44 Leyba Pou, "Disciplina y dirección," RFADR (January–February 1950): 3–5; and García Villasmil, "La psicología y su utilidad," RFAV (Venezuela) (May 1951): 362–63.

45 Hernández, "Disciplina militar," *Revista Militar* (Guatemala) (January–March 1953): 5–10. Hereafter RMGU. Baldezón Valle, "Disciplina," RMGU (April–June 1953): 19–20. Also see Hernández, "Moral militar y espíritu de grupo," RMGU (July–September 1953): 27–29.

46 "El valor, la disciplina, y la lealtad del soldado dominicano," RFADR (January 1954): 79. Also see Captain Rafael Rojas Rodríguez, "La disciplina en el ejército dominicano," RFADR (February 1954): 10–12; and Lieutenant Luis Curet Colón, "Disciplina," RFADR (April 1954): 10–12.

47 "Ejército," REM (July 1955): 13–21. The citation is from p. 19. See also his "Disciplina," REM (May 1955): 17–27; and "Virtudes militares," REM (March 1956): 4–11; and (April 1956): 5–13.

48 "Factor moral predominante," RFAV (February 1956): 22–23. See also his "Disciplina," RFAV (January–February 1957): 14.

49 "Disciplina," RMA (October–December 1958): 7–10.

50 See Major Rafael Navarro Mendoza, "Consejos a un comandante," REM (December 1959): 53–57. Also see the André Maurois excerpts entitled "El dificil arte del mando," REM (December 1959): 58–59.

51 General Alfonso Corona del Rosal, "El valor," REM (April 1960): 18–25.

52 Corona del Rosal, "La disciplina," REM (March 1960): 51–56.

53 "El mando," GN (September–October 1961): 17–20.

54 "Reflexiones sobre comando y estado mayor," RESGP (April–June 1966): 24–32.

55 Julián Martínez, "La disciplina como ideal del buen ciudadano," RFAV (1969): 14.

56 See, for example, "Disciplina y cortesía militar," RFADR (November 1970): 95–108.

57 Lieutenant Colonel Ramón Iriarte Alana, "Disciplina y subordinación," RFAV (October–December 1973): 85–86; General José Antonio Olavarría, "El liderazgo militar," RFAV (August–December 1984): 21–28.

58 Colonel Servio Júpiter Camey Sierra, "La disciplina," RMGU (April–June 1975): 6–9.

59 Lieutenant Colonel H. Hernández Méndez, "Disciplina militar," *Armas* (May–June 1976): 33–35.

60 Colonel Renato Picón Ruiz, "El comandante-lider," MECH (May–August 1983): 63–67.

61 "Soldier," "What Makes a Good Unit," AAJ (June–July 1948): 36–37.

62 C. A. Moureau, "L'autorité," RMI (April 1962): 19–22 and (June 1962): 11–13.

63 Commander (medical corps) Joaquín Anel Urbez, "La aptitud para el mando: Base psicológica para la selección de los cuadros," *Ejército* (April 1962): 13–18.

64 "Discipline in the Soviet Army," SMR (August 1970): 7–9.

65 (September 1970): 458–62.

66 "Piu meritate l'obbedienza e piu sarete obbediti," RMIT (April 1971): 521–23.

67 Captain (navy) Giorgio de Benedictis, "Sul principio d'autorità," RMIT (February 1972): 207–23; Major Diego Bertoncin, "La psicologia como supporto nella soluzione dei problema di comando," RMIT (April 1972): 561–70.

68 "Pour réhabiliter la discipline," FAF (April 1973): 26–29.

69 "Ist Führung lernbar?" *Truppenpraxis* (July 1974): 492–96.

70 "Contributo della psicologia alla formazione del militare," RMIT (September–October 1974): 50–54.

71 "Une adhésion et non une contrainte," AA (October 1978): 50–51.

72 "La spécificité du commandement militaire," AA (March 1981): 30–32.

73 Colonel Francisco Belza y Ruiz de la Fuente, "El mando: Su responsabilidad moral," *Ejército* (July 1982): 57–61.

74 Colonel P. Simkenchov, "Commander: The Organizer of Combat Training," SMR (January 1984): 18–19.

75 "Junior Leadership," AAJ (August–September 1948): 55.

76 See Lochlin MacGlynn, "My Idea of an Officer," ACE (March 1961): 109–11.

77 "Leadership: Everyday Aspects and Problems: A Young Officer's View," CAJ (April 1962): 44–47. See also Captain M. Rioux, "The Qualities of Leadership: An Essay," CAJ (July 1962): 2–7.

78 ACE (November 1966): 583–86.

79 Colonel D. G. Levis (OBE), "Military Purpose and Human Factors," AAJ (April 1968): 25–36. See also Captain J. G. Menzies, "Leadership," AAJ (December 1970): 27–36; Air Commodore R. G. Funnell, "The Professional Army Officer in Australia," DFJ (July–August 1980): 23–39; and Funnell, "Leadership: Theory and Practice," DFJ (July–August 1982): 5–22.

80 General Sir Frank King (GCB, MBE), "Thoughts on Leadership," TAQDJ (April 1984): 135–47. The quotation appears on p. 147.

81 Major Gurbachan Singh, "The Right Type and Some Thoughts on Indianisation," JUSII (July 1946): 443–45.

82 "A Lesson in Leadership," PAJ (January 1961): 7–8.

83 "The Leader and His Men," PAJ (December 1962): 5–8.

84 See "Devotion: The Greatest Single Weapon of War," PAJ (June 1963): 1–3.

85 Major Mansoor Ahmed, "Conferences or Orders," PAJ (December 1963): 1–2. See also Captain Tariq A. Rehman, "Motivation and Leadership," PAJ (September 1977): 50–58; and Major Shajar Hussain, "Man: The Key to Success," PAJ (September 1977): 15–20.

86 Major K. Brahma Singh, "The Wind of Change," JUSII (October–December 1972): 317–23.
87 "The Paternalistic Society of the Army and Its Implications," JUSII (January–March 1973): 56–62.
88 "Notes sur la manière de former le soldat," BMBC (October 1954): 635–38.
89 "Le respect des règles qui régissent les rapports devant exister entre le chef et le subordonné," *Frères d'Armes* (May–June 1973): 24–25. Hereafter FA.
90 "The Value of Man in the Islamic Military Thought," *Islamic Defence Review* (January 1982): 9–12. See also Dewitt C. Ellinwood and Cynthia H. Enloe, *Ethnicity and the Military in Asia* (New Brunswick, N. J.: Transaction Books, 1981).
91 "Prejudice and the Soldier," MR (August 1965): 63–66.
92 Bradley, "Leadership," MR (September 1966): 48–53; Ridgway, "Leadership," MR (October 1966): 40–49. See also Bradley's "Leadership," *Parameters* (December 1972): 2–8; and "On Leadership," *Parameters* (September 1981): 2–7. See also Staff Report, "What Makes a Good Leader," AD (February 1968): 36–40.
93 "Machiavellian Views on Leadership," MR (January 1970): 26–33.
94 MR (September 1970): 9–14.
95 "A Do-It-Yourself Professional Code for the Military," *Parameters* (December 1980): 10–15.
96 Colonel Richard J. Kattar, "The First Commandment of Leadership: Love Thy Soldier," MR (July 1980): 65–68; Colonel Charles D. Bussey, "Leadership for the Army," ibid., 69–76; Major James L. Narel, "Values and the Professional Soldier," *Parameters* (December 1981): 74–79.
97 "Leadership: A Personal Philosophy," MR (November 1984): 17–24. The cited passage is from p. 17.
98 "Necesidad de la preparación profesional y general," RFAC (January–March 1959): 177–81.
99 See "Despedida de la Escuela Superior de Guerra a los jefes y oficiales egresados del curso de estado mayor de 1947," RESGA (January–February 1948): 3–9.
100 Carmen Marín, "Preparación para el alto mando," RMP (April 1956): 1–13; Pando Egusquiza, "La Junta Interamericana de Defensa como una garantía de paz en el continente," ibid., ix–xxix.
101 "Vocación y profesión militar," RMGU (January–March 1959): 9–12. See also Colonel Guillermo Reyes Santa Cruz, "Concepto sobre el ejercicio del mando," RMGU (October–December 1959): 20–21.
102 Colonel Vicente Marchelli Padrón, "La institución armada y el ejército-nación," REV (March–April 1959): 17–22. See also Monsignor José María Pibernat S., "Ejército y libertad," RFAV (August–September 1959): 4–5.
103 "Amor, fidelidad, y servicio," RFAV (January 1960): 4–5.
104 "Al joven oficial egresado del Colegio Militar," RMA (January–March 1960): 46–56.
105 "Palabras del comandante en jefe del ejército," RFAV (1967): 3–5; and "Agradecimiento del ministro de defensa," ibid., 6–8.
106 "Palabras," RMGU (July–September 1970): 35–37.
107 "La carrera del oficial del ejército," MECH (January–April 1979): 87–95. The cited passage is from p. 94.
108 "El ejército ante la dinámica de la revolución mexicana," *Armas* (January–February 1979): 8–10.

109 *El relevo de las fuerzas armadas: Conceptos del jefe del estado en ceremonias en el Fuerte Tiuna y en la Escuela de Aviación Militar* (Caracas: Ministerio de la Defensa, 1982), 4–5.

110 "O Ofício de Oficial do Exército Brasileiro," *Revista do Exército* (Brazil) (July–September 1983): 22–29. The quotation is from p. 27. Hereafter REB.

111 Captain Geraldo L. Amaral, "Reflexões sobre a Formação Cultural do Oficial," RMB (July–December 1946): 466–74.

112 Lieutenant Colonel Rodolfo Sejas, "¿Cómo unificar la cultura militar del ejército?" RMBO (September–November 1950): 88–90.

113 Captain Federico Juárez Rodos, "La educación del oficial del ejército," RMGU (May 1951): 69–71.

114 Captains Jorge Elizagaray, Juan Carranza Zavalía, and José M. Menéndez, "La preparación profesional," RMA (July–August 1954): 45–50; and "Preparación del oficial argentino," RMA (May–June 1954): 30–36.

115 Vice Commodore Dardo Eugenio Ferreyra, "Cultura general y cultura profesional," RMA (July–September 1960): 110–14.

116 Major De Bow Freed, "El oficial completo," GN (November–December 1961): 28–38.

117 "Cultura y técnica en los estudios militares," RCMA (January–April 1966): 15–18.

118 "El libro leído," RFAC (1969): 123–26.

119 Colonel Homar Segrista, "La educación en el ejército," RESGA (September–October 1973): 53–64.

120 RMP (November–December 1974): 94–104.

121 "O Homem Militar, o Futuro, e a Guerra," ADN (March–April 1984): 7–15. The quotation is from p. 15.

122 "The Good Commander," CAJ (August 1951): 23–31. The citation is from p. 23. See also Captain P. H. Rubie, "Some Thoughts on Leadership," CAJ (April 1953): 74–77; and Colonel E. R. Rivers-MacPherson, "Some Thoughts on Morale," CAJ (October 1953): 72–76.

123 "Post-War Conditions in the Army," TAQDJ (October 1945): 89–98. See also General G. S. Bushnell (CBE, MC), "Officers for the Regular Army," TAQDJ (January 1946): 278–85.

124 "The Average Officer," JUSII (July–September 1950): 176–80. The citations are from p. 177.

125 "The Officer's Problem," TAQDJ (January 1951): 206–12.

126 "Revolution in the Military Profession," AAJ (June 1954): 5–9.

127 "Soldier, Scientist or Socialite," AAJ (October 1954): 5–12.

128 "De la formation du chef," RMI (10 May 1956): 27–33. The citation is from p. 32. See also the original version of Freed's essay cited in n. 116, "The Compleat Officer," MR (December 1960): 24–29.

129 "Army Officer: Mercenary or Missionary?" AAJ (September 1956): 20–28. The cited material is from pp. 25, 27.

130 "The Officer's Career," BAR (March 1959): 17–25.

131 "Armée, la parade et la riposte psychologique," RMI (June 1960): 20–35 and (August–September 1960): 16–35. The citation is from p. 27 of the second installment. See also Captain Neyron de Saint-Julien, "Évolution du corps des officiers," RMI (December 1964): 38–53.

132 "The Great Warrior," PAJ (December 1961): 1–3.

133 Martin Blumenson, "Some Thoughts on Professionalism," AAJ (February 1965): 44–48.

134 "Military Professionialism," PAJ (June 1965): 18–22.

135 Captain Francesco Albarosa, "La formazione degli ufficiali dell'esercito della Repubblica Federale Tedesca," RMIT (October 1967): 1165–78; and General Rodolfo Rufino, "Prepararsi alla carriera," RMIT (September 1973): 1079–89. See also Major Alessio Antonutti, "Ufficiali dell'esercito: Rapporto informale sulla situazione in Italia nel 1971," RMIT (November–December 1971): 79–93.

136 Lieutenant Colonel E. H. Dar, "Service in the Ranks?" PAJ (June 1970): 60–62.

137 General (ret.) André Gribius, *Une vie d'officier* (Paris: Éditions France Empire, 1971), 16. See also J. C. Rocqueplo, "Perspectives actuelles de l'évolution de la fonction militaire en France," RDN (March 1972): 389–98.

138 Lieutenant Colonel W. A. Piper, "An Army Career: Is it Worthwhile?" AAJ (October 1971): 34–38.

139 See Major Richard P. Diehl, "Military Professionalism in the U. S. Army," MR (March 1974): 60–71. The citation is from p. 71. The Spanish version, published nine months later, is cited in n. 120.

140 "The Soviet Officer Corps," SMR (January 1977): 5–9.

141 Commander Francisco Laguna Sanquirico, "Reflexiones sobre la vocación militar," *Ejército* (January 1979): 3–8.

142 General P. W. Blyth (MBE), "The Professional Army Officer," DFJ (March–April 1979): 11–19. The quotation is from p. 12.

143 Brigadier Usman Khan, "The Charms of the Profession of Arms," PAJ (April 1979): 20–21.

144 "The Pride and the Privilege," PAJ (May 1981): 42–45.

145 Captain Marcial Figueroa Arévalo, "El oficial de ejército y la integración del indígena a la nacionalidad," RMP (September 1955): 104–9.

146 General Benjamín Rattenbach, "Sociología militar," RCMA (January–March 1964): 5–24.

147 "Decálogo del soldado argentino: Orden general no. 14," RMA (November–December 1954): 4–5.

148 Captain Poumeyrol, "La formación del oficial y su rol social," RMBO (January–February 1943): 104–21.

149 "Función de las ff. aa. de la nación en la hora presente," RMBO (July–September 1951): 5–6. See also Lieutenant Colonel Arturo Arévalo, "La contextura moral del oficial," RMBO (January–February 1946): 71–84.

150 See Colonel Félix Edmundo Martínez, "El oficial como instructor y educador," RFAV (January 1950): 3–4; Major Antonio Croce R., "La disciplina: Virtud de virtudes," RFAV (February 1950): 68–69; and Major Tomás Pérez Tenreiro, "La cultura del jefe," RFAV (March 1950): 129–31. Also see Gonzalo Canal Ramírez, "Oficiales y soldados," RFAC (March–April 1965): 139–41.

151 See Colonel Heriberto Florentín, "Paraguay y la guerra de guerrillas," RFAP (March–May 1968): 8–16; Lieutenant Colonel Aparicio Rolón, "La apreciación de la situación en la solución de los problemas militares," ibid., 22–29; and the editorial, "La paz, fecundo instrumento del desarrollo," RFAP (January–June 1983): 2–3.

152 "Semblanza de la escuela militar," *Revista Militar* (Honduras) (1979–80): 28–38. Cited passages are from p. 33.

153 "National Service and the Regulars," AAJ (August 1955): 25–26.
154 "Le rôle éducatif de l'armée," RMI (25 June 1950): 22–27.
155 "Aspect social de la profession militaire," RMI (10 April 1951): 26–27.
156 Lieutenant Colonel Mathey, "Pedagogie et instruction militaire," RMI (10 January 1956): 29–34.
157 RMI (June 1960): 48–66. The cited passage is from p. 66.
158 Major Joachim Jäschke, "Gedanke eines Bataillons Kommandeurs zur Erziehung und Weiterbildung seiner jungen Offiziere," *Wehrkunde* (February 1960): 88–92.
159 "Offizierausbildung in der Truppe: Gedanken-Erfahrungen-Anregungen," *Truppenpraxis* (March 1963): 205–8.
160 "Der jugend Offizier der Bundeswehr," *Wehrkunde* (April 1964): 211–14.
161 *Bundeswehr-Elite der Nation? Determination und Funktionen elitärer Selbsteinschätzungen von Bundeswehrsoldaten* (Berlin: Herman Luchterhand Verlag, 1970), 57.
162 See V. Petroukhine, "Educator and Friend of the Soldier," SMR (December 1968): 14–16.
163 See K. Moskalenko, "Loyal Sons of the People," SMR (September 1971): 2–5.
164 SMR (July 1972): 3–5.
165 See Lieutenant Colonel V. Lutsenko (M.Sc.), "The Young Officer's Prestige," SMR (September 1973): 20–21; Colonel I. Babenko, "The Commander as Educator," SMR (September 1979): 8–10; and Lieutenant Colonel V. Amelchenko," An Honorable Profession," SMR (December 1978): 5–6.
166 See "Land of Fulfillment," PAFJ (February 1956): 23–25. Ramos, "The New Look in Citizen Soldier Training," PAFJ (March 1956): 32–42. Mendoza and Gunabe, PAFJ (May 1956): 42–46. Coloma, "Leadership at the Crossroads," PAFJ (June 1956): 41–44.
167 "Professional Competence and Self-Improvement," PAFJ (December 1956): 4–10. The citation is from p. 5.
168 Counet, "Le soldat congolais: Quelques réflexions sur la psychologie," RMCB (June 1959): 332–36. Marlier, "Connaître sa troupe," ibid., 325–31.
169 Hubert Lyautey, "On the Social Role of the Officer," tr. William Kyer West, MR (September, 1974): 14–24. See also Major Gordon L. Rogers, "The Leader as Teacher," MR (July 1983): 2–13; and Major Robert A. Fitton, "Military Leadership and Values," MR (October 1983): 56–61.
170 *Captains and Kings: Three Dialogues on Leadership* (*Dialogues sur le commandement*), tr. J. Lewis May (London: The Bodley Head, 1925), 19, 47–48, 49.
171 See Lieutenant Bernardo Perdomo y Granela, "Psicología del mando," *Boletín del Ejército* (Cuba) (November–December 1950): 30–35 (hereafter BEC); Colonel Enrique Borbonet y Echeverría, "El capitán," BEC (January–February 1951): 6–10; and "ABC, El arte del jefe," BEC (September–October 1952): 7–23. See also Major Antonio Ramírez Barrera, "Un problema de mando: La moral," REM (January–March 1951): 63–67; Major Mario Carballo Pozos, "El ejercicio del mando," REM (December 1958): 60–72; Lieutenant Colonel Enrique Escobar Pereyra, "Virtudes castrenses," REM (March 1958): 38–41; General F. Calleja, "Compendio sintético del arte de mandar," RMBO (April–May 1972): 7–13; and Colonel Emilio Bolón Varela, "Canon de conductor (el bien y el mal)," RMA (July–August 1953): 12–25.
172 See Lieutenant Carlos Moreira L., "El militar y los políticos," RMGU (April–June 1960): 19–21. See as well Lieutenant Colonel Felipe Alfonso Aceituno Q., "El

prestigio y dignidad del ejército," RMGU (January–March 1960): 62–63; Lieutenant Marco Antonio Ortiz Andrino, "Fundamentos psicológicos del don de mando" and "El determinismo y el hombre máquina," RMGU (July–September 1964): 39–45, 46–47, respectively; and Lieutenant Colonel Sergio Obregón Carrillo, "El don de mando," RMGU (October–December 1964): 11–18; (January–March 1965): 5–15; (April–June 1965): 10–17; (January–March 1966): 5–18; (April–June 1966): 5–14; (October–December 1966): 18–25; (January–June 1967): 5–18; (October–December 1967): 5–15; (January–March 1969): 5–10.

173 Major Augusto Baldoceda Sedano, "Fundamentos del don de mando," RESGP (January–March 1961): 8–25.

174 "El don de mando, un desafío para el comandante de división," RECEMMEA (April–June 1963): 24–29.

175 General Martín García Villasmil, "El militar y la política," REV (April–May 1964): 13–20.

176 Major Raimundo Barúa, "El mando y la lealtad," RFAP (August–December 1964): 3–7; and Major Alejandro Peralta Arellano, "Generalidades sobre el don de mando," ibid., 9–14.

177 See "Consejos prácticos sobre el arte de mandar," REM (July 1968): 3–4.

178 See "Reflexiones sobre don de mando," RECEMMEA (June 1969): 11–21.

179 "La cultura y el arte de mandar," RESGA (July–September 1969): 21–33.

180 (Santiago: Estado Mayor del Ejército de Chile, 1971): vol. 2, 172. Gavet's work was republished by the Chilean army as *El arte de mandar: Principios del mando para el uso de los oficiales de todos los grados* (Santiago: Estado Mayor del Ejército de Chile, 1973).

181 Colonel Antonio López Salas, "El arte de mandar," RFAV (February 1971): 33–39. The citation is from pp. 35, 39.

182 RMP (January–February 1972): 7–11.

183 See General Carlos de Meira Mattos, "Chefia Militar," ADN (September–October 1973): 43–62; Colonel Jorge Luongo, "O oficial é um Lider," ADN (July–August 1974): 39–64; General Tácito Theóphilo Gaspar de Oliveira, "Princípios de Chefia," ADN (September–October 1974): 3–18.

184 "El don de mando," REFAM (October 1975): 4–14. See also General Antonio Gómez García, "Algo sobre el mando," REFAM (April 1973): 3–6; and Lieutenant Colonel Arturo Saavedra Vieyta, "La dificil facilidad del arte de mandar," REFAM (September 1977): 4–11 and (October 1977): 40–49.

185 See Major Rafael A. Paniagua Araujo, "El mando militar," *Revista de las Fuerzas Armadas* (El Salvador) (July–September 1979): 2–3 (hereafter RFAES); and Captain (ret.) Federico Luna Orozco, "El arte de saber mandar y el arte de saber dirigir," RMBO (January–March 1979): 67–69.

186 "Mensaje del general de ejército don Alfredo Stroessner a la honorable convención extraordinaria de la Asociación Nacional Republicana," RFAP (July–November 1982): 7–11.

187 MECH, 1983, no. 1: 34–40.

188 "Offizier und Politik," WR (July 1956): 380–89. The quotation is from p. 382.

189 See, for example, Captain (navy) A. du Vigier, "Le militaire, sa tête, son coeur . . . et le reste," FAF (April 1974): 10–17.

190 Núnez G. Maturana, "El militar y la política," *Ejército* (October 1964): 43–46; Martínez Tenreiro, "La formación política del oficial," *Reconquista* (May 1965): 5–9.

191 "Los militares y la política," *Ejército* (January 1975): 11–16. See also his "El jefe y sus funciones," *Ejército* (May 1975): 25–30.

192 Herminio Redondo, "Apuntes sobre el concepto actual de la profesión militar," *Ejército* (May 1979): 30–33.

193 Colonel Y. Smyrnov, "The Soldier in Politics, SMR (December 1973): 6–7.

194 Interview, SMR (September 1976): 34–46. See also Colonel Sh. Nurullin, "The Commander and the Party Organization," SMR (June 1984): 30–31; and Colonel N. Tabunov (D.Sc., Phil.), "The Soviet Officer's World Outlook," SMR (May 1974): 22–23.

195 See RMI (25 March 1956), esp. J. Weygand, "L'officier des affaires indigènes," 63–66.

196 "The Defence of Independent National Africa," TAQDJ (October 1969): 98–107. The citation is from p. 102.

Chapter Four

1 *Mars, or the Truth About War* (tr. Doris Mudie and Elizabeth Hill) (London: Jonathan Cape, 1930), 34.

2 Colonel (ret.) Román Rodríguez Muñiz, "La profesión militar," *Ejército* (October 1978): 49–53.

3 Sublieutenant Fernando Suárez, "Razones para que el 27 de febrero sea considerado día del ejército nacional," *Revista de las Fuerzas Armadas del Ecuador* (1969): 41–50. The cited passage is from p. 50. Hereafter RFAEC.

4 Colonel Leobardo C. Ruiz, "La obra patriótica y cultural del Heróico Colegio Militar: El soldado como factor de unidad nacional," REM (June 1954): 7–9. See also General Alfonso Corona del Rosal, "La disciplina," REM (March 1960): 51–56.

5 Captain Antonio Suárez Loa, "El deber social y el deber militar: Definición del deber," REM (November 1965): 25–34. The quoted material is from p. 29.

6 "La voz sincera y franca de las fuerzas armadas," EL (September–October 1968): 55.

7 General Bruno Galindo Trejo, "Del civismo en el ejército," REM (September 1970): 39–45.

8 Editorial, REM (January 1971): 1–2. See also the editorial, "El ejército mexicano fue en sus inicios un pueblo en armas . . . ," REM (February 1967): 1–3.

9 Colonel Raúl Lira Villarespe, "La lealtad," REFAM (April 1976): 5–6.

10 Anon., "El ejército ante la dinámica de la revolución mexicana," *Armas* (January–February 1979): 8–10.

11 Major Carlos Castillo Armas, "Depuración, unión, trabajo," RMGU (January–February 1945): 8–10. Author's own italics.

12 See "La doble personalidad del soldado," RMGU (1947): 317–19.

13 Editorial, RMGU (October–December 1967): n. p.

14 Lieutenant Colonel Manuel de J. Girón T., "La constitución de la república y el ejército," RMGU (December 1968): 31–33.

15 Major Mamerto Marroquín, "Misión del ejército," RMGU (July–September 1963): 40–45.

16 Editorial, *Boletín del Ejército* (El Salvador) (20 January 1950): 1. Hereafter BEES. See also "El ejército y sus detractores," BEES (27 January 1950): 1–2; "Pueblo y ejército:

Columnas centrales de la revolución," BEES (17 March 1950): 1; and "El ejército y el pueblo," BEES (14 April 1950).

17 See Lieutenant Víctor Chamorro V., "Importancia de la cortesía militar en el desempeño de la disciplina," *Guardia Nacional* (November–December 1961): 23–27. Hereafter GN.

18 See General Alfonso Corona del Rosal, "Moral militar y civismo," GN (November–December 1960): 26–46.

19 Editorial, GN (January–February 1962): 13.

20 Captain Angel Castillo Maradiaga (sic), "La dimensión exacta de la patria debe comenzar por sus hombres," *Revista Militar* (Honduras) (1979–1980): 26–27.

21 See Carmen Melchor de Díaz de Vera, "A los soldados de nuestro glorioso ejército," BEC (September–October 1952): 24–29.

22 J. F. Alcorta, *Biblioteca militar: La biblia del soldado* (La Habana: Molina y Cía., 1940), 89.

23 Ibid., 54.

24 See "Moral militar: El soldado," RFADR (July–August 1964): 10–12; and "Moral militar: El ejército," RFADR (September–October 1964): 9. See also Lieutenant Viterbo Peña Medina, "El valor, la disciplina, y la lealtad del soldado dominicano," RFADR (January 1954): 7–9.

25 See Major José Antonio Rodríguez F., "Las fuerzas armadas ante la ciudadanía," RFADR (October–November 1969): 75–76.

26 See Colonel Diógenes Noboa Leyba, "Las fuerzas armadas y su misión en una democracia," RFADR (January 1969): 8–10.

27 Editorial, "Las fuerzas armadas y la sociedad," RFADR (April 1976): 3–4.

28 See Lieutenant Rafael Angarita Trujillo, "La política en el medio militar," RFAV (August 1951): 134–36.

29 Major Tomás Pérez Tenreiro, "Nacionalismo y ejército," RFAV (January 1953): 60–61.

30 Colonel (sic) Marcos Pérez Jiménez, "Jerarquía y misión de los institutos militares," RFAV (October 1954): 36–39.

31 Lieutenant Colonel Tomás E. Cheguín, "El ejército del futuro," RFAP (October–December 1957): 13–19. The cited passages are from pp. 13, 18.

32 Colonel Hernán Delgado Sánchez, "Juguemos la guerra," RFAV (1968): 3–4.

33 Colonel José Andrés Adarmes Pérez, "Sistema de educación militar," RFAV (February 1971): 10–13.

34 See "Una fuerza para combatir la fuerza," REV (December 1976): 4–9.

35 Senator Pedro Pablo Aguilar, "Las fuerzas armadas y el sistema democrático," RFAV (March–April 1983): 30–38.

36 *El relevo de las fuerzas armadas: Conceptos del jefe del estado en ceremonias militares en el Fuerte Tiuna y en la Escuela de Aviación Militar* (Caracas: Ministerio de la Defensa, 1982), 13–14. See also "Vocación militar," RFAV (July–August 1981): 88–96.

37 See the editorial, "Necesidad de la preparación profesional y general," RFAC (January–March 1959): 177–81.

38 Alberto Lleras Camargo, "Misión de las fuerzas armadas," RMC (May 1959): iv–vii.

39 Colonel Gonzalo Canal Ramírez, "Misión civil de las fuerzas armadas," RFAC (August 1960): 139–43.

40 Lieutenant Colonel Silvio Rosero, "Las fuerzas militares y la defensa de la soberanía nacional," RFAC (July–September 1972): 364.

41 Editorial, "Es ciertamente hermoso este nobilísimo oficio de soldado," RFAC (July–September 1984): 313–18.

42 "El ejército y la nación," RMBO (January–February 1948): 80–82.

43 "El soldado boliviano," RMBO (May–July 1948): 65–70. See also Bilbao's "El actual soldado boliviano,"RMBO (November–December 1947): 38–45.

44 "Virtudes olvidadas," RMBO (December 1950): 60–64.

45 Editorial, "El ejército de Bolivia," RMBO (June–July 1952): 5–6. Theological implications of the doctrine of consubstantiation dating from the Lutheran Reformation of the sixteenth century were apparently of no concern to the predominantly Roman Catholic Bolivian officer corps.

46 "Hablemos del ejército," ibid., 60–81. The cited material is from pp. 61, 63.

47 Colonel Clemente Inofuentes, "Necesitamos un ejército que sea síntesis del anhelo popular," RMBO (February–March 1953): 63–69. The citation is from p. 63.

48 Sublieutenant Jorge Terrazo Alborta, "Consideraciones breves sobre el ejército nacional," RMBO (January–February 1955): 16–17.

49 Colonel Clemente Inofuentes, "La revolución nacional y las fuerzas armadas de Bolivia," RMBO (March–April 1955): 85–89.

50 "Mensaje dirigido a las ff. aa. de la nación por el excmo. sr. ministro de defensa nacional con motivo de fin de año," RFAP (October–December 1959): 109–13.

51 "Etica profesional y corrección en los procederes del militar," RESGA (October–December 1954): 384–421. The quoted passage appears on p. 397. See also Carullo's "Cultura y técnica en los estudios militares," RCMA (January–April 1966): 15–18.

52 "Decálogo del soldado argentino: Orden general no. 14," RMA (November–December 1954): 4–5.

53 "La conciliación de intereses sociales, económicos, y financieros de la nación con la organización y desarrollo de la fuerza ejército," RESGA (January–March 1957): 71–78.

54 Lieutenant Colonel (ret.) Julio A. Sarmiento, "Las fuerzas armadas y algunos caracteres de su obra progresista," RMA (January–March 1959): 18–26.

55 Major Luis Alberto Leoni, "Encuadre de la institución ejército en el estado moderno," RCMA (July–September 1960): 116–29.

56 See Lucio V. Mansilla, "Lo que es el ejército," RESGA (March–April 1971): 11–13.

57 General José M. Vega Rodríguez (a Spaniard), "La filosofía y el mando militar," RESGA (September–October 1971): 11–26.

58 Colonel Robert Viel (a Frenchman), "Las fuerzas armadas y la sociología," RESGA (July–August 1972): 23–44. The quotation is from p. 39.

59 General Juan E. Gugliamelli, "Nación y soberanía: Reflexiones para ingenuos y desprevenidos," *Estrategia* (May–August 1980): 5–9.

60 See Jorge Diez, "Política y militares en el Uruguay," *Estrategia* (May–June 1973): 39–48; and Lieutenant Colonel Juan A. Cambiasso, "La defensa de la paz," RMNU (December 1951–April 1952): 70–87.

61 Major Gustavo A. Díaz Feliú, "El soldado alemán: El ejército chileno debe conservar su tradición prusiana," MECH (May–June 1971): 126–27.

62 "Mensaje de s. e. el presidente de la república, dr. Salvador Allende Gossens," MECH (September–October 1971): 3–5.

63 "O Exército e a Conjuntura Nacional, RMB (July–September 1970): 61–68. Cited material is from pp. 62–63.

64 Henrique Paula Bahiana, *As Forças Armadas e o Desenvolvimento do Brasil* (Rio de Janeiro: Edições Bloch, 1974), 15. Three recent well-documented sources dealing with the Brazilian army's official self-perception as representative of nation, state, and society are Frank D. McCann, "The Formative Period of Twentieth-Century Brazilian Thought," *Hispanic American Historical Review* (November 1984): 737–65; McCann's *A Nação Armada: Ensaios Sobre a História de Exército Brasileiro* (Recife: Editora Guararapes, 1989) and Robert A. Hayes, *The Armed Nation: The Brazilian Corporate Mystique* (Tempe: Center for Latin American Studies, Arizona State University, 1989).

65 See Ministério do Exército, Centro de Comunicação Social, *O Seu Exército* (Brasília: Ministério do Exército, 1982), passim.

66 See Colonel Fernando de Maya Pedrosa, "O Exército e a Sociedade Brasileira," ADN (July–August 1984): 139–48.

67 General Vinícius Lemos Kruel, "As Forças Armadas Reverenciam as Víctimas de 1935," *Revista do Clube Militar* (November–December 1982): 18–19. Hereafter RCMB.

68 Colonel Juan Mendoza Rodríguez, La escuela militar en su obra de la educación nacional," RMP (April 1948): 259–67. The cited material is from p. 261.

69 Captain Erasmo Herrera B., "El ejército, celoso guardián de nuestra heredad territorial," RMP (September 1950): 81–82.

70 "El ejército, el ofical, y la política," RMP (January–February 1972): 7–11.

71 "The Army and Politics," SMR (August 1968): 44–47.

72 "Loyal Sons of the People," SMR (September 1971): 2–5.

73 "Las fuerzas armadas de la Unión Soviética de la segunda guerra mundial a su misión actual," *Estrategia* (May–August 1975): 93–103. The citation is from p. 100.

74 V. V. Shelyag, A. Glotochkin, K. K. Platonov, *Military Psychology: A Soviet View* (Moscow: Military Publishing House, Ministry of Defense, 1972), 311.

75 See General V. Novikov, "Unity of the Army and the People," SMR (January 1981): 5–8; and V. Borisov, "A School of Courage and Heroism," SMR (April 1985): 6–7.

76 "The American Military Profession: An Egalitarian View," MR (November 1974): 18–29. Cited material appears on p. 27.

77 Major Pereira Botelho, "O Exército, Centro Fundamental de Cultura e Educação," RMPO (May 1952): 313–21.

78 Editorial, "L'esercito italiano oggi," RMIT (October 1963): vii–ix.

79 Brigadier Alfredo Pereira da Conceição, "Os Estados e a Força Armada," RMPO (February–March 1968): 113–27. See also Nascimento Garcia, "Velhos Princípios, Princípios de Sempre," RMPO (February–March 1951): 143–52.

80 See Cruz Martínez Esteruelas, "Vida cultural militar: Ejército y sociedad," *Reconquista* (August–September 1968): 36–38; and Commander (air force) Luis de Miramón Riera, "Misión del ejército español," *Ejército* (January 1971): 19–28. The citation is from Miramón, p. 23.

81 See "Las fuerzas armadas ante su excelencia el generalísimo," *Ejército* (February 1975): 3–5.

82 General Luigi Poli, "Profesione militare negli anni ottanta," RMIT (January–February 1980): 4–11. The citation is from p. 7. See also Captain (navy) Falco Accame, "Che cos'è la filosofia militare," RMIT (May–June 1975): 89–95.

83 "De la compétence de l'armée," RMI (25 January 1950): 24–27.

84 "Essai sur la propagande et la mission politique des officiers," RMI (10 December 1951): 10–15.

85 General L. M. Chassin, "Du rôle idéologique de l'armée," RMI (10 October 1954): 13–19, esp. 18–19.

86 General Jean Valluy, "Le corps des officiers devant la nation," RMG (December 1958): 591–611. Cited passages are from pp. 591, 596.

87 See Jean-Maurice Martin, "Soldats et citoyens," RMI (October 1960): 39–51.

88 "La défense nationale: Réflexions sur une formule," RMI (January 1961): 2–15. The quotation is from p. 11.

89 Daniel Guérin and Roland Gengenbach, *L'armée en France* (Paris: Éditions Filipucchi, 1974), 10.

90 General Marcel Bigeard, *Pour une parcelle de gloire* (Paris: Plon, 1975), 472.

91 Ludwig Scholte, "Innere Führung: Ein demokratisches Prinzip," *Wehrkunde* (May 1969): 245–46.

92 See Major Henry G. Gole, "Leadership from Within," MR (February 1973): 83–91.

93 See Richard Jaeger, *Soldat und Bürger: Armee und Staat* (n.p., n.d.), 13.

94 See Colonel Erich Pruck, "Der Offizier in der Sowjetgesellschaft," RMG (January 1966): 89–108.

95 See Ferdinand E. Marcos, "The Armed Forces in the New Society," *Philippine Army Digest* (January–March 1973): 7–12. Hereafter PAD.

96 Major K. Brahma Singh, "The Wind of Change," JUSII (October–December 1972): 317–23. This quotation is from p. 321.

97 Brigadier Mohammad Sardar Hussain, "Technology and National Military Potential," PAJ (December 1974): 12–16. See also his "Science and Technology for Development," PAJ (June 1978): 39–43.

98 PAJ (March 1981): 42–45. See as well Brigadier Usman Khan, "The Charms of the Profession of Arms," PAJ (April 1979): 20–21.

99 Brigadier F. W. Speed, "Indonesian Armed Forces," TAQ (July 1982): 311–19.

100 See, for example, G.-P. Jouannet, "Le maréchal de Lattre: Formateur de la jeunesse," RMI (January 1958): 93–99; and General Paul Ely, "Former les chefs," RDN (December 1960): 1913–22.

101 Of numerous examples, see René Marie, "L'objection de conscience," RMI (October 1963): 41–49; Claude Albert Moreau, "Le service militaire," RMI (July–August 1964): 32–37; and "L'esprit de corps," RMI (April 1964): 35–39; Batallion Chief E. Walter, "Notre enthousiasme," RDN (May 1970): 763–68; France, Ministère de la Défense Nationale, *Le livre blanc sur la défense nationale* (Paris: Ministère de la Défense nationale, 1972); Michel Debré, "À propos du service militaire," FAF (January 1973): 2–3. Interview with General Paul Etcheverry, "La conscription: Un devoir national lié à la dissuasion," AA (July–August 1981): 43–45, and General Jean-Germain Salvan, "Réflexions sur le service militaire," AAH (January–February 1982): 62–64.

102 Lieutenant Colonel (ret.) A. Barber, "The Recruiting Problem," TAQDJ (July,

1963): 193–99. The citation is from p. 194. See also Brigadier A. R. W. Low (CBE, DSO, MP), "Army Man-Power: The Case Against the Wishful Thinkers," TAQDJ (October 1949): 33–40; and Lieutenant Colonel B. S. Jerome, "The Army as a Career," TAQDJ (April 1950): 72–81.

103 W. Correlli Barnett, "The Military Profession in the 1970s," in J. N. Wolfe and John Erickson, eds., *The Armed Services and Society: Alienation, Management, and Integration* (Edinburgh: Edinburgh University Press, 1970), 14. See also Lieutenant Colonel W. A. Piper, "An Army Career: Is It Worthwhile?" AAJ (October 1971): 34–48; and Hawley C. Black, "Unification and the Canadian Land Forces," TAQDJ (October 1980): 436–44.

104 See General von Stolzmann, "Ist die allgemeine Wehrpflicht die militärische Lebensform eines modernen Industriestaats?" RMG (November 1956): 249–69.

105 The term was employed by Martin Kitchen in *A Military History of Germany from the Eighteenth Century to the Present Day* (London: Weidenfeld and Nicholson, 1975), 339. See, on obligatory service, "Innere Führung und soldatischer Gehorsam: Diskussion über eine grundsätzliche Frage," *Truppenpraxis* (March 1961): 216–18; Hans-Joachim von Merkatz, "Vom Sinn der Tradition," WR (November 1961): 609–16; Berthold Schirmer, "Der Soldat und das Vaterland," WR (March 1967): 132–49; "Das Deutsche Heer, 1978," *Wehr Technik* (April 1978): 35–39; Chaplain Albert Pesch and Captain (navy) Armin Kolb, "Zum Begriff und zur Konzeption der Inneren Führung," *Truppenpraxis* (August 1980): 620–24; and Heinrich Bolz, *Soldat und Student: Offizierausbildung und Konfliktbereiche an Hochschulen der Bundeswehr* (Heidelberg and Hamburg: R. V. Dicker's Verlag, G. Schenck, 1983).

106 See V. Nikolayev, "Universal Military Duty," SMR (August 1984): 26–30. See also Colonel Mikhail Zyzin, "Citizens Enjoying Full Rights," SMR (September 1984): 14–17.

107 Lieutenant Colonel R. T. Jones, "Tradition and Reality," AAJ (January 1968): 33–52; Lieutenant Colonel I.B. Ferguson, "Are You in a Training Rut?" AAJ (December 1955): 14–16; Major F. E. Cochran, "The Young Officer Programme: Who Will Take Your Place," CAJ (April 1959): 74–78; and Commandant J. P. Duggan, "The Soldier and the State," AC (February 1968): 43–45.

108 See Captain Fidel V. Ramos, "The New Look in Citizen-Soldier Training," PAFJ (March, 1956): 32–42. See also Pedro G. Javier, "Military Training and Citizenry," PAFJ (July 1950): 21–24; Colonel J. Nazareth, "A Citizen Army for India," JUSII (July–September 1965): 93–106; Major G. S. Kapur, "Man and the Army," JUSII (October–December 1965): 253–59, 265; Lieutenant Colonel S. K. Sinha, "Compulsory Military Training," JUSII (April–June 1967): 1214–26; Major S. A. El-Edroos, "A Plea for a People's Army," PAJ (June 1962): 19–25; and Lieutenant M. Abdul Hameed, "Education Is an Investment in Human Resources," PAJ (February 1979): 1–7.

109 Captain (med.) Luis Macias Teixeira, "A Assistência Médico-Social no Exército," RMPO (April 1952): 257–59; Colonel Júlio Martins Mourão, "Educação Militar," RMPO (May 1961): 277–86; Captain Jesús Baeza López, "Vocación y selección en la carrera militar," *Ejército* (February 1970): 37–40; Lieutenant Colonel Benvenuto Pecorni and Lieutenant Colonel Norberto Perugini, "Necessità e tecnica di formulazione dell'idea colletiva," RMIT (February 1971): 207–15; and General Manuel Díaz Alegría, *Ejército y sociedad* (Madrid: Alianza Editorial, 1972).

110 Major Alejandro Medina V., "La instrucción pre-militar en el Perú," RMP (September 1946): 23–30. The quotation is from p. 24.

111 See Colonel Juan Mendoza Rodríguez, "Servicio militar vocacional," RMP (November 1946): 31–42; Colonel Néstor Gambetta, "En torno a la ley del servicio militar obligatorio," RMP (June 1952): 67–73; Lieutenant Colonel José I. Iturralde, "Educación moral del militar," RMA (November 1947): 1461–62; Lieutenant Rafael Angarita Trujillo, "El recluta y sus problemas," RFAV (April 1951): 297–98; Colonel Juan Jones Parra, "Universidad y fuerzas armadas," RFAV (January 1959): 8–11; General Leobardo C. Ruiz, "La juventud de México y nuestros Niños Heroes," REM (September 1954): 29–32.

112 Lieutenant Colonel Novoa M., "El comandante y el mando," RMC (September 1956): 39–44; Colonel Humberto Seabra, "Preliminares da Introdução do Serviço Militar Obrigatório," RMB (January–June 1958): 19–32.

113 Colonel Aníbal Suárez Galindo, "Al joven oficial egresado del Colegio Militar," RMA (January–March 1960): 46–56; General Jorge A. Giovanelli, "Los grandes problemas de la defensa nacional," RESGA (April–June 1960): 135–46; and "El servicio militar obligatorio en las filas: Algunas ideas sobre su duración," RCMA (April–June 1964): 7–12.

114 Colonel Eduardo Bendfeldt, "El hombre como elemento indispensable en la defensa de la nación," RMGU (July–September 1960): 39–42; Lieutenant Colonel Mario Modesto Chacón Arévalo, "Consideraciones sobre la defensa civil," RECEMMEA (April–June 1963): 39–42.

115 Admiral Antonio J. Aznar Zetina, "Del servicio militar nacional: Lo que no se ha dicho: Su razón de ser," REM (February 1967): 13–19. The citation is from p. 14.

116 "Fe en una patria soberana," RMP (July–August 1969): 2–6; Colonel Luis Enrique Sira Suárez, "El sesquicentenario y la conciencia patriótica del pueblo," RFAV (June–July 1971): 105–7; Lieutenant Colonel Jorge Muñoz Pontony, "¿Ejército profesional?" MECH (January–April 1976): 33–38.

117 Colonel Davis Ribeiro de Sena, "Serviço Militar Obrigatório e Exército Profissional," ADN (September–October 1984): 29–39. The cited passage is from p. 39.

118 Colonels Carlos J. Peñaloza Z., Juan Torres S., and Luis R. Rodríguez P., *Formación de la seguridad de un estado* (Santiago: Biblioteca Militar Interamericana, 1985), 29.

119 See Major Benjamín Videla V., "La intervención del ejército en obras de beneficio público," MECH (September–October 1947): 64–80. The citation is from p. 67.

120 Major Luis Valenzuela Reyes, "Misión de las fuerzas armadas y su participación en el desenvolvimiento normal de nuestra vida democrática," MECH (May–June 1958): 22–36. The quoted passage is from p. 28.

121 Major Claudio López Silva, "Las fuerzas armadas en el tercer mundo," MECH (July–August 1970): 11–51. The citation appears on p. 12.

122 See the rev. ed. (New York: Frederick A. Praeger, 1961).

123 See Lieutenant Colonel Hugo Moya V., "Participación, en teoría, de las fuerzas armadas en la política de los estados modernos," MECH (October–December 1972): 65–68.

124 See Hugo Tagle Martínez, "Patria, fuerzas armadas, y política económica," *Política y Geoestrategia* (successor to *Seguridad Nacional*) (October–December 1972): 53–60. Hereafter PG.

125 See his "Ejército y libertad," RFAV (August–September 1959): 4–5.

126 Major Santos Solon Guanipa Mora, "La acción cívica en la guerra irregular," REV (June–July 1964): 49–54.

127 "La seguridad y las políticas de la integración internacional," REV (December 1967): 13–22. See also Lieutenant Humberto Cárdenas Zambrano, "Acción cívica en la guerra irregular," RFAV (1967): 23–35.

128 Colonel Juan Antonio Lossada Volcán, "Contrainsurgencia," RFAV (1967): 103–10.

129 Chaplain Major José del Carmen Manzanares, "¿A quién apoyan las fuerzas armadas?" RFAV (1968): 16–17.

130 Cardinal Quintero, "Las fuerzas armadas constituyen poderosa garantía para la libertad de la patria," RFAV (January–April 1978): 27–29. See also Colonel Orlando José Pérez Suárez, "Siempre estamos en campaña," ibid., 45–51; and General (defense minister) Luis Enrique Rangel Bourgoin, "La colectividad aspira a encontrar en la guardia nacional un modelo guía," RFAV (April–August 1979): 65–68.

131 "El arte de mandar solo se obtiene aprendiendo a obedecer," RFAV (October 1980): 2–12.

132 "La unidad moral: Nación-fuerzas armadas," RMA (May–June 1956): iv–ix.

133 Estado Mayor del Ejército, "La obra del ejército en la educación, la investigación científica, la tecnología, la industria, la economía, y la acción cívica," RESGA (January–April 1964): 75–93.

134 "La acción cívica en los movimientos insurreccionales," RCMA (January–March 1964): 78–86. The citation is from p. 84.

135 "Discurso del director del Centro de Estudios y Escuela Superior de Guerra, general de brigada Juan Enrique Guglialmelli, el 15 de diciembre de 1965, con motivo del cierre del año lectivo," RESGA (January–February 1966): 5–14. The quotation appears on p. 9.

136 See Colonel Emilio Bolón Varela, "Un hombre superior," RCMA (December 1973): 16–19.

137 General Edgardo Mercado Jarrín, "Reflexiones sobre la seguridad y el desarrollo en América Latina," *Estrategia* (September–October 1973): 29–40.

138 "Argentina: Objetivo orgánico del ejército para el largo plazo," *Estrategia* (September–October 1979): 37–43. The quoted material is from pp. 37–38.

139 Editorial, "El ejército y la defensa nacional," RMP (August 1946): iii–iv.

140 See Lieutenant Colonel Antonio Medina Ruiz, "Comisión nacional de cartografía," RMBO (May–June 1954): 11–16; and Major Carlos Rueda La-Rotta, "Hacia una colonización militar," RFAC (February 1961): 651–59. The quotation appears on p. 653.

141 Basilides Brites Fariña, "El guaraní y los problemas educacionales," RFAP (September–December 1966): 104–44. The cited passage is from p. 105.

142 "Exército: Fator de Integração Nacional," RCMB (June 1969): 10–11.

143 General Ruperto Cabrera, "Nuestro ejército," BEC (September–October 1950): 7–9.

144 Colonel Luis Lazo Sánchez, "El absurdo de considerar improductivo el ejército," GN (September–October 1961): 68–72; and Lieutenant Oscar Cifuentes R., "Consideraciones sobre la función y la responsabilidad del ejército en la sociedad," GN (May–June 1961): 46–56.

145 Major Jorge Hernández M., "Nobleza del servicio militar," RMGU (February 1951): 78–79.

146 See Major Mamerto Marroquín, "Misión del ejército," RMGU (July–August 1963): 40–45. See also Colonel Juan Paredes Cordero, "Razón de ser y existir del ejército," RMGU (January–June 1979): 25–26.

147 "La fuerza armada," RECEMMEA (December 1967): 30, 40.

148 "La razón de ser de las fuerzas armadas: Actualidad y futuro de las fuerzas armadas," RFADR (August 1973): 24–28 and (September 1973): 13–21; and Alfredo de Jesús Balcácer Vega, "Acción cívica militar," RFADR (July 1974): 15–23.

149 See Captain Juan Ismael Morales López, "Situación general del indígena en Guatemala," RMGU (April–December 1976): 7–12. See also Captain José Luis Quilo Ayuzo, "Trascendencia del servicio militar," RMGU (October 1975, January–March 1976): 47–52.

150 Colonel Armando Jirón Saballos, "Acción cívica militar: Ayuda positiva al pueblo," *Acción Cívica* (Nicaragua) (March 1978): 6–10. Hereafter ACN. See also Captain José Rolando Mejia Carranza, "La integración del indígena al desarrollo nacional, ACN (January–March 1979): 51–62.

151 General (subsecretary, national defense) Juan José Gastelum Salcedo, "Doctrina filosófica de la revolución mexicana," EL (August 1966): 7–13. The citations are from p. 9.

152 See Saúl Castorena Monterrubio, "El ejército mexicano: Baluarte de la soberanía nacional," *Armas* (November–December 1978): 33–34.

153 S-2, Estado Mayor de Defensa Nacional, "El ejército mexicano de hoy: Sus actividades," REFAM (September 1980): 8–15. The quoted passage is from p. 9.

154 See Marcel Clément, "Les valeurs que nous défendons," RMI (February 1960): 7–13; Colonel Suire, "Vertu des traditions militaires," RMI (September 1963): 68–77. See also Colonel Fernand-Thiebaut Schneider, "Problèmes et perspectives de la Bundeswehr," *Revue Militaire Suisse* (June 1971): 253–63.

155 See, for example, General E. Saulais, "La gendarmerie outre-mer et la défense nationale," FAF (October 1973): 28–37.

156 Captain A. Juyon, "Le militaire dans la cité: Ou des relations entre une ville et sa garrison," FAF (November 1973): 2–10.

157 Colonel M. Riuquet, "Pour un nouveau 'rôle social' de l'armée," FAF (December 1973): 9–11.

158 See General J. Beauvallet, "Pourquoi les armées douteriant-elles de leur mission," FAF (January–February 1974): 4–7. See also Roger Tebib, *L'armée de la France: Sa philosophie et ses traditions* (Paris: Christine Bonneton Éditeur, 1982); and Paul Stehlin, *La force d'illusion* (Paris: Éditions Robert Laffont, 1973).

159 Ministère de la Défense, État Majeur de l'Armée de Terre, Service Historique, *Le réarmement et la réorganisation de l'armée de terre française (1943–1946)* (Château de Vincennes: n. p., 1980), 102.

160 G. M. C. Sprung, "Gedanken über die militärische Tradition in der heutigen Zeit," WR (March 1963): 121–30.

161 See Eberhardt Wagemann, "Ewiger Wert 'Soldatentum'?" *Wehrkunde* (March 1966): 124–28. See also Lieutenant Heiner Hirtsiefer, "Der Bundeswehrsoldat: Ein Arbeitnehmer?" *Wehrkunde* (July 1967): 359–62.

162 See Erich Hermann, "Innere Führung: Erläuterungen zu einer kurzen Begriffsumschreibung," WR (September 1969): 492–507. See as well General Ulrich de Maizière, "Armee, Staat, und Gesellschaft," IT (March 1979): 3–23; and Lieu-

tenant Colonel Dieter Portner, "Soldaten als Mandatsträger," EW (August 1977): 407–10.

163 "Le forze armate: Analise di una realità: Problemi e perspettive," RMIT (January–February 1977): 2–7; "Forze armate e sicurezza," RMIT (July–August 1977): iii–iv; and "Le forze armate e le sfide de nostro tempo," RMIT (November–December 1977): 2–8.

164 "The Fighting Man's Moral Character," SMR (April 1969): 3–5.

165 "Army of Developed Socialism," SMR (April 1977): 10–11, 62.

166 Field Marshal Sir William Slim (GBE, KCB, DSO, MC), "Liberty and Discipline," AAJ (October 1950): 45–48.

167 Major (ret.) H. B. C. Watkins (MBE), "A Case for Integration: *Autres temps, autres moeurs*," TAQ (January 1957): 183–99.

168 "A Acção Psicossocial do Exército como Exemplo e Contributo para a Formação do Espaço Portugues," *Boletim do Estado Maior do Exército* (Portugal) (October 1963): 201–14. The cited passage is from p. 212.

169 See General Gino de Luca, "Difesa civile," RMIT (July–August 1964): 814–23; Umberto Capuzzo, "Il ruolo dell'esercito nella protezione civile," RMIT (July–August 1983): 2–8; "Messagio del ministro della difesa alle forze armate nella ricorrenza del xxv anniversario della repubblica," RMIT (June 1971): 797–98; and Colonel Raffaele Farina, "La difesa della patria e sacro dovere del cittadino," RMIT (October 1971): 1295–1304.

170 Captain Gerardo Torres Bados, "Soldado soy de España," *Ejército* (August 1980): 2–5.

171 See Commander d'Allones, "Psichari, un colonial," *Tropiques* (September 1950): 30–36.

172 See, as examples, Colonel Masud Akhtar Shaikh, "Military Uses of Language Study," PAJ (December 1971): 61–65; Captain R. Sachi, "Destroying the Communist Terrorist: The Primary Task of the Malaysian Army," ADJ (April 1976): 18–19; General Jose G. Syjuco, *Military Education in the Philippines* (Quezon City: New Day Publishers, 1977); Tan Sri Ghazali Shafi (Minister of Home Affairs), "On Development and Security," ADJ (September 1981): 16–17; General K. L. Kochar, "Civil-Military Relations," JUSII (July–September 1983): 221–29; Herman Oehling, *La función política del ejército* (Madrid: Instituto de Estudios Políticos, 1967); Heinrich Wilhelm Nobel, *Heer und Politik in Indonesien: Zielsetzung und Zielverwirklichung einer militärischen Organisation, 1945–1967* (Boppard am Rhein, n. p., 1975).

173 K. J. Roghmann, "Armed Forces and Society in West Germany: Program and Reality, 1955–1970," in Morris Janowitz and Jacques van Doorn, eds., *On Military Intervention* (Rotterdam: Rotterdam University Press, 1971), 117–52. The quotation is from p. 147.

Chapter Five

1 "Subversión y guerra revolucionaria," MECH (1981): 97–107. The citation is from p. 99.

2 "Advice to Gentlemen Cadets," *Journal of the United Services Institution of India and Pakistan* (October 1948): 331–33.

3 Lieutenant Colonel Omar E. Parada, "Ejército y sistema educativo," RESGA (May–June 1973): 17–26. The quoted material is from p. 26.

4 See, for example, essays in Claude E. Welch, Jr., *Civilian Control of the Military* (Albany, N.Y.: State University of New York Press, 1976).

5 André Maurois, *My Latin American Diary* (London: The Falcon Press, 1953), 10.

6 See Guido Vicario, *Militari e politica in America Latina* (Roma: Editori Riuniti, 1978), esp. 48–49.

7 See *Politics of the Sword; A Personal Memoir on Military Involvement in Ghana and of Problems of Military Government* (London: Alex Collings, 1977), 138.

8 See "Porque actuó el ejército," RMGU (January–February 1945): 3–7; and Captain Alfredo Niederheitman, "¿Lealtad o automatismo?" RMGU (January–February 1945): 12–13.

9 See Lieutenant Colonel Arturo Arévalo, "La contextura moral del oficial," RMP (May 1945): 27–39; and the editorial, "El ejército frente a la crisis política," RMP (October 1945): xi–xiv.

10 General Froilán Calleja Castro, "Compendio sintético de moral militar adaptado a nuestro ejército nacional," RMBO (July–October 1946): 443–52; (November–December 1946): 598–602.

11 See M. Seabra Fagundes, "As Forças Armadas na Constituição," RMB (July–December 1948): 333–70; and the editorial, "La revolución del 27 de octobre," RMP (October 1948): xv–xviii.

12 "Saludo del presidente de la república al Colegio Militar con motivo de su aniversario," RMBO (April–June 1951): 15.

13 Víctor Paz Estenssoro, "Situación del país," RMBO (January 1953): 7–13.

14 "Ningún cuerpo armado puede deliberar," MECH (July–August 1953): 79–84.

15 See Dr. Jose Arze Murillo, "La revolución nacional," RMBO (September–October 1954): 62–65; and Lieutenant Colonel Luis Quirós, "El ejército y la revolución nacional," RMBO (September–December 1957): 48–50.

16 "Inquietud profesional," MECH (May–June 1958): 3–4.

17 "Apartes del mensaje del sr. presidente de la república a la primera legislatura de 1959," RMC (August 1959): iii–vii.

18 In Major Antonio Aceituno A., "El ejército y la política," RMGU (October–December 1959): 25–28.

19 "El ejército y la democracia," RMP (May–June 1961): 87–94.

20 "¿A quién apoyan las fuerzas armadas?" RFAV (1968): 16–17. See as well on this subject, Lieutenant Carlos Moreira L., "El militar y la política," RMGU (April–June 1960): 19–21; Dr. Segundo V. Linares Quintana, "Los partidos políticos," RESGA (January–March 1961): 5–44; Captain (navy) M. Pérez Ugueto, "Deliberancia e institución," RFAV (October–December 1961): 2–7; Lieutenant Colonel Alvaro Pito Fonseca, "Reflexiones sobre el sistema de gobierno democrático," RESGP (January–March 1964): 117–21; Colonel Gastón Ibáñez O'Brien, "El congreso y la fuerza armada," RESGP (April–June 1965): 33–41; "El ejército es totalmente ajeno a la contienda política," RMGU (July–September 1969): 2; Colonel Mario Enrique Siliezar Ríos, "Los partidos políticos," RMGU (January–March 1972): 63–70; and "El nuevo régimen gubernamental," RMBO (April–June 1972): 1–2.

21 In Dr. Alberto Conil Paz, "Fuerzas armadas y política," RESGA (March–April 1973): 11–26. The citation is from p. 17.

22 Major Ernesto Ramírez, "Régimen orgánico fundamental," RESGA (November–December 1972): 63–72; and Colonel (ret.) Héctor J. Piccinali, "Las políticas nacionales desde el punto de vista estratégico," RESGA (January–February 1973): 31–42.

23 General Edgardo Mercado Jarrín, "Reflexiones sobre la seguridad y el desarrollo en América Latina," RMP (September–October 1973): 2–19. The citation is from p. 5.

24 See Diogo de Figueiredo Moreira Neto, "Teoria do Poder," RCID (February 1979): 37–50; and General Golbery do Couto e Silva, "Conjuntura Política Nacional," ADN (March–April 1981): 61–75.

25 "If We Rest We Rust," JUSII (July–September 1972): 213–35. The cited passage is from pp. 230–31.

26 "The Armed Forces in the New Society," PAD (January–March 1973): 7–12.

27 General Jesús Vargas, "On the Need for Preparedness," PAFJ (October 1956): 9–16.

28 Lieutenant Colonel Majumdar, "Brass Hats and Frocks," RMG (November 1961): 447–59. The citation is from p. 450. See also Reginald Hargreaves, "The Abiding Flaw," TAQDJ (January 1969): 203–17; and Lieutenant Colonel Robert P. Hand, "Cast Your Ballot," AD (August 1970): 8–9.

29 Lieutenant Colonel (chaplain) R. J. Wood, "Citizenship in Democracy," AID (December 1966): 11–12.

30 General Horst Hildebrandt, "Führen in einer modernen Armee," IT (February 1979): 3–9. Quoted material appears on p. 9. See also Franz Pöggeler, "Politische Bildung in den Streitkräften," *Wehrkunde* (August 1969): 394–98; Hans-Helmut Thielen, *Der Verfall der Inneren Führung: Politische Bewusteinbildung in der Bundeswehr* (Frankfurt am Main: Europäische Verlagsanstalt, 1970); General Rudolf Jenett, "Der Soldat zwischen Staat und Gesellschaft," *Wehrkunde* (October 1972): 510–13; and Lieutenant Colonel Otto Münter, "Das Primat der Politik," *Wehrkunde* (June 1975): 302–7.

31 See Arthur Conte, *Sans de Gaulle* (Paris: Plon, 1970); and Marie Madeleine Martin, *Charles de Gaulle cité au tribunal de l'histoire en l'année de Saint-Louis* (Paris: Éditions Reconquista, 1972).

32 Commander Rafael Gravalos Guzmán, "Ejército, juventud, participación," *Ejército* (August 1979): 44–45. See as well "Anti-militarismo," *Reconquista* (September 1981): 5.

33 Lieutenant Colonel Andrew P. O'Meara, Jr., "Civil-Military Conflict within the Defense Structure," *Parameters* (March 1978): 85–92.

34 As an example, see Senator Pedro Pablo Aguilar, "Las fuerzas armadas y el sistema democrático," RFAV (March–April 1983): 30–38.

35 See General (ret.) Erich Dethleffsen, "The German Armed Forces and Democracy," AAJ (December 1953): 19–22.

36 "Was ist Innere Führung?" *Truppenpraxis* (May 1962): 344.

37 Walter Rehm, "Offizier und Politik," WR (July 1956): 380–89; and Hans-Jürgen von Mitzlaff, "Zur Regelung des Befehls und Gehorsams im Soldatengesetz," WR (February 1957): 84–92.

38 "Innere Führung in der Deutschen Bundeswehr," RMG (April 1958): 521–40.

39 "Europa als Aufgabe der Soldaten," RMG (May 1958): 621–31; and his "Das Abendland verpflichtet," RMG (July 1959): 212–24; Captain (navy) Paul-E. Lenkeit, "Innere Führung und Künstlichkeit," *Wehrkunde* (October 1959): 537–40; Captain

(navy) Carl Kamps, "Innere Führung als erzieherische Aufgabe," *Wehrkunde* (January 1960): 28–31; Helmut Ibach, "Innere Führung: Ein Beitrag zur Begriffsklärung," *Truppenpraxis* (November 1965): 826–27; and Franz Pöggeler and Otto Wien, eds., *Soldaten und Demokratie: Die Bundeswehr in Gesellschaft und Staat* (Frankfurt am Main: Bernard & Graefe Verlag, 1973).

40 "Éducation civique et formation morale du soldat," RMG (October 1966): 332–52. The citation is from p. 339. See also Carl-Gero von Islemann, *Die Bundeswehr in der Demokratie: Zeit der Inneren Führung* (Hamburg: R. V. Decker's Verlag, 1971).

41 In *Soldat für den Frieden: Entwurfe für eine zeitgemässe Bundeswehr* (München: R. Piper Verlag, 1969).

42 Paul Roth, "Die politische Bildung in der Bundeswehr und die Verantwortung des Offiziers," *Wehrkunde* (February 1973): 82–87; Captain Claus Freiherr von Rosen, "Die Stabsakademie der Bundeswehr: Sternstunde oder Provisorium," *Wehrkunde* (January 1974): 29–37; General Andrea Viglione, "Le forze armate: Analisi di una realità: Problemi e perspettive," RMIT (January–February 1977): 2–7; "La Repubblica Federale di Germania," RMIT (July–August 1980): 4–16; Hans Jürgen Schulz, *Militarismus und Kapitalismus in der Bundeswehr* (Frankfurt am Main: ISP Verlag, 1977); Rudolf Haman, *Armee im Abseits?* (Hamburg: Hoffmann und Campe Verlag, 1972); and Wolfgang R. Vogt, *Militär und Demokratie: Funktionen und Konflikte der Institution des Wehrbeauftragen* (Hamburg: R. V. Decker's Verlag, 1972).

43 General Eberhard Wagemann, "Tradition und Bundeswehr," EW (September 1977): 455–59. See also Lieutenant Colonel Hans Hermann Krieger, "Allgemeine Führungslehre und Innere Führung," WR (May–June 1977): 65–67.

44 General Werner Lange, "Die Schule der Bundeswehr für Innere Führung," IT (February 1980): 15–25; Colonel G. Werner von Scheven, "Grundsätze der Inneren Führung," IT (March 1980): 3–31.

45 "Die Schule der Bundeswehr für Innere Führung," IT (November 1979): 40–53.

46 See Baudissin's "Gedanken zur Tradition," in Klaus-M. Kodalle, *Tradition als Last?: Legitimations probleme der Bundeswehr* (Köln: Verlag Wissenschaft und Politik, 1981).

47 See Helga G. Rockenbach, *Komponenten der gesellschaftlichen und wirtschaftlichen Integration der Bundeswehr* (München: Minerva-Publikation, 1983): 29–30.

48 Werner Heurmann and Wilhelm Niggemeyer, "Soldatische Erziehung aus der Sicht der Inneren Führung," WR (August 1965): 433–37. See also Major Henry G. Gole, "Leadership from Within," MR (February 1973): 83–91.

49 See Ralf Zoll, "Politische Bildung in the Bundeswehr," in *Civic Education in the Military: The German Case* (München: Sozial-Wissenschaftliches Institut, Heft 28, 1982), 1–87.

50 Georgy Mirsky, "The Army and the Revolution," SMR (August 1967): 53–55.

51 General P. Zhilin, "Cornerstone of the Development of the Soviet Armed Forces," SMR (January 1968): 2–5.

52 "Embodiment of Lenin's Ideas on Military Developments," SMR (February 1968): 2–5.

53 "The Soldier's Labour," SMR (September 1968): 2–3. See as well Colonel M. Lisenkov, "Culture and the Army," SMR (February 1969): 2–5.

54 "The Party, People and Army Are One," SMR (May 1971): 2–5.

55 Interview with Marshal K. S. Moskalenko, SMR (September 1971): 2–5. See also Colonel L. Eremeev, "Lessons in Valor," SMR (January 1973): 21–23.

56 Colonel M. Goryachev, "Socialist Unity of Command," SMR (July 1973): 6–8.

57 Colonel V. Mikheyev, "The Making of A Soldier: The Moral Strength of the Soviet Soldier," SMR (June 1976): 30–31. See also Admiral A. Sorokin, "Moral Potential of the Soviet Army," SMR (April 1978): 2–5; and Colonel V. Zhuravel, "Marxist-Leninist Training of Officers," SMR (June 1978): 30–31.

58 General N. Shapalin, "The Internationalist Mission of the Soviet Armed Forces," SMR (July 1983): 5–7.

59 General L. Vinogradov, "Political Information in the Armed Forces," SMR (January 1984): 34–36.

60 General Nikolai Gusev, "Leninist Principles of Soviet Military Development," SMR (November 1984): 1–13. See as well General Alexei Agafanov, "The Political Worker in the Life of the Military Collective," SMR (December 1984): 10–12; and Vladimir Borisov, "A School of Courage and Heroism," SMR (April 1985): 26–27.

61 Colonel E. Sulimov, "Armies: Their Origin and Essence," SMR (January 1966): 10–13.

62 See, for example, Colonel O. Rubstov, "The Bundeswehr Unmasked," SMR (September 1969): 58–59.

63 See João Assis Gomes, ed., *O Exército ao Serviço de Quem?* (Lisboa: Preto Editôra, 1974).

64 See Jack Waddis, *Armies and Politics* (London: Lawrence and Wisehart, 1977).

65 Gerhard Baumann, "Der Strukturwandel in den Zonenstreitkräften nach dem 13 August 1961," WR (May 1962): 245–61. The citation is from p. 261. See also Walter E. Schmitt, "Das Schlagwort vom 'Westdeutschen Militarismus,' in der kommunistischen Propaganda," WR (June 1962): 313–27; and Lieutenant Colonel Roy B. Root, "The 'Peace Loving' Chinese Communists," AD (October 1966): 5–8.

66 Lieutenant Colonel (hon.) Lucien Gespann, "Les fondements politico-militaires et idéologiques de l'armée nationale populaire de la DDR," RMG (December 1966): 611–25; Klaus Fielenbach, "Wehrerziehung in der DDR," *Wehrkunde* (April 1970): 186–90; and Ernst Leghan, "Drill = 'brutales System des Preussisch-Deutschen Militarismus,'" WR (June 1970): 332–33; and Leghan's "Politische Erziehung in der Nationalen Volksarmee," *Wehrforschung* (April 1971): 15–17.

67 See, as examples, N. von Ostrowska, "The Development of the Chinese Red Army," MR (January 1960): 82–87; Major Edgar O'Ballance, "The Officer Cadre of the Chinese Red Army," TAQDJ (October 1965): 50–57; Ellis Joffe, "Party and Military in China: Professionalism in Command?" *Problems of Communism* (September–October 1983): 48–63.

68 "La política en el medio militar," RFAV (August 1951): 134–36.

69 Captain Arturo Castilla Pizarro, "El Perú como nación: Nacionalismo y conciencia nacional: Sus factores formativos," RMP (January–March 1955): 89–101. The citation is from p. 93. See also General (ret.) Jorge A. Giovanelli, "La guerra psicológica entre oriente y occidente," RMA (November–December 1957): 5–10.

70 "Necesidad de la preparación profesional y general," RFAC (January–March 1959): 177–81.

71 General Lyman L. Lemnitzer, "One Army and the National Security," AID (January 1960): 2–9. The quotation is from p. 5.

72 "Discurso del jefe de la guardia nacional, General A. Somoza Debayle . . . el 30 de julio," GN (July–August 1960): 308.

73 Lieutenant Carlos Moreira López, "El por qué de la acción civica," GN (March–April 1962): 44–47.

74 "El pueblo liberal recibe con jubilo al mayor general Anastasio Somoza Debayle, al regresar a su patria," 5–10.

75 Colonel Julio Eladio Aguirre, "El comunismo en Gran Bretaña," RESGA (January–March, 1961): 62–78; Lieutenant Colonel Antonio Federico Moreno, "El 'lavado del cerebro,'" ibid., 45–61; and Rogelio Tristeny, "El despertar político de Africa," ibid., 79–100.

76 Claude Delmas, "Le communisme à l'assaut de l'Amérique Latine," RDN (May 1962): 817–32.

77 Colonel Tomás A. Sánchez Bustamante, "La situación mundial: El cerco estratégico," RESGA (January–March 1962): 1–11. The citation is from p. 5, Sanchez's emphasis.

78 Lieutenant Colonel Ricardo Peralta Méndez, "El comunismo como arma de dominación mundial," RMGU (October–December 1962): 27–33. See also Defense Minister Kai-Uwe von Hassel, "Deutsche Sichertsheitspolitik und Atlantische Verteidigung," *Wehrkunde* (July 1963): 346–48.

79 "Breve síntesis sobre el comunismo," RESGA (October–December 1963): 81–95.

80 "La seguridad y las políticas de integración internacional," REV (December 1967): 13–22. The quoted material is from p. 19.

81 Colonel Bruno Galindo Trejo, "El ejército y los disturbios del 2 de octubre," REM (January 1969): 3–13. The quotation is from p. 10. See as well Major S. Andrejulio Azahar, "El soldado salvadoreño y su misión histórica," RFAES (April 1970): 10–11.

82 Lieutenant Colonel José L. Sexton, "Marxismo: Contradicciones," RESGA (March–April 1969): 85–88.

83 See Werner Haupt, "Moskaus Griff nach Lateinamerika," WR (July 1970): 349–62. The citation is from p. 359.

84 See, as examples, Captain (navy) Roberto Gomes Pereira, "Ação do Movimento Comunista Internacional na Africa Austral-Occidental," ADN (July/August 1978): 35–53; and his "O Brasil e a Africa Subsahárica," ADN (November–December 1978): 89–102; and General Jonas de Morais Correia Neto, "A Guerra Revolucionária Comunista," RCMB (January–February 1982): 37–43.

85 General Paulo Campos Paiva, "O Comunismo e Seu Sonho de Domínio Mundial," ADN (November–December 1982): 123–31. The cited passage is from p. 130.

86 Lieutenant Colonel Alfonso Plazas Vega, "La guerra que el mundo libre está perdiendo," RFAC (July–September 1984): 357–79.

87 Justo de la Espriella, "Cuba e influencia comunista en el Caribe," RFAC (October–December 1984): 45–53. The quotation is from p. 52.

88 Major Luiz Carlos Aliandro, "Segurança Nacional e Sociedade Solidária," ADN (May–June 1984): 27–41. The cited material appears on p. 40.

89 Major J. D. Lunt, "Post-War Conditions in the Army," TAQDJ (October 1945): 89–98. The quotation appears on p. 90.

90 See Pastor Valencia Cabrera, "Las clases en la hora actual," 4 parts, RMBO (January–March 1949): 65–75; (April–June 1949): 41–49; (July–September 1949): 78–84; (October–December 1949): 41–48.

91 Colonel Alfredo Castellanos Alfaro, "Moral militar y civismo," REM (July–September 1951): 98–104. The cited passage comes from p. 101.

92 Departamento 5, "Algunas consideraciones sobre la democracia," RFAC (January–February 1964): 539–42.
93 See Lieutenant P. Shekleton, "The Case for Social Studies," AAJ (January 1956): 33–37.
94 "The Unseen Foe," AAJ (March 1963): 24–33. The quotation is from p. 33. See also Warrant Officer J. P. Sheddick, "Communism Versus Australia," AAJ (July 1963): 31–38.
95 Lieutenant Colonel Y. A. Mande, "The Paternalistic Society of the Army and Its Implications," JUSII (January–March 1973): 56–62. The quotation is from p. 57.
96 See General Alzir Benjamin Chaloub, "O Militar e o Momento Atual," ADN (May–June 1980): 41–53. The cited passage is from pp. 45–46. Chaloub's emphasis. See also General Adolpho João de Paula Couto, "A Guerra Política," ADN (September–October 1975): 29–62.
97 Hugo Tagle Martínez, "Patria, fuerzas armadas, y política económica," PG (October–December 1982): 53–60. Cf. Brigadier P. K. Gupta, "Right Officer Material," JUSII (April–June 1984): 103–19.
98 Batallion Chief Yemeniz, "Étude sur l'antimilitarisme," RMI (25 February 1950): 27–29.
99 Lieutenant Colonel Riograndino Da Costa e Silva (Brazilian), "Los militares y los problemas sociales," RMBO (January–June 1952): 34–39.
100 Major (air force) Carlos Carreño Monasterios, "La delincuencia como fenómeno social," RFAV (March–April 1971): 46–51.
101 Major Claudio Moreira Bento, "O Culto dos Tradições no Exército," RMB (January–June 1973): 35–48.
102 Colonel Hugo I. Pascarelli, "Características fundamentales de los valores del hombre y de la sociedad: Situación en el mundo de hoy," RCID (February 1979): 22–35.
103 See Captain Andrew Bacevich, Jr., "Progressivism, Professionalism, and Reform," *Parameters* (March 1979): 66–71.
104 "Mensaje del general de ejército don Alfredo Stroessner a la honorable convención extraordinaria de la asociación nacional republicana . . . 18 de septiembre de 1982," RFAP (July–November 1982): 7–11.
105 Directorate of Military Training, "Democracy and Communism," AAJ (January 1951): 16–18. See as well Lieutenant N. G. Maloy, "Significance of Political Parties in a Democracy," AAJ (May 1954): 29–31.
106 See Colonel Francisco Romero, "Hablemos del ejército," RMBO (January 1952): 60–81.
107 "Las centinelas de paz y democracia," BEC (May–June 1956): 14–21.
108 As examples, see Major Roberto Escobar G., "El poder como fenómeno social: El poder estatal," RECEMMEA (December 1967): 71–78; "Agradecimiento del ministro de defensa," RFAV (1967): 3–5; untitled editorial in RFAES (July 1968): 1–2; General L. Larrea Alba, "La política norteamericana y América Latina," RFAEC (1969): 127–31; and General Heberto Sánchez Barquero, "El rector de la Universidad de Honduras es agente de subversión comunista en Centroamérica," ACN (February 1977). See also Lieutenant Colonel Marlier, "La défense du Congo et l'avenir de la force publique," BMBC (April 1960): 184–89; and General Harold K. Johnson, "The Army's Role in Nation Building and Preserving Stability," AID (November 1965): 6–13.

109 Editorial, "Al pan, pan y al vino, vino," RFADR (April–May 1981): 2. See also General Herbert von Brockmann, "Krieg und Politik," WR (January 1953): 11–14.

110 "Motivation of Armed Forces Towards Our Ideology," PAJ (December 1973): 58–63.

111 See Major Rómulo Zanabria Zamudio, "Algo sobre guerra de guerrillas," RESGP (January–March 1956): 37–42.

112 Lieutenant Colonel Frances Patrice Naurois (French), "Algunos aspectos de la estrategia y de la táctica aplicadas por el Viet-Minh durante la campaña de Indochina," RESGA (January–March 1958): 97–128; and Lieutenant Colonel Manrique Miguel Mom, "Guerra revolucionaria: El conflicto mundial en desarrollo," RESGA (October–December 1958): 641–65.

113 See H. E. Wolf, "Zur Psychologie und Taktik des Kalten Kriegs," WR (April 1959): 204–10.

114 Lieutenant Colonel Fernando Louro de Silva, "Rumo ao Ultramar," RMPO (June 1959): 335–48; and Major José Luis Almiro Canelhas, "O Que é a Guerra Psicológica," RMPO (August–September 1963): 613–42.

115 See, as examples, Colonel Manrique Miguel Mom, "Guerra revolucionaria: Proceso, desarrollo," RESGA (July–September 1959): 489, 515; and Lieutenant Colonel Alcides López Aufranc, "Guerra revolucionaria en Argelia," RESGA (October–December 1959): 611–48.

116 Major Manuel Alfonso Rodríguez, "¿Será efectiva la defensa móvil ante la guerrilla?" RECEMMEA (April–June 1963): 30–38. Cf. Major Marcello Eydalin, "Opinioni: Gli opposti blocchi ideologici di fronte alla propaganda," RMIT (November 1963): 1337–44. And see Lieutenant Colonel Luis Alberto Leoni, "Filosofia comunista: Coexistencia pacífica o guerra abierta," RCMA (January–March 1964): 60–68; Colonel R. Fournier, "L'Amérique Latine face au communisme," RDN (November 1964): 1800–20; Lieutenant Colonel Irvin M. Kent and Major Richard A. Jones, "The Myth of the Third Man," MR (May 1966): 48–56; and Lieutenant Colonel Renato Marques Pinto, "A Acção Psicológica: Uma Arma de Combate," RMPO (June 1970): 478–89.

117 General Moacir Araújo Lopes, "A Grande Opção," RMB (April–June 1966): 7–24. See as well Colonel Oswaldo de Araújo Souza, "A Guerra Revolucionária e a Subversão Comunista Internacional," ibid.: 25–56.

118 Colonel Antonio López Salas, "Anatomía de la traición," RFAV (1966): 68–74. The cited material is from p. 70.

119 Major Jacinto R. Pérez Arcay, "Mística, nuestra verdadera fortaleza," SF (May–August 1968): 16–22. The quotation is from p. 17.

120 Major J. L. Epagniol, "Not by Arms Alone," AAJ (July 1971): 3–5. See also General J. Beauvallet, "La violence et la force: Réflexions sur la défense," FAF (October 1973): 3–7; Lieutenant Colonel Federico Quintero Morente, "Empleo de la violencia urbana por la subversión," RFADR (October 1973): 10–19; and Major Manuel Antonio Cuervo Gómez, "Guerra subversiva y revolucionaria," RFADR (December 1973): 10–17.

121 See General Hélio Lemus, "Psicopolítica e Contrapsicopolítica," ADN (November–December 1975): 3–40; Lieutenant Colonel Rashid Ali Malek, "Islamic Renaissance in Muslim World," PAJ (June 1980): 85–104; and General José Maria de Toledo Camargo, "O Que Dizer a um Jovem Sobre Comunismo," RMB (May–August 1979): 3–20.

122 Captain Arturo Grandinetti, "Aspectos político-militares de los conflictos en la guerra revolucionaria," RESGA (March–April 1976): 69–78. The quotation is from p. 71.

123 General Eliodoro A. Guerrero Gómez, "La profesión militar," REV (January–June 1985): 4–8.

124 General Octávio Pereira da Costa, "O Ofício de Oficial do Exército Brasileiro," REB (July–September 1983): 22–29.

125 See Major Jae-Ho-Chung, "La ética comunista de Corea del Norte," RFAC (1975?): 305–15; and Valencia Cabrera (chaplain), "Los antiguos testamentos y la clase obrera," RMBO (April–May 1950): 70–78.

126 See Colonel Santiago F. Baigorria, "Fuerza moral del frente interno," 4 parts, RMA (May–June 1952): 301–8, (July–August 1952): 463–69, (September–October 1952): 613–16; and (November–December 1952): 765–68; Major Constante Ma. Cruz, "The Story of Communism in the Philippines," PAFJ (October 1956): 2–8; Renaud-Joseph de Pesquidoux, "Guerre révolutionnaire et lutte anti-religieuse," RMI (January 1959): 23–40; General Baillif, "Forces armées et psychologie," RDN (May 1960): 819–29; and Dr. J. Guillermand, "Humanisme et condition militaire," FAF (January 1973): 4–9.

127 See Lieutenant Colonel Víctor Sánchez Marín (Peruvian), "Introducción al estudio de la guerra revolucionaria," GN (November–December 1961): 39–49; Lieutenant Colonel (ret.) Arturo S. Pasqualis Politi, "El problema marxista y su incidencia en nuestra resolución de estrategia cordial," RMA (July–September 1961): 45–79; Colonel Osiris Guillermo Villegas, "Guerra revolucionaria comunista," RMA (January–March 1960): 3–26; General L. M. Chassin, "De Nietzsche à Lenin," RDN (October 1962): 1480–1501; and General Sir Richard Hill, "Leadership in the Army of the Sixties," BAR (April 1963): 4–5.

128 See, for example, Colonel Ferdinando de Carvalho, "Por que Devemos Lutar Contra o Comunismo," 2 parts, ADN (January–February 1971): 39–52; and (March–April 1973): 47–54; Walter Rehm, "Der NVA-Soldat und sein Vaterland," *Wehrkunde* (September 1970): 444–49; Major C. C. M. Peters, "Communism and the Military Efficiency of the Soviet Armed Forces," AAJ (May 1973): 3–27; "Terrorisme," *Paratus* (Union of South Africa) (August 1974): 2–12; Colonel Clovis Borges de Azambuja, "O Marxismo-Leninismo e as suas Modalidades," RCID (January 1975): 2–16; Colonel Iván Dobud, "Causas sicosociales de la subversion," RCID (June 1976): 37–50; and "A Juventude e a Subversão Comunista," ADN (January–April 1977): 115–20.

129 Lieutenant Colonel Juan Antonio Mandraccio, "Pensamiento y acción contra la obra nefasta del comunismo," RCMA (October–December 1962): 48–51.

130 "El papel de acción cívica militar en el desarrollo de la comunidad," RMGU (July–September 1967): 52–61.

131 See "Communism and the AMF," AAJ (January 1953): 32–35. See also Max Lejeune, "La mission de l'armée en Algérie," RMI (November 1956): 85–87; Captain Raúl F. Cardoso Cunero, "El concepto marxista ante las fuerzas armadas," RMA (January–March 1959): 58–65; General José Díaz de Villegas, "El ejército: Valladar de la revolución," GN (March–April 1961): 59–68; and "La estabilidad del estado y el ejército profesional," RMGU (January–June 1967): 3–4.

132 "El perfeccionamiento del sistema militar interamericano: Análisis de la situación actual, orientación para su mejoramiento," RESGA (September–December 1968): 5–15. The cited passage appears on p. 14.

133 *Bekenntnis zum Soldaten: Militärische Führung in unserer Zeit,* 3d ed. (Hamburg: R. von Decker's Verlag, G. Schenck, 1971), 9–10, 87.

134 See Brigadier A. J. F. McDonald, "The Indonesian Army: A Brief History of Its Role in Indonesian Society," AAJ (April 1974): 17–32; A. de Lannes, "Conhecendo o Inimigo Interno," ADN (July–September 1977): 95–102; Colonel Edmirson Maranhão Ferreira, "Partido Político e Expressão Militar do Poder Nacional," ADN (November–December 1980): 35–42; General Romeo C. Espino, "A Call for the Return to Old Virtues," PAD (December 1978): 35–38; and Admiral Alfredo Landa Saa, "Reflexiones sobre algunas amenazas que atentan contra la seguridad y defensa nacional," RFAV (July–December 1981): 22–26.

Chapter Six

1 Lieutenant Colonel C. J. Johnson, "The Source of Military Morale, " AAJ (January 1952): 5–20. The citation is from p. 15

2 General (chaplain) Frank A. Tobey, "Character Guidance Program," AID (October 1959): 2–6.

3 General Eberhard Wagemann, "Soldat, ein Beruf wie jeder andere?" *Wehrkunde* (January 1971): 2–9.

4 Captain R. C. McNeill, "What's Going on at Cornwallis?" *Sentinel* (formerly CFS) (January 1971): 4–8. See also Captain Marsha Dorge, "They Wear the Cross," *Sentinel* (March 1981): 7.

5 Longinus, "Christianity and Militarism," TAQDJ (January 1978): 47–61. The citations are from pp. 56, 59.

6 General Ralph E. Haines, Jr., "Christian Leadership in the Armed Forces," DFJ (July–August 1984): 9–14.

7 See Chaplain Florencio Infante Durán, "Año santo militar," *Armas y Servicios del Ejército de Chile* (January 1976): 81–85. Hereafter ASEC.

8 "Pablo VI habla a los militares católicos," RFAP (January–June 1983): 86–91.

9 See Manuel Fernández Cambeiro, "El papel de la iglesia en el mundo de hoy," RFADR (February 1971): 45–46; Lieutenant Colonel (chaplain) Jaime Tovar Patrón, "XIV peregrinación militar internacional a Lourdes," *Ejército* (November 1972): 3–6; Rev. E. Innocenti, "La religione, componente importante del morale," RMIT (July–August 1974): 68–71; and Chaplain Ugo Crestani, "1975 anno santo: Un grande evento storico fra tradizione e progresso," RMIT (January–February 1975): 105–8.

10 See "Pablo VI habla a los militares católicos," ASEC (January 1976): 84.

11 Major Juan Tello Johnson, "El carácter frente a la actividad del oficial," RMP (December 1952): 55–56.

12 See Eulogio D. Carizo, "Milicia y servicio," RCMA (January–April 1966): 88–92.

13 Colin Beer, "The Portuguese Army in Angola," TAQDJ (October 1969): 109–11.

14 See Major Luis Alberto Leoni, "Encuadre de la institución del ejército en el estado moderno," RCMA (July–September 1960): 16–29; Colonel R. E. Saldaña J., "Las fuerzas armadas y la sociedad," RFARD (April–May 1966): 17–18; and General Raffaele Binetti, "La preparazione spirituale della forze armate," RMIT (June 1965): 846–57.

15 Lucio V. Mansilla, "Lo que es el ejército," RESGA (March–April 1971): 11–13.

16 Un Groupe d'Officiers Chrétiens, "Réflexions sur la défense," RDN (October 1973): 17–46. The cited passage is from p. 27. See also General J. Beauvallet, "Le chrétien et la défense nationale," FAF (July–August 1972): 2–9; General Wilhelm Hess, "Frieden mit oder ohne Waffen? Illusionare und Klarende Stimmen von Christen und Kirchen," EW (August 1981): 357–61.

17 See, for example, Chaplain Horst Scheeffler, "Funktionen und Leistungen der Religion in der soldatischen Existenz," EW (September 1980); 452–58. And see Commander (chaplain) Albino Fernández Fernández, "Valores religiosos de los soldados," *Ejército* (August 1982): 23–28.

18 "L'Algérie n'est pas l'Indochine," RMI (10 April 1956): 40–44. See also Lieutenant Colonel (air force) C. Jomain, "Essai sur le sentiment patriotique," FAF (April 1974): 2–9; Paul Rego, *Militares e Paisanos, Ou O Militarismo e Outras Forças de Violência na Sociedade Portuguesa* (Lisboa: Perspectivas e Realidades, 1981).

19 General (deacon) Dr. Bernhard Gramm, "Christ in Uniform," EW (May 1981): 211–16; and Hans Ulrich von Erlach, "L'arme idéologique qu'il nous faut: Le réarmament moral," RMG (April 1960): 438–54.

20 See Lieutenant Hernan Arbeláez Arbeláez, "Bajo la red del comunismo," RFAC (August 1962): 493–500; B. Chakravorty, "Is Political Indoctrination of Our Armed Forces Necessary?" JUSII (October–December 1968): 410–14; General (ret.) T. N. R. Nayar, "Reflections on the Generation Gap in Our Times," JUSII (October–December 1973): 353–60; General A. Baldini, "Autorità e libertà: Il milennio cristiano e la reforma," RMIT (September–October 1975): 48–56; and General Carlos de Meira Mattos, "Os Princípios do Realismo Político ou da *Realpolitiker*," RCID (April 1977).

21 Editorial, "Taiwan es la salvaguardia de la cultura mas antigua del mundo," RFAP (January–June 1983): 97–100.

22 "A Matter of Priorities," PAJ (January 1961): 4–6. Cf. Susheela Kanshik, "Democracy vs. Authoritarianism in Pakistan," JUSII (April–June 1963): 173–82.

23 "Devotion: The Greatest Single Weapon of War," PAJ (June 1963): 1–3.

24 Colonel Bushir Ahmad, "Morale in the Muslim Campaigns," PAJ (December 1963): 6–13.

25 Lieutenant Colonel Mohammad Safdar Iqbel, "Motivation of the Pakistani Soldier," PAJ (December 1966): 6–15. The citation is from p. 11.

26 See Brigadier Ihsan ul Haq, "Quran and War," PAJ (June 1968): 11–15; and also his "Mohammad the Ideal Soldier," PAJ (June 1969): 1–7. The final citation is from p. 15.

27 "Armed Forces of an Ideological State," PAJ (June 1969): 28–32.

28 "You and Your Heart," ibid., 46–49; and "Obesity," PAJ (December 1969): 67–73. The quotation is from p. 68.

29 "The Code of Ethics for Government Officials," PAJ (June 1970): 8–16.

30 Major Usman Shah, "Will of a Nation: How to Develop Its Attributes in Our Nation," ibid., 63–66.

31 "The Soldier, the Battlefield, and Leadership," AAJ (September 1971): 15–23. The citation is from p. 17. See also Justice (ret.) Hamodur Rahman, "Ideology of Pakistan: The Raison D'Être of Our Country," PAJ (June 1978): 1–9; and Lieutenant Colonel S. M. A. Rizvi, "Oneness of God," PAJ (September 1978): 1–4.

32 General Nawabazda Sher Ali Khan Pataudi, "Islam and Military Power," MR (November 1979): 66–73. The quoted passage appears on p. 73.

33 See Lieutenant Colonel Muhammad Hafeez, "Islamic Renaissance in Muslim World," PAJ (March 1980): 81–105. The quote is from p. 87.

34 General Muhammad Gamal El-Din Mahtouz, "The Value of Man in the Islamic Military Thought," *Islamic Defence Review* (January 1982): 9–12.

35 "The Pakistan Army in the 1980s," 2 parts, TAQDJ (July 1984): 287–94; (October 1984): 412–17. The citation is from p. 289.

36 See the commemorative issue of *Ejército* dedicated to the twenty-fifth anniversary of the rising of 1936 (*Nuestra Cruzada*) (July 1961). The cited passage is from a speech by Generalissimo Francisco Franco, 3 April 1961.

37 See Commander Manuel Patilla, "Cruzada frente a guerra revolucionaria," *Ejército* (August 1963): 11–16; and Captain José Aparicio Olmos, "Guerra de liberación: Conceptos sintéticos," *Ejército* (February 1964): 3–10; General José Díaz de Villegas, "25 años de paz: El milagro español," *Ejército* (April 1964): 3–14.

38 Commander Sánchez-Díaz, "Patria, patriotismo, cristiandad," *Reconquista* (January 1965): 23–26.

39 Lieutenant Colonel (chaplain) Roberto A. Wilkinson, "Psicología del mando," RIA (September–October 1953): 552–75. The quotations come from pp. 554–58.

40 "¿Se puede hablar de una vocación a las armas?" RMA (May–June 1954): 22–24.

41 General (ret.) Raúl A. González, "Panorama económico, político, y social argentino," RCMA (July–September 1962): 8–25.

42 See Colonel Justo P. Briano, "El humanismo integral americano," RCMA (July 1972): 51–54.

43 Juan Rafael Llerena Amadeo, "La política al servicio del hombre," RESGA (March–April 1978): 47–56.

44 "El humanismo," RESGA (January–February 1979): 91–95.

45 See "Vocación militar," RFAV (July–December 1981): 88–96.

46 See Major D. Lunt, "The Training of the Young Officer Cadet after the War," TAQDJ (April 1944): 115–22. The citation is from p. 16.

47 Lieutenant D. G. R. Teisseire, "Influencia del ejército en el desarrollo de los valores materiales y morales del pueblo argentino," RMA (January–February 1953): 33–39. The cited material appears on p. 37.

48 General Lionel C. McGarr, "Ethical and Moral Aspects of the Service," MR (August 1960): 3–8. See also Brigadier B. S. Gill, "The Average Officer," JUSII (July–October 1950): 176–80.

49 See, for example, bi-weekly editorials and brief essays in BEES, esp. during 1950–1954.

50 As examples, see Colonel Sinforiano Bilbao Rioja, "La paz y la guerra: Las instituciones armadas," RMBO (February–March 1953): 32–37; and "Mensaje de navidad del jefe del estado," RFAP (October–December 1957): i–vi.

51 Dr. Wilhelm Ritter von Schramm, "Bundeswehr und Tradition," *Wehrkunde* (October 1959): 505–13. Along this line, see also General A. S. Naravane, "Motivation in Military Leadership," JUSII (October–December 1964): 395–403; General Manoel Pedroso Gonçalves, "O Patriotismo," RMPO (May 1966): 276–82; and Major José Oscar Aguilar M., "Virtudes militares," RECEMMEA (December 1967): 15–16.

52 General (ret.) Som Dut, "The Military Mind," JUSII (July–September 1973): 242–

45. In this vein, see as well Dadjit Singh, "Military Education in India: Changes from the British Tradition," JUSII (July–September 1974): 227–37; Peter J. Prior, "Your Country Needs You," TAQDJ (January 1976): 44–50; Commander Francisco Laguna Sanquirico, "Apuntes sobre educación militar," *Ejército* (September 1977): 9–15; Brigadier (ret.) N. B. Grant, "An Officer and a Gentleman," JUSII (October–December 1978): 317–23; Lieutenant Colonel N. V. Bal, "Education in the Indian Armed Forces," JUSII (April 1947): 310–15; Lieutenant Colonel Rodolfo Sejas, "¿Cómo unificar la cultura militar del ejército?" RMBO (September–November 1950): 42–46; Captain Federico Juárez Rodos, "La educación del oficial del ejército," RMGU (May 1951): 69–71; (June 1951): 43–46; and Lieutenant Colonel Risstel, "Debe fomentarse la cultura militar y técnica de nuestros suboficiales y demás clases instructores," RMBO (January 1953): 15–19.

53 Brigadier Rajendra Singh, "About Military Thinking," TAQDJ (July 1961): 218–22. See also Major Gurbachan Singh, "The Right Type and Some Thoughts on Indianisation," JUSII (July 1946): 443–45.

54 See Major A. W. John, "Army Education: Its Value to Soldier and Nation,"AAJ (November 1952): 32–35. See also Warrant Officer N. F. Clarke, "The Dynamic of Education in the Army," AAJ (April 1953): 42–44; Lieutenant Colonel N. E. V. Short, "The Owl and the Sword," TAQDJ (January 1958): 233–42; Adjutant J.-M. Pottiez, "Scoutisme et Force Publique: De la théorie à la pratique," BMBC (April 1956): 194–204; and Colonel (ret.) Virgil Ney, "Soviet Military Education: A Source of Communist Power," MR (December 1959): 3–12.

55 See Colonel Jackson E. Shirley, "Brainpower and Manpower," AID (August 1960): 25–29. See as well Vice Commodore Dardo Eugenio Ferreyra, "Cultura general y cultura militar," RMA (July–September 1960): 110–14; Captain E. M. McCormick, "Political Education in the Army," AAJ (June 1961): 5–9; Colonel Alexandre, "De la pensée militaire et des impératifs," RMI (March 1962): 4–7; Major H. E. D. Harris, "The Value of History to the Soldier," TAQDJ (October 1962): 79–87; Friedrich Forstmeier, "Hochschulstudium für Offiziere: Eine Forderung der Gegenwart," WR (September 1963): 489–509; Otto Zwengel, "Bundeswehr und Universität," WR (March 1964): 177–80; and Captain O. H. Wieser, "Social Studies: Necessity or Humbug?" AAJ (March 1964): 31–35.

56 See Colonel Donato Solluzi, "Il Centro Alti Studi Militari," RMIT (November–December 1978): 4–8; Colonel Juan Antonio Lossada Volcán, "Un paso adelante: La educación sobre la defensa nacional," REV (October–December 1966): 33–36; Major Fernando Bernal Petrelli, "La educación, la cultura, y la profesión militar," RFAC (March–April 1967): 83–87; and Colonel Ricardo Benza Carreras, "Importancia de la educación moral militar," RFAP (January–May 1967): 7–11.

57 General Hans Speidel, "Estado Mayor y cultura," RESGA (March–April 1969): 29–44. The citation is from p. 36. See also Colonel de Bloisfleury, "Réflexions sur la formation des officiers," RDN (December 1969): 2012–21; Colonel Luigi De Mari, "Il problema della formazione, della preparazione, e della stabilità nell'incarico de docenti militari," RMIT (April 1971): 507–15; Colonel Homar Sagrista, "La educación en el ejército," RESGA (September–October 1973): 53–64; Captain Robert R. Begland, "Officer Education and Training in the Army: An Alternative Solution," MR (October 1978): 15–26; and General M. L. Thopan, "Academic Recognition of Service Education," JUSII (July–September 1980): 216–20.

58 See General Guy Mery, "The Future of the French Army," *Atlantic Community Quarterly* (Fall 1979): 317–30. And see Brigadier F. W. Speed, "The Australian Defence Force Academy," TAQDJ (January 1982): 31–36.

59 Admiral Alfredo J. Landa Saa, "Reflexiones acerca del Instituto de Altos Estudios de la Defensa Nacional," RFAV (April–June 1981): 31–36.

60 Major Luis Ramos Arce, "Ciencia y arte militar en sus relaciones con los estudios universitarios," RMBO (January–February 1947): 41–44; (March–April 1947): 49–52; (May–June 1947): 54–57; (August–October 1947): 100–103. Cf. Captain Gonzalo Borges Ramos' argument for more places in universities in "Los estudios universitarios y la educación militar," RFAV (March–May 1961): 30–32.

61 See General L. M. Chassin, "Réflexions sur l'éducation militaire," RMI (10 July 1950): 25–28; and his "Du rôle idéologique de l'armée," RMI (10 October 1954): 13–19.

62 Dr. R. A. Preston, "Academics and Culture in Cadet Colleges," TAQDJ (April 1955): 97–111.

63 Captain Domingo López, "Educación y defensa nacional," RMA (October–December 1958): 20–23. See also Jean Sarrilh, "Éducation nationale et civisme," RMI (April 1959): 11–16.

64 Captain James E. Smith, Jr., "Teaching Military Science," MR (September 1961): 41–44.

65 See Lieutenant Colonel Héctor E. Contreras Corrales, "La defensa nacional en torno a una ley," RFAV (1968): 24–32.

66 Major U. B. S. Ahluwalia, "Man the Deciding Factor," JUSII (April–June 1971): 108–16.

67 General J. D. Lunt (CBE), "An Army in Transition," TAQDJ (April 1974): 280–84.

68 Lieutenant Colonel (ret.) Sam Sarkesian, "Changing Dimensions of Military Professionalism," MR (March 1979): 44–56. The citation is from p. 50. Cf. the views on differences between military and civilian education in Major Craig Wills, "The Emphasis Is on Leadership," *Sentinel* (April 1982): 3–7.

69 General José Julio Mazzeo, "Educar para la democracia," RESGA (January–February 1982): 7–14. The quoted material comes from pp. 209–10.

70 "Educação e Democrácia," ADN (May–June 1985): 45–57.

71 Anon., "Languages in the Services," TAQDJ (July 1944): 180–86; "KRGM," "The Study of Foreign Languages," JUSII (January–April 1951): 87–90; Major J. M. da Costa, "Training in Foreign Languages," AAJ (January 1961): 16–18; Sergeant D. W. Roy, "The Use of Foreign Languages in the Australian Forces," AAJ (March 1966): 14–17; Lieutenant Colonel Antonio Polimeni, "Opinioni: Il problema linguistico in campo militare," RMIT (February 1963): 211–15.

72 General (ret.) Jorge A. Giovanelli, "El movimiento moderno de las ideas: Algunas reflexiones destinadas a los jóvenes oficiales de nuestro ejército," RCMA (October–December 1963): 9–18.

73 "A Necessidade do Estudo de um Idioma Estrangeiro no Exército," ADN (July–August 1974): 91–94.

74 General H. E. N. Bredin (CB, DSO, MC), "The First Job of an Officer," AAJ (February 1975): 29–35. The citation is from p. 35.

75 Major Gustav Lünenborg, "Gedanke zur Offizierausbildung im Heer," *Truppenpraxis* (January 1972): 33–34.

76 General Giorgio Liuzzi, "Caracteristiche ed esigenze di un esercito moderno," RMIT (May 1961): 561–67.

77 See Major Mamerto Marroquín, "Misión del ejército," RMGU (July–September 1963): 40–45.

78 See Lieutenant Colonel Julio Sanguinetti, "El potencial humano," RMA (October 1945): 767–82; Colonel Juan Mendoza Rodríguez, "La escuela militar en la obra de la educación nacional," RMP (April 1948): 259–67; Commander Rogelio Soto Barreto, address, *Ejército* (Cuba) (10 March 1952): 5–15; Colonel Emilio Bolón Varela, "Canon del conductor (el bien y el mal)," RMA (July–August 1953): 12–15; Lieutenant Colonel Geoffrey Cox, "Training France's Military Elite: The École Militaire," TAQDJ (October 1983): 421–27; and Lieutenant (ret.) Domingo I. de J. López, "Educación civil y educación militar," RMA (October–December 1959): 65–68.

79 See, as selected examples, Squadron Chief Chaudessais, "Considérations sur le moral," RMI (10 July 1951): 17–21; General d'Astier de Villate, "Défense nationale et défense d'outre mer," *Tropiques* (March 1955): 33–35; Lieutenant Colonel Matthey, "Pédagogie et instruction militaire," RMI (10 January 1956): 29–34; General (ret.) André Gribius," *Une vie d'officier* (Paris: Éditions France Empire, 1971): passim; Lieutenant Colonel Vincenzo Morelli, "Piu meritate l'obbedienza e piu sarete obbediti," RMIT (April 1971): 521–23; Maxime Laborde, "Université de la défense nationale," RDN (April 1960): 591–604; Governor General Chauvet, "Réforme administrative et réforme de l'état," RDN (January 1961): 22–44; Lic. Adolfo López Mateos, "El ejército, baluarte revolucionario," REM (September 1960): 1–3; and Captain R. T. Jones, "Countering the Spread of Communism," AAJ (March 1962): 34–38. See also Lieutenant Colonel Enrique Gallegos Venero, "Un combate victorioso en guerra revolucionario," RESGP (July–September 1962): 7–26; Colonel Suire, "Honneur et patrie," RDN (August–September 1963): 1290–1305; Colonel Ernesto del Castillo Fernández, "Misión militar del ejército," REM (July 1969): 8–13; General Cristóbal Guzmán Cárdenas, "La educación militar," REM (November 1962): 20–47; and the entertaining editorial on the occasion of the birthdays of Luis and Anastasio Somoza Debayle, GN (November–December 1961): 5–6.

80 "La preparación militar y las profesiones paralelas," RFAC (May–June 1966): 273–78.

81 See General Martín García Villasmil, "Exposición del ministro de defensa ante el congreso de la república," RFAV (1970): 5–13.

82 "Ligeiro Ensaio sobre a Doutrina Nacionalista da Revolução Brasileira," RCMB (January 1970): 12–13.

83 Fritz-Rudolf Schultze, "Probleme der Bundeswehr am Anfang der siebziger Jahre," *Wehrkunde* (December 1970): 627–30. See also Lieutenant Colonel Humberto J. Lobaiza, "Características generales de los diferentes regímenes políticos y económico-sociales," RESGA (July–August 1972): 75–88.

84 General Carlos E. Celis Noguera, "Doctrina militar," RFAV (March–April 1971): 30–34. See also J. Guillermand, "Humanisme et condition militaire," FAF (January 1973): 4–9.

85 Alejandro Leloir, "Brasil: Ejército y política," *Estrategia* (May–June 1971): 23–38.

86 "Pérennité et nécessité de la défense," RDN (July 1973): 21–34. The quotation is

from p. 26. Cf. the antimilitary arguments in David Guérin and Roland Geigenbach, *L'armée en France* (Paris: Éditions Filipacchi, 1974).

87 See Colonel M. Rouquet, "Pour un nouveau rôle social de l'armée," FAF (December 1973): 9–11. See as well Major Agneldo Del Nero Augusto, "A Política Militar Francesa," ADN (July–August 1976): 3–24.

88 General Fred C. Weyand, "America and Its Army: A Bicentennial Look at Posture and Goals," *Parameters* (March 1976): 2–11. The citation is from p. 11.

89 Squadron Leader Nak Parik, "Armed Forces and Ideals," JUSII (January–March 1976): 72–76.

90 Departamento de Reglamentación y Doctrina, Escuela Superior de Guerra, "La profesión militar," RFAC (September–December 1976): 327–30. See as well Captain P. C. Cameron, "The Military and Political Development," DFJ (September–October 1977): 26–30; and Major A. Holmes, "Political Developments in Third World Countries," DFJ (January–February 1983): 25–30; and Major Shajar Hussain, "Man: The Key to Success," PAJ (September 1977): 15–20.

91 General Ariel Pacca da Fonseca, "O Comunismo e a Formação de Lideranças Militares com Convicções Democráticas," ADN (March–April 1980): 31–45. The cited passage is from p. 43.

92 See "Values and the Professional Soldier," *Parameters* (December 1981): 74–79.

93 As selected examples, see discussions in Christopher Clapham and George Philip, eds., *Political Dilemmas of Military Regimes* (London: Croom Helm, 1984). See as well [H]Asan Astari Rizvi, *The Military and Politics in Pakistan* rev. ed. (Lahore: Progressive Publishers, 1976); Stuart Drummond, "The Role of the Indonesian Army in Society and Its Attitude towards the Use of Force," TAQDJ (October 1975): 423–32; Kenneth W. Grundy, *The Rise of the South African Military Establishment: An Essay on the Changing Locus of State Power* (Capetown: South African Institute of International Affairs, 1983).

94 See General Francisco Batista Torres de Mello, "O Medo, A Disciplina, e A Liberdade," ADN (January–February 1982): 177–81.

95 Adolfo López Mateos, Lic., presidential message, REM (February 1961): 3.

96 "Doctrina filosófica de la revolución mexicana," EL (August 1966): 7–13. The citation is from p. 9.

97 "El pasado y el presente," REM (April 1967): 31–35.

98 General Javier Echeverría Adame Marquina, "¡20 de noviembre de 1910!" EL (November–December 1967): 56–58.

99 General Raúl Madero González, "Conferencia," EL (April 1968): 23–25.

100 See Major Alberto Santander Bonilla, "La juventud de México," REM (May 1970): 33–34. See also Colonel Bruno Galindo Trejo, "El ejército y los disturbios del 2 de Octubre," REM (January 1969): 3–13; Galindo, "De nuestros deberes para con la patria," REM (February 1969); and the views expressed in two installments of a multipart commentary, in Anon., "Constitución política de los Estados Unidos Mexicanos y comentarios a cada uno de sus artículos," REM (June 1970): 5–13, and (July 1970): 41–49.

101 See this speech in REM (October 1970): 5–8. See as well "Un ejército doblemente constitucionalista," *Armas* (March–April 1976): 9–15; and "El ejército ante la dinámica de la revolución mexicana," *Armas* (January–February 1979): 8–10.

102 Cf. Colonel Hermes de Araújo Oliveira, "O Homem Branco, O Homem Preto,

Frente a Frente," RMPO (January 1969): 9–28. See also General José del Carmen Marín, "Preparación para el alto mando," RMP, 3 parts, (April 1956): 1–13; (September–October 1956): 1–16; (November–December 1956): 1–16; Captain Cogniet, "L'avenir politique du Sahara," *Tropiques* (August–September 1954): 49–51; Georges R. Manue, "Le rôle de l'armée en Algérie," RMI (July 1956): 12–13; "La francophonie et l'Afrique," FA (March–April 1969): 4–11; Batallion Chief Pourichkevitch, "Les rouges et l'Afrique Noire," RMI (April 1960): 4–16.

103 See, for example, General José del Carmen Marín, "El Perú y la defensa hemisférica," RMP (June 1955): 110–20.

104 See Luis Mericq Seoane, ed., *Edgardo Mercado Jarrín: Seguridad-Política-Estrategia* (Santiago: Estado Mayor del Ejército de Chile, 1975); Captain André Souyris, "La acción sociológica y las fuerzas armadas," RMP (September–October 1959): 73–89: Colonel Martín García Villasmil, "El militar y la política," RMP (November–December 1959): 75–82; Major Enrique Gallegos Venero, "¿Debe preocuparnos la guerra subversiva?" RESGP (January–March 1960): 18–20; Frederick M. Nunn, *Yesterday's Soldiers: European Military Professionalism in South America, 1890–1940* (Lincoln: University of Nebraska Press, 1983), passim; Lieutenant Colonel Artemio García Vargas, "Programas de acción cívica," RMP (January–February 1962): 49–56; and Major Orellana Ariza, "El soldado convencional frente al comunismo," RMP (May–June 1962): 43–44.

105 See "Introducción al estudio de la guerra revolucionaria," RMP (March–April 1961): 132–51. The citation is from p. 141.

106 "El ejército y la aviación en 1964: Su acción frente al subdesarrollo, frente al sistema panamericano y frente al orden interno," *Revista del CIMP* (October–December 1964): 205–14. The quoted passage appears on p. 209. See also General Edgardo Mercado Jarrín, "La política y la estrategia militar en la guerra contrasubversiva," RESGP (October–December 1967): 77–104.

107 See Frederick M. Nunn, "Professional Militarism in Twentieth-Century Peru: Historical and Theoretical Background to the *Golpe de Estado* of 1968," *Hispanic American Historical Review* (August 1979): 391–417.

108 "Educación militar y fuerzas armadas: Reflexiones para los alumnos que egresan de la Escuela Militar de Chorrillos," RMP (January–February 1972): 11–14. Cf. Lieutenant Colonel Jorge Lucas Figueroa, "La Escuela Militar: Cuna de la proyección futura del oficial," MECH (May–August 1977): 10–30.

109 "La vocación militar y algunos juicios de extranjeros sobre el Ejército de Chile," MECH (May–August 1973): 133–42. The citation comes from p. 142.

110 See Colonel Raúl Toro Arriagada, "¿Capacidad ciudadana? ¿Desarrollo y expansión?" MECH (January–April 1975): 3–6.

111 See "11 de septiembre," MECH (September–December 1979): 11–12. See also Nunn, "Latin American Militarylore: An Introduction and a Case Study," *The Americas* (April 1979): 429–74.

112 General Adel Edgardo Vilas, "Reflexiones sobre la subversión cultural," MECH, 3 parts, (September–December 1979): 40–45; (January–April 1980): 54–62; (May–August 1980): 43–64.

113 "La lucha anti-comunista en el campo de espíritu," MECH (September–December 1980): 138–45. The citation is from p. 141.

114 "Un breve vistazo en el mundo en que vivimos," MECH (January–April 1981): 100–108. The cited passage appears on p. 101.

115 "Marxismo: Análisis político, económico, y religioso," MECH (May–August 1983): 38–53.

116 "La infiltración y destruccion de las fuerzas armadas," MECH (January–April 1985): 25–34.

117 See, as examples of this, General Augusto Pinochet Ugarte, *Política, politiquería y demagogia* (Santiago: Editorial Renacimiento, 1983); Lieutenant Colonel Carlos Molina Johnson, *1973: Algunas de las razones del quiebre de la institucionalidad política* (Santiago: Estado Mayor General del Ejército de Chile, 1987); and General Roberto Guillard Marinot, "La intervención del ejército en los acontecimientos del presente siglo," mimeo (La Reina: Academia de Guerra del Ejército de Chile, 1988).

Chapter Seven

1 "Army Nationbuilders," MR (August 1967): 47–53.

2 See RMP (November–December 1968): 1–20.

3 Ibid., 6–7.

4 "Resumen de un programa de desarrollo industrial y regional para El Perú: Transcripción del resumen del informe presentado al gobierno del Perú por Arthur D. Little, Inc.," RESGP (April–June 1961): 7–38. The cited passage is from pp. 7–8.

5 See, as examples of military developmental mobilization, Colonel Julio E. Mavila Durand, "Nuestra riqueza ictiológica y la defensa nacional," RMP (June 1953): 1–12; Major Abel Carrera Naranjo, "La minería peruana y la defensa nacional: Proyecciones geopolíticas de la riqueza mineral del Perú," RMP (October 1953): 80–95; (November 1953): 5–34; and Lieutenant Colonel Luis Bustos G., "La industrialización y la guerra," RMP (October 1953): 74–79.

6 "El departamento de movilización integral de la nación, elemento básico del ministerio de la defensa nacional," RESGP (July–September 1955): 30–53. The citation is from p. 33. See also Captain Arturo Castilla Pizarro, "Geopolítica: El heartland y la teoría del control terrestre," RMP (September 1955): 66–79; Lieutenant Colonel Alejandro Medina Valderrama, "Actualización de los nuevos conceptos de la ciencia geográfica en El Perú," RMP (May 1956): 45–52; and Colonel César A. Pando Egusquiza, "La declaración de las 200 millas de mar territorial frente a la defensa nacional y al derecho," RMP (November–December 1956): 19–43.

7 Colonel Víctor Odicio T., "Ensayo sobre lo que podría ser una ley de seguridad o de defensa nacional," RMP (January–February 1957): 23–31. The quotation comes from p. 23.

8 "Pensamiento estratégico," RESGP (January–March 1963): 7–12.

9 See Major Wilfredo Contreras A., "Geopolítica," RMP (May–June 1960): 65–81; Lieutenant Colonel Sergio Cornejo, "El problema nacional e institucional de movilización," RMP (July–August 1960): 71–78; and "Clausura del año académico en el CAEM," RMP (January–February 1961): 48–50.

10 Lieutenant Colonel Gastón Ibáñez O'Brien, "Comando y delegación de autoridad y responsibilidad," RESGP (April–June 1963): 9–26. See as well Colonel Angel Valdivia Morriberón, "El estado en la planificación," RESGP (October–December 1963): 113–20.

11 Colonel Edgardo Mercado Jarrín, "La política de la seguridad nacional," RESGP (October–December 1964): 83–112. The quotation is from p. 89. See also Lieutenant Colonel Alvaro Pito Fonseca, "Reflexiones sobre el sistema de gobierno democrático," RESGP (January–March 1964): 117–21; Colonel Edgardo Mercado Jarrín, "Las relaciones entre la política y la estrategia militar," RESGP (July–September 1965): 37–61; Colonel Armando Cueto Zevallos, "Movilización de recursos humanos," RESGP (January–March 1964): 7–54; Lieutenant Colonel Gastón Ibáñez O'Brien, "Movilización económica," ibid., 55–59; and (April–June 1964): 25–64; Lieutenant Colonel Víctor Sánchez Marín, "Potencial nacional," RMP (March–April 1964): 73–79; Colonel Oscar Ceberos Rueda, "Algunos aspectos del problema agropecuario," RMP (March–April 1964): 80–86; and the Colombian General Alberto Ruiz Novoa, "Economía y defensa nacional," RMP (September–October 1964): 71–83.

12 Lieutenant Colonel Oscar Torres Llosa, "¿Debe el ejército participar en la colonización?" RESGP (October–December 1966): 21–40. See also his "Plan de colonización del ejército y sus alcances en provecho del país," RMP (May–June 1967): 7–19.

13 See Lieutenant Colonel Napoleón Urbina Abanto, "La regionalización del país y el desarrollo económico nacional," RESGP (January–March 1967): 7–13. See also Colonel Lorenzo Morachimo T., "La producción industrial en el ejército," RMP (July–August 1967): 40–46.

14 "El ejército y la empresa," RESGP (April–June 1968): 7–23.

15 In "Exposición hecha el 5 de noviembre de 1968 por el ministro de hacienda, general de brigada Angel Valdivia Morriberón, a nombre del gobierno revolucionario del Perú sobre reforma de la administración publica," RMP (November–December 1968): 40–49. See as well General Edgardo Mercado Jarrín, "Reflexiones sobre la seguridad y el desarrollo en América Latina," RMP (September–October 1973): 2–19. A good treatment of the post-1968 military-civilian experience in Peru is Cynthia McClintock and Abraham Lowenthal, eds., *The Peruvian Experiment Reconsidered* (Princeton: Princeton University Press, 1983).

16 General Jorge Chávez Quelopana, "Reflexiones sobre el CAEM: Objetivo, política, y estrategia," RESGP (October–December 1973): 13–63 (April–June 1974): 19–47. See also Lieutenant Colonel Carlos Bobbio Centurión, "El ejército, el oficial, y la política," RMP (January–February 1972): 7–11.

17 Captain Usureau, "De la compétence de l'armée," RMI (25 January 1950): 24–27.

18 *A Nova Constituição do Brasil de 17 de Outobro de 1969*, Chap. VII, Sec. VI, Arts. 90–83. See also the discussion in Colonel Waldir da Costa Godolphim's "Institucionalidade, Destinação, e Bases Constitucionais para a Atuação das Forças Armadas Brasileiras," RMB (January–March 1971): 81–92.

19 See Lieutenant Colonel Jaime Ribeiro da Graça, "A Geopolítica como Ciência da Paz: Como a Estudar e Interpretar," RMB (January–June 1950): 49–56; and Major Ituriel Nascimento, "O Brasil e o Seu Petróleo," RMB (July–December 1947): 435–38.

20 See "A Educação da Elite Militar," RCMB (January 1970): 21–24; and also his "Doutrina Política Revolucionária: Brasil Potência," RCMB (April 1970): 16–18.

21 Cited in Major Levy Bittencourt Junior, "Colonização Militar na Faixa da Fronteira do Oeste Brasileiro," RMB (January–March 1971): 71–79.

22 Colonel Miguel Monori Filho, "La movilización nacional," RESGA (May–June

1971): 79–94. The citation is from p. 84. See also General Antônio Carlos de Silva Muricy, "O Exército e Sua Missão Constitucional," RCMB (August 1971): 1–4; and also his "Revolução, Desenvolvimento, Democrácia, e Poder," RCMB (March–April 1972): 5–7; and Meira Mattos' "Nossa Viabilidade para Grande Potência," RCMB (March 1971): 3–6.

23 Major Claudio Moreira Bento, "O Culto das Tradições no Exército," RMB (January–June 1973): 35–48. The quotation is from p. 36.

24 See, for example, Major Waldeck Nery de Medeiros, "Rondon: Uma Lição de Civismo," RCMB (May–June 1973): 42–43; Meira Mattos, "A Geopolítica e a Teoria da Forma e Espaço dos Estados," RMB (July–December 1974): 29–58; Darino Castro Rebelo, "O Exército e a Integração Nacional," RCMB (July–August 1975): 4–15; General Carlos de Meira Mattos, "Uma Geopolítica Panamazónica," ADN (May–June 1978): 5–13; Colonel Waldir da Costa Godolphim, "Fundamentos Filosóficos na Formação da Geografia Moderna e da Geopolítica," ibid., 89–107.

25 See Lieutenant Colonel Herbert Orellana Herrera, *Brasil: Un país que aceptó el desafio del desarrollo* (Santiago: Estado Mayor General del Ejército de Chile, 1974), 252. See as well General Obino Alvares, "Desenvolvimento e Subdesenvolvimento," ADN (September–October 1975): 63–70; and Antônio de Arruda, "A Doutrina da Escola Superior de Guerra," ADN (September–October 1978): 65–73.

26 Getúlio Carvalho, "Poderes do Estado: O Exército Forte," ADN (January–February 1979): 25–43.

27 See Major Luiz Carlos Aliandro, "Projeto Nacional Brasileiro: Ideias Básicas," ADN (January–February 1979): 75–77.

28 General Carlos de Meira Mattos, "A Continentalidade do Brasil," ADN (March–April 1979): 15–19. See also his "Desinformação Histórica e Segurança Nacional," ADN (July–August 1979): 61–65; Therezinha de Castro, "Amazônia: O Grande Desafio Geopolítico," ADN (September–October 1981): 23–27; and General Golbery do Couto e Silva, "Questões sobre 'Geopolítica do Brasil,'" ADN (November–December 1981): 33.

29 Cited in Lieutenant Colonel William L. Hauser, "The French Army after Algeria," MR (August 1972): 2–12. The cited passage appears on p. 2. It originally appeared in *Le Monde* (24 November 1961). Hauser cited George A. Kelly's *Lost Soldiers: The French Army and Empire in Crisis* (Cambridge, Mass., M.I.T. Press, 1965), p. 361, as his own source.

30 General Osiris Guillermo Villegas, "La seguridad nacional y los recursos hídricos," RESGA (July–September 1969): 5–20. The citation is from p. 20. The best work on the recent role(s) of Brazil's generals remains Alfred Stepan, *The Military in Politics: Changing Patterns in Brazil* (Princeton: Princeton University Press, 1971).

31 General Juan Enrique Guglialmelli, "Nación y soberanía: Reflexiones para ingenuos y desprevenidos," *Estrategia* (May–August 1980): 5–9.

32 Lieutenant Colonel Miguel A. Pérez Tort, "El potencial económico-industrial argentino y la defensa nacional," RIA (September–October 1948): 610–36; and his "La industria pesada y los materiales críticos: Sus perspectivas en nuestra actualidad," RIA (September–October 1949): 591–610.

33 See his "La teoría del 'espacio vital,'" RIA (May–June 1951): 273–87; and his "La importancia del estudio de la geopolítica," RIA (September–October 1948): 637–40.

34 Lieutenant Colonel Julio César Salvadores, "Defensa nacional: La reestructuración

del poder ejecutivo y la existencia del consejo de la defensa," RESGA (January–March 1955): 18–26.

35 General Jorge A. Giovanelli, "La unidad moral: Nación-fuerzas armadas," RMA (May–June 1956): iv–ix; and "La moral de los pueblos y la capacidad de recuperación nacional," RMA (July–August 1957): 5–9.

36 Giovanelli, "El ambiente profesional en el ejército," RMA (July–September 1961): 7–10.

37 "El conocimiento geopolítico y sus propósitos," RCM (January–March 1964): 47–59.

38 "Instancias de un proceso nacional: Filosofía, política, y estrategia," RESGA (March–April 1967): 98–117.

39 See Comando de Ingenieros, "La acción cívica, el ejército, y el arma de ingenieros," RESGA (March–April 1969): 105–8. See also Major Edgardo Bautista Matute, "Eficaz respuesta al Castro-comunismo," RESGA (May–August 1967): 109–12; and Escuela Nacional de Guerra, "La seguridad nacional: Un concepto de palpitante actualidad," RESGA (May–June 1969): 5–8.

40 General Osiris Guillermo Villegas, "Política nuclear, desarrollo, y seguridad nacional," RCMA (April–June 1969): 53–62. The cited passage appears on p. 62. Villegas' emphasis. See also his "Política de fronteras, desarrollo, y seguridad nacional," RCMA (October–December 1969): 126–38.

41 Colonel Máximo A. Garro, "La hora de la Patagonia: Nuestro norte está en el sur," RCMA (April–June 1970): 129–42.

42 "Reflexiones sobre la situación argentina y la obtención de los objetivos políticos nacionales," RESGA (July–October 1970): 41–46. The quotation is from p. 43. See also his "Reflexiones de planeamiento: El desarrollo y la seguridad de América Latina," RESGA (May–June 1971): 33–44.

43 General Juan Enrique Guglialmelli, "Las fuerzas armadas en América Latina: Fuerzas armadas y revolución nacional," *Estrategia* (July–August 1972): 9–20. The citation is from p. 10. See also Lieutenant Colonel José Julio Mazzeo, "Reflexiones sobre seguridad nacional," RESGA (May–June 1973): 11–16; Colonel (ret.) Horacio P. Ballester, "El ejército y el proceso nacional," *Estrategia* (May–June 1973): 7–10; Lieutenant Colonel Elbio E. Ojeda, "Las comunciaciones en la defensa nacional," RESGA (May–June 1976): 69–88; and General Roberto R. Knopfelmacher Benítez, "Paraguay: El hierro es el poder de los pueblos," *Estrategia* (September–October 1976): 35–39.

44 General Tomás Sánchez de Bustamante, "El ejército nacional civilizador," RESGA (November–December 1976): 17–24. The quotation is from p. 23.

45 See the already-cited Juan Ramón Muñoz Grande (pseud.), "Argentina: Objetivo orgánico del ejército para el largo plazo," *Estrategia* (September–October 1979): 37–43.

46 See Captain José Guillermo Lamoglia, "A los soldados, suboficiales, y oficiales argentinos (¡¡soldados todos!!) caídos durante la primera batalla por las Islas Malvinas" (a poem), RESGA (March–June 1984): 108. The best source on any aspect of the Argentine army's role(s) since World War II remains Robert A. Potash, *The Army and Politics in Argentina, 1945–1962: Perón to Frondizi* (Stanford: Stanford University Press, 1980).

47 General V. Kourfakis, "An Outline of the Organisational and Training Goals of the Hellenic Army," *Military Technology* (October 1981): 17–21.

48 "Política," PG (May–August 1985): 43–62. The citation comes from p. 43. See also Colonel Julio César von Chrismar Escuti, "Algunos problemas geopolíticos de Chile y su trascendencia en la seguridad nacional," PG (January–March 1984): 13–42.

49 General Claudio López Silva, "Discurso de graduación de los cursos año 1981 del sr. director de la Academia Superior de Seguridad Nacional, SN (January–March 1982): 5–9.

50 See Colonel Aniceto Muñoz F., "El departamento de movilización económica y los problemas de la defensa nacional," MECH (March–April 1943): 239–42; and Enrique Alvarez Vásquez de Prada, "El problema del fierro en la economía chilena," MECH (March–April 1944): 225–91.

51 General Horacio Arce Fernández, "La fuerza armada y la seguridad nacional," MECH (March–April 1957): 102–12.

52 See Frederick M. Nunn, *The Military in Chilean History: Essays on Military-Civilian Relations, 1810–1973* (Albuquerque: University of New Mexico Press, 1976), esp. 260–66.

53 "El estado y la seguridad nacional," SN (August 1976): 29–42. See also Colonel Gerardo Cortés Rencoret, "Introducción a la seguridad nacional," MECH (May–August 1976): 44–63.

54 General Gastón Zúñiga Paredes, "Importancia de la seguridad nacional," SN (April–June 1977): 25–28.

55 Captain (navy) Aldo Montagne Bargetto, Colonel (carabineros) José Vargas Concha, and Colonel Roberto Bonilla Bradanovic, "La nueva institucionalidad de Chile y la seguridad nacional," SN (October–December 1977): 83–108. The citation is from p. 85. See also Colonel Daniel Gastón Frez Arancibia, "Algunas consideraciones sobre economía de defensa," SN (April–June 1977): 29–42; General Gastón Zúñiga Paredes, "El sistema de seguridad nacional," SN (July–September 1977): 9–16; General Horacio Toro Iturra, "Seguridad nacional y política exterior en los objetivos nacionales," ibid., 17–48; Colonel (carabineros) Carlos Donoso Pérez, "Orden público y seguridad nacional," ibid., 49–56.

56 See, as additional examples, Captain (navy) Francisco García Huidobro G., "Consideraciones geopolíticas de Chile," SN (July–September 1978): 17–37; and Colonel Julio César von Chrismar Escuti, "El país, la nación, y el poder nacional: Fenómenos fundamentales del estado," SN (January–March 1980): 45–78.

57 "Discurso del señor director de la Academia Superior de Seguridad Nacional . . . con motivo del 5° aniversario de su creación," SN (April–June 1979): 70–74. See also Rafael Augusto López Faúndez and Captain (carabineros) Juan I. González Errázuriz, "Naturaleza filosófica de la seguridad nacional," SN (January–April 1981): 11–19.

58 "La relación entre el desarrollo político, económico, social, y la seguridad nacional en el contexto de la regionalización chilena," SN (January–April 1981): 1–35. The quotation is from p. 23. See also Colonel Julio César von Chrismar Escuti, "El perfeccionamiento del estado," SN (May–August 1981): 19–31.

59 "Los pequeños estados en el concierto internacional," MECH (September–December 1980): 36–39. See also Major Juan E. Cheyre Espinosa "Política exterior, estrategia política, y estrategia militar," MECH (September–December 1982): 54–64; Colonel Julio César von Chrismar Escuti, "La armonía del estado: Uno de los principios fundamentales de la geopolítica," PG (January–March 1983): 13–62; and

his "Vigencia de las leyes geopolíticas y su aplicación en la seguridad nacional," PG (April–June 1983): 39–62. The most oft-cited Chilean source on geopolitics is, of course, General Augusto Pinochet's derivative *Geopolítica,* 2d ed. (Santiago: Editorial Andrés Bello, 1974).

60 Recent comparative monographic works treating Uruguay with a degree of success are Roberto Calvo, *La doctrina militar de la seguridad nacional: Autoritarismo político y neoliberalismo económico en el Cono Sur* (Caracas: Universidad Católica Andrés Bello, 1979); and Alain Roquié, *l'État militaire en Amérique Latine* (Paris: Seuil, 1982).

61 "Discurso de s. m. el Rey," *Ejército* (January 1978): n. p.

62 "Mensaje de s. m. el Rey," *Ejército* (January 1980): i–iv.

63 "Discurso del ciudadano presidente de la república . . . en el acto de retiro y ascenso de oficiales," RFAV (February 1971): 7–12. Despite the passage of time, the best single treatment of the military in Venezuela since World War II is still Winfield J. Burggraaff, *The Venezuelan Armed Forces and Politics, 1935–1959* (Columbia: University of Missouri Press, 1972).

64 General Carlos Soto Tamayo, "Vamos a la vida civil con fe en los valores de la república," RFAV (February 1971): 75–78.

65 Lieutenant Colonel Rubén Rueda Sáenz, "Colonización militar," RMC (April 1957): 40–46. The quoted passage is from p. 41. See also Captain Víctor Maldonado Michelina, "Problemas de nuestra movilización industrial," RFAV (June 1951); 479–81; Major Tomás Pérez Tenreiro, "Nociones de geopolítica venezolana," RFAV (April 1952): 354–64; and Major Luis Manuel Bruzual Martínez, "El papel de las ff. aa. en la superviviencia nacional," RFAV (October–December 1962): 32–35.

66 Colonel Juan Antonio Lossada Volcán, "El ferrocarril en la defensa nacional," RFAV (n. d., 1965): 76–83. The citation is from p. 83. See as well General Martín García Villasmil, "La seguridad y las políticas de integración internacional," REV (December 1967): 13–22; also see Colonel (ret.) Alfonso Littuma Arizaga (an Ecuadoran), "Doctrina de seguridad nacional," REV (June 1968): 89–99; Lossada Volcán's "Movilización económica," RFAV (n.d., 1968): 59–64; Colonel Angel Rodríguez García, "Los problemas de la defensa de los recursos nacionales," RFAV (n.d., 1969): 28–34; Lieutenant Colonel Luis Enrique Sira Suárez, "Las fan [fuerzas armadas nacionales] y la economía," RFAV (n.d., 1969): 4–8; General Carlos Noguera, "Doctrina militar," RFAV (March–April 1971): 30–34; Mássimo Severo Giannini, "Las fuerzas armadas y el papel que desempeñan en el estado contemporáneo, con especial referencia a las instituciones militares que cumplen funciones policiales," *Revista de la Escuela Superior Fuerzas Armadas de Cooperación* (July–December 1973): 13–19.

67 Captain Jovino Navas Meleán, "Algo más sobre carreteras," REV (n.d., 1976): 51–60; General Fernando Paredes Bello, "Consolidar logros y avanzar hacia nuevas metas," RFAV (January–April 1968): 38–39; Lieutenant Colonel Eduardo Sánchez Chacón, "Reforma agraria, conservación, y desarrollo," RFAV (April–June 1981): 63–65; and Colonel Littuma Arizaga's "La movilización en la guerra moderna," RFAV (June–December 1957): 20–37.

68 Lieutenant Colonel Miguel A. Peña B., "Defensa nacional," RMC (April 1957): 35–39. See also Colonel Francisco Gómez Laverde, "Sentido de la movilización," RFAC (October 1960): 31–40.

69 Lieutenant Colonel Camilo Acevedo Vélez, "Premovilización y movilización," ibid.,

41–54. The citation is from p. 49. See also Departamento de Reglamentación y Doctrina, Escuela Superior de Guerra, "La profesión militar," RFAC (September–December 1976): 327–30; and Lieutenant Colonel Benjamín Medina Angarita, "El planeamiento: Necesidad nacional," RFAC (March–April 1966): 117–22.

70 See Gonzalo Canal Ramírez, "Sesenta años después: La Escuela Militar de Cadetes marca el final de las guerras civiles y el principio del civilismo," RFAC (June 1967): 263–66.

71 "Colombia, un país sin conciencia geopolítica," RFAC (April–June 1973): 459–62.

72 José Vicente Rangel, Luis Esteban Rey, Pompeyo Márquez, and Germán Lariet, *Militares y política: Una polémica inconclusa* (Caracas: Ediciones Centauro, 1976), 11.

73 See Alvaro Echeverría U., *El poder y los militares: Un análisis de los ejércitos del continente y Colombia* (Bogotá: Fondo Editorial Suramérica, 1978); General Alberto Ruiz Novoa, *El gran desafío* (Bogotá: Ediciones Tercer Mundo, 1965); and Alfredo Peña, *Democracia y golpe militar* (Bogotá: Carlos Valencia Editores, 1979).

74 Major Ricardo Humberto Torres S. and Captain (navy) Justino Eduardo Villalba, "El poder de la ilegalidad en la economía," RFAC (n.d., 1980): 245–64.

75 "Fuerzas armadas en la defensa y desarrollo de los países subdesarrollados," RFAC (October–December 1981): 3–15. The citation comes from p. 9. See also Lieutenant Colonel Humberto González Rojo, "Creación de un 'instituto de estudios de la política de defensa,'" RFAC (April–June 1981): 159–62; Majors Mauro V. Fajardo Sánchez and Florentino Flórez Jiménez, "Política de desarrollo científico y tecnológico en Colombia," RFAC (October–December 1981): 117–33.

76 See General Jorge E. Alba Hernández, "Los estados y sus espacios geopolíticos," RFAC (April–June 1983): 39–46; Major Augusto Bahamón Durán, "Importancia geopolítica de la amazonia colombiana," ibid., 47–58; and General Eduardo Pedraza Neira, "Apuntes sobre movilización nacional," RFAC (October–December 1983): 371–81.

77 See Guillermo Boils, *Los militares y la política en Mexico (1915–1974)* (México, D. F.: Ediciones el Caballito, 1975). For a good, recent monographic source on the Mexican military and its late-twentieth-century role(s) see also David Ronfeldt, ed., *The Modern Mexican Military: A Reassessment* (La Jolla: Center for U. S.–Mexican Studies, University of California, San Diego, 1984).

78 See Colonel Alfredo Castellanos, "Moral militar y civismo," REM (running in issues from March 1950 through October–December 1952). See also Lic. Adolfo López Mateos, "El ejército: Baluarte revolucionario," REM (September 1960): 1–3; and Major Juan Jose Carbonell López, "La influencia militar en la historia cartográfica de nuestro país," REM (October 1969): 4–12.

79 Lieutenant Colonel Rama, "Defendámonos contra la propaganda injusta," RMBO (January–March 1951): 23–24; Lucio Diez de Medina, "Las fuerzas armadas de la nación y objetivos en la recuperación de la hegemonía nacional y la diversificación económica del país," RMBO (July–December 1953): 95–100; "Ejército de producción," RMBO (July–August 1955): 47–49; and an editorial foreword, in RMBO (January–March 1962): 3.

80 See, as examples, Major Aminodow Feller Nickelberg, "El estado y la defensa nacional," RECEMMEA (April–June 1963): 5–23; Lieutenant Colonel José Francisco René Chacón, "El estado y las comunicaciones," RECEMMEA (June 1969): 45–53; Lieutenant Colonel Carlos Aníbal Méndez Cabrera, "Población y analfabetismo,"

RMGU (January–March 1974): 63–70; and Captain Carlos Abel Cabrera Padilla, "El analfabetismo como problema nacional," RMGU (January–March 1979): 13–22. The best monographic work in English on a Central American military organization remains Richard Millett, *Guardians of the Dynasty: A History of the Guardia Nacional and the Somoza Family* (Maryknoll, N.Y.: Orbis Books, 1977).

81 See, for example, General Sindulfo Pérez Moreno, "La geopolítica: Arma poderosa del estadista, del político, y del militar," RFAP (April 1966): 64–67; and Lieutenant Colonel Juan E. González M., "Algunos aspectos doctrinarios sobre defensa interna y del territorio," RFAP (January–June 1983): 40–51, 72–75.

82 "Resunción del mando presidencial," RFAP (July–August 1958): n.p. There is no full-fledged study of the military profession in Paraguay. On Ecuador, see John Samuel Fitch, *The Military Coup as Political Process: Ecuador, 1948–1966* (Baltimore: The Johns Hopkins University Press, 1977).

83 *Captains and Kings: Three Dialogues on Leadership*, tr. J. Lewis May (London: The Bodley Head Limited, 1925), 124.

84 See Colonel Wilmot R. McCutcheon, "The National Purpose," MR (November 1965): 13–17.

85 Lieutenant Colonel Roy K. Flint, "Army Professionalism for the Future," MR (April 1971): 3–11. The quoted passage appears on p. 4.

86 Lieutenant Colonel John H. Moellering, "Future Civil-Military Relations: The Army Turns Inward?" MR (July 1973): 68–83.

87 Lieutenant Colonel Harold R. Lamp, "Some Managerial Aspects of Command," *Parameters* (Spring 1971): 42–49.

88 See Lieutenant Colonel James B. Channon, "Preparing the Officer Corps for the 1990s," MR (May 1978): 10–23; and Lieutenant Colonel Joel E. L. Roberts, "Managing Soldiers: A Personal Philosophy of Management," MR (July 1980): 44–50.

89 General Edward C. Meyer, "Leadership: A Return to Basics," MR (July 1980): 4–9. The cited material comes from pp. 6–7. See also Colonel Richard J. Kattar, "The First Commandment of Leadership: Love Thy Soldier," MR (July 1980): 65–68.

90 Lieutenant Colonel (chaplain) Malcolm J. Brummit, "The Army's Ethical Dilemma," MR (July 1981): 44–47. See also Lieutenant Colonel Anthony L. Wermuth, "The Army's Profile in Changing Times," MR (October 1960): 19–36.

91 See Lieutenant Colonel Boyd M. Harris, "A Perspective on Leadership, Management, and Command," MR (February 1984): 48–57; and Lieutenant Colonel (ret.) Robert M. Walker, "In Defense of the Military Mind," MR (April 1969): 55–62.

92 See Colonel James H. Short, "Young Soldiers Fade Away," MR (October 1969): 44–53; Lieutenant Colonel James S. White, "Race Relations in the Army," MR (July 1970): 3–12; and Colonel Donald F. Bletz, "Military Professionalism: A Conceptual Approach," MR (May 1971): 9–17.

93 See General R. W. Porter, Jr., "Post-Retirement Teaching Careers," AID (December 1958): 42–46. See as well General Lionel C. McGarr, "Education and National Security," MR (July 1960): 3–4.

94 For example, see Colonel Harry G. Summers, Jr., "To Provide for the Common Defense," *Parameters* (September 1982): 2–9; and Lieutenant Colonel (ret.) Sam Sarkesian, "An Empirical Reassessment of Military Professionalism," MR (August 1977): 3–20.

95 See David E. Engdahl's "Foundations for Military Intervention in the United

States," in Peter J. Rowe and Christopher J. Whelan, eds., *Military Intervention in Democratic Societies* (London: Croom Helm, 1985), 1–50.

96 Lieutenant Colonel Heinz Karst, "Partnerschaft und Kameradschaft," *Wehrkunde* (January 1961): 27–30.

97 See Colonel Glauco Pridasso, "Contributo dell'esercito alla preparazione morale e tecnico-profesionale del cittadino," RMIT (June 1968): 661–81.

98 As examples, see Major Jürgen Schreiber, "Moderne Menschenführung als Problem der Inneren Führung und der Personalpolitik," *Truppenpraxis* (February 1967): 81–83; Major Francesco Scala, "Psicologia militare," RMIT (February 1968): 227–30; Major Heinz Kluss, "Zur Führungsproblematik in Armee und Gesellschaft," *Wehrkunde* (March 1968): 1335; Jean-Paul Moreigne, "Officiers, pour quel office?" RDN (May 1971): 718–27; Ugo Rende, "Le forze armate e la psico-sociologia," RMIT (March–April 1974): 48–51; Dr. Michele Musto, "Aspetti e metodi della selezione attitudinale del personale per le forze armate," RMIT (February 1972): 198–206; Lieutenant Colonel (air force) Werner Breindl, "Führung aus Sozialpsychologischer Sicht," *Truppenpraxis* (August 1976): 529–33; Colonel Johannes Pfeiffer, "Bessere Führung: Eine Analyse des Gesamtproblems," WR (January–February 1976): 9–13; General Eberhard Wagemann, "Wissenschaft und Offizierausbildung," WR (March–April 1977): 33–35; General Eugenio Rambaldi, "Esercito e società," RMIT (January–February 1978): 2–6; General Günther Kiesling, "Personalführung und Innere Führung," EW (February 1981): 64–69; General Jürgen Schreiber, "Über die Verantwortung des militärischen Führers," WR (March–April 1981): 33–36; Lieutenant Colonel Klaus-Jürgen Preusschoff, "Innere Führung und Sozialarbeit," *Truppenpraxis* (March 1983): 175–81; and Giampolo Giannetti, "L'ufficiale: Comandante o manager," RMIT (May–June 1983): 50–56.

See, for further comparison, Colonel Kirpel Singh, "Toughening of Mind of Soldiers," JUSII (April–June 1974): 172–80; Squadron Leader A. N. Veerma, "Shortcomings in the Staff Officer of Today: Their Causes and Remedial Measures," JUSII (January–May 1979): 50–61; and Edward L. Warner III, *The Military in Contemporary Soviet Politics* (New York: Praeger Publishers, 1977).

99 Captain Helmut Leonhardt, "Haben wir noch eine Chance? Gedanken eines jungen Offiziers," *Truppenpraxis* (June 1973): 422–23.

100 Captain Prudencio García Martínez de Munguía, "El militar profesional hoy y mañana," *Ejército* (March 1975): 36–42; Captain Miguel Martín Fernández, "La formación profesional hoy: Objetividad y subjetividad ocupacional," *Ejército* (January 1977): 59–61; and General Jesús Montero Romero, "La disciplina hoy," *Ejército* (July 1977): 5–11. And compare General S. D. Verma, "Retiring," JUSII (April–June 1978): 143–49.

101 Colonel K. Vorobyov, "Social Progress and the Army," SMR (July 1981): 17–19. See also Colonel Zakir Gafurov, "Party Structuring in the Armies of Socialist-Oriented Countries," SMR (July 1986): 45–47, 55.

102 *Constitución política de la República de Chile, 1980,* Chap. X, Art. 90.

103 See, as examples, Colonel Carlos M. Aguilar, "Relaciones públicas y fuerzas armadas," RESGA (January–March 1964): 13–26; Lieutenant Colonel Ernesto Manuel Gordillo, "El ejército y sus relaciones con la comunidad," RESGA (April–May 1964): 106–15; Major Manuel Levi Plaza, "El ejército mexicano," REM (March 1971): 21–22; General A. J. Paulo Couto, "O Impacto da Revolução de 31 de Março

no Campo Psicosocial," RCMB (March–April 1973): 5–7; and General Tomás Abreu Rescaniere, "El arte de mandar solo se obtiene aprendiendo a obedecer," RFAV (October 1980): 2–12.

104 Defense Minister Michel Debré, "La fonction militaire dans la France d'aujourd'hui," RDN (April 1972): 523–43. The quoted passage appears on p. 529.

Chapter Eight

1 Colonel A. Korkeshkin, "With the Party, With the People," SMR (February 1976): 4–6.

2 General Edward B. Atkeson, "Military Art and Science: Is There a Place in the Sun for It," MR (January 1977): 71–81. The citation is from p. 77.

3 General Wolfgang Altenburg, "30 Jahre Friedenssicherung: Verpflichtung für die Zukunft," *Soldat und Technik* (October 1985): 583.

4 See A. Olugboyega Banjo, *The Potential for Military Disengagement in Africa: A Nigerian Case Study* (Lagos: Nigerian Institute of International Affairs, 1980).

5 Michel-L. Martin, *Le militarisation des systèmes politiques africains (1960–1972): Une tentative d'interprétation* (Sherbrooke, Que.: Éditions Naaman, 1974).

6 See Major Adewale Ademoyega, et al., *Why We Struck: The Study of the First Nigerian Coup* (Ibadan: Evans Brothers-Nigeria Publishers, 1981); and A. M. Mainsara, *The Five Majors: Why They Struck* (Zaria: Hudahuda Publishing Company, 1982); A.[lbert] K.[wesi] Ocran, *Politics of the Sword: A Personal Memoir on Military Involvement in Ghana and of Problems of Military Government* (London: Rex Collings, 1977); and Samuel Decalo, *Coups and Army Rule in Africa: Studies in Military Style* (New Haven: Yale University Press, 1976).

7 See, for example, S. J. Baynham, "The Military in Ghanaian Politics," TAQDJ (October 1976): 428–39; and Colonel J. J. Packard, "Scholarships for Foreigners at Our Military Schools," TAQDJ (April 1959): 96–98.

8 S. J. Baynham, "The Military in Black African Politics," TAQDJ (July 1975): 304–16; and Brigadier E. Logan, "Some Thoughts on Africa," AAJ (September 1962): 29–36.

9 Major Iain Grahame, "Uganda and Its President," TAQDJ (July 1974): 480–90. The quoted passage is from p. 482.

10 See, for example, Colonel L. Dullin, "Pour une OTAS," RMG (November 1959): 435–58; Batallion Chief Guyot, "Réflexions sur certains aspects du problème militaire outre-mer," *Tropiques* (November 1960): 13–17; and Edward M. Corbett, *The French Presence in Black Africa* (Washington, D.C.: Black Orpheus Press, 1972).

11 "Despair of a Free Volunteer" (*Hosties noires*, 1948), in Léopold Sédar Senghor, *Selected Poems*, trans. and with intro. by John Reed and Clive Wake (New York: Atheneum, 1969), 33–34.

12 Editorial, RFAP (1983): 2. And see the fervent birthday greetings of 1961 to the Somoza brothers in GN (November–December 1961): 5–6; and Major (ret.) José T. Vera Fretes, "Stroessner–de Gaulle: Dos figuras para la historia," RFAP (January–April 1965): xxi–xxiii.

During the Pinochet government Chilean scholars were pointing out meticulously the transition from professional militarism to what might be termed (ominously) "professional personalism." See, for example, the following publications of the Facultad Latinoamericana de Ciencias Sociales (FLACSO): Augusto Varas, Felipe Agüero, and Fernando Bustamante, *Chile, democracia, fuerzas armadas* (Santiago,

1980); Varas and Agüero, *El proyecto político militar* (Santiago, 1982); Hugo Frühling, Carlos Portales, and Varas, *Estado y fuerzas armadas en el proceso político* (Santiago, 1983). Also see Varas, *Los militares en el poder* (Santiago: Pehuén, 1978); J. Samuel Valenzuela and Arturo Valenzuela, eds., *Military Rule in Chile: Dictatorship and Oppositions* (Baltimore: The Johns Hopkins University Press, 1986); Genaro Arriagada, *Pinochet: The Politics of Power*, trans. Nancy Morris with Vincent Ercolano and Kristen A. Whitney (Boston: Unwin Hyman, 1988); Esteban Tomic, *1988 . . . y el general bajó al llano* (Santiago: Ediciones ChileAmérica, 1989); and Hernán Vidal, *Mitología militar chilena: Surrealismo desde el superego* (Minneapolis: Institute for the Study of Ideologies and Literature, 1989). See as well A. Pinochet U., *Política, politiquería, y demagogia* (Santiago: Editorial Renacimiento, 1983); Giselle Munizaga, *El discurso público de Pinochet: Un análisis semiológico* (Santiago: CESOC/CENECA, 1988); and Varas, "Crisis de legitimidad del autoritarismo y transición democrática en Chile" (typescript, Santiago, 1991).

Recent Pinochet apologia include General Santiago Sinclair Oyaneder, "Homenaje a s. e. el presidente de la república, Capitán General Augusto Pinochet Ugarte, con motivo de cumplir 15 años de mando de la institución," MECH (May–August 1988): 5–17; Centro de Estudios Sociopoliticos, *Presidente Pinochet: Transición y consolidación democrática, 1984–1989* (an anthology of excerpts from speeches and decrees) (Santiago: Zig-Zag, 1989); Raquel Correa and Elizabeth Subercaseaux, *Ego sum Pinochet* (interviews with two journalists) (Santiago: Zig-Zag, 1989); and the autobiographical Augusto Pinochet Ugarte, *Camino recorrido: Memorias de un soldado, Vol. 1* (Santiago: Instituto Geográfico Militar, 1990). There is no end in sight to works on Pinochet, beyond doubt the most controversial Chilean military-political figure of the twentieth century.

13 In "O Czar e o Russia," *Cartas e Bilhetes de Pariz* (Porto: Livraria Charderon-Dr. Lello e Irmãos, 1907). Cf. Colonel Víctor Chaves Dailhe, "El poderío naval soviético: La seguridad de occidente y el Pacífico Sur," MECH (January–April 1981): 109–18.

14 "El empleo de las fuerzas armadas en el futuro," RMNU (April–June 1948): 26–43.

15 See his "Carta abierta al señor Jimmy Carter, presidente de los Estados Unidos de América," MECH (1978): 43–51; Major Octávio Tosta's oft-reprinted (Bolivia, Brazil) "América del Sud: Salvaguardia de los EE. UU. de Norte América," RESGA (July–September 1960): 401–8; Colonel Mario Modesto Chacón Arévalo, "Fuerza interamericana de paz," RECEMMEA (December 1967): 23–30; Captain Boris Rebbio Porta España (a Guatemalan), "El consejo de defensa centroamericana," RECEMMEA (December 1967): 51–57; General (ret.) Hélio Lemos, "Educação no Futuro," ADN (January–April 1977): 93–101; Colonel Gribaldo Miño Tapia, "Realidades y problemática económica de Latinoamérica," RCID (April 1977): 7–11; Chacón Arévalo's "El Colegio Interamericano de Defensa," RECEMMEA (December 1968): 149–51; and General Juan de Dios Barriga Muñoz, "¡Prospectiva! y su relación con la seguridad nacional," MECH (May–August 1982): 89–121.

16 General Osiris Guillermo Villegas, "El regionalismo, el desarrollo, y la seguridad," RESGA (March–April 1968): 5–14; General (ret.) Víctor F. Aulestia, "Aspectos generales de la seguridad nacional," RFAE (1969): 9–18.

17 Lieutenant Colonel Gribaldo Miño, "A las fuerzas armadas de mi patria," ibid., 30–31.

18 General Eduardo José Catún, "Desarrollo industrial argentino," RCMA (December 1973): 4–15.

19 General Osiris Guillermo Villegas, "Cuenca del Plata: Política nacional sin rumbo," RESGA (May–June 1974): 9–40.

20 Paulo Henrique da Rocha Correa, "O Brasil e os Caminhos para o Oceano Pacífico," ADN (May–June 1980): 127–33.

21 See Captain (navy) Dino Willy Cozza, "A Geoestrategia do Brasil," ADN (May–June 1982): 79–110; Therezinha de Castro, "Terceir Mundo: Quem é Quem," ADN (September–October 1982): 45–59; Aristides Pinto Coelho, "O Brasil e a Antártida," ADN (November–December 1982): 59–70; Therezinha de Castro, "O Brasil e a Bacia do Prata," ibid., 73–91; "América Central-Caribe: Area Vulnerável do Hemisfério Occidental," ADN (March–April 1981): 77–86; and "O Caribe em Ritmo de Guerra Fria," ADN (November–December 1983): 35–54; Captain (navy) Ricardo Ramos Ormeño, "O Pensamento Político de Mercado Jarrín," ADN (March–April 1984): 89–110; and Colonel Luiz Paulo Macedo Carvalho, "O Atlântico do Sul," ADN (November–December 1983): 57–68.

22 Captain (navy) Eddie Ramírez Poveda, "¿Porqué es importante el Caribe para Venezuela?" RFAV (August–December 1984): 29–30; Colonel (air force) Luis Angel Díaz Díaz, "Importancia de la posición geográfica de Colombia para la defensa continental," RFAC (October–December 1984): 83–89.

23 Jorge Eduardo Hernández Méndez, "Geopolítica," RECEMMEA (December 1968): 59–83. See also his earlier "El Bloque del Caribe en la defensa continental," RMGU (July–August 1963): 5–17; and Colonel Alejandro Ureta L., "Nociones de geopolítica: La frontera como periférica de tensión y fricción," ibid., 18–32.

24 General Edgardo Mercado Jarrín, "Uma Potência no Horizonte," RCMB (March–April 1977): 13–17.

25 General Carlos de Meira Mattos, *A Geopolítica e as Projeções do Poder* (Rio de Janeiro: José Olympio, 1977). See also General Golbery do Couto e Silva, *Aspectos Geopolíticos do Brasil* (Rio de Janeiro: José Olympio, 1957).

26 Captain (navy) Luiz Sanctos Döring, "Algumas Lições de Angola," ADN (March–April 1978): 139–47. See also Therezinha de Castro, "Vocação Atlântica de América do Sul," ADN (January–February 1979): 53–72; Captain (navy) Aguinaldo Aldighieri Soares, "O Continente Africano ou Muitas Africas," ADN (January–February 1979): 119–40; Lieutenant Colonel Ramiro José Marcelino Mourato, "O Continente Africano: Espaço e Posição," ADN (March–April, 1980): 47–59; and Meira Mattos' "Atlântico Sul: Sua Importância Estratégica," ADN (March–April 1980): 73–90.

27 See Eurípides Cardoso de Meneses, "A Antártica e os Desafios da Era Oceânica," ADN (May–June 1981): 121–29; Captain (navy) Wintceas Villaca Barbosa de Godois, "Considerações Geopolíticas," ADN (July–December 1981): 43–63; Colonel Luiz Paulo Macedo Carvalho, "Intereses e Responsabilidades do Brasil no Atlântico-Sul," ADN (January–February 1984): 75–80; Colonel Octávio Tosta, "Geopolítica do Brasil," ibid., 107–22; Therezinha de Castro, "O Cono Sul e a Conjuntura Internacional," ADN (March–April 1984): 17–34; Lieutenant Colonel Theo Espindola Basto, "Malvinas: Uma Guerra Para Reflexão," ADN (March–April 1984): 75–108; Ricardo R. Caillet-Bois, "Las Malvinas y la Antártida Argentina," RESGA (July–September 1956): 333–75; also see essays in most issues of *Estrategia*; and Captain

José B. Richter, "Porqué los argentinos tenemos un sector en la Antártida," RESGA (July–December 1976): 75–86.

28 Captain (navy) Luis Bravo Bravo, "Vision geopolítica mundial," SN (July–September 1979): 21–44.

29 Bravo Bravo, "Visión geopolítica de Chile en el Pacífico," SN (January–April 1981): 75–89. See also General Ramón Cañas Montalva, "El Pacífico: Epicentro geopolítico de un nuevo mundo en estructuración," SN (October–December 1979): 105–13; Colonel Julio César von Chrismar Escuti, "Geopolítica y seguridad nacional," SN (May–August 1981): 21–44; and Bravo Bravo's "Teorías geopolíticas para lograr el dominio mundial," SN (September–December 1981): 39–50.

30 Admiral José Toribio Merino Castro, "Geopolítica oceánica de Chile," SN (April–June 1982): 5–12; General Julio Canessa Robert, "Visión geopolítica de la regionalización de Chile," SN (April–June 1982): 13–35; Admiral José Toribio Merino Castro, "La Antártica y el futuro de Chile," PG (January–April 1987): 5–18; and General Fernando Arancibia Reyes, "La seguridad hemisférica en la decada de los noventa," PG (January–December 1990): 87–94.

31 See Captain (navy) Guilherme Eugénio Barbosa Dumont, "Importância Estratégica do Atlântico Sul na Segurança e no Desenvolvimento do Continente Americano," RCID (June 1976): 63–80. The quotation is from p. 77.

32 See the Brazilian General Alfredo Souto Malan's "Comunidade Luso-Brasileira," RMPO (July 1969): 375–80.

33 See "Golbery do Couto e Silva, el 'destino manifiesto' brasileño y el Atlântico Sur," *Estrategia* (March–April 1976): 5–24; Colonel Hermes de Araújo Oliveira (a Portuguese), "O Brasil e o Atlântico-Sul," ADN (September–October 1978): 37–43; Therezinha de Castro, "Quo Vadis Africa," ADN (July–August 1979): 5–25; Captain (navy) Gilberto Rocque Carneiro, "O Apartheid na República Sul Africana," ADN (July–August 1984): 109–18; and Denis Martin, *Os Militares e o Poder na América Latina e na Africa* (Lisboa: Publicações Dom Quixote, 1975), esp. 85–94.

34 See Fabiola Cuvi Ortiz, "La mujer en las sociedades del continente americano y su participación en el desarrollo," RCID (August 1982): 1–33.

35 See "Eva Perón: Jefe espiritual de la nación," RMA (July–August 1952): 434–35; and General (ret.) Juan Domingo Perón, "Fortalecer el ser nacional y desarrollar un profundo nacionalismo cultural," (an address of 1 May 1974) *Estrategia* (November 1978–February 1979): 59–67.

36 Colonel Luis Gozzoli, *Reflexiones sobre el mando,* Chilean ed., 2 vols. (Santiago: Estado Mayor General del Ejército de Chile, 1971), 1: 11–13.

37 In "Mensaje de la primera dama de la nación, señora Lucia Hiriart de Pinochet, a las esposas de los miembros del ejército," ASEC (September 1975): 44–48.

38 Lieutenant Angélica Yevenes Gutiérrez, "La mujer en el ejército," ASEC (July–December 1980): 190–93. See also Martín Rodríguez González, "La mujer chilena: Alma de la patria," ASEC (December 1984): 129–30; and "Homenaje a la mujer chilena," MECH (September–December 1976): 31–32. A key source on women in Chilean military service is María Elena Valenzuela, *La mujer en el Chile militar* (Santiago: Ediciones Chile y América, 1987).

39 See Hugo Tagle Martínez, "Seguridad nacional y matrimonio," SN (January–March 1982): 83–93.

40 See Colonel (air force) Alberto Spoerer Covarrubias, Colonel (carabineros) Pablo

Atria Ramírez, and Captain (navy) René Muguieles Orellana, "Planificación familiar en la seguridad nacional," SN (January–March 1978): 77–108.

41 Colonel Víctor Manuel Martínez Morfín, "La actuación de la mujer dentro del medio militar," REFAM (November–December 1973): 3–6.

42 Lieutenant Colonel Rubén Darío Castillo Ferrera, "La mujer dentro de nuestra sociedad," REFAM (February 1971): 2–6.

43 See Captain (nurse) María de Lourdes Martínez Vargas, "La mujer: Su participación política social y económica," REFAM (September 1975): 10–16; Captain (nurse) María del Refugio González M., "La mujer y la sociedad," REFAM (October 1975): 37–41; and Captain Mario Eduardo Chavero Ceballos, "La importancia de la mujer en la vida del militar," REFAM (May 1976): 37–41. Cf. "La mujer paraguaya: Heroína de todos los tiempos," RFAP (January–May 1975): 93.

44 "The Use of Woman Power in the Army," TAQDJ (July 1948): 217–26.

45 AAJ (September 1973): 28–31.

46 See "Army Women: A Decade of Progress," AAJ (June 1975): 27–34; Colonel K. M. Fowler, "The Changing Role of Women in the Armed Forces," AAJ (October 1975): 23–33; and Captain S. I. Horner, "Women in the Services: A Majority View," AAJ (February 1976): 43–46.

47 "After All Is Said and Done," MR (November 1978): 46–52.

48 "Woman Soldier, Quo Vadis?" *Parameters* (June 1983): 58–64. The citation is from p. 59.

49 See Guy Garonne, "De la femme guerrière . . . aux militaires féminins des armées," FAF (October 1973): 8–15. The cited passage appears on p. 15. See also a special issue of AA (August 1975), "Femmes militaires et femmes des militaires."

50 Colonel Raymond Caire, "La condition féminine dans les armées," AA (December 1980): 58–62. See as well Lieutenant Colonel Marie Christian Meric, "Le service national féminin," AA (April 1980): 14–15.

51 See Peter Kurt Wurzbach, "Frauen in die Bundeswehr?" EW (March 1980): 129–36; and Lieutenant Colonel Fabio Mini, "Soldato Joe e soldato Jane," RMIT (May–June 1983): 37–45.

52 "Women and the Armed Forces," SMR (March 1984): 24–25.

53 María del Carmen González Ribas, "Ser militar: La ilusión de una vida: El papel de la mujer en las fuerzas armadas," *Ejército* (February 1981): 28–29.

54 "El arte de mandar," RFAV (February 1971): 33–39. The quotation is from p. 38.

55 "Reflexiones sobre la seguridad y el desarrollo en América Latina," *Estrategia* (September–October 1973): 29–40.

56 "El nacionalismo, intereses y aspiraciones: Sus concurrencias en el campo psicosocial de América Latina," RCID (April 1977): 31–43.

57 Ramiro de la Espriella, *Conciencia subversiva: Ejército y pueblo* (Bogotá: n.p., 1976), 32.

58 Luis Herrera Campíns, *El relevo de las fuerzas armadas: Conceptos del jefe de estado en ceremonias militares en el Fuerte Tiuna y en la Escuela de Aviación Militar* (Caracas: Ministerio de Defensa, 1982).

59 *Relación de España,* Spanish ed. (Madrid: Librería de los Bibliófilos, 1879), 197–98.

60 *South American Meditations: On Hell and Heaven in Man's Soul*, trans. Therese Duerr (London: Jonathan Cape, 1932), 102.

61 David Craig, "Lukacs' Views on How History Moulds Culture," in G. H. R. Parkinson, ed., *Georg Lukacs: The Man, His Work, His Ideas* (London: Weidenfeld and Nicolson, 1970), 193.

62 *The Book of the Courtier* (1528), trans. Charles S. Singleton (New York: Anchor Books, 1959), 72.

63 "I shall remove from the promotion list any officer whose name I have read on the cover of a book." Cited in Charles de Gaulle, *France and Her Army*, trans. F. L. Dash (London: Hutchinson, 1940), 77.

64 "Fiction Reading in the Foreign Area Specialty Program," MR (September 1976): 71–78. The cited passage appears on pp. 72–73.

65 *Ejército y sociedad* (Madrid: Alianza Editorial, S. A., 1972), 151–72. The citation appears on pp. 163–64.

66 Milan Kundera, *The Art of the Novel*, trans. Linda Asher (New York: Grove Press, 1988), 9.

67 Carlos Fuentes, "The Discovery of Mexico," *Granta* (Autumn 1987), 225.

68 Mario Vargas Llosa, *La guerra del fin del mundo*, trans. Helen R. Lane (New York: Farrar Straus Giroux, 1984), 83.

69 *The Ill-Fated Peregrination of Fray Servando Teresa de Mier*, trans. Andrew Hardy (New York: Avon Books, 1987), xvii.

70 Christopher Hampton, *Savages, Scene 10* (London: Faber and Faber, 1974), 53.

71 Manlio Argueta, *Cuzcatlán Where the Southern Sea Beats*, trans. Clark Hansen (New York: Aventura, 1987), 5.

72 Carlos Fuentes, *High Noon in Latin America* (Los Angeles: The Manos Publishing Co., 1983), 12.

73 Mario Vargas Llosa, "A Media Stereotype," *The Atlantic Monthly* (February 1984): 21–24.

74 Trans. George R. Shivers and Ariel Dorfman (New York: Penguin Books, 1987), 32. See also his *Viudas* (1981) for a study of the impact of militarism on the role of women in opposition groups.

75 José Donoso, *El jardín de al lado* (1981).

76 Ernest Renan, "Prayer on the Acropolis," *Recollections of My Youth*, trans. C. B. Pitman (London: Chapman, 1883), 59.

77 Trans. Ellen Watson (New York: Avon Books, 1985), 173.

78 Gabriel García Márquez, "The Crux of Our Solitude" (Oslo: The Nobel Foundation, 1982).

79 Octavio Paz, "The Barricades and Beyond," *The New Republic* (9 November 1987): 26–30.

80 Recent works taking into account the ability of the military to endure as an institution through times of change are Philip O'Brien and Paul Cammack, eds., *Generals in Retreat: The Crisis of Military Rule in Latin America* (Manchester, Eng.: Manchester University Press, 1985); Alfred Stepan, *Rethinking Military Politics: Brazil and the Southern Cone* (Princeton: Princeton University Press, 1988); and Louis W. Goodman, Johanna S. R. Mendelson, and Juan Rial, eds., *Los militares y la democracia: El futuro de las relaciones cívico-militares en América Latina* (Montevideo: PEITHO, 1990). Countries dealt with are Argentina, Brazil, Chile, and Uruguay.

Postscript

1 (Lincoln: University of Nebraska Press, 1983), 296. See also comments on p. 286.

2 Tobías Barros Ortiz, *Recogiendo los pasos: Testigo político y militar del siglo xx*, Colección

Espejo de Chile (Santiago: Editorial Planeta, 1988), 15. This passage was also part of the interview referred to in the preface.

3 (New York: Random House, 1987). The review appeared in "Book World," *The Washington Post*, 27 December 1987.

4 LaRocque was cited in Studs Terkel, *The Good War: An Oral History of World War II* (New York: Pantheon Books, 1984), 191.

5 See Edward W. Said, *Beginnings: Intentions and Method* (New York: Columbia University Press, 1985), 7; Augusto Roa Bastos, *I the Supreme*, trans. Helen Lane (New York: Aventura, 1986), 32.

6 If views expressed from 1985 to 1990 by Chilean officers close to the Pinochet regime indicate concerns accurately, Marxism-Leninism Chilean-style, leftist terrorism, any challenge to the constitutionally mandated military role in all matters subsumed under "national security," liberation theology, liberal democracy, and human rights may all be considered threats to the armed forces, and to all Chileans. For a representative selection of officer corps thought and self-perception, see Major Eduardo Aldunate Herman, *Las fuerzas armadas de Chile, 1891–1973: En defensa del consenso nacional* (Santiago: Estado Mayor General del Ejército de Chile, 1988); General Julio Canessa Robert, El partido comunista y el sistema institucional democrático chileno," MECH (May–August 1989); 26–79; Canessa, "El estado según Marx y Hegel," PG (July–September 1989): 5–37; Lieutenant Colonel Germán García Arriagada, "El consejo de seguridad nacional: Pivote del equilibrio de poderes en la constitución de 1980," MECH (January–April 1989): 17–27; Lieutenant Colonel Jaime García Covarrubias, "La seguridad nacional en el marco de la institucionalidad," PG (April–June 1989): 5–13; Admiral Francisco Ghisolfo Araya, "Hacia una democracia protegida," PG (January–March 1988): 31–37; Captain (navy) Omar L. Gutiérrez Valdebenito, "La profesión militar," PG (July–September 1989): 67–74; General Alejandro Medina Lois, "Las fuerzas armadas como garantes de la institucionalidad bajo el concepto de seguridad nacional," *Revista de Estado Mayor* (Chile) (November 1989): 111–19; Medina, "Seguridad nacional en Chile, la subversión y el terrorismo," PG (January–March 1987): 19–31; Medina, "Seguridad nacional y la visión ideológica de la defensa," PG (January–April 1989): 11–29; Lieutenant Colonel Carlos Molina Johnson, "La acción desestabilizadora del comunismo: Una constante en la vida política nacional," MECH (May–August 1987): 87–95; Molina, *Chile: Unidad nacional y fuerzas armadas* (Santiago: Estado Mayor General del Ejército de Chile, 1989); Molina (as colonel), "Misión constitucional de las fuerzas armadas," PG (January–December 1990): 25–39; Lieutenant Gerardo José Molina Trivelli, "Teología de la liberación," MECH (January–April 1987): 12–17; Brigadier Herbert Orellana Herrera, "Opinión pública y seguridad nacional," MECH (May–August 1986): 22–34; General Augusto Pinochet Ugarte, "La participación del ejército en la organización y desarrollo del estado de Chile," MECH (September–December 1990): 5–15; General Javier J. Salazar Torres, "Discurso del director de la Academia Nacional de Estudios Políticos y Estratégicos con motivo de conmemorarse el XV aniversario de la creación del instituto," PG (January–December 1990): 5–13; and Major (ret.) Juan Carlos Stack, "Los derechos humanos en la URSS," MECH (January–April 1985): 13–21.

INDEX